The United Nations World Water Development Report 2021

VALUING WATER

Published in 2021 by the United Nations Educational, Scientific and Cultural Organization,
7, place de Fontenoy, 75352 Paris 07 SP, France

This report is published by UNESCO on behalf of UN-Water. The list of UN-Water Members and Partners can be found on the following website: www.unwater.org.

Print ISSN: 2159-9084
Online ISSN: 2707-0816
ISBN 978-92-3-100434-6

Suggested citation:
United Nations, The United Nations World Water Development Report 2021: Valuing Water. UNESCO, Paris.

Cover artwork by Davide Bonazzi.

Printed by UNESCO, Paris.

This publication is printed on 100% recycled, chlorine-free paper.

Climate neutral
Production
ClimatePartner.com/12066-2002-1001

Contents

Contents

Contents

Boxes, figures and tables

Boxes

Figures

Tables

Foreword

by **Audrey Azoulay**, *Director-General of UNESCO*

What is water worth? There is no easy answer to this deceptively simple question. On the one hand, water is infinitely valuable – without it, life would not exist. On the other, water is taken for granted – it is wasted every single day.

According to economic theory, the value of a good is determined by scarcity – the gap between limited resources and unlimited needs. Humans certainly use water as if it was limitless: an estimated 80% of all industrial and municipal wastewater, for example, is released into the environment without prior treatment.

But fresh water is in fact scarce, and becoming scarcer. Over 2 billion people already live in areas subject to water stress. Some 3.4 billion people, 45% of the global population, lack access to safely managed sanitation facilities. According to independent assessments, the world will face a global water deficit of 40% by 2030. This situation will be worsened by global challenges such as COVID-19 and climate change.

More importantly, economic theory is not the only way of determining worth. Cultural values are equally, if not more, significant. Many indigenous peoples, for example, accord special status to water and waterways. This is the case in New Zealand, where the Te Awa Tupua Act, passed in 2017, recognizes the Whanganui River as "an indivisible and living whole from the mountains to the sea". The Ganges and Yamuna Rivers, in India, are also considered living entities with the same rights as human beings. For these groups, bodies of water are like loved ones, and therefore priceless.

How, then, should we value water? The 2021 *World Water Development Report* focuses on this crucial issue. It assesses the ways water in which is valued across different sectors and identifies how this process can be improved, with a view to better evaluating what water is worth to our societies.

As the Report underlines, there are few standardized approaches to the valuation of water, whether within or between sectors. Moreover, these approaches do not always acknowledge the perspectives of different belief systems, cultures, genders and scientific disciplines. Only by incorporating these viewpoints can we achieve more sustainable, inclusive, gender-responsive and equitable decision-making processes – and take a step towards attaining Sustainable Development Goal 6, clean water and sanitation for all.

This report, coordinated by UNESCO, was made possible thanks to the Government of Italy and the Regione Umbria, which have long supported UNESCO's World Water Assessment Programme. I wish to thank all those who participated in this common endeavour, especially the UN-Water family for its close and continued collaboration. This publication recognises that water is not a question of development, but also a basic human right. By working together, we can identify solutions to help us on our way to a sustainable and prosperous world, without leaving anyone behind.

Because the fate of humans and water is inextricably linked. In the words of the Whanganui River tribe's proverb, *"Ko au te awa, ko te awa ko au"* – I am the river, the river is me.

Audrey Azoulay

Foreword

by **Gilbert F. Houngbo,** *Chair of UN-Water* and
President of the International Fund for Agricultural Development

Achieving the 2030 Agenda for Sustainable Development is a moral imperative. We owe it to our children and to future generations.

There is no life on earth without water. Sustainable Development Goal 6 (SDG 6) calls for the availability and sustainable management of water and sanitation for all. Unless we reach SDG6, we risk failing to attain many of the other Sustainable Development Goals, including those related to poverty reduction, food and nutrition, human health, gender equality, energy, economic growth, sustainable cities and the environment. The devasting COVID-19 pandemic reminds us of the importance of access to water, sanitation and hygiene facilities, and that far too many people are still without them.

The 2021 edition of the United Nations World Water Development Report focuses on valuing water. There is enough water for all provided we use and manage it efficiently. But we don't. We invest too little, and ineffectively. We use too much water, creating scarcities. Quality is suffering and so is the environment.

The value we place on water varies, depending upon who is using it, and why. Value can be a guide to what our goals should be, what actions are needed, and where we should invest. Many of our problems arise because we don't value water highly enough; all too often water is not valued at all.

The time has come for stakeholders to identify, articulate and share perspectives of the values of water.

This report explains various approaches to valuing water for environmental considerations, water-related infrastructure, drinking water, sanitation and hygiene. It looks at valuation issues in food and agriculture, business, industry, energy and financing. And it highlights the perspectives of different value systems and cultures, and associated social and gender-based considerations.

I am grateful to UNESCO and its World Water Assessment Programme for coordinating the production of this report and would like to thank UN-Water Members, Partners and other contributors for their important work.

I am confident that the report will facilitate a better appreciation of the values of water and accelerate our progress towards the Sustainable Development Goals.

Gilbert F. Houngbo

Preface

by **Michela Miletto**, *UNESCO WWAP Coordinator*
and **Richard Connor**, *Editor-in-Chief*

It has often been stated that water is undervalued, or that we somehow need to recognize the 'true' value of water in order to make better decisions about how we protect, share and use it. But what does this really mean? Can the value of water be measured? And if so, how? Who actually gets to determine water's value? In other words, what *is* water worth – and to whom?

While these questions may appear clear and simple enough, the answers are anything but. The bottom line is that there is no one 'true' value of water. Rather, water holds a myriad of values that can differ greatly based on where the water is located, its level of abundance or scarcity, its quality, and its availability. Its values also depend upon the purpose it is used for and the benefits generated by these uses.

Some values can be quantified and even monetized, such as when water is used as an input in specific industrial processes or for irrigated agriculture, and expressed as a unit of production (or profit) per volume used. Yet, even across and within different economic sectors, such metrics can easily fall short of providing a comprehensive 'value' for water. For example, while food security is of vital importance to any household, community or nation, the value of water for food security is rarely (if ever) factored in when assessing the value of water for agriculture.

The values of water to human well-being extend well beyond its role in supporting direct physical life-sustaining functions or economies, and include mental health, spiritual well-being, emotional balance and happiness. The often-intangible nature of these sociocultural values attributed to water regularly defies any attempt at quantification, but they can nevertheless be regarded amongst the highest values.

Which leads us to the concept of 'perception'. Even when water from the same source is used for the same purpose under the same circumstances, its value can be perceived differently from one user to the next. Personal and sociocultural differences often lay at the root of this, with variables such as gender, age, race, class, status, or even belief, playing a determining role. The highly subjective nature of the concept of 'value' underscores the need to accommodate the different perspectives of various stakeholders.

As the eighth in a series of annual, thematic reports, the 2021 edition of the United Nations World Water Development Report (WWDR) examines the value of water across a broad range of water-related perspectives, ranging from water resources, infrastructure, and supply and sanitation services, through to economic uses and cultural values. It offers insights in the different methods for valuing water and provides guidance in how to use them.

The report presents a number of methodologies and approaches to valuing water across different use sectors and shows how these tools have been applied to improve water management. It also describes how valuation can potentially lead to better decision-making in terms of financing, governance, and knowledge and capacity-building.

We have endeavoured to produce a balanced, fact-based and neutral account of the current state of knowledge, covering the most recent developments, and highlighting the challenges and opportunities that a greater attention to valuing water can provide. Although primarily targeted at policy- and decision-makers, water resources managers, academics, and the broader development community, we hope that this report will also be useful to economists, social scientists, and those who are engaged in the alleviation of poverty and humanitarian crises, in the pursuit of the human rights to water supply and sanitation, and in the advancement of the 2030 Agenda for Sustainable Development.

This latest edition of the WWDR is the result of a concerted effort between the Chapter Lead Agencies: FAO, GWP, IHE Delft, UNDP, UNESCO-IHP, UN-Habitat, UNIDO, WWAP and the World Bank, with regional perspectives provided by UNECE, UNECLAC, UNESCAP, the UNESCO Office in Nairobi and UNESCWA. The report also greatly benefitted from the inputs and contributions of several other UN-Water members and partners, as well as from numerous scientists, professionals and NGOs who provided a wide range of relevant material.

On behalf of the WWAP Secretariat, we would like to extend our deepest appreciation to the afore-mentioned agencies, members and partners of UN-Water, and to the writers and other contributors for collectively producing this unique and authoritative report during the COVID-19 pandemic, with all the additional difficulties the situation has imposed on each and all of us.

We are profoundly grateful to the Italian Government for funding the Programme and to the Regione Umbria for generously hosting the WWAP Secretariat in Villa La Colombella in Perugia. Their contributions have been instrumental to the production of the WWDR.

Our special thanks go to Ms Audrey Azoulay, Director-General of UNESCO, for her ongoing support to WWAP and the production of the WWDR, and to Mr Gilbert F. Houngbo, President of the International Fund for Agricultural Development (IFAD) and Chair of UN-Water.

We extend our most sincere gratitude to all our colleagues at the WWAP Secretariat, whose names are listed in the Team page. The report could not have been completed without their professionalism and dedication.

We would like to thank the institutions who have graciously agreed to translate the WWDR into several different languages. Their support and efforts to broaden the dissemination of the report are very much appreciated.

Last but not least, we dedicate this report to the front-line healthcare providers and essential service workers whose tireless efforts allowed us to remain as safe as possible during the COVID-19 pandemic.

Michela Miletto

Richard Connor

WWDR 2021 Team

Director of the Publication
Michela Miletto

Editor-in-Chief
Richard Connor

Process Coordinator
Engin Koncagül

Publications Assistant
Valentina Abete

Graphic Designer
Marco Tonsini

Copy Editor
Simon Lobach

UNESCO World Water Assessment Programme (WWAP) Secretariat (2020–2021)

Coordinator: Michela Miletto

Programmes: Richard Connor, Laura Veronica Imburgia, Engin Koncagül, Paola Piccione and Laurens Thuy

Publications: Valentina Abete, Martina Favilli and Marco Tonsini

Communications: Simona Gallese

Administration and support: Barbara Bracaglia, Lucia Chiodini and Arturo Frascani

IT and Security: Fabio Bianchi, Michele Brensacchi, Francesco Gioffredi and Tommaso Brugnami

Interns: Marianna Alcini, Hanouf Alyami, Giulia Cadoni, Han Chen, Lorenzo Barrasso Mazza, Ahmed Assah Quatah and Yani Wang

Acknowledgements

This Report is published by the United Nations Educational, Scientific and Cultural Organization (UNESCO), on behalf of UN-Water, and its production is coordinated by the UNESCO World Water Assessment Programme (WWAP). Gratitude goes to UN-Water Members and Partners and other Contributors that made the content preparation of this Report possible.

Chapter Lead Agencies

Food and Agriculture Organization of the United Nations (FAO), Global Water Partnership (GWP), IHE Delft Institute for Water Education (IHE-Delft), United Nations Human Settlements Programme (UN-Habitat), United Nations Development Programme (UNDP), UNESCO (Intergovernmental Hydrological Programme – IHP, Nairobi Office and WWAP), United Nations Industrial Development Organization (UNIDO), United Nations Regional Commissions (Economic Commission for Europe – UNECE, Economic Commission for Latin America and the Caribbean – UNECLAC, Economic and Social Commission for Asia and the Pacific – UNESCAP, Economic and Social Commission for Western Asia – UNESCWA), and the World Bank

Contributors

Asia-Pacific Water Forum (APWF), FAO, GWP, GWP Global Technical Committee, Human Right 2 Water/WaterLex, International Association for Hydro-Environment Engineering and Research (IAHR), International Association of Hydrological Sciences (IAHS), International Centre for Water Cooperation (ICWC), International Federation of Private Water Operators (AquaFed), IHE Delft, International Institute for Applied Systems Analysis (IIASA), International Labour Organization (ILO), International Organization for Migration (IOM), International Union for Conservation of Nature (IUCN), International Water Management Institute (IWMI), IWMI South Africa, Stockholm International Water Institute (SIWI), UNDP, UNDP-SIWI Water Governance Facility, UNECE, UNESCO, UNESCO-IHP, UNESCO-WWAP, United Nations Children's Fund (UNICEF), University of Mpumalanga, University of Oxford, United Nations University Institute for Integrated Management of Material Fluxes and of Resources (UNU-FLORES), UNU Institute for the Advanced Study of Sustainability (UNU-IAS), UNU Institute for Water, Environment and Health (UNU-INWEH), Valuing Water Initiative (VWI), Water.org, WaterAid, Water Supply and Sanitation Collaborative Council (WSSCC), Women for Water Partnership (WfWP), World Business Council for Sustainable Development (WBCSD), and World Youth Parliament for Water (WYPW)

Donors

The development of the Report was financially supported by the Government of Italy and the Regione Umbria. All who have provided in-kind contributions, and their respective donors, are gratefully acknowledged.

Executive summary

Perspectives, challenges and opportunities

The current status of water resources highlights the need for improved water resources management. Recognizing, measuring and expressing water's worth, and incorporating it into decision-making, are fundamental to achieving sustainable and equitable water resources management and the Sustainable Development Goals (SDGs) of the United Nations' 2030 Agenda for Sustainable Development.

Those who control how water is valued control how it is used. Values are a central aspect of power and equity in water resources governance. The failure to fully value water in all its different uses is considered a root cause, or a symptom, of the political neglect of water and its mismanagement. All too often, the value of water, or its full suite of multiple values, is not prominent in decision-making at all.

Whilst the term 'value' and the process of 'valuation' are well defined, there are several different views and perspectives of what 'value' specifically means to various user groups and stakeholders. There are also different methods for calculating value and different metrics to express it.

Differences in the way water is valued occur not only between stakeholder groups but are widespread within them. These divergent perspectives on water value and the best ways to calculate and express it, coupled with limited knowledge of the actual resource, present a challenging landscape for rapid improvements in valuing water. It is, for example, futile to attempt to quantitatively compare the value of water for domestic use, the human right to water, customary or religious beliefs, and the value of maintaining flows to preserve biodiversity. None of these should be sacrificed for the sake of achieving consistent valuation methodologies.

Traditional economic accounting, often a key means of informing policy decisions, tends to limit water values to the way that most other products are valued – using the recorded price or costs of water when economic transactions occur. However, in the case of water, there is no clear relationship between its price and its value. Where water is priced, meaning consumers are charged for using it, the price often reflects attempts for cost recovery and not value delivered. Yet, regarding valuation, economics remains a highly relevant, powerful and influential science, even though its application needs to be made more comprehensive.

Nevertheless, the different values of water need to be reconciled, and the trade-offs between them resolved and incorporated into systematic and inclusive planning and decision-making processes. The way forward, therefore, will be to further develop common approaches to valuation where feasible, but also to prioritize improved approaches to compare, contrast and merge different values, and to incorporate fair and equitable conclusions into improved policy and planning.

This report groups current methodologies and approaches to the valuation of water into five interrelated perspectives: valuing **water sources**, *in situ* water resources and ecosystems; valuing **water infrastructure** for water storage, use, reuse or supply augmentation; valuing **water services**, mainly drinking water, sanitation and related human health aspects; valuing **water as an input to production and socio-economic activity**, such as food and agriculture, energy and industry, business and employment; and other **sociocultural values of water**, including recreational, cultural and spiritual attributes. These are complemented with experiences from different global regions; opportunities to reconcile multiple values of water through more integrated and holistic approaches to governance; approaches to financing; and methods to address knowledge, research and capacity needs.

Valuing the environment

The source of all water is the environment and all water abstracted by humans eventually returns there, together with any impurities added to it. The environment–water interface can be proactively managed in order to address water-related challenges through what has become known as 'nature-based solutions'.

But the status and trends of the environment–water interactions clearly indicate the need for much better incorporation of the value of the environment in water resources management. In most studies, water-related ecosystem services are not treated as a distinct or separate category, and clusters or bundles of services must often be combined from the underlying results to obtain relevant analyses and conclusions regarding water.

There are several different views and perspectives of what 'value' specifically means to various user groups and stakeholders

Significant values can also be attributed to ecosystem services that relate to supporting resilience, or reducing risks. Many disaster risks are exacerbated by the loss of relevant ecosystem services, as these services played a role in preventing disasters in the first place. The values of these services can be calculated, but they are often not recognized or adequately included in economic planning, which tends to favour short-term gains over longer-term sustainability.

Expressing the values of ecosystem services in monetary terms enables values to be more easily compared with other economic assessments, which often use monetary-based units. However, the environment can have important values that cannot, or should not, be constrained or defined by monetary-based approaches.

The existence of different value systems infers that it would be problematic to develop a unified system of, and metrics for, valuing water and/or the environment. What is feasible is to develop a common approach under which different environmental values or value systems can be compared, contrasted and used.

Valuing hydraulic infrastructure

The value of water to society is underpinned by hydraulic infrastructure, which serves to store or move water, thus delivering substantial social and economic benefits. Socio-economic development is curtailed in countries that have insufficient infrastructure to manage water. While more infrastructure is needed, past experience shows that the valuation of hydraulic infrastructure has been seriously flawed.

In spite of the large sums of money invested in water infrastructure, the valuation of costs and benefits are not well developed, standardized or widely applied. Societal benefits delivered are often unquantified, costs (particularly external costs) are not adequately accounted for, options are often not appropriately valued and compared, and hydrological data are often poor and outdated.

The valuation of hydraulic infrastructure is beset with conceptual and methodological difficulties, particularly regarding non-consumptive use, and indirect and non-use values. Most methods of valuing water infrastructure centre on a cost–benefit approach, but there is a tendency to overestimate benefits and underestimate costs, and in particular to not include all costs.

One of the most critical questions is 'value to whom'. Valuations tend to excessively focus on target beneficiaries while other stakeholders may benefit less or even be negatively impacted.

A major shortcoming in many approaches is that they focus mainly on financial costs (cash flows, and capital and operational expenditure) and financial returns. They often omit indirect costs, and in particular social and environmental costs, which are treated as externalities.

A key question in valuation is whether large capital and operational and maintenance (O&M) costs are included in subsequent valuations of end uses. Full-cost charging for water services is the exception rather than the rule. In many countries, only part or all of the operational costs are recovered, and capital investments are covered by public funds.

Valuation is only of use if the decision-making process in question is based on a fair assessment of values. Too many projects, particularly for high-profile water infrastructure such as dams, remain essentially vanity projects, politically motivated and/or potentially subject to corruption. Under such circumstances, values, if assessed, are opaque, selective, manipulated or ignored. No amount of guidance on valuation will change that. Fundamentally, valuation of water infrastructure is about good governance. At least, the attempt to govern well must be in place for proper valuations to play their part.

Valuing water supply, sanitation and hygiene (WASH) services

The role of water within households, schools, workplaces and health care facilities is often overlooked or not assigned a value comparable with other uses

The role of water within households, schools, workplaces and health care facilities is often overlooked or not assigned a value comparable with other uses. Water is a basic human need, required for drinking and to support sanitation and hygiene, sustaining life and health. Access to both water and sanitation are human rights. A direct extension of access to WASH services not only improves educational opportunities and workforce productivity, but also contributes to a life of dignity and equality. WASH services also indirectly add value in the form of a healthier environment.

It has been estimated that achieving universal access to safe drinking water and sanitation (SDG Targets 6.1 and 6.2) in 140 low- and middle-income countries would cost approximately US$1.7 trillion from 2016 to 2030, or US$114 billion per year. The benefit–cost ratio of such investments has been shown to provide a significant positive return in most regions. Returns on hygiene are even higher, as they can greatly improve health outcomes in many cases with little need for additional expensive infrastructure.

The year 2020 saw the rise of the COVID-19 pandemic, which hit the world's most vulnerable people the hardest – many of them living in informal settlements and urban slums. Hand hygiene is extremely important to prevent the spread of COVID-19. Globally, over three billion people and two out of five health care facilities lack adequate access to hand hygiene facilities.

Because access to WASH is so fundamental to life and public health, in many countries WASH services are considered the realm of governments and therefore often subsidized, even in high-income countries.

However, subsidies do not necessarily ensure that the poor are able to access basic services. Water subsidies can end up benefiting those with existing connections to sewerage or water networks, many of whom are non-poor. As a result, the poor do not benefit from the subsidy and the water service provider loses the tariff revenue it could have collected from wealthier households. Value is lost in terms of revenue to the provider, while the negative impacts of not having access to WASH services, such as school and work absenteeism, are not mitigated.

It is important to examine affordability from the perspective of disadvantaged groups, based on their income, their location and the socio-economic challenges they face.

Valuing water for food and agriculture

Agriculture uses the major share (69%) of global freshwater resources. However, water use for food production is being questioned as intersectoral competition for water intensifies and water scarcity increases. Moreover, in many regions of the world, water for food production is used inefficiently. This is a major driver of environmental degradation, including depletion of aquifers, reduction of river flows, degradation of wildlife habitats, and pollution.

The value assigned to water in food production is generally low compared to other uses. It is usually very low (typically less than US$0.05/m^3) where water is used for irrigating food grains and fodder, while it can be relatively high (of the same order of magnitude as values in domestic and industrial uses) for high-value crops such as vegetables, fruits and flowers.

Estimates of values of water for food production normally only consider the direct economically beneficial use of water (i.e. value to users of water), while many of the other direct and indirect benefits associated with water, which may be economic, sociocultural or environmental, remain unaccounted for or only partially quantified. Some of those benefits include improving nutrition, accommodating shifts in consumption patterns, generating employment and providing livelihood resilience especially for smallholder farmers, contributing to alleviating poverty and revitalizing rural economies, and supporting climate change mitigation and adaptation. The food security value of water is high but rarely quantified – and it is often a political imperative irrespective of other values.

Improving water security for food production in both rainfed and irrigated systems can contribute to reducing poverty and closing the gender gap

Several management strategies that could maximize the multiple values of water for food production could be implemented, including improving water management in rainfed areas; transitioning to sustainable intensification; sourcing water for irrigated agriculture, especially from nature-based and non-conventional sources; improving water use efficiency; reducing demand for food and its consequent water use; and improving knowledge and understanding of water use for food production.

Improving water security for food production in both rainfed and irrigated systems can contribute to reducing poverty and closing the gender gap directly and indirectly. Direct effects include higher yields; reduced risk of crop failure and increased diversity of cropping; higher wages from enhanced employment opportunities; and stable local food production and prices. Indirect effects include income and employment multipliers beyond the farm, and reduction of migration. Enhanced and more stable incomes could help improve education and the skillsets of women, and thus foster their active participation in decision-making. Although increasing water productivity can have substantial positive impacts, care should be taken to account for possible perverse effects and implications on poverty alleviation (i.e. land grabbing and increasing inequality).

Energy, industry and business

In the energy, industry and business (EIB) sector, water is seen as both a resource with withdrawal and consumption costs determined by prices, and a liability involving treatment costs and regulatory penalties, leading to a perception that water is a cost or risk to sales and compliance. Business tends to focus on operational savings and short-term revenue impacts, and tends to pay less attention to water value in administrative costs, natural capital, financial risk, future growth and operations, and innovation.

There are drivers that push and others that pull businesses towards valuing water. The former are trends, both global and regulatory, involving natural capital accounting, water valuation and water pricing. The latter is the growing business case for prospective benefits including better decision-making, higher revenues, lower costs, improved risk management and a better reputation.

The higher costs, lower earnings and financial losses related to water risks are significant. The risks associated with increased water scarcity, flooding and climate change include higher operating costs, supply chain disruption, water supply disruption, constraints to growth and brand damage.

The higher costs, lower earnings and financial losses related to water risks are significant

Due to its character, the EIB sector is highly focused on monetization. This provides a predisposition towards certain aspects of value (e.g. price of a cubic metre of water) and sometimes an indifference to others (e.g. the tangible and intangible value of water to other stakeholders). The most straightforward monetary valuation is volumetric – price per cubic metre, multiplied by the volume of water used, plus the cost to treat and dispose of wastewater. The metrics for the commercial performance of water use in EIB are relatively simple. They include water productivity, defined as profit or value of production per volume ($/m^3); water use intensity, defined as volume to produce a unit of value added (m^3/$); water use efficiency, defined as value added per volume ($/m^3); and the change in water use efficiency over time (SDG Indicator 6.4.1).

The overall economic productivity of water (GDP/m^3) in the EIB sector also leads at local, regional and national levels to various co-benefits, such as job creation and new enterprises. These are not easy to quantify, as many factors come into play, of which water is only one.

A better understanding of the motivations behind corporate interests in water management should align with those of water management agencies pursuing Integrated Water Resources Management (IWRM) planning approaches. The circular economy will value water to the extent that each litre is reused again and again, making water itself almost become part of the infrastructure rather than a consumable resource.

Cultural values of water

Culture directly influences how the values of water are perceived, derived and used. Every society, group or individual exists in their own cultural setting that is moulded by a varying mix of heritage, tradition, history, education, life experience, exposure to information and media, social status, and gender, among many other factors.

Some cultures can hold values that are difficult to quantify or indeed, in some cases, to articulate. Water can appeal to people for spiritual reasons, or through scenic beauty, because of its importance for wildlife or recreation, among others, or combinations of these. These values can be problematic to compare with values derived through other formal means, such as economics, and are therefore often excluded from value assessments that favour those. Moreover, culture changes and evolves over time, sometimes rapidly.

There is a close relationship between religion, or faith, and ethics. For example, narratives originating from regions characterized by water scarcity often feature illustrations of lawful and morally correct living beings, often as characterized by the local religion, rewarded with rainfall and access to water. By contrast, the modern economic conception of water can be characterized by its abstraction from social, cultural and religious contexts. Water in the global economic development context is often considered a resource at the disposal of society and is therefore distinct from water as it may be recognized by religions or the belief systems of many indigenous peoples, creating quite diverse, and potentially contradictory, perspectives of values.

The values of water to human well-being extend well beyond its role in supporting direct physical life-sustaining functions, and include mental health, spiritual well-being, emotional balance and happiness

The values of water in the context of conflict, peace and security are paradoxical. Whilst much has been written about the positive value of water in promoting peace, in many cases water itself was a contributing factor to the conflict in the first place. It has been argued that a spirit of dialogue helps to transform water-related conflicts into cooperation.

The values of water to human well-being extend well beyond its role in supporting direct physical life-sustaining functions, and include mental health, spiritual well-being, emotional balance and happiness.

After understanding, categorizing or codifying cultural values, there is a need to identify ways and means of incorporating these values into decision-making. These tools, such as cultural mapping, can help to better understand cultural values of water, reconcile antagonistic values, and build resilience with regard to current and future challenges, such as climate change. A fundamental need is the full and effective gender-sensitive participation of all stakeholders in decision-making, allowing everyone to express their own values in their own way.

Regional perspectives

Sub-Saharan Africa

Africa's freshwater resources are estimated to be nearly 9% of the world's total. However, these resources are unevenly distributed, with the six most water-rich countries in Central and Western Africa holding 54% of the continent's total resources and the 27 most water-poor countries holding only 7%.

The *Africa Water Vision 2025* offers a context within which water security and sustainable management of water resources could be achieved. However, rapid population growth, inappropriate water governance and institutional arrangements, depletion of water resources through pollution, environmental degradation, deforestation, and low and unsustainable financing of investments in water supply and sanitation are some of the main challenges to the achievement of SDG 6 on the continent.

In Sub-Saharan Africa, valuing water has been a challenging task for many researchers and development experts, due at least in part to limited baseline historical data. Researchers studying the value of water have focused mainly on using the actual price paid or the willingness to pay from the consumer's point of view by adopting the contingent valuation method. Studies valuing water in Sub-Saharan Africa have mostly focused on domestic water use.

Pan-European region

Valuing water is a challenging task within any single jurisdiction, hence doing so across borders presents even greater challenges. While increasing significance is being placed on valuing water within the Pan-European region, efforts to value water, especially in a transboundary basin context, remain limited in scope and often use different approaches. The discernable approaches to valuing water quantitatively in transboundary basins are more targeted on flood management, disaster risk reduction (DRR), early-warning systems and ecosystem services. The collective economic benefits of transboundary cooperation on these aspects outweigh the collective investment costs of unilateral action by several times.

Quantitatively valuing water is significantly more challenging within transboundary contexts as the data required to base calculations are often lacking. The countries that share a water resource often put different emphases on values, needs and priorities attached to water-related sectors. Many elements that can be valued, are done so on the basis of approximations and thus often undervalued, especially due to the lack of data and the inability to quantify indirect benefits. However, several broad-based approaches exist for identifying the intersectoral benefits of transboundary water cooperation on a case-by-case basis. These benefits, when strengthened, can consequently help increase the value of transboundary water management by reducing the economic and other costs of 'inaction' or insufficient cooperation in shared basins.

Latin America and the Caribbean

Water stress in the region has fuelled a number of conflicts, as various sectors, including agriculture, hydroelectricity, mining, and even drinking water and sanitation, are competing over scarce resources.

Most countries in Latin America and the Caribbean have not assigned sufficient funds for proper law enforcement in cases of pollution or overexploitation

Some of the major obstacles in securing effective allocation processes are connected to poor regulation, missing incentives and/or lack of investment. All these factors ultimately reflect the low value that is largely attributed to water resources in the region. The costs of water use or maintenance (once the concession or right of use is granted), are usually nil or insignificant for hydroelectric plants, mining companies and even farmers; and sometimes these costs are not even included in their economic balances. The latter represents an implicit subsidy that does not reflect the strategic value of water in the multiple production processes and under a context of climate change.

Most countries in the region have not assigned sufficient funds for proper law enforcement in cases of pollution or overexploitation. While legal precepts are of extreme relevance, regulation and monitoring as well as well-aligned incentives are essential in the region, not only to ensure a better appreciation of the role and value of water but also to prevent its overexploitation and pollution, particularly given the increasing climate instability.

Asia and the Pacific

Due to population growth, urbanization and increased industrialization, water competition among sectors has become more severe in the region, threatening agricultural production and food security while also affecting water quality. Water is often a relatively scarce and valuable resource in the region, and water scarcity is likely to worsen due to the impacts of climate change.

Unsustainable water withdrawals are a major concern in the region, as some countries withdraw unsustainable proportions of their freshwater supply – exceeding half of the total water availability – and seven of the world's 15 biggest abstractors of groundwater are in Asia and the Pacific.

Wastewater remains an underutilized resource in the region. There is therefore an urgent need in Asia and the Pacific to tap into wastewater, as well as to tackle water pollution and promote water efficiency, including from the industrial sector. This is particularly urgent in the region's least developed countries, on islands and in countries where water resources are particularly scarce.

The region has seen the emergence of diverse positive water-valuing initiatives that leverage new financial, governance and partnership models, notably in Australia, China, Japan and Malaysia.

The Arab region

Few other regions value water as much as the water-scarce Arab region, where over 85% of the population live under conditions of water scarcity. This scarcity has increased dependency on transboundary waters, non-renewable groundwater resources and non-conventional water resources. The quantity of freshwater that can be abstracted in a sustainable way would probably even be lower if water quality considerations were included.

Water is so highly valued in the region that it is considered a topic of security in bilateral and multilateral discussions among states. This is amplified by the fact that over two thirds of freshwater resources available in Arab states cross one or more international boundaries. However, joint methodologies for the economic valuation of transboundary waters have not yet been incorporated into cooperation arrangements, and funding to inform joint management efforts remains limited. Furthermore, national security considerations and a water rights perspective tend to dominate the discourse among riparian states, although nascent initiatives exist to value transboundary water cooperation and analysis focused on climate security and risk mitigation in transboundary water contexts in the Middle East and North Africa.

For the full value of water to be captured and considered by all to be a human right, there is a need for considerable investment in infrastructure, appropriate technologies and the use of non-conventional water resources to improve productivity, sustainability and access for all.

Governance

The use of multi-value approaches to water governance entails acknowledging the role of values in driving key water resources management decisions as well as a call for active participation of a more diverse set of actors

Global momentum is evolving towards an understanding that a diverse set of values drives the economic and financial considerations in water-related decision-making. Coupled with a recognition of water's multiple values, there is also a call for more robust measurement and valuation methods to help resolve trade-offs. The use of multi-value approaches to water governance entails acknowledging the role of values in driving key water resources management decisions as well as a call for active participation of a more diverse set of actors, thereby also incorporating a more diverse set of values into water governance. Including the intrinsic or relational values of diverse groups to better inform and legitimize water and related land resources management decisions would typically involve the direct participation of groups or interests that are often excluded from water-related decision-making. It may bring greater emphasis on ecological and environmental processes, and refocus efforts on sharing water resource benefits, rather than allocating water quantities for highest-value economic priorities.

Transitioning to a system of water governance that recognizes multiple values and the active participation of a varied set of actors presents a set of challenges. The first relates to acknowledging that the governance of water is driven by a set of implicit or explicit values. The second involves the value or worth of using water in different ways, which is fraught not only with measurement issues, including what can – and should – be measured, and by whom. The third relates to the common disconnect between public decision-making processes and actions on the ground, including the risk of agendas being controlled by vested interests.

Nations can transition into multi-value governance by building on existing governance frameworks such as IWRM, which integrates interests of diverse stakeholder groups operating at various political levels and policy sectors. IWRM is most often represented as cutting across water for people, food, nature, industry and other uses, and aims to encompass all social, economic and environmental considerations. It is essential to broaden and strengthen multi-stakeholder processes that recognize and reconcile a comprehensive mix of values, including benefit-sharing in water governance, as well as integrating ecological and environmental values into climate-resilient water management.

Financing and funding water services

In cases where benefits cannot be monetized, other valuation tools can be used, such as cost–effectiveness analyses

Maximizing the value of water in investment decisions requires careful valuation of the costs and benefits that a project provides. For this, all benefits need to be taken into account, including those that are economic, social or environmental. Many of the unintended consequences of these investments, both negative and positive, must also be considered. Aggregating these types of benefits can be difficult, as they are not all easily converted into monetary amounts. In cases where benefits cannot be monetized, other valuation tools can be used, such as cost–effectiveness analyses, which compare costs with non-pecuniary outcomes such as lives saved, people served or environmental metrics achieved. Another critical factor for determining benefits of a project is comparing it to what would happen if the project were not undertaken.

How a project will be funded is another critical component to the valuation analysis, as a project that does not have a means for funding will eventually see a service disruption when operations and maintenance are unfunded and capital costs cannot be repaid. Similarly, the dynamics of the funding type will impact the net benefits of the investment itself, and who receives them.

For investments in water supply, sanitation or irrigation services, designing an appropriate water tariff structure is a challenge, as there are multiple, often competing, policy goals that need to be taken into consideration. When supplying these services, care should also be taken to ensure affordability for the poor, expansion to the widest number of individuals, and funding to ensure reliability and network improvements. The water tariff (i.e. price) must be carefully designed to accomplish as many of these goals as possible – the price of water, its cost of delivery and its value are not synonymous, and price is merely one tool for aligning water's use with its values.

Large subsidies for WASH service provision are justifiable from an economic as well as a social and moral standpoint; however, they are often poorly targeted, resulting in poor outcomes. In fact, large, untargeted WASH subsidies can be counterproductive, reducing the benefits of water services, and thus the valuations of WASH investments. Indeed, in countries where piped water is deemed to be very low-cost or free, the poor are often unserved or underserved, and are compelled to pay a much higher price for their water than the rich.

Knowledge, research and capacity development

As a core component of knowledge building and sharing, water-related data and information are central to understanding and valuing the resource. Water-related data and information can also be generated by other sources such as earth observations, sensor networks and citizen data, including on social media. But data and information relating to social, economic and environmental demands and uses for water are also needed to complete the picture for potential value generation from water. Further efforts and investments are required to sustain the supply chain of data and information from its collection, analysis, sharing and application across sectors and scales.

To promote inclusive and transformative change in valuing water, it is strategically important to recognize the unique role of local and indigenous knowledge, in addition to the mainstream or traditional scientific or academic knowledge. Another part of the solution is to expand citizen science. The involvement of representative local stakeholders in ground-truthing data and information is also important.

Within the context of valuing water, capacity development concerns the establishment of know-how to inclusively and properly value water and to effectively manage it on the basis of those values, applied at different levels and under diverse conditions, leading to variable outcomes.

Conclusions

Unlike most other natural resources, it has proven extremely difficult to determine water's 'true' value

Unlike most other natural resources, it has proven extremely difficult to determine water's 'true' value. As such, the overall importance of this vital resource is not appropriately reflected in political attention and financial investment in many parts of the world. This not only leads to inequalities in access to water resources and water-related services, but also to inefficient and unsustainable use and degradation of water supplies themselves, affecting the fulfilment of nearly all the SDGs, as well as basic human rights.

Consolidating the different approaches and methods for valuing water across multiple dimensions and perspectives will likely remain challenging. Even within a specific water use sector, different approaches can lead to strikingly different valuations. Trying to reconcile valuations across sectors would normally increase the overall level of difficulty, as would taking account of some of the more intangible values attributed to water in different sociocultural contexts. While there may be scope to reduce complexities and standardize metrics in some circumstances, the reality is the need for better means to recognize, maintain and accommodate different values.

Coda

Even though it is not always recognized by all, water clearly has value. In some perspectives the value of water is infinite, since life does not exist without it and there is no replacement for it. This is perhaps best exemplified by the efforts and investments made in the search for extra-terrestrial water and the recent elation in finding it on the Moon and Mars. It is a shame that all too often, it is taken for granted here on Earth. The risks of undervaluing water are far too great to ignore.

Prologue

The state of water resources

WWAP

Richard Connor and David Coates

Water demand and use

Global freshwater use has increased by a factor of six over the past 100 years (Figure P1) and continues to grow at a rate of roughly 1% per year since the 1980s (AQUASTAT, n.d.). While the rate of increase in freshwater use had tapered off in most Member States of the Organisation for Economic Co-operation and Development (OECD), where per capita water use rates tend to be among the world's highest, it continues to grow in the majority of the emerging economies, as well as in middle- and lower-income countries (Ritchie and Roser, 2018). Much of this growth can be attributed to a combination of population growth, economic development and shifting consumption patterns.

Figure P1

Global water withdrawals, 1900–2010

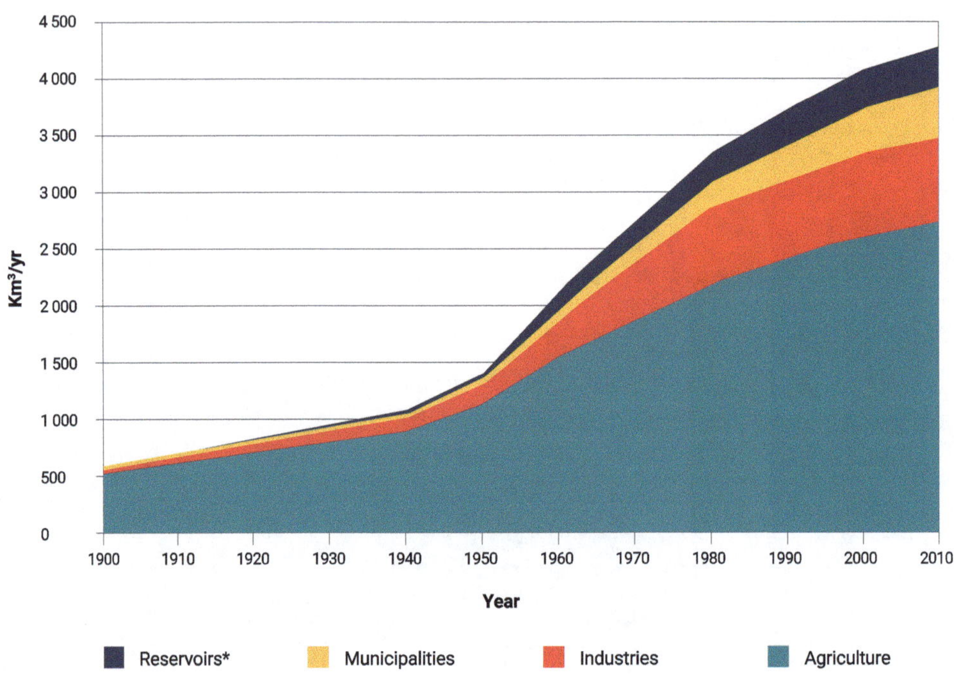

*Evaporation from artificial lakes.

Source: AQUASTAT (2010).

Agriculture currently accounts for 69% of global water withdrawals, which are mainly used for irrigation but also include water used for livestock and aquaculture. This ratio can reach up to 95% in some developing countries (FAO, 2011a). Industry (including energy and power generation) accounts for 19%, while municipalities are responsible for the remaining 12%.

Studies attempting to project trends in future water use have yielded varying results. For example:

- The 2030 Water Resources Group (2009) concluded that the world would face a 40% global water deficit by 2030 under a business-as-usual scenario.
- The OECD (2012) projected that global water demand would increase by 55% between 2000 and 2050.
- Burek et al. (2016) estimated that global water use would likely continue to grow at an annual rate of about 1%, resulting in an increase of 20 to 30% above the current level of water use by 2050.

While the exact magnitude of the actual increase in global water use remains uncertain, most authors agree that agricultural water use will face increasing competition and that most of the growth in water use will be driven by increasing demand by the industry and energy sectors, as well as by municipal and domestic uses, mainly as a function of industrial development and improving water and sanitation service coverage in developing countries and emerging economies (OECD, 2012; Burek et al., 2016; IEA, 2016).

Changes in agricultural water demand are among the most difficult to predict. The Food and Agriculture Organization of the United Nations (FAO) estimates, based on a business-as-usual scenario, that the world will need about 60% more food by 2050, and that irrigated food production will increase by more than 50% over the same period (FAO, 2017a). The necessary amounts of water for these developments are not available. FAO recognizes that the amounts of water withdrawn by agriculture can only increase by 10%. Fortunately, there is substantial room for improvements in water use efficiency in irrigated, and especially rainfed, systems (FAO, 2017a), as well as in eliminating food waste and shifting consumption towards less water-demanding diets (FAO, 2019a). Together, these responses would enable projected food demands to be met within sustainable limits and even present the potential to reduce current withdrawals over the longer term, thereby reducing competition with other uses.

Water availability

Water stress, essentially measured as water use as a function of available supply, affects many parts of the world (Figure P2). Over two billion people live in countries experiencing water stress (United Nations, 2018). However, physical water stress is often a seasonal rather than an annual phenomenon, as exemplified by the seasonal variability in water availability (Figure P3). An estimated four billion people live in areas that suffer from severe physical water scarcity for at least one month per year (Mekonnen and Hoekstra, 2016).

It should also be noted that about 1.6 billion people face 'economic' water scarcity, which means that while water may be physically available, they lack the necessary infrastructure to access that water (Comprehensive Assessment of Water Management in Agriculture, 2007).

Climate change is likely to increase seasonal variability, creating a more erratic and uncertain water supply, thus exacerbating problems in already water-stressed areas and potentially generating water stress in places where it has not yet been a recurring phenomenon.

Several of the world's main aquifers are under increasing stress and 30% of the largest groundwater systems are being depleted (Richey et al., 2015). The areas experiencing the highest levels of decline are shown in Figure P4. Water withdrawals for irrigation are the primary driver of groundwater depletion worldwide (Burek et al., 2016).

Water quality

While global water quality data remain sparse due to a lack of monitoring and reporting capacity, especially in many of the least developed countries, a number of trends have nonetheless been reported. Water quality has deteriorated as a result of pollution in nearly all major rivers in Africa, Asia and Latin America. Nutrient loading, which is often associated with pathogen loading, is among the most prevalent sources of pollution (UNEP, 2016).

Globally, an estimated 80% of all industrial and municipal wastewater is released into the environment without any prior treatment, with detrimental effects on human health and ecosystems. This ratio is much higher in least developed countries, where sanitation and wastewater treatment facilities are grossly lacking (WWAP, 2017). Managing excess nutrients in agricultural runoff is also considered as one of the most prevalent water quality-related challenges globally (OECD, 2017a). Hundreds of chemicals are also negatively impacting water quality. Risks related to emerging pollutants, including micropollutants, have been acknowledged since the early 2000s (Bolong et al., 2009).

Figure P2 Annual baseline water stress

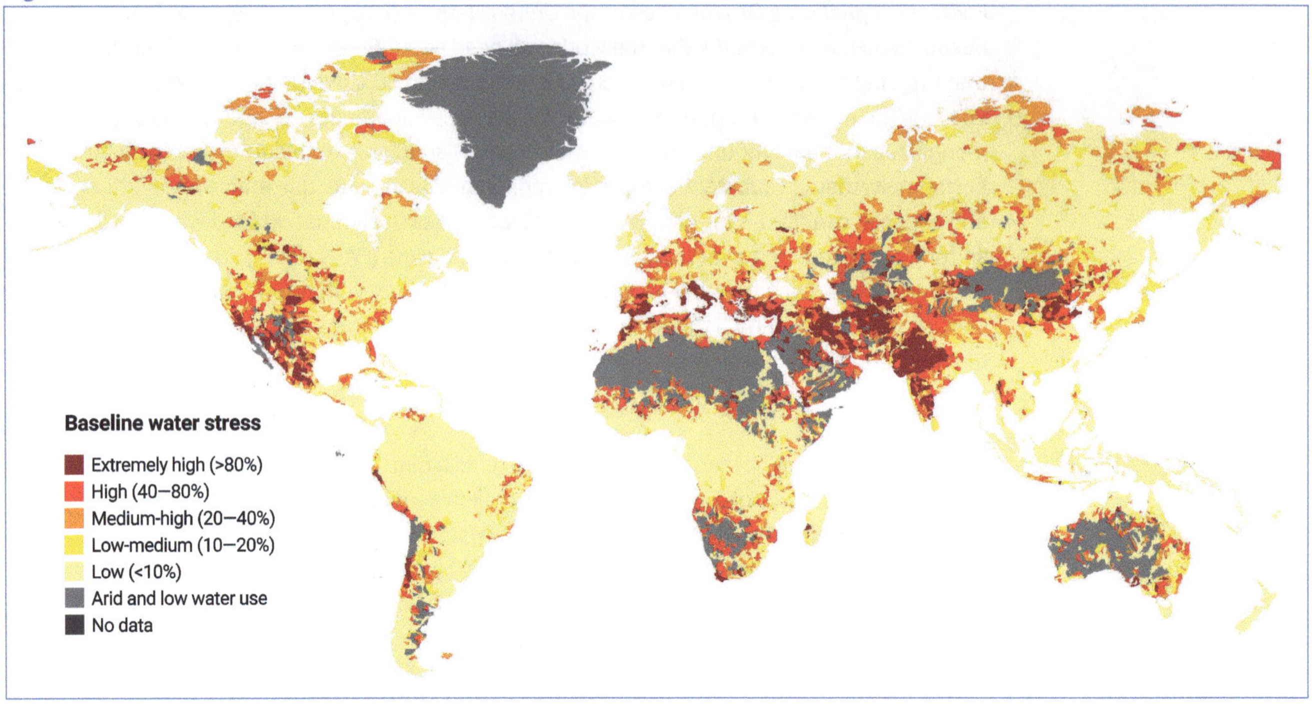

Note: Baseline water stress measures the ratio of total water withdrawals to available renewable water supplies. Water withdrawals include domestic, industrial, irrigation and livestock consumptive and non-consumptive uses. Available renewable water supplies include surface and groundwater supplies and considers the impact of upstream consumptive water users and large dams on downstream water availability. Higher values indicate more competition among users.

Source: WRI (2019). Attribution 4.0 International (CC BY 4.0).

Figure P3 Seasonal variability in available water supply

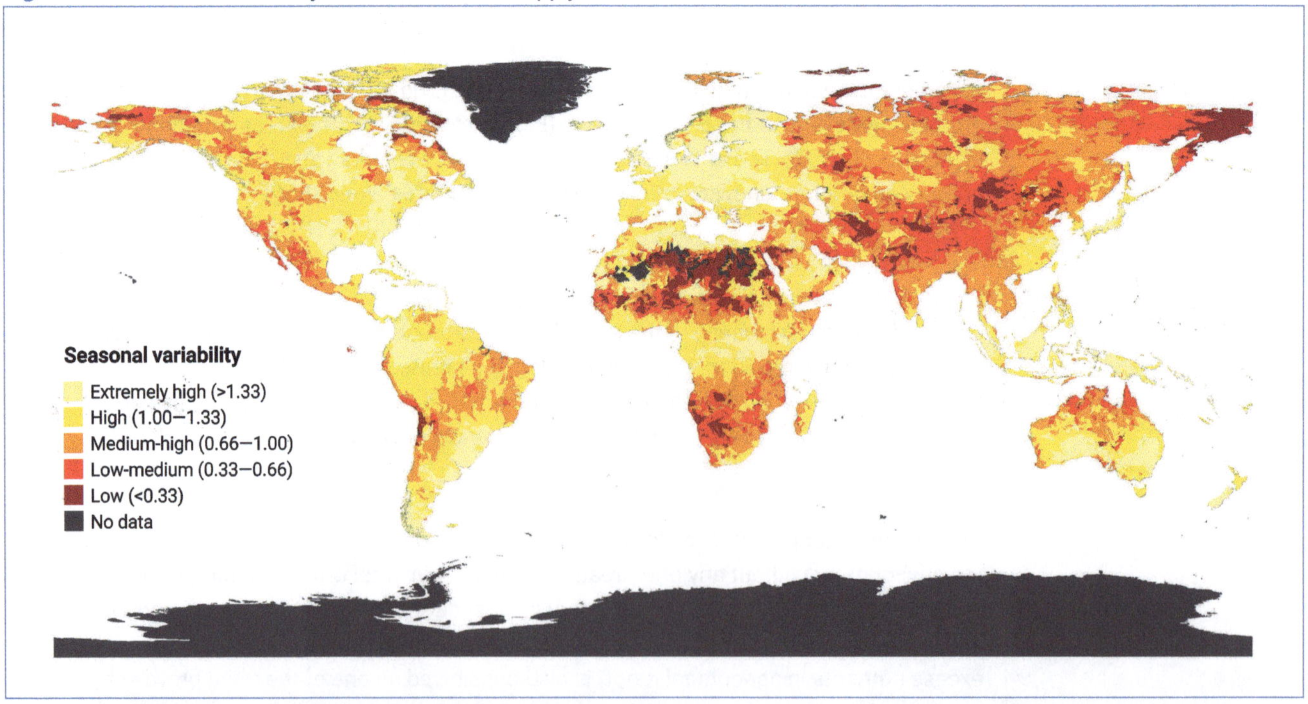

Note: Seasonal variability measures the average within-year variability of available water supply, including both renewable surface and groundwater supplies. Higher values indicate wider variations of available supply within a year.

Source: WRI (2019). Attribution 4.0 International (CC BY 4.0).

Figure P4 Groundwater table decline

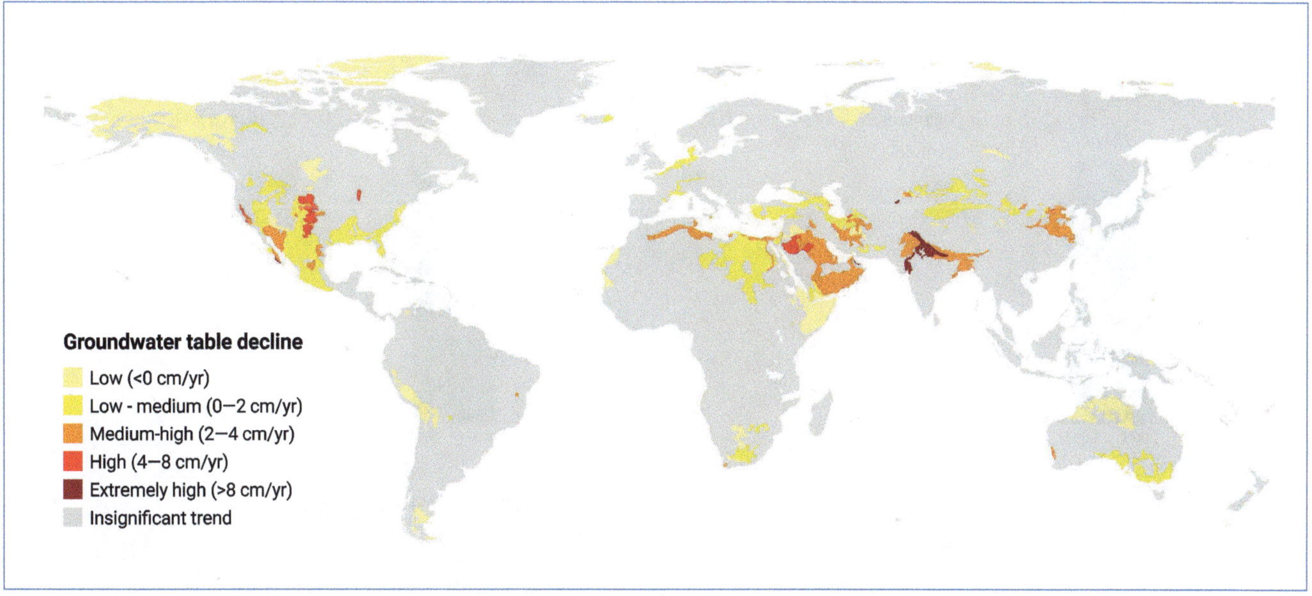

Note: Groundwater table decline measures the average decline of the groundwater table as the average change for the period of study (1990–2014). The result is expressed in centimetres per year. Higher values indicate higher levels of unsustainable groundwater withdrawals.

Source: WRI (2019). Attribution 4.0 International (CC BY 4.0).

Extreme events

Floods and droughts represent the two main water-related disasters. Over the period 2009–2019, floods caused nearly 55,000 deaths (including 5,110 in 2019 alone), affected another 103 million people (including 31,000 in 2019 alone) and caused US$76.8 billion in economic losses (including US$36.8 billion in 2019 alone) (CRED, 2020). Over the same period, droughts affected over 100 million people, killing over 2,000 people more, and directly causing over US$10 billion in economic losses (CRED, 2020).

Globally, floods and extreme rainfall events have increased by more than 50% over the past decade, occurring at a rate four times greater than in 1980 (EASAC, 2018). Climate change is expected to further increase the frequency and severity of floods and droughts (IPCC, 2018).

Water, sanitation and hygiene (WASH)

In 2017, 5.3 billion people (71% of the global population of 7.55 billion) used a safely managed drinking water service – one located on premises, available when needed and free from contamination (Figure P5). 3.4 billion people (or 45% of the global population) used safely managed sanitation services – an improved toilet or latrine that is not shared, from which excreta are safely disposed of in situ or treated off-site (Figure P6).

Figure P5 Global drinking water coverage, 2000–2017 (%)

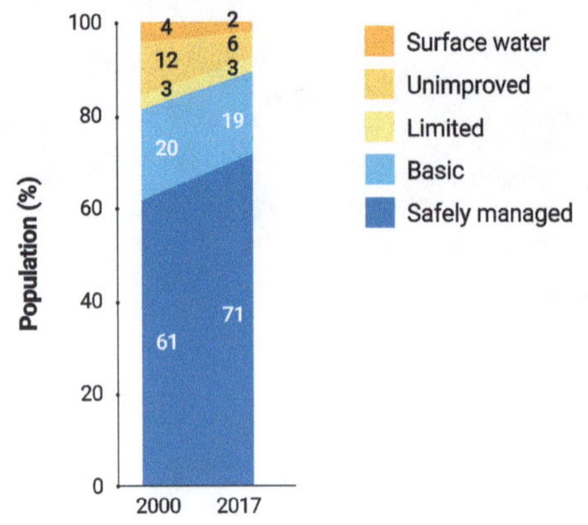

Source: WHO/UNICEF (2019a, fig. 1, p. 7).

Figure P6 Global sanitation coverage, 2000–2017 (%)

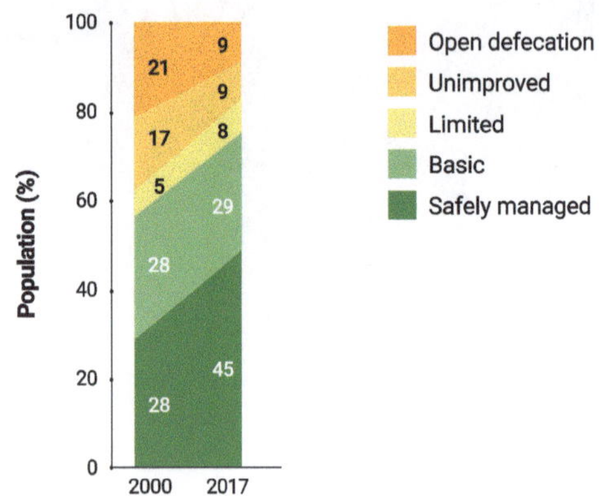

Source: WHO/UNICEF (2019a, fig. 4, p. 8).

Water-related ecosystem services

Of the 18 categories of 'nature's contributions to people' (which include bundles of ecosystem services), 14 are in decline. These include the three explicitly water-related categories: regulation of freshwater quantity, coastal and freshwater quality, and hazards and extreme events (IPBES, 2019a). Declines in these categories also contribute to declines in most other services categories, threatening the sustainability of those currently increasing (energy, food, animal feed and materials). Taking into consideration that the Sustainable Development Goals (SDGs) are integrated, indivisible, and nationally implemented, current negative trends in biodiversity and ecosystems will undermine progress towards 80% (35 out of 44) of the assessed targets of SDGs related to poverty (SDG 1), hunger (2), health (3), water (6), cities (11), climate (13), oceans (14) and land (15) (IPBES, 2019a).

Chapter 1

Valuing water: Perspectives, challenges and opportunities

WWAP
David Coates, Rebecca Tharme
and Richard Connor

With contributions from:
David Hebart-Coleman (SIWI)

1.1 Introduction

Water's worth is arguably infinite – without water life ceases to exist. Recognizing, measuring and expressing water's worth, and incorporating it into decision-making, are fundamental to achieving sustainable and equitable water resources management. Whilst the term 'value' and the process of 'valuation' are well defined (Box 1.1), there are multiple uses, and often reuses, of water and the very many different stakeholders involved usually have different views of what 'value' specifically means to them. There are also different methods for calculating value and different metrics to express it. Identifying and reconciling these differences is the subject of this *World Water Development Report*.

Box 1.1 Value and valuation: definitions

Valuation is the process by which a person or entity assigns value to something.
In the context of natural resources, the term 'value' is used in three main ways:

i. ***Exchange value:*** the price of a good or service in the market (i.e. market price);

ii. ***Utility:*** the use value of a good or service, which can be very different from the market price (e.g. the market price of water is very low, but its use value very high; the reverse is the case, for example, for diamonds or other luxury goods);

iii. ***Importance:*** the appreciation or emotional value we attach to a given good or service (e.g. the emotional or spiritual experience some people have when viewing water landscapes, or the importance given to water through culture or religion).

Source: Oxford English Dictionary

Recognizing, measuring and expressing water's worth, and incorporating it into decision-making, is fundamental to achieving sustainable and equitable water resources management

It is well recognized that water underpins most aspects of economies and sustainable development. The valuation of water, at least at a fundamental level, is implicit in most water resources management decisions. Therefore, the valuation of water connects with, for example, human rights frameworks, with the 2030 Agenda for Sustainable Development and its five pillars (people, prosperity, planet, peace and justice, and partnership), and with Integrated Water Resources Management (IWRM), among others. In order to provide more refined and quantitative information to support decision-making, some recent initiatives have focused more explicitly on the valuation of water. Examples include, the High Level Panel on Water (HLPW, 2017a) and its Bellagio Principles (HLPW, 2017b), the Global High-Level Panel on Water and Peace (2017), numerous water sector and/or private sector initiatives, and for ecosystems the recent global assessment of the Intergovernmental Science-Policy Platform on Biodiversity and Ecosystem Services (IPBES, 2019a), among others. The most advanced work on the valuation of water, in the context of accounting, is the System of Environmental Economic Accounting that has been developing detailed accounts for water since 2003 – the SEEA-Water (UNDESA, 2012).

This report groups current methodologies and approaches to the valuation of water into five inter-related perspectives: valuing **water sources**, *in situ* water resources and ecosystems (Chapter 2); valuing **water infrastructure** for water storage, use, reuse or supply augmentation (Chapter 3); valuing **water services**, mainly drinking water, sanitation and related human health aspects (Chapter 4); valuing **water as an input to production and socio-economic activity**, such as food and agriculture, energy and industry, and business and employment (Chapters 5 and 6); and other **sociocultural values of water**, including recreational, cultural and spiritual attributes (Chapter 7). These are complemented with experiences from different global regions (Chapter 8). Chapter 9 addresses the interdependency of these five perspectives and the obvious need to reconcile multiple values of water through more integrated and holistic approaches to governance. Chapter 10 covers financing, while Chapter 11 focuses on knowledge, research and capacity. Chapter 12 presents overall conclusions and ways forward.

1.2 Why value water?

The real worth of water, combined and contrasted across all stakeholder perspectives, has often been neglected, leading to its wastage, misuse and misappropriation by certain interests. Sometimes the contention around the value of water resides in the measurement of its worth. Other times, contention, or even conflict, resides in comparing differing value domains, for example, economic versus more intangible cultural values. Those who control how water is valued control how it is used. Values are a central aspect of power and equity in water resources governance.

The current status of water resources (see Prologue) highlights the need for improved water resources management. The cascading negative impacts of increasing water stress, water scarcity, flooding, pollution, loss of biodiversity and ecosystem services, and other aspects of water-related environmental degradation continue to be inadequately accounted for. This strongly underscores the need to change the way water is valued (Damania et al., 2017). For example, despite the challenges of increasing water scarcity, farmers, businesses, and households often have few incentives to consume less water, maintain water quality, or allocate it to ecosystems or social objectives (HLPW, 2018). Examples abound of countries where water is scarce and yet is used more intensively and wastefully than in countries where it is abundant (Figure 1.1). This is often a consequence of inappropriate policies, regulations and incentives that condone waste and over-use, instead of efficient and prudent use of scarce water resources. Technical solutions often exist, but the challenge is to translate them into concrete plans: who does what, at which level, and how. These questions often remain unanswered (HLPW, 2018).

Figure 1.1

Comparison of water-scarce and water-intensive economies

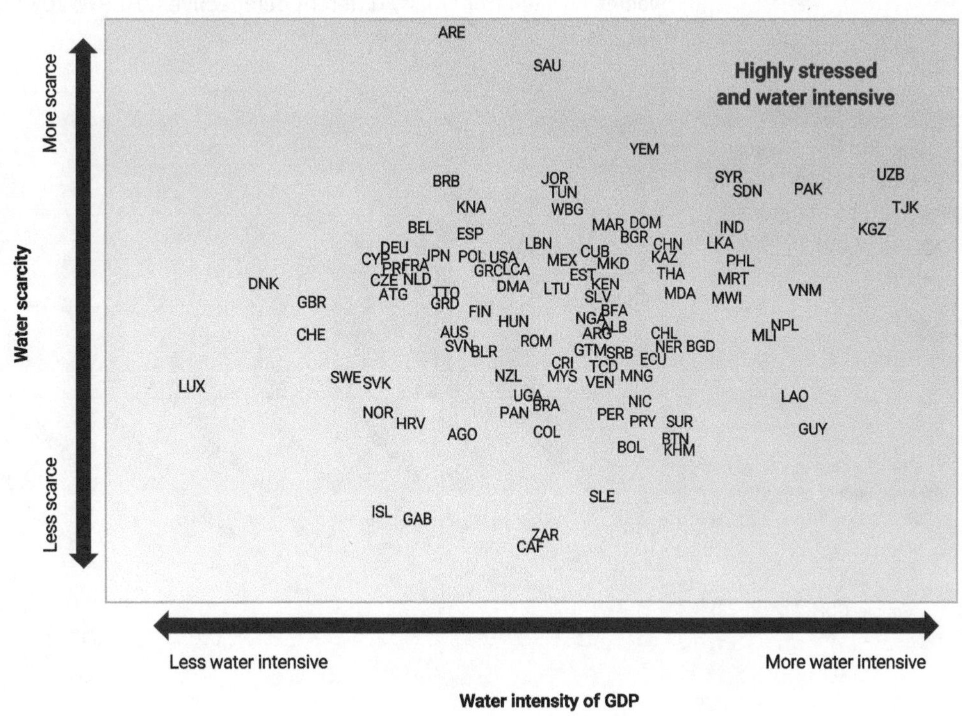

Note: Figure 1.1 compares water intensity of Gross Domestic Product (GDP) with water scarcity. Water intensity of GDP is measured as the ratio of total economic output to total water withdrawals, and water scarcity is measured as the ratio of total water withdrawals to renewable freshwater resources. Country abbreviations are the International Organization for Standardization's.

Source: Damania et al. (2017, fig. 1.1, p. 10).

The failure to fully value water in all in its different uses is considered a root cause, or a symptom, of the political neglect of water and its mismanagement (WWAP, 2012). It is argued that a primary reason for limited successes in attaining IWRM and other water-related goals and targets, and failures in water governance, is the omission of a full representation of the values of water. Water governance fundamentally concerns values (Groenfeldt, 2019).

Polarization of views on value can either constrain good governance, or be exacerbated by poor governance, and can lead to: insufficient appreciation of the importance of water; a low priority being given to water policy in country development programmes, poverty reduction strategies, and other policies; suboptimal levels of investment in water infrastructure; and even failure in meeting international socioeconomic goals (WWAP, 2012).

There is some recognition of the overall value of water and its contribution to human well-being. For example: "*Water is life. It is a fundamental condition of human survival and dignity, and is the basis for the resilience of societies and of the natural environment*" (Global High-Level Panel on Water and Peace, 2017, p. 11). The right to safe and clean drinking water and sanitation was recognized by the United Nations General Assembly in 2010 (UNGA, 2010) as a human right that is essential for the full enjoyment of life, forming a basis from which all human rights essentially stem. There is a plethora of other similar declarations of the overall value of water. However, the current status of water resources shows that these fundamental perceptions of value have done little to improve management. All too often, the value of water, or its full suite of multiple values, is not prominent in decision-making at all. Fragmented approaches, and in particular dominance of water resources management decisions by specific sectors or political classes, have been identified as a key challenge in every *World Water Development Report* so far.

As the drivers of water insecurity have accelerated apace (Figure 1.2), water has similarly grown in importance in terms of its essential and diverse values to society. This growth has placed more attention globally, regionally and at basin and local levels on how societies value water, why, and to what end purpose. It has underlined a pressing need for a more balanced, transparent, inclusive and nuanced characterization and reconciliation of water's diverse values as seen from many different perspectives (HLPW, 2017a).

Figure 1.2

The top ten drivers of water-related risk as perceived by businesses, reported in the 2019 CDP survey

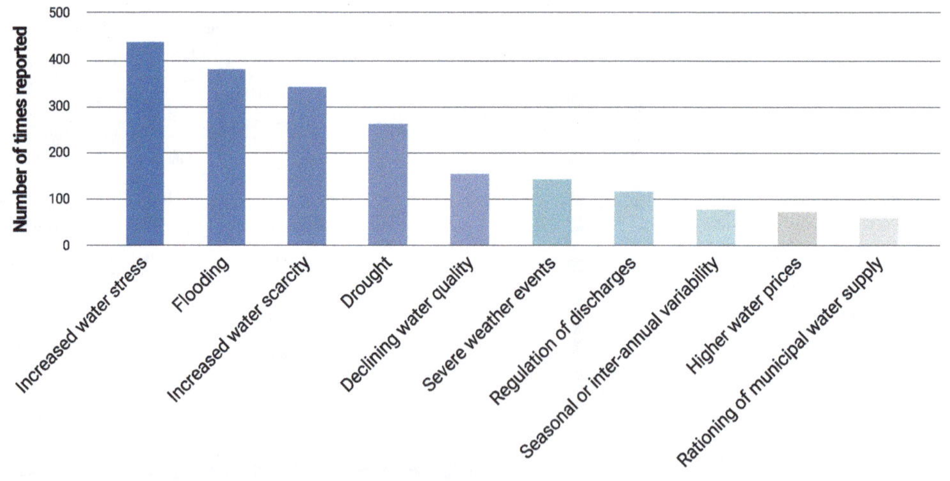

Note: The categories are not necessarily independent of each other.

Source: CDP (2020, p. 33).

This *World Water Development Report* argues that better measurement, monitoring and understanding of the values of water, and their incorporation into improved decision-making frameworks enable the equitable comparison of multiple values of water held by multiple stakeholder groups, and are essential for achieving sustainable water resources management.

1.3 The values of water to society

1.3.1 Differing perspectives on valuing water

Policy, management and investment decisions are compounded by differences among, and often within, stakeholder groups on priorities among different values, the specifics of what value means and how it can be measured, and the metrics for expressing it. Individuals intuitively recognize that water is *"more than a substance: it carries multiple values and meanings"* (HLPW, 2017a, Preamble, p. 1). People's cultural heritage, world views, codes of ethics, and established norms frame their relationships with water, influencing their perspectives and the ways in which they think about and value this natural resource (Johnston et al., 2012; Bakker, 2012; Krause and Strang, 2016). Different cultures, societies and communities around the world, including indigenous peoples, understand and define the values of water in quite different ways, according divergent values to the resource and its uses, which may be hard or even inappropriate to attempt to reconcile.

There are a number of ways of categorizing value concepts such as assigned (or instrumental/economic), moral (notions of what is right), held (fairness, courage) and relational values (Chan et al., 2018). *Relational values* encompass a wide range of values that are embedded in desirable relationships, including those between people and those involving the notion of values held because of specific principles or moral duties and regardless of whether those relationships imply trade-offs. For this reason, they may depart from an economic valuation framework (IPBES, 2019a). Relational values can be a bridge between intrinsic and instrumental values. However, others have considered cultural and religious values, and other intangible benefits of belief systems, to be cultural ecosystem services and therefore amenable to economic analysis (e.g. Russi et al., 2013). None of these concepts, categorizations or approaches are necessarily more important than others. For example relational, cultural or other intangible values can trump 'economic' values in decision-making (examples are provided in chapters 2 and 9). But the weight given to different value concepts has a major impact on values assessed and decisions taken. Practitioners need to be acutely aware of the value system that they, and others, are adopting.

In the case of water there is no clear relationship between its price and its value. Where water is priced, meaning consumers are charged for using it, the price often reflects attempts for cost recovery and not value delivered

Economics is the most widely applied framework for valuing water. This report takes a comprehensive view of its scope. There are a number of economic categories of 'value' (Box 1.2). In practice, economic approaches can often be more limited in scope and often furnish an incomplete indication of water's true economic value. Traditional economic accounting, often a key means of informing policy decisions, tends to limit water values to the way that most other products are valued – using the recorded price or costs of water when economic transactions occur. However, in the case of water there is no clear relationship between its price and its value. Where water is priced, meaning consumers are charged for using it, the price often reflects attempts for cost recovery and not value delivered (see Section 1.5 and Chapter 10). Yet regarding valuation, economics remains the most relevant, powerful and influential science. Its application, therefore, needs to be made more comprehensive.

The unique characteristics of water also make it difficult to value using market prices. It is a heavily regulated commodity, usually without free markets. Due to economies of scale, water storage and distribution are often under the control of monopolies. Moreover, property rights, essential for competitive markets, are often absent. Water is also a bulky commodity with very high weight to value ratio, limiting markets to those in a local area. Finally, large amounts of water abstracted can be unrecorded (UNDESA, 2012).

Differences in the way water is valued occur not only between stakeholder groups but are widespread within them. For example, there are multiple ways of expressing and calculating values of water used by agriculture and variation in what is included in accounting. This results in a wide range of approaches (Box 1.3).

Box 1.2 Categories of economic values

In this report, *economics* is a social science concerned with the production, distribution and consumption of goods and services (Oxford English Dictionary); *goods and services* are interpreted comprehensively and include any benefit received from water, material or otherwise. Importantly, economic assessment and analysis are not limited to monetary valuation.

There are a number of categories for the economic values associated with water such as:

Use values:

Direct use values relate to the direct use of water resources for consumptive uses, such as input to agriculture, manufacturing and domestic use; and non-consumptive uses, such as generating hydroelectric power, recreation, navigation and cultural activities.

Indirect use values relate to the indirect environmental services provided by water, such as waste assimilation, habitat and biodiversity protection, and hydrologic function (UNDESA, 2012, Box VIII.2, p. 123).

Option value is the value of maintaining future choices – today's value of maintaining the future option for the use of water, directly or indirectly; for example, pollution of a groundwater store that is not currently being used incurs no immediate loss of direct value, but reduces the value of the resource for future use (UNDESA, 2012, Box VIII.2, p. 123).

Non-use values:

Bequest value is the value of water-related ecosystems left or sustained for the benefit of future generations; the concept of intergenerational equity is a related value system.

Existence value is the intrinsic value of water and water ecosystems, including biodiversity; for example, the value people place simply on knowing that a wild river exists, even if they never visit it.

There is a strong economic case to invest in water use efficiency gains that make more water available to, or reduce competition with, other uses that have a higher value

Robust water measurement, modelling and accounting constitute the foundation for water valuation, and a necessary enabling step towards sustainable development of water resources. However, there are gaps in our knowledge about the storage and fluxes of water in the landscape and human-built infrastructure, which are especially surprising when we consider the important role of water in human welfare (Garrick et al., 2017).

These divergent perspectives on water value and the best ways to calculate and express it, coupled with limited knowledge of the actual resource, present a challenging landscape for rapid improvements in valuing water.

1.3.2 Reconciling water value and use

Low values for use based on economic efficiency do not necessarily imply foregoing that use. Better valuation of water helps identify the case for necessary investments in water use efficiency, including moderating impacts on water quality. In the example of water use for food, the very low economic returns ($/m^3 of water) do not mean food production to be sacrificed in order to allocate water to uses with higher returns, since that would jeopardize food security and livelihoods in developing countries. It means that there is a strong economic case to invest in water use efficiency gains that make more water available to, or reduce competition with, other uses that have a higher value. In this example, valuing water helps identify the value of investment in its management.

Box 1.3 Values of water in food and agriculture – Showcasing the diversity of approaches and the main challenges to estimations

Which parameters should be used to value water use in agriculture, and how? All have their merits, but few can be easily compared. It is inevitable that different groups will select the value and method that best support their particular interests.

Agriculture accounts for 69% of global water withdrawals. Yet, globally, agriculture accounts for only about 4% of global Gross Domestic Product (GDP) with an average contribution per country of 10.39%, with the highest contribution of 57.39% (Sierra Leone) and the lowest of 0.03% (Singapore), the trend being a decreasing share of GDP (World Bank, 2020). Such figures suggest that the value added of water use in agriculture is very low.

Rwanda, for example, has recently prepared detailed water accounts (Government of Rwanda, 2019). Agriculture uses 96% of water withdrawn from the environment (including soil water), mostly for the low-value crops that are essential to the country's food needs and the rural economy (see Figure below).

Figure: Water consumption in Rwanda by sector

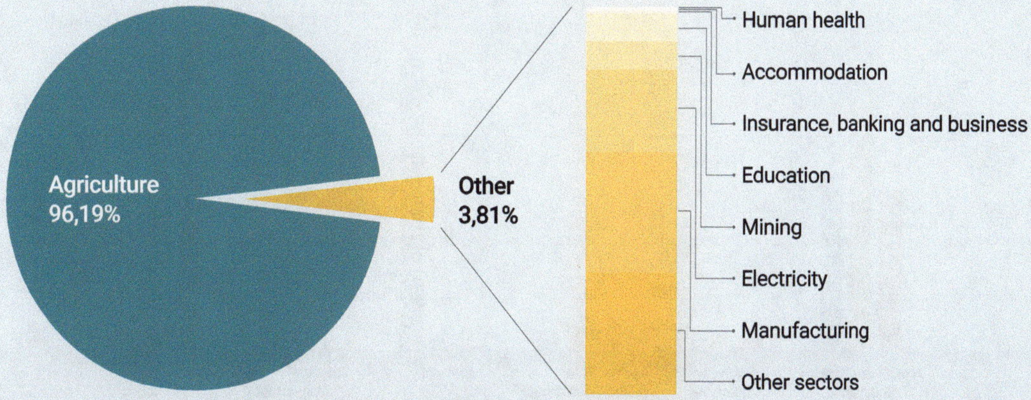

Source: Based on Government of Rwanda (2019, fig. 8, p. 34).

However, agriculture delivers the lowest returns on use efficiency among all the sectors, usually by a considerable margin (see Table below).

Table: Water productivity or 'total water use' efficiency (RWF/m³) for 2015 by sector in Rwanda

Economic sector	Productivity or use efficiency = GDP/m³ of water used (RWF/m³)	% of water used
Agriculture	118.4	91.12%
Mining	6 236.1	0.15%
Manufacturing	523.0	4.36%
Electricity	138.4	2.41%
Water and waste management	576.1	0.35%
Accommodation	6 297.8	0.11%
Financial services	2 352 460.5	0.0005%
Education	699.3	1.47%
Human health	33 876.9	0.03%
Cultural, domestic and other services	2 133 843.5	0.001%
Value added (GDP) per m³ of water used for the selected industries (RWF/m³)	**204.0**	

Source: Government of Rwanda (2019, Table 11, p. 37).

However, there are important nuances that should be applied when interpreting such data. For example, the water supply and waste management sector is not using water to produce economic output directly, but rather treating and distributing water primarily for the use of other sectors. For this reason, the measure of 'contribution to GDP' may be misleadingly narrow in this case. Further, there are water losses in the process from abstraction to purification to distribution that contribute to a higher measure of water 'use' relative to the economic gains.

A very different picture emerges if value is considered in terms of contribution to overall GDP or employment. When applying these criteria, it appears that agricultural use of water scores better through its high contribution to total GDP and high levels of employment; electricity (mainly hydropower) scores very poorly (although the electricity delivers much value added and most water is actually returned to the environment); and the service sectors deliver the highest gains in water use efficiency (see Figure below).

Figure: Shares of GDP, employment and water abstracted (2015) by industrial sector in Rwanda

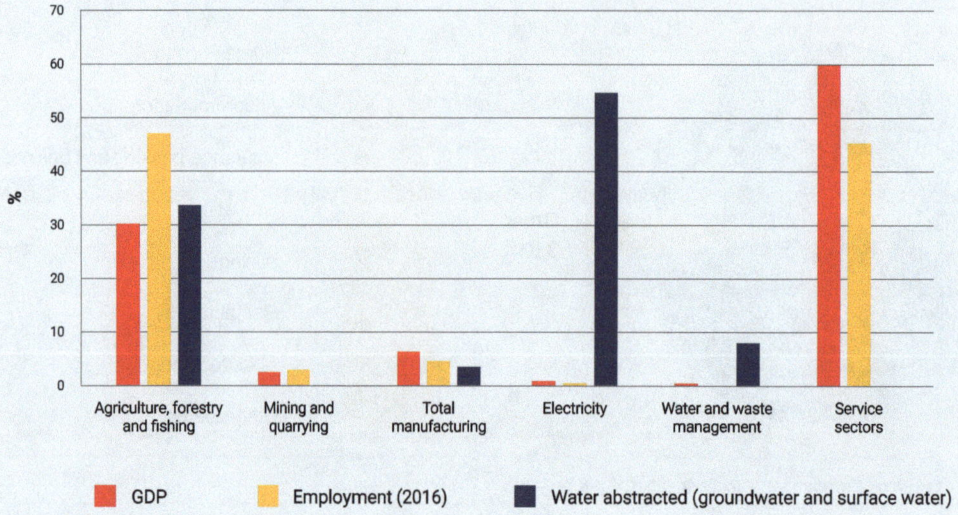

Source: Government of Rwanda (2019, fig. 9, p. 36).

There are a number of options when considering farm produce values, and hence water use efficiency values: for example, farm gate, wholesale or retail price, or value added (e.g. price of prepared food in the services sector). These values can differ by orders of magnitude. An added factor is whether to use gross farm income or residual (net) income when calculating value delivered. In Namibia, for example, based on gross income, farms returned US\$3.88/m^3 of water but after factoring in the costs of inputs, the residual value was only US\$0.14–0.51/m^3 (Lange, 2006).

Things get even more complicated when considering how to calculate water 'used' when determining value per unit of water. For example, for irrigated agriculture return flow needs to be factored into consumption (i.e. use net withdrawals), but its degraded state factored in as a cost. In accounting terms, water infrastructure capital as well as operation and maintenance costs should be factored in – but rarely are. In rainfed systems, withdrawals (soil moisture/rainfall) are not usually considered part of water 'abstraction/withdrawal' in use calculations. But land use in rainfed farming can decrease local surface and groundwater storage and flows, and therefore has a 'consumption' element. On the other hand, it can also increase local water storage and flows, in which case water availability is augmented. As a final example, in both rainfed and irrigated systems most consider the water evapotranspired by crops as water actually 'consumed', but in both cases this will return again somewhere else as rainfall – so is it 'consumed' or 'recycled'?

1.3.3 Recognizing that values of water can be negative

'Value' in itself is neutral, but all too often it is assumed to be positive (a benefit). But where water is in the 'wrong' place at the wrong time, or is contaminated, its value can be significantly negative; that is, involve net costs. Floodwater can, for example, have a positive benefit (for example by supporting fisheries production or replenishing nutrients across floodplains to support seasonal livestock grazing), but also a high negative impact. The value of investment in flood mitigation, therefore, is reflected in the reduction of this negative value of water. Arguably, the value of certain water bodies could be considered negative if it interrupts transport – the cost of building a bridge over it reflects that negative value. Although wastewater should be considered a resource (WWAP, 2017), the value of untreated wastewater released to the environment is negative and can be estimated based on how it reduces the value of water in the environment (pollution impact cost, including how this affects human health). In effect, the net value of wastewater treatment, above recovering valuable substances from wastewater, is reflected in the reduction of that negative value of wastewater. Other examples include where water use results in a negative economic return; for example, where accounting for all associated inputs and costs (e.g. subsidies) reveals that the water being used delivers a net economic loss (examples are provided below).

1.4 Methods for calculating the values of water

There are a number of methods commonly in use for calculating the value of water (Box 1.4). However, there can be large differences between values obtained through different methods. In addition, values derived are not necessarily those that drive investment. For example, the value of domestic water supply is generally perceived by households to be higher than that of sanitation and especially wastewater treatment (UNESCO/UN-Water, 2020), but investments in sanitation deliver about twice the return of investments in drinking water supply (WHO, 2012).

For some values, or value domains, no 'methodologies' are applied – value just exists. This applies, for example, to some intrinsic values or intangible values held under customary or religious belief systems. These can be more influential than values derived through scientific assessment.

1.5 Accounting for subsidies and other incentives in valuations

Governments often subsidize the costs of critical inputs and fix the price paid for major commodities, often below their marginal value. In other countries, trade protection is used to maintain high prices (Box 1.5). For example, Chapter 3 highlights that the operational costs of water infrastructure, and in particular capital costs, are often not recouped from users and therefore not reflected in their valuations of water at point of use. These distortions must be factored into valuations if an accurate picture of values is to be obtained.

1.6 Reconciling different values and perspectives

The diversity in perspectives, value systems or world views, and methods for calculating values and measurement metrics encourage stakeholders to select those approaches to valuation that best suit their own agendas. Difficulties in valuation and fragmented approaches to water resources management go hand in hand. Given even an optimistic view of the levels of impartiality in play, it is unlikely that all stakeholders will easily agree on a common method of expressing value. But there is a strong argument that diversity in perspectives on value should be maintained: it is, for example, futile to attempt to quantitatively compare the value of water for domestic use, the human right to water, customary or religious beliefs, and the value of maintaining flows to preserve biodiversity. None of these should be sacrificed for the sake of achieving consistent valuation methodologies.

Box 1.4 Some examples of methods to calculate values of water

Residual value estimates change in net income; that is, the difference (the residual) between the value of the output and the costs of all non-water inputs to production. The approach is quite sensitive to small variations in the parameters used and assumptions about the market and the policy environment. If an input into production is omitted or underestimated, its value would be wrongly attributed to water. For example, based upon data quoted in UNDESA (2012) for farming in Namibia, assuming a 5% cost for capital investments, the residual value of water appeared to be 19 Namibian cents per cubic metre. However, if the real cost of capital rose to 7%, farmers would not earn enough to cover even the capital costs and the value of the water would be negative – meaning that its use in farming would result in economic losses.

Mathematical programming models have been developed to inform decisions on water allocation and infrastructure development. They specify an objective, such as maximizing the value of output, subject to production inputs such as water supply, and institutional and behavioural constraints. Economy-wide approaches may use linear programming or simulation to compare marginal values of water among sectors (e.g. Renzetti and Dupont, 2003). More commonly, a computable general equilibrium model is used, as was done in Morocco in order to determine the impact of trade reform on the shadow value[1] of water in agriculture (Diao and Roe, 2000).

Replacement cost or ***replacement value*** refers to the amount that an entity would have to pay to replace an asset at the present time, according to its current worth. The approach is often used when the market or shadow price of water cannot be accurately assessed. For example, the absence of drinking water piped to a household could be estimated by the cost of supplying the same water in bottled form. The method is commonly applied to estimate the value of ecosystem services (Russi et al., 2013). For example, the value of loss of watershed water purification services can be estimated, partly, through the capital and operational costs of water treatment facilities.

Contingent valuation does not rely on market data but asks individuals how much they would be willing to pay for the item in question. The method is especially useful for determining the value of ecosystem goods and services that have no market prices, for example, biodiversity, good water quality or recreation. It has some utility for valuing consumer water demand by asking consumers how much they would be willing to pay for water.

Demand functions approaches use a demand curve either from actual sales of water (revealed preference) or from the use of the contingent valuation approach (stated preference) and involves econometric analysis to measure total economic value. However, it is often impossible to obtain the circumstances under which a demand curve can be accurately derived, even in developed countries (Walker et al., 2000).

Tradeable water rights attempt to capture markets in the derivation of the value of water. Examples can be found in Australia, Chile, Iran, South Africa and Spain's Canary Islands, as well as in some of the western states of the United States of America where water trading schemes are in place. Some countries, especially in South Asia, also have informal water trading schemes (Carey and Bunding, 2001). Australia's water market in the Murray-Darling Basin is recognized as the most advanced globally (Seidl et al., 2020a), but the absence of standardized approaches to valuation leads to considerable divergence in water values (Seidl et al., 2020b). There are varying opinions about how well markets for water function, as well as about their impact on consumers and the environment, and the morals of applying them (e.g. Garrick et al., 2020a).

The ***water footprint*** is an indicator of freshwater use that looks at both direct and indirect water use of a consumer or producer, and can be calculated for a particular product, for any well-defined group of consumers or producers. It can be expressed in terms of water volume and monetary unit, for example, when the water footprint per unit of time is divided by income (for consumers) or turnover (for businesses). A water footprint sustainability assessment will further evaluate whether the water footprint is sustainable in terms of an environmental, social and economic perspective such as biodiversity, human health, welfare and security, thus adding an important additional dimension to value (Hoekstra et al., 2011).

---

[1] The calculated price of a good or service for which no market price exists (Collins English Dictionary).

Box 1.5 The impact of including subsidies and other incentives in accounting for the values of water

When accounting for the costs of agriculture subsidies in the European Union, it was found that the value of water used in irrigation in part of the United Kingdom was negative for winter wheat, barley, oilseed and sugar beet (Bate and Dubourg, 1997). For these crops, net negative value varied between 2.5 and 15 times the positive value calculated without subsidies. This means that using water to irrigate crops, in this case, results in a net economic loss. Only potatoes produced a net positive value when including subsidies but, even then, the subsidies reduced that value by about half. On the other hand, correcting the effects of trade distortion on the value delivered per unit of water for crops in Jordan resulted in a reduction of 7% for fruits and 50% for vegetables, but in both cases net value was still positive (Schiffler, 2014).

Nevertheless, the different values of water need to be reconciled, and the trade-offs between them resolved and incorporated into systematic and inclusive planning and decision-making processes. The way forward, therefore, will be to further develop common approaches to valuation where feasible, but to prioritize improved approaches to compare, contrast and merge different values, and to incorporate fair and equitable conclusions into improved policy and planning.

Gender-sensitive stakeholder consultation and the active involvement of all users and beneficiaries, including disadvantaged and marginalized groups, are critical to ensure full representation of perspectives and values from the outset, and throughout the development process (Horne et al., 2017a). All stakeholders and socio-economic sectors, from water supply and sanitation to agriculture, energy and industry stand to benefit from an improved integration of the values of water across the full water development or engineering cycle, from planning and pre-feasibility, through to adaptive management and monitoring. Water opportunities and risks cannot be managed by a single institution and require collective action at a meaningful scale.

1.7 Principles for valuing water for sustainable development

Valuing water has been a longstanding general theme and one of great relevance to development. Efforts to value water have advanced over the past 30 years, ranging from willingness to pay for drinking water and ecosystem services, to participatory processes that capture water's diverse cultural benefits. Yet valuing water remains difficult and contentious owing to water's physical, political and economic characteristics (Garrick et al., 2017). There is still a surprising lack of clarity as to the recognition, measurement and reconciliation of the full range of values on the ground. Debate reigns over how best to capture, and give due attention to, the values of water.

The values given to water are at the heart of the United Nations 2030 Agenda for Sustainable Development (see Section 7.5). Valuing water is a shared societal responsibility (HLPW, 2017a). The High Level Panel on Water's Bellagio Principles on Valuing Water presents a global opportunity to rethink the values of water through five fundamental principles (Box 1.6). These broad principles build a more explicit articulation of best practices and experience in ascertaining and maximizing the benefits to be gained from water.

Box 1.6 The Bellagio Principles for Valuing Water

1. ***Recognize water's multiple values***: Consider the multiple values to different stakeholders in all decisions affecting water. There are deep interconnections between human needs, economic well-being, spirituality and the viability of freshwater ecosystems that must be considered by all.
2. ***Build trust***: Conduct all processes to reconcile values in ways that are equitable, transparent and inclusive of multiple values. Trade-offs will be inevitable, especially when water is scarce. Inaction may also have costs that involve steeper trade-offs. These processes need to be adaptive in the face of local and global changes.
3. ***Protect the sources***: Value and protect all sources of water, including watersheds, rivers, aquifers and associated ecosystems for current and future generations. There is growing scarcity of water. Protecting sources and controlling pollutants and other pressures are necessary for sustainable development.
4. ***Educate to empower***: Promote education and public awareness about the essential role of water and its intrinsic value. This will facilitate better-informed decision-making and more sustainable water consumption patterns.
5. ***Invest and innovate***: Increase investment in institutions, infrastructure, information and innovation to realize the full potential and values of water. The complexity of the water challenges should spur concerted action, innovation, institutional strengthening and re-alignment. These should harness new ideas, tools and solutions while drawing on existing and indigenous knowledge and practices in ways that nurture the leaders of tomorrow.

Source: HLPW (2017b).

1.8 The approach of the *World Water Development Report*

This *World Water Development Report* assesses the opportunities and challenges to determining the multiple values of water. Subsequent chapters view valuation through the lenses of the broad perspectives of key stakeholders or interest groups. Each perspective addresses how value has been, and is currently being, attributed to water, with which measures and approaches, and with what degree of success, as well as the opportunities for, benefits of and methodologies for integrated or nexus approaches. Important gaps in areas such as data and monitoring, potentially constraining any future action agenda on valuing water, are identified. Chapter 12 identifies further options for responding to the current challenges to valuing water.

Chapter 2

Economic valuation of the source

WWAP

David Coates and Richard Connor

With contributions from:

Rebecca Welling (IUCN) and Manzoor Qadir (UNU-INWEH)

> ***We use nature because it is valuable – but we lose it because it is free***
>
> ***Pavan Sukhdev***[1]

2.1 Introduction

The environment is central to water resources management. The environment is both the source of water and a competitor for its use. The value of water as an integral component of an ecosystem, the role of the environment in driving flows of water, sediments, nutrients, energy and biota, as well as the interconnections between these flows in the landscape, are central to water resources challenges. Most water allocation mechanisms nowadays include the allocation of environmental water as a value domain. These mechanisms include: water reserves, caps on consumption, sustainable abstraction limits, water markets, licence conditions on infrastructure operators, and flow release rules and regimes for dams (Horne et al., 2017a). Legislation on water pollution is among the most widespread and oldest of water-related rules and regulations (WWAP, 2017).

But the status and trends of the environment–water interactions (see Prologue) clearly indicate the need for much better incorporation of the value of the environment in water resources management. The value of the diverse environmental aspects of water, including the value of biodiversity, are particularly neglected (Arthington et al., 2018; IPBES, 2019a).

This chapter looks at the valuation of the nature–water relationship principally from an economic perspective. However, Chapter 1 has noted that the scope of 'economics' in this regard should be understood comprehensively and holistically. In particular, 'economics' should not be seen as limited to monetary valuation, nor to determining values solely through market-based approaches. There are important values associated with water and nature, held by communities or societies, that cannot be properly captured through economic frameworks. These include, for example, spiritual, religious and cultural values or belief systems (Chapter 7). These are not limited to indigenous peoples and can also exist, and be powerful, in a broad range of societies. These values are often held without a valuation process – they just exist. They are important to consider and can trump economic values.

2.2 The environmental dimensions of the resource – A key consideration

The environment is central to the water cycle and an integral part of all aspects of water management. The source of all water is the environment and all water abstracted by humans eventually returns there, together with any impurities added to it. Changes to the environment can influence the location, amount, timing and quality of water available for human use. Human influences on the environment are usually negative for water resources. However, the environment–water interface can be proactively managed in order to address water-related challenges through what has become popularly known as 'nature-based solutions' (WWAP/UN-Water, 2018). This approach centres on the concept of green, or natural, infrastructure that can function in the same way as built/physical or grey infrastructure (Figure 2.1).

---

[1] Pavan Sukhdev is an environmental economist, founder of The Economics of Ecosystems and Biodiversity (TEEB) initiative, President of the World Wide Fund for Nature (WWF) International, and former head of the United Nations Green Economy Initiative, among others. Please see R. Cohn, 2012. "Putting a price on the real value of nature". Interview with Pavan Sukhdev. Yale Environment. 360. yale.edu/features/putting_a_price_on_the_real_value_of_nature.

Figure 2.1 Natural infrastructure for water management

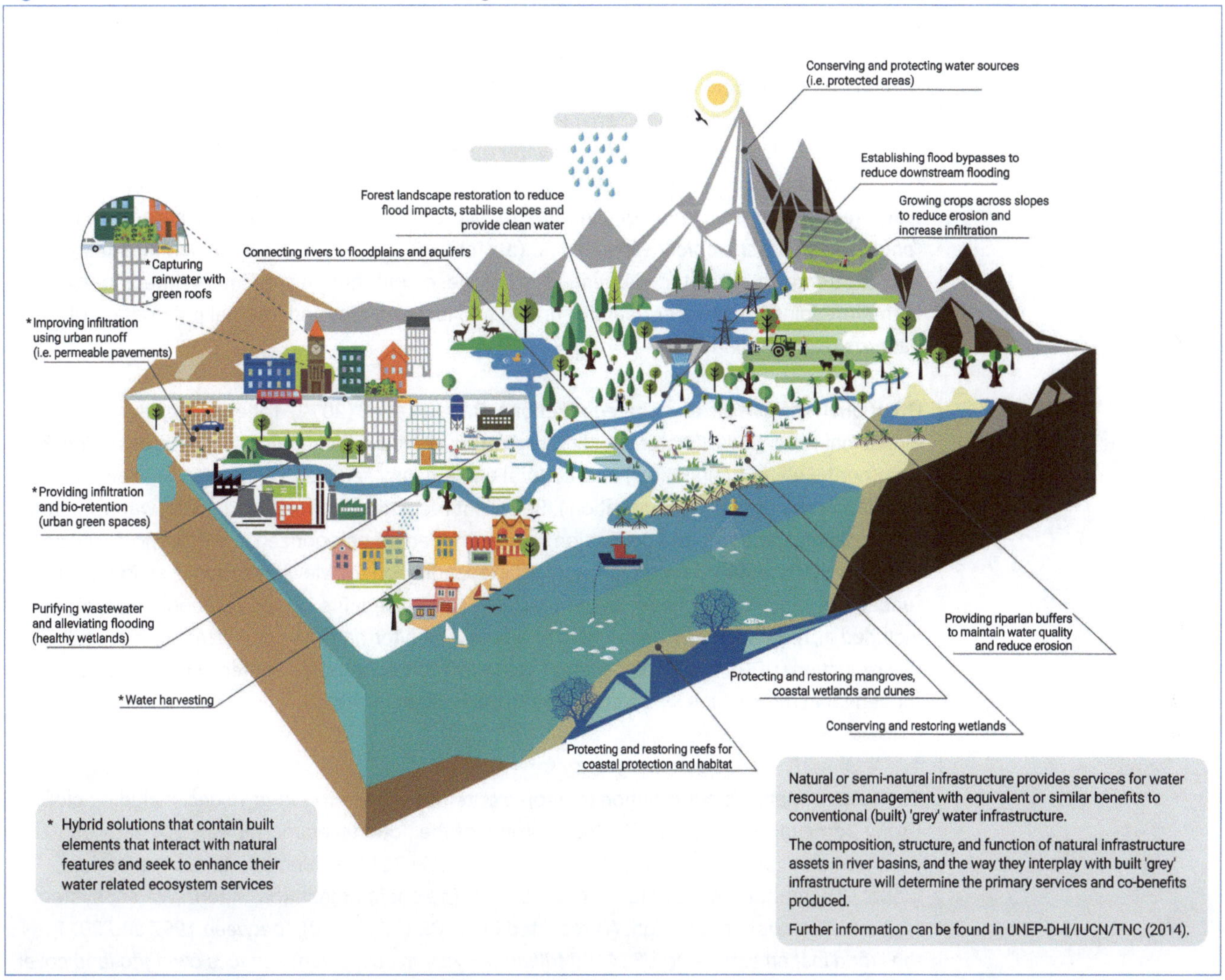

Source: Infographic 'Natural Infrastructure for Water Management', © IUCN 2015.

2.3 Valuing the environment

The environment's value can be expressed in terms of the role it plays in delivering water for direct human uses, such as for drinking, irrigation or industrial use, dealing with extremes such as flooding, or helping to deal with pollution. But the environment can also be a competing user of water if, for example, demands are made to allocate water to the environment to support fisheries or for aesthetic reasons. These are not entirely independent of each other and in both cases the approach to valuation is similar.

2.3.1 The basis of valuation – nature's contribution to people, including ecosystem services

The various values of the environment, or ecosystems, are usually categorized and measured as benefits delivered to people. 'Nature's contributions to people' is the currently intergovernmentally accepted terminology and *"refers to all the benefits that humanity obtains from nature: ecosystem goods and services, considered separately or in bundles, are included in this category"* (IPBES, 2019a, p. 51). Water-related ecosystem services, or bundles of them, are those that play a particular role in the water cycle through the regulation of water flows and water quality: for example, flood regulation and coastal storm protection, water erosion control and sediment transport, water supply, water purification (nutrient recycling and pollution absorption), and regulation of climate and precipitation. These groups of services influence the amount of water, its location, timing of availability, and quality. In addition, all ecosystem services are water-dependent, irrespective of their role in hydrology. Without water, ecosystems cease to function.

In most studies, water-related ecosystem services are not usually treated as a distinct or separate category and clusters or bundles of services must often be combined from the underlying results to obtain relevant analyses and conclusions regarding water. Inter-relationships of different ecosystem processes and functions can be complex. There are also varying categorizations of the benefits these functions deliver to people. For example, IPBES (2019a, p. 23) lists *"regulation of freshwater quantity, location and timing"* and *"regulation of freshwater and coastal water quality"* as nature's contributions to people that are explicitly water-related, but *"regulation of climate"*, *"regulation of hazards and extreme events" and "physical and psychological experiences"* (as, for example, relating to water landscapes) also have a strong water-related element. Many of these contributions are inter-related; for example, in the foregoing, freshwater quantity, timing and location are fundamental parameters of hazards (e.g. flooding).

Significant values can be attributed to ecosystem services that relate to supporting resilience, or reducing risks

Other analyses use different categorizations. Barredo et al. (2019), for example, use 'provisioning services' ('water supply'), 'regulating services' ('regulation of water flows, waste treatment – water purification') and 'cultural and amenity services' (e.g. 'spiritual experience, inspiration and aesthetic information'). Sediment regulation, both on land and in water, including its formation, transport and deposition, is often not easily categorized and its importance as a water-related service is often overlooked. Depending on the viewpoint, this is an important function of, or service provided by, ecosystems and its benefits can be categorized as, or included in, regulation of water quality or erosion, land formation or stabilization, and/or disaster risk reduction (DDR). It is important that values attributed to water-related ecosystem services must bear in mind which services are being included or excluded.

2.3.2 Overall values of ecosystem services

The value of nature's contribution to people outstrips other economic values, including global Gross Domestic Product (GDP). One estimate of the notional economic value of nature's contribution to people was US$125 trillion per year in 2011, around two-thirds higher than global GDP at that time (Costanza et al., 2014). The costs of inaction, in terms of ecosystem loss and degradation, are high. As reported by OECD (2019, p. 9), *"between 1997 and 2011, the world lost an estimated US$4–20 trillion per year in ecosystem services owing to land cover change and US$6–11 trillion per year from land degradation."*

Significant values can be attributed to ecosystem services that relate to supporting resilience, or reducing risks. In 2019, environment-related risks accounted for three of the top five risks by likelihood and four of the top five by impact (World Economic Forum, 2019). Most disaster risks and costs are water-related. For example: between 2000 and 2006, there were 2,163 water-related disasters, costing US$422 billion in damages and affecting 1.5 billion people (Adikari and Yoshitani, 2009); 45% out of the 820 natural catastrophes registered in 2019 by Munich Re were related to floods, flash floods and landslides (MunichRe, 2020). Many of these disaster risks are exacerbated by the loss of relevant ecosystem services (WWAP/UN-Water, 2018), as these services played a role in preventing disasters in the first place. The values of these services can be calculated (e.g. Batker et al., 2010), but they are often not recognized or adequately included in economic planning, which tends to favour short-term gains over longer-term sustainability (IPBES, 2019b).

Estimates of value for ecosystem services vary depending on the location of the study, the methods used, and the clusters and categories of services and biomes considered. In a review of published valuation studies, De Groot et al. (2012) showed that different biomes have widely varying total economic values (TEV) per unit area, ranging from less than US$1,000 to over US$1,000,000 per hectare per year. Wetlands are by far the most valuable biomes per unit area, by several orders of magnitude. However, this category includes coral reefs, which are an outlier due to high tourism values.

The proportion of the total value that can be attributed to water-related ecosystem services has not been systematically calculated but it is probably the majority of all ecosystem services: the proportion (including water provisioning, climate regulation, erosion prevention, disturbance moderation, waste treatment and nutrient cycling) averaged between studies is 89% in the case of coastal systems and coastal wetlands, 83% for tropical forests, 65.5% for inland wetlands and 46% for rivers and lakes, but less than 15% for temperate forest, woodlands and grasslands (De Groot et al., 2012).

2.4 Methods used to calculate values

The ecosystem services concept has given considerable impetus to continuing efforts to document the value of ecosystems, including as natural infrastructure within water management systems (Russi et al., 2013; Gilvear et al., 2017). These values and benefits are being documented in increasingly transparent, sophisticated economic terms (Vörösmarty et al., 2018).

Various methods are used to calculate ecosystem service values. These methods are similar across ecosystem types. Some of those commonly used for water-related services from forests (Barredo et al., 2019), a wide range of ecosystem types (De Groot et al., 2012) and wetlands (Russi et al., 2013) include: contingent valuation, choice modelling, averting behaviour,[2] value transfer, related goods approaches, production functions, indirect opportunity costs, restoration costs, hedonic pricing, replacement costs and preventive/defensive expenditures.

2.4.1 Monetary valuation

Expressing the values of ecosystem services in monetary terms enables values to be more easily compared with other economic assessments that often use monetary-based units. Research on the monetary valuation of ecosystem services dates back to the early 1960s but received wide attention with the publication of Costanza et al. (1997). Since then, there has been increasing recognition of the monetary valuation of natural resources and ecosystem services. Some reject monetary valuation because it undervalues nature, commodifies it or suggests it can be traded (Conniff, 2012; Bresnihan, 2017), although this is not necessarily the intention. But monetary valuation has been a major driver of elevating attention to the environment because of the high values often generated, particularly regarding water.

The environment can have important values that cannot, or should not, be constrained or defined by monetary-based approaches

2.4.2 Non-monetary values

The environment can have important values that cannot, or should not, be constrained or defined by monetary-based approaches. This applies particularly to such things as spiritual experiences, inspiration for culture, art and design, aesthetic values, information for cognitive development, and other ecosystem services generally categorized as cultural services (TEEB, 2010). Such aspects as option, existence or bequest value, or intrinsic or relational values (see Chapter 1) are particularly difficult to value in monetary terms. Most of these values are also difficult to quantify. Nevertheless, they are important to include in estimates of overall value and comparison between different measures of value.

Value can be determined primarily by religious beliefs such as, for example, the revering of the Ganges River in the Hindu faith. Some societies reject the validity of the application of economics to nature and the commodification of its benefits, such as, for example, concepts of the rights of 'Mother Earth', whilst others reflect the value of natural resources by giving them legal rights. Such value systems can be powerful in influencing policy and can override any assessments based on economic or monetary approaches. Chapter 7 discusses these aspects of value in further detail.

---

2 Averting behaviour analyses the rate of substitution between changes in behaviour, and expenditures on and changes in environmental quality, in order to infer the value of certain non-marketed environmental attributes.

The existence of different value systems infers that it would be problematic to develop a unified system of, and metrics for, valuing water and/or the environment. What is feasible is to develop a common approach under which different environmental values or value systems can be compared, contrasted and used to identify wise policy choices. A fundamental ingredient of this is the full and meaningful participation of relevant stakeholder groups in assessments and gender-sensitive decision-making. This is perhaps the most effective, and equitable, means to capture the full spectrum of values. Often stakeholders alone know the true values in play to them.

Regarding nature as natural capital enables nature, and its benefits, to be compared and understood in terms of the more traditional economic thinking that often dominates water-related decision-making

2.4.3 Natural capital accounting

Regarding nature as natural capital enables nature, and its benefits, to be compared and understood in terms of the more traditional economic thinking that often dominates water-related decision-making. *Natural capital* is the stock of renewable and non-renewable resources (e.g. plants, animals, air, water, soils, minerals) that combine to yield a flow of benefits to people (United Nations, 2014). *Natural capital accounting* systematically measures and reports on stocks and flows of natural capital. As in traditional economics, capital is valued in terms of its production or potential production of benefits, including non-use, future use or option values, which in this context are (potential) ecosystem services. These are effectively the interest on the capital. Both monetary and non-monetary valuation methods can be used. The underlying premise is that the environment should be recognized as an asset that must be maintained and managed, with its contributions (services) better integrated into commonly used accounting frameworks that support economic analysis (Box 2.1).

Box 2.1 The System of Environmental Economic Accounting for Water – The SEEA-Water

The SEEA-Water can be used to derive water-related indicators such as: access; use per capita or Gross Domestic Product (GDP) and value added; supply rates; availability per capita and by type; productivity and use efficiency (Sustainable Development Goal (SDG) 6.4); water emissions (pollution loads) by GDP or per capita; water stress (SDG 6.4); and indicators for most of the other SDG 6 targets and overlapping SDGs (UNDESA, 2012). SEEA-Water has been recently applied in different countries for various goals: as a reference guide or tool to organize relevant statistics to assess water at a national scale (e.g. Statistics Canada, 2016), for compiling national water accounts (e.g. Government of Rwanda, 2019), for an integrated assessment of water security in an aquifer-scale case study in Iran (Mahdavi et al., 2019), as a procedure for the compilation of highly disaggregated water accounts in Finland (Salminen et al., 2018), and to support decision-making processes of urban water management in Ecuador (López et al., 2019).

Natural capital accounting approaches are commonly applied to nature-based solutions (WWAP/UN-Water, 2018) in order to calculate values in play. The impacts of environmental degradation on water-related costs are often well known; as is often the case, for example, when estimating the value of watershed services and calculating the potential for, and scale of, payments for ecosystem services schemes (examples are provided in Chapter 3).

As cases from the United Kingdom (UK) show, natural capital accounts can be generated for countries, large organizations and businesses, cities, protected areas, and smaller-scale areas of land and water (e.g. private estates and public parks).[3] The World Bank-led Wealth Accounting and the Valuation of Ecosystem Services (WAVES) partnership encourages the incorporation of the value of the environment in national economic accounts and development planning.

[3] See for example: ecosystemsknowledge.net/resources/themes/accounting.

Figure 2.2 Examples of some key considerations in assessing total economic value (TEV) of the environment or an ecosystem asset

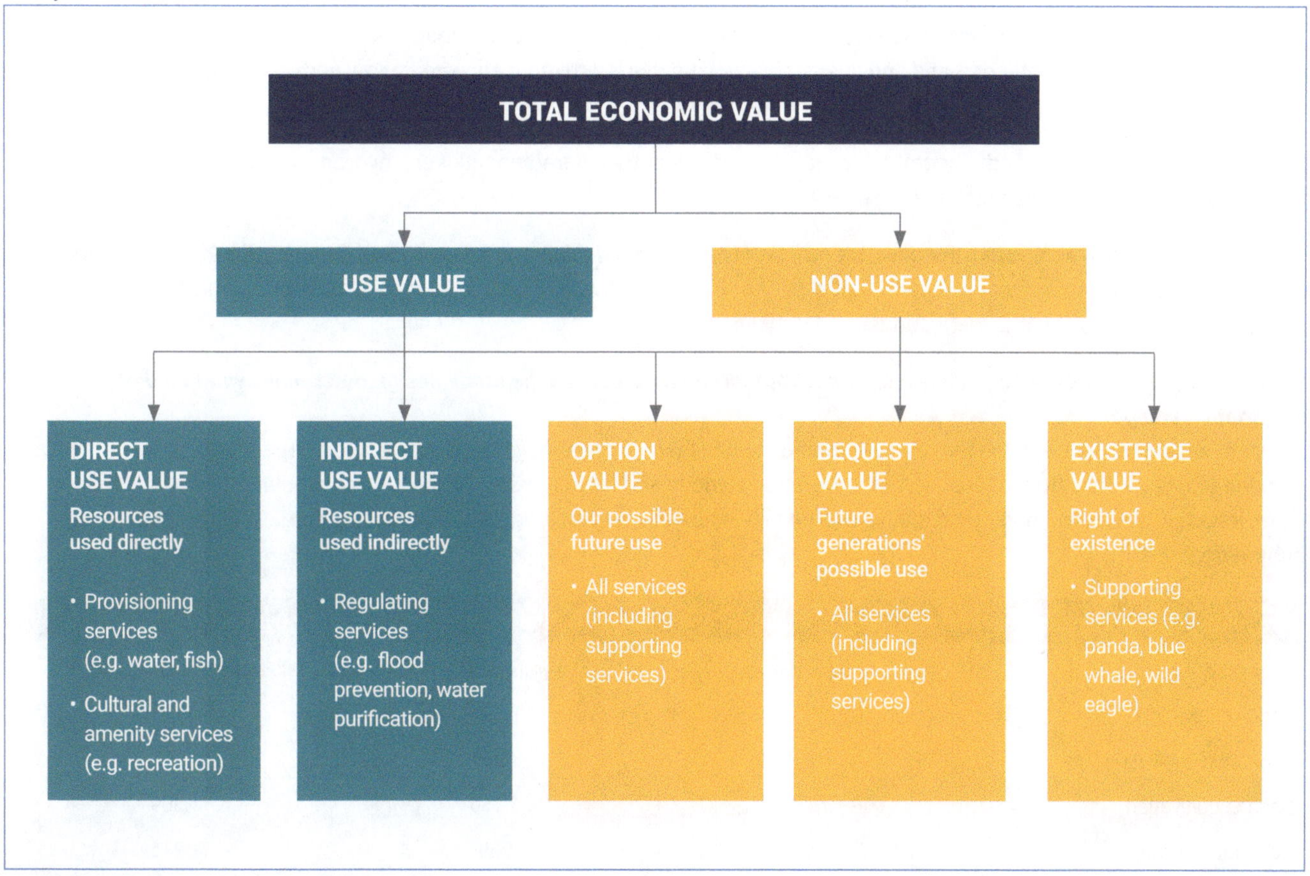

Source: Adapted from De Groot et al. (2006, fig. 6, p. 23). Reproduced with permission from the Ramsar Convention on Wetlands Secretariat/Secretariat of the Convention on Biological Diversity (CBD).

2.4.4 Assessing aggregate values

Multiple methods and approaches can be combined to reflect overall values for the environment. This is usually achieved through the estimation of TEV that reflects the overall suite of values involved, each of which may be calculated using a different method (Figure 2.2).

2.4.5 Levels of precision required

It can be quite challenging to undertake a comprehensive assessment of the value of water-related ecosystems and their full range of services. But different uses require different spatial scales and methods of precision. Costanza et al. (2014), for example, suggest: low levels of precision are required for raising awareness and interest at regional to global scales using total values and macro-aggregates; low to medium levels for urban and regional land use planning using values for changes by land use scenario; and, medium to high levels for payments for ecosystem services at multiple scales using data for changes by actions.

2.4.6 Methods for integrating values into decision-making frameworks

At some stage it is necessary to compile information on the values of water and ecosystems under a coherent decision-making framework. McCartney et al. (2019) provide a comprehensive example of how to assess the ecosystem services people derive from the Tana River basin, in Kenya, which enabled the benefits of natural and built infrastructure to be optimized, thereby increasing overall economic gains.

TEEB (2010) outlines a six-step approach to navigate through the available options for integrating ecosystem services in local and regional management. Box 2.2 explains the approach with an example of the Kala Oya River basin in Sri Lanka.

Box 2.2 Application of a stepwise approach to identify options for optimizing ecosystem services in the Kala Oya River basin in Sri Lanka

The Kala Oya River basin in Sri Lanka has a traditional irrigation system with human-made wetlands for water storage (known as water tanks). Increasing water demand and unsustainable land use led to reduced water inflow and an increased sediment load.

Step 1: Specify and agree on the problem with stakeholders
Two challenges were identified: (i) competing water demands between traditional users, hydropower and modern agriculture; and (ii) the need for improved tank management.

Step 2: Identify which ecosystem services are most relevant (to the decision to be made and covering the key stakeholders)
It became clear that, apart from the water tanks' benefit for rice cultivation, the wetland provided other important ecosystem services – fish stocks, lotus flowers, fodder and drinking water.

Step 3: Identify the information needs and select appropriate methods, as the study design determines what kind of information you get
First, assessing the value of the tanks' provisioning services would offer insights about people's dependence on them. It was decided to use participatory appraisal methods, market prices and labour costs. Second, three regulating/habitat services were selected for a qualitative trend analysis (using literature and expert judgement): water recharge, soil retention and habitat services.

The value of tank water and biological resources in Rajangana and Angamauwa sub-catchments of the Kala Oya basin (per tank)

Resource	% of households	Value per household (US$/hh/yr)	Value per unit area (US$/ha/yr)
Paddy cultivation	13%	177	161
Vegetable cultivation	7%	86	39
Banana cultivation	3%	1 150	209
Coconut cultivation	13%	239	216
Domestic water	93%	226	1 469
Livestock water	13%	369	335
Commercial water	2%	132	12
Fishery	16%	309	351
Lotus flowers	10%	106	72
Lotus roots	7%	235	107
		Total	**2 972**

Step 4: Assess expected changes in availability and distribution of ecosystem services
Rice production had been considered the principal benefit. But results showed that rice accounted on average for about US$160 per hectare per year, while other provisioning services, including water supply, accounted for an average value of about US$2,800. This was important for future water allocation negotiations.

Step 5: Identify and appraise policy options based on the analysis of expected changes in ecosystem services
To improve tank management, four scenarios were examined and probable future costs and benefits were jointly considered (see table below) with qualitative information on the regulating/habitat services (indirect use trends in the table, estimated based on likely outcomes through expert opinion; -7 equals worst case outcome: continued loss and decline, +7 equals best case outcome: restoration and recovery).

Scenario 4 (i.e. removing silt and rehabilitating the tanks' water storage capacity) was the best option with regard to all criteria.

Cost–benefit assessment of alternative task management scenarios					
Scenario	Net present value in thousand US$			Indirect use trends (Index)	Natural capital in 30 years
	Cost	Incremental tank benefits	Quantifiable net benefit		
S1: Do nothing	0	0	0	-7	↓↓
S2: Raise spill	0.4	24.2	23.8	-4	↓
S3: Raise spill and rehabilitate	35.8	64.6	28.8	6	↑
S4: Remove silt and rehabilitate tank reservation	62.8	120.7	57.9	7	↑↑

Step 6: Assess social and environmental impacts of policy options, as changes in ecosystem services affect people differently
The scenario of rehabilitating the tanks' water storage capacity was also the most expensive option, requiring labour for silt removal (see Table above). As the tanks constituted a fully functioning secure water supply for 93% of households, these costs were accepted locally.

Source: Extracted from Russi et al. (2013, Box 3.9, pp. 32–33). Reproduced with permission from the Secretariat of the Ramsar Convention on Wetlands/Institute for European Environmental Policy (IEEP AISBL).

2.4.7 Valuing the environmental services of water for waste assimilation and water quality

Ecosystems have a certain assimilation capacity towards contaminants, depending on the chemical in question, the natural background concentrations and the ambient water quality standards. This ecosystem service is highly valuable – avoiding costs of treating all releases – but is hardly ever quantified because it is considered 'free'. Polluters also appropriate themselves of freshwater volumes that are required to dilute pollutants to such an extent that the quality of the water remains above the agreed water quality standards, negatively impacting water availability. Transgressing beyond this background carrying capacity causes pollution that creates health hazards, detrimentally affects biodiversity, raises the cost of treating water and increases water stress (WWAP, 2017).

Biological oxygen demand (BOD) is commonly used as one indicator of water quality. BOD measures to what extent pollution loads exceed ecosystem carrying capacity, resulting in an oxygen deficit (demand). Data on BOD can be used in various ways to calculate values associated with environmental pollution; for example, in a recent study assessing the impact of BOD on GDP growth (Box 2.3).

Box 2.3 Estimating the impact of upstream biological oxygen demand (BOD) on downstream Gross Domestic Product (GDP)

To estimate the impact of increasing levels of BOD on downstream economic activity, local GDP data were matched to the nearest upstream water quality monitoring station with data on BOD. Other factors that are known to impact GDP growth were added as a set of controls, including weather variables, population, geography, intra-annual variations in water quality and country-specific time trends that capture economic transitions. The results are striking, if not surprising. When the BOD level exceeds 8 mg/L—a level at which rivers are considered heavily polluted— GDP growth falls by about a third. For middle-income countries, where BOD is a bigger problem, the impact increases to almost half of growth lost. In high-income countries, where levels of BOD are lower, GDP only declines marginally.

In effect, this approach estimates the costs of pollution, in this case using GDP, and therefore the value that would be delivered were the environment less polluted.

Source: Adapted from Damania et al. (2019a, p. 10).

Box 2.4 Estimating the value of surface water pollution accidents (SWPAs) in China

Estimation of economic losses due to SWPAs is referenced in China's Environmental Protection Law. SWPA damages can be divided into eight types: damage to human health; water supply suspension; damage to fisheries, to recreational functions, to biological diversity; environmental property loss; accidents; and other, indirect losses. The same procedure for compensation for traffic accidents was used in the valuation of damage to people's lives. The functional replacement cost method was used in economic estimation of the losses due to water supply suspension and loss of water's recreational functions. Damage to biological diversity was estimated by recovery cost analysis and damage to environmental property losses was calculated using pollutant removal costs. The valuation procedure can be used by decision-makers for the economic estimation of losses in SWPAs. Estimates of the economic losses of pollution accidents also help quantify potential costs associated with increased risk sources along lakes/rivers and highlight the value of clean water to society as a whole.

Source: Adapted from Yao et al. (2016, p. 1).

The direct valuation of environmental degradation arising from water pollution is usually based on the cost of damage: either through costs in preventing it (the maintenance cost approach, e.g. infrastructure costs to reduce damage) or from the benefits of averting the damage (such as human illness and premature death or any loss of productivity attributable to changes in water quality) (UNDESA, 2012). A combination of approaches can be used to estimate the costs of pollution (Box. 2.4). These reflect, at least in part, the value of water in its natural state in the environment.

The cost-based approach has three variants: *abatement cost* – the most widely used approach, which measures the cost of introducing technologies to prevent water pollution; *structural adjustment costs* – the costs incurred to restructure the economy (production and/or consumption patterns) in order to reduce water pollution or other forms of environmental degradation to a given standard, which often requires complex economy-wide modelling; and *restoration cost* – which measures the cost of restoring a damaged body of water, or ecosystem, to an acceptable state (UNDESA, 2012).

2.5 Approaches that support valuing the environment–water relationship

Improving attention to values of the environment–water relationship involves improved valuation and mechanisms for incorporating those values into improved decision-making frameworks.

2.5.1 Nature-based solutions

Nature-based solutions use, or mimic, natural processes. They are being deployed at an ever-increasing rate and are attracting an improved, if still too peripheral, proportion of water-related financing (WWAP/UN-Water, 2018). *The Green Infrastructure Guide for Water Management* (UNEP/UNEP-DHI/IUCN/TNC, 2014) describes various ecosystem-based management approaches for water-related infrastructure projects. Innovation in nature-based solutions is continuing with little sign of a slow-down (Vörösmarty et al., 2018). Specific principles and standardized implementation guidelines have been developed for application in flood risk management (Van Wesenbeeck et al., 2017). Nature-based solutions also play a significant role in climate change adaptation and mitigation (UNESCO/UN-Water, 2020).

Valuation of ecosystem services plays a central role in evaluating nature-based options and can be calculated from the reduction of water-related operational or capital cost, or increased productivity gained (examples are provided in Chapter 3). The protection of high-value catchments and water sources is increasingly recognized for conferring benefits to downstream rural and urban users (Abell et al., 2017). The value of source protection is usually calculated through measurably improved supplies for downstream users, as well as cost savings associated with higher water quality and thus lower treatment costs. Investment in watershed conservation could generate a positive return on investment for one in every four cities (McDonald and Shemie, 2014). Water funds are innovative tools for promoting these benefits (TNC, 2018). These approaches usually adopt payments for ecosystem services as the mechanism to transfer benefits from beneficiaries to suppliers of services (see Box 3.2).

Nature-based solutions can deliver significant environmental secondary co-benefits: that is, the conjunctive delivery of multiple water-related and other ecosystem services (WWAP/UN-Water, 2018). For example, they often deliver improved benefits such as biodiversity conservation, fisheries, or recreation and tourism, which can tip investment decisions in their favour (UNEP/UNEP-DHI/IUCN/TNC, 2014; WWAP/UN-Water, 2018). As such, they deliver the social, economic and environmental co-benefits required under the Sustainable Development Goals (SDGs), including: access to water supply and sanitation services, food and energy security, human health and livelihoods, economic growth, job creation, improved human settlements, reduction in water-related disasters and climate risks, and last but not least, ecosystem restoration and the protection of biodiversity. They also tend to support overall system resilience.

Valuation of ecosystem services plays a central role in evaluating nature-based options and can be calculated from the reduction of water-related operational or capital cost, or increased productivity gained

2.5.2 Environmental flows

A specific flow regime in a river, capable of sustaining a complex set of aquatic habitats and ecosystem processes, is referred to as an environmental flow or 'e-flow'. Similar, but not necessarily identical, concepts include in-stream flow needs, ecological reserves, the ecological demand of water, environmental water allocation (or requirement), compensation flow and minimum flow (WMO, 2019). Interdisciplinary bridges between the eco-hydrological and social sciences have enabled a better integration of sociocultural and ecological values of water (Poff et al., 2017; Jackson, 2017; Arthington et al., 2018). The growing ability of markets to accommodate environmental water needs when supported by capable institutions (Garrick et al., 2017; Horne et al., 2017b) has created ways to shift water back to the environment without compromising urban water demands and increasing agricultural productivity.

An evaluation methodology that enables the hydrological, ecological and ecosystem services relationships in given rivers, including estuaries, is central to the effectiveness of an e-flow (Acuña et al., 2013). Valuation of these services enables the identification of a desired suite of ecosystem services and subsequently the hydrological regime required to deliver it. There is a progression from the point where stresses are introduced into the ecosystem, to how these impact on the ecosystem and, in turn, on the value of benefits to society (Figure 2.3). E-flows represent the amount of water where this progression is optimal and sustainable.

Estimates of environmental flow requirements are being explicitly integrated into SDG Indicator 6.4.2, to generate national datasets for monitoring water stress (FAO, 2019b). The provision of environmental flows supports the achievement of other water-related goals and targets, such as those addressing food security and nutrition from fisheries and flood recession agriculture, and human health (Arthington et al., 2018; Vörösmarty et al., 2018).

Figure 2.3 Model linking flow alterations to effects on the ecosystem, resulting in impacts to endpoints and finally the value of benefits

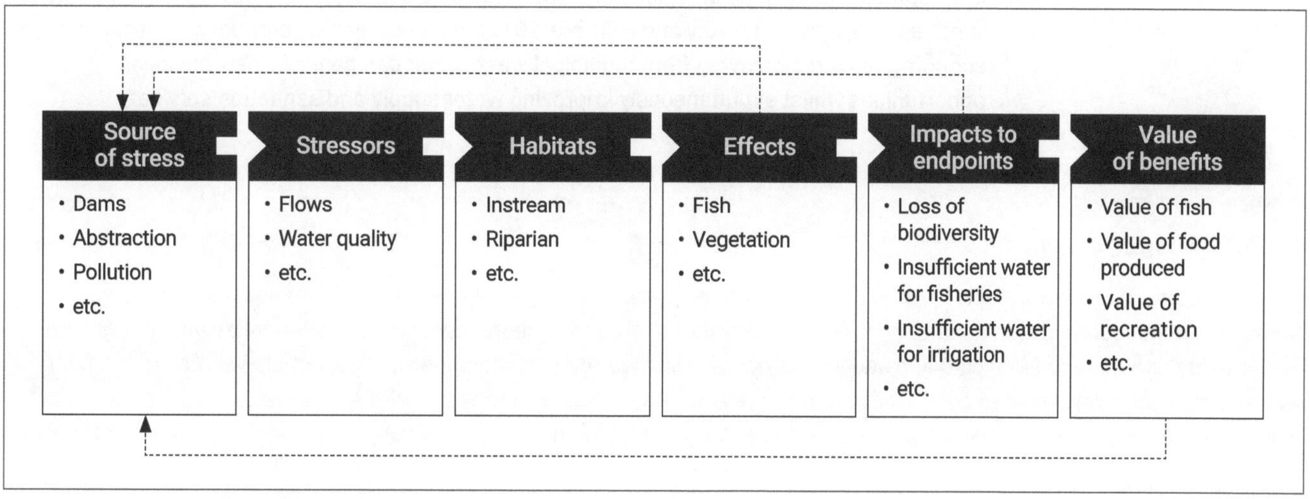

Note: Dotted lines represent feedback opportunities to manage the sources of stress.

Source: Based on O'Brien et al. (2020).

2.5.3 Private sector initiatives and water stewardship

Business has become increasingly aware, beyond corporate social responsibility, of the risks of not considering water-related impacts, which has prompted action towards associated alliance building (Newborne and Dalton, 2016). Water stewardship refers to an approach to support major water users to understand their water use and its impacts, and to work collaboratively and transparently for sustainable water management within a catchment context (Box 2.5). Several initiatives are active in this space: for example, the *CEO Water Mandate* and the *Business for Water Stewardship*. The latter has over 1,200 companies in the United States of America (USA) engaged in environmental water stewardship efforts that have improved the quality of 72 billion litres of water, generating a purported economic value of US$1.4 trillion.

2.6 Alternative sources: Water reuse, desalination and supply augmentation

Reusing water is the key to water conservation and enhancement opportunities that lead to fit-for-purpose use of treated municipal wastewater and agricultural drainage water. Additional opportunities to develop water resources exist in the form of desalinated potable water. The volumes of some unconventional water resources, such as municipal wastewater and desalinated water are 380 km^3 and 35 km^3, respectively. Accessing such sources can help alleviate water scarcity in dry areas (UN-Water, 2020).

2.6.1 Water reuse

Recovering water, nutrients, precious metals and energy from waste streams are means of delivering value added (WWAP, 2017). About 380 billion m^3 of water can be recovered from the annual volumes of wastewater produced. This type of water recovery is expected to reach 470 billion m^3 by 2030 and 574 billion m^3 by 2050 (Qadir et al., 2020). The full recovery of nitrogen, phosphorus and potassium from wastewater can offset 13.4% of the global demand for these nutrients in agriculture, but current technologies of nutrient recovery from wastewater have yet to reach 100% efficiency levels (Fernández-Arévalo et al., 2017; Ward et al., 2018). Beyond nutrient recovery and economic gains, there are critical environmental benefits, such as a reduction in eutrophication (Mayer et al., 2016).

The energy potential of wastewater is yet to be fully exploited (Frijns et al., 2013). Wastewater contains more energy than is needed for its treatment and more and more wastewater treatment plants are reaching internal energy self-sufficiency (Tarallo et al., 2015). There are good opportunities of intensifying energy recovery from wastewater (Maktabifard et al., 2018). Wastewater treatment facilities have the potential to produce surplus energy beyond self-supply. Investments in energy efficiency and recovery activities based on life cycle cost analysis in wastewater systems have the potential to deliver high rates of return. By implementing current best management practices and integrating energy considerations through step-by-step programmes, there is an opportunity to leapfrog sustainable development, particularly in regions and countries where wastewater collection and treatment is not always a given (Lackey and Fillmore, 2017). As an essential component of a circular economy, resource recovery from municipal wastewater can generate new business opportunities whilst simultaneously improving water supply and sanitation services.

Box 2.5 Water stewardship

The Alliance for Water Stewardship (AWS) has developed a detailed set of guidelines, the AWS *International Water Stewardship Standard 2.0*, that aims to drive economic, social and environmental benefits at catchment scale, by engaging 'water-using sites' in understanding and addressing not only site water risks and opportunities, but also shared catchment water challenges. Water-related costs and revenues are holistically assessed together with shared value creation that considers economic value, social value and environmental value, including values that benefit stakeholders outside of the site.

Source: Alliance for Water Stewardship (n.d.).

Saline drainage water produced by irrigated agriculture can be reused for growing salt-tolerant crops, particularly for energy crops and renewable energy production, thereby relaxing the growing pressure on already stretched water and energy resources (Qadir et al., 2010). A range of plant species can be irrigated with saline water for biomass and renewable energy production. Some promising examples are jatropha, toothbrush tree, Russian olive, and sweet-stem sorghum (Lamers and Khamzina, 2008). Such use of saline water can also contribute to carbon sequestration via biomass production and buildup of soil carbon stocks, thereby reducing the impact of global warming. In addition, the hydraulic pressure heads located at the regulated gated points in the saline drainage and collector networks can be used for operating micro-turbines. As a source of decentralized and off-grid energy production, these hydro-turbines represent an environmentally clean source of energy for pumping water, lighting and heating, and have the potential to make the associated farming communities more resilient to climate change impacts (Qadir et al., 2010).

Over the past decade, seawater desalination has experienced an accelerated growth driven by advances in membrane technology and material science

2.6.2 Desalination

Desalinated water is an important water resource, which extends water supplies beyond what is available from the hydrological cycle, providing a climate-independent and steady supply of high-quality water (UN-Water, 2020). With around 16,000 operational desalination plants, daily production of desalinated water stands at 95 million m^3 (35 billion m^3 annually) of clean water for use in industry, commerce, households, tourism, and high-value agriculture. Almost half of the desalination capacity (44%) is in the still-growing Middle East market, but markets in other regions are growing even faster, particularly in China, the USA and Latin America (Jones et al., 2019).

Over the past decade, seawater desalination has experienced an accelerated growth driven by advances in membrane technology and material science. A steady downward trend in desalination costs, coupled with increasing costs of conventional water treatment and water reuse driven by more stringent regulatory requirements, is expected to accelerate the current trend of reliance on the ocean as an attractive and competitive water source (see Box 3.5). These trends are likely to continue and to further establish seawater desalination as a reliable drought-proof alternative for coastal communities worldwide in the next 15 years (UN-Water, 2020).

Currently, more than 174 countries use desalination in one form or another to meet sector water demand, supplying over 300 million people with potable water (IDA, 2020). Despite declining costs, most desalination facilities are in high-income countries (67%), accounting for 71% of the global desalination capacity. Conversely, less than 0.1% of the capacity occurs in low-income countries (Jones et al., 2019).

2.6.3 Augmenting supply

Nature-based solutions, including catchment management, are the key means of augmenting supply by, for example, recharging groundwater, sustaining surface water flows, improving soil moisture retention or managing regional precipitation (see Chapter 2 and WWAP/UN-Water 2018). There are also various other infrastructure approaches to augment water supply. Rainwater harvesting, usually involving the construction of micro-impoundments, often in conjunction with green infrastructure such as groundwater or soil water storage, can be a useful alternative to larger dams.

2.7 Constraints and challenges

Despite growing experience and improvements in valuation tools, some limitations still exist. Barredo et al. (2019) list these as: (i) gaps in knowledge of *interdependence of ecosystems and their services* – the value of one service may not easily take into account how other services are being affected; (ii) preventing *double-counting* – the full range of complementary and competitive services must be distinguished before any aggregation of values is completed; (iii) *spatial issues* – ecosystem services are best evaluated across their full geographical extent, which may not fit well with the spatial scale of valuation; (iv) *temporal issues* – impacts on ecosystems and their services may extend well beyond a standard time period of a given policy (project) appraisal; (v) *environmental limits* – the services that ecosystems provide depend not only on the scale and function of the ecosystem but also, crucially, on its conditions and biodiversity levels, and studies typically estimate marginal change at a few points along the demand curve but applying these values to non-marginal changes is not appropriate; (vi) *dealing with uncertainty* – there is often no consensus on certain aspects, but an option for estimating uncertainty is to conduct a sensitivity analysis; and (vii) *data transfer and knowledge gaps* – data transfer is challenging because of differing social and environmental contexts, characteristics and time periods, as well as the inability to deal with the valuation of novel impacts – a number of initiatives are attempting to build databases to support knowledge transfer, such as a database on Forest Ecosystem Service Valuation Studies (Thünen Institute, n.d.), woodland valuation tools (Scottish Government, n.d.) and The Economics of Ecosystems and Biodiversity Valuation Database (Van der Ploeg and De Groot, 2010).

All too often water-related policy decisions are based on a limited suite of values. In many cases, other values are known but not included

Various practical barriers are reported for integrating valuation of ecosystem services in policy decisions (e.g. Russi et al., 2013; Costanza et al., 2014; Barredo et al., 2019). These include: (i) *cultural barriers* – there are often reservations to considering economic approaches for solving environmental challenges; (ii) *methodological barriers* – often, there are no generally accepted procedural rules amidst the methodological complexities of valuation; and (iii) *political barriers* – difficulty in implementing and communicating political decisions based on intangible values, including from the monetization of services with private and public goods characteristics.

The Intergovernmental Science-Policy Platform on Biodiversity and Ecosystem Services has provided a comprehensive overview of gaps in knowledge (IPBES, 2019b). These include gaps in data, inventories and monitoring on: nature and the drivers of change; biomes and units of analysis; taxonomy; links between nature, nature's contributions to people and drivers with respect to targets and goals; integrated scenarios and modelling studies; potential policy approaches; and the incorporation of knowledge of indigenous peoples and local communities.

All too often water-related policy decisions are based on a limited suite of values. In many cases, other values are known but not included. There is little point improving environmental valuation if the policy context is not sensitive to incorporating diverse values. Value-based policy-making is a prerequisite for subsequently enabling environmental values, or any values, to be properly considered and reflected in decisions.

Environmental values inescapably need to include different perspectives of economic valuation, including monetary and non-monetary values, as well as other cultural and societal beliefs or value judgements. The greatest need, therefore, is for tools that compare and contrast diverse values. This need is common to many other aspects of water values and considered further in Chapter 7.

Chapter 3

Valuation of hydraulic infrastructure

WWAP

David Coates and Richard Connor

With contributions from:

Chris Dickens and Karen Villholth (IWMI); Neil Dhot (AquaFed); and Gordon O'Brien (University of Mpumalanga)

3.1 Introduction

The value of water to society is underpinned by hydraulic infrastructure that serves to store or move water. This can be either built (grey) or natural (green). 'Soft' infrastructure, such as organizational infrastructure (e.g. institutions or social networks), is not covered here.

There is little doubt that, overall, hydraulic infrastructure has delivered substantial social and economic benefits. It is argued (e.g. by Muller et al., 2015) that socio-economic development is curtailed in countries that have insufficient infrastructure to manage water, as a result of which many developing countries are held hostage to their hydrology. Therefore, more infrastructure is needed. However, past experience shows that the valuation of hydraulic infrastructure has been seriously flawed, particularly for large dams (Box 3.1).

Box 3.1 Experiences with the valuation of large dams

The World Commission on Dams (2000) concluded that: inadequate valuation was a significant factor in the poor or negative performance of many large dams; in too many cases social and environmental costs have been unacceptable; substantive evaluations of completed projects are few in number, narrow in scope, poorly integrated across impact categories and scales, and inadequately linked to decisions on operations; there were a significant number of shortcomings in the valuation of dams in the proposal, design and implementation stages; and many dams were not built based on a comprehensive assessment and evaluation of the technical, financial and economic criteria applicable at the time, much less the social and environmental criteria that apply in today's context.

It is doubtful that things have substantially improved in practice in the meantime. For example, key findings of an assessment of dam building under the Programme for Infrastructure Development in Africa (PIDA), using known standards from the World Commission on Dams (2000) and the International Hydropower Association's Sustainability Assessment Protocol (IHA, 2010) included that: whereas a laudable development rationale has emerged, benefits tend to be overstated and skewed; risks often outweigh the rewards; costs to communities and the environment have been high; and assessments were not based on a robust assessment of options (International Rivers, 2012).

By 2030, investment in water and sanitation infrastructure will need to be around US$0.9–1.5 trillion per year, roughly 20% of the total requirement for all types of infrastructure investment (OECD, 2017b). About 70% of this total infrastructure investment will be in the global South, with a large share in rapidly growing urban areas (GCEC, 2016). In developed countries, large investments will be required for renovation and upgrade. The number of large water infrastructure projects is expected to increase in world regions where precious natural resources are located, requiring significant trade-offs (Opperman et al., 2015). Yet, the values of ecosystem services and social impacts remain insufficiently addressed in major water engineering projects (Hansjürgens et al., 2016), despite social and environmental safeguards (Skinner and Haas, 2014).

Considering the sums of money invested in water infrastructure, it could be reasonably expected that the valuation of costs and benefits would be well developed, standardized at least to some degree, and widely applied. This is not so, and, as will be shown, societal benefits delivered are often unquantified, costs (particularly external costs) are not adequately accounted for, options are often not adequately valued and compared, and data are often poor with almost universally outdated or unrepresentative hydrological data. According to the *Water Integrity Outlook* (Water Integrity Network, 2016), no part of the water financing system, public or private, is immune from corruption or integrity failures and about 10% of investment is lost to corruption, equalling about US$75 billion each year.

This chapter discusses how improved attention to the valuation of hydraulic infrastructure can help identify the full range of costs and benefits in play and thereby help maximize its economic, social and environmental benefits.

3.2 Values of global benefits of water infrastructure

Whilst there are various estimates of global investments in hydraulic infrastructure (see above), less is known about global benefits. There are some estimates of national water infrastructure value that can be implied from projected benefits delivered. For example, in the United States of America (USA), current national water infrastructure capital needs are US$123 billion per year, with an aggregate economic impact of US$220 billion in annual economic activity and 1.3 million jobs, and an added indirect benefit of US$140 billion (The Value of Water Campaign, 2017). But these kinds of estimates are not available for the majority of countries.

Some indications of global values can be implied from the costs of infrastructure deficits or infrastructure failure. In 2015, the economic losses caused by water risks were estimated at approximately US$500 billion annually (Sadoff et al., 2015). Water-related losses in agriculture, health, income and property could result in a decline by as much as 6% of Gross Domestic Product (GDP) by 2050 and lead to sustained negative growth in some regions of the world (World Bank, 2016a). In the USA, service disruptions put US$43.5 billion in daily economic activity at risk (The Value of Water Campaign, 2017). Water shortages consistently rank among the global risks of greatest concern to policy-makers and business leaders (World Economic Forum, 2019). These concerns are real. The global population experiencing severe water scarcity is increasing from 32 million people in 1900 to a projected 3.1 billion people by 2050 (Kummu et al., 2010; Gosling and Arnell, 2016). Costanza et al. (2014) valued the water-related services provided by nature at US$29 trillion per year, and between 1997 and 2011 the estimated loss in annual services from ecosystems was US$2.7 trillion for swamps and floodplains, and US$7.2 trillion for tidal marshes and mangroves. Asia's poor river health alone could threaten US$1.75 trillion in ecosystem services annually (ADB/APWF, 2013). With financing needs for water infrastructure ranging from US$6.7 trillion to US$22.6 trillion by 2030 (WWC/OECD, 2015), these previous figures on benefits suggest that investments in both grey and green water infrastructure have the potential to deliver a good economic return, in addition to often unquantifiable social and human welfare returns.

3.3 Methods and approaches to the valuation of hydraulic infrastructure

The valuation of hydraulic infrastructure is beset with conceptual and methodological difficulties, particularly regarding non-consumptive use, and indirect and non-use values. At an empirical level, the value of this infrastructure can be determined through the cumulative value it represents to the various end uses of the water. But these values are often not well established.

3.3.1 General concepts and approaches

Well-established methodologies are available for valuing hydraulic infrastructure. For natural, or green, infrastructure, and for assessing many environmental impacts of built (grey) infrastructure, the methodologies centre on the valuation of ecosystem services, which is covered in more detail in Chapter 2. Onuma and Tsuge (2018) present a methodology to identify the conditions under which introducing green infrastructure is desirable, and the point at which it is preferable to grey infrastructure. On the other hand, WWAP/UN-Water (2018) stresses that separating green from grey infrastructure is a false dichotomy and that the values of both should be considered together, with their deployment being mutually supportive (Box 3.2).

The most widely published approaches for the valuation of grey infrastructure relate to large dams (World Commission on Dams, 2000) and include direct methods, such as market-based or stated preference approaches, and indirect methods, such as revealed preferences or choice modelling (see Chapter 1 for further details). Most methods of valuing water infrastructure centre on a cost–benefit approach, but there is a tendency to overestimate benefits and underestimate costs, and in particular to not include all costs (e.g. World Commission on Dams, 2000). The most common shortcomings in valuations relate to social and environmental costs. One of the most critical questions is 'value to whom'. Valuations tend to excessively focus on target beneficiaries while other stakeholders may benefit less or even be negatively impacted.

Box 3.2 Valuations help identify how green infrastructure supports grey infrastructure – The case of the Itaipu Dam in Brazil

The Itaipu Dam in Brazil is among the world's largest in terms of hydropower generation. However, due to the nature of the soils in its catchment area and land use practices of local farmers, the Itaipu Reservoir (like most others) is vulnerable to excessive sediment loads that gradually fill it and reduce the storage capacity, and therefore shorten the reservoir's life expectancy, while increasing maintenance costs.

Itaipu Dam, Brazil. *Photo: © nicolasdecorte/Shutterstock.com*

Natural capital accounting (described further in Chapter 2) identified relevant natural capital flows (ecosystem services). Farmers in the watershed were able to develop a quantified scoring system that could account for how much each farm might contribute to reducing siltation (Laurent et al., 2011). This enabled farmers to be considered as 'water producers' by the National Water Agency, which assigns values to the ecosystem services generated by farms participating in the programme based on their contribution to savings in terms of dam maintenance, operational costs and capital depreciation (ANA, 2011). The resulting programme, Cultivando Água Boa (*"cultivating good water"*), has established a partnership with farmers to achieve mutual goals of sustainability based largely on the adoption of no-till farming (Mello and Van Raij, 2006). The life expectancy of the dam complex has now been increased from 60 years to 350 years. Additionally, other environmental benefits are delivered (such as reduced nutrient runoff and biodiversity conservation) and, importantly, farm productivity and sustainability have also increased – presenting a win-win scenario for farmers and the hydropower company.

One of the most critical questions is 'value to whom'. Valuations tend to excessively focus on target beneficiaries while other stakeholders may benefit less or even be negatively impacted

Because water infrastructure assets are not commonly traded, evidence of their market-based fair value may be limited. Therefore, most water business accounting methods estimate fair value based on the Net Present Value of expected incomes, on depreciated replacement cost, or current replacement cost (Box 3.3). When the business operation is effectively not-for-profit, it is inappropriate to value water supply infrastructure assets on the basis of future expected earnings. In such case, a valuation based on depreciated replacement cost gives a better idea of the future expected benefits arising from holding these assets. It also provides a better idea of the exposure of the government/community to loss due to extreme events (Comisari et al., 2011).

Unit Reference Value (URV) approaches have been used to identify the cost of water per unit volume for water management schemes. For example, in South Africa a URV was developed in the 1980s. In its most basic form, it is calculated as the discounted present value of the total (capital and operational) life-cycle cost of a water augmentation or management scheme, divided by the discounted incremental increase in water supply (Bester et al., 2020).

However, a major shortcoming in many approaches, including most of those listed immediately above, is that they focus mainly on financial costs (cash flows, and capital and operational expenditure) and financial returns. They often omit indirect costs, and in particular social and environmental costs, which are treated as externalities. As noted in Chapter 1, neither the price of water, nor the costs of its delivery, accurately reflect value. Value needs to be assessed based on balancing the full suite of all costs and benefits, monetary and non-monetary, direct and indirect. Using 'total economic value' is one approach that can better reflect these broader considerations as detailed further in Chapters 1 and 2. A full cost–benefit analysis of a water infrastructure project will therefore involve complex economic assessments. It will also necessarily involve assumptions regarding such things as risks, discount rates, project longevity, depreciation rates and interest rates. Not only does this allow for a high degree of latitude, and potential bias, in estimates, it also leads to the significant problem that the circumstances upon which assumptions are based can change (Box 3.4).

The costs of dam removal are rarely, if ever, factored into valuations at design stage. Dam removal can be required where structures become unsafe or redundant.

Box 3.3 Why and how to value water infrastructure assets?

Asset value can vary dramatically depending on the valuation basis and the nature of the assets involved. Therefore, it is necessary to determine for which reasons the asset value is being estimated. Possible reasons for valuing water infrastructure assets include:

- To measure the net worth; that is, to inform the owners (private or public) of their wealth held;
- To establish a possible sale price for the assets in question;
- To appraise owners of the likely replacement cost of the asset in the event of its destruction or damage;
- To generate estimates of return on the asset; and
- As a basis for generating ongoing measures of productivity.

Key economic and accounting concepts include:

Fair value – The amount for which an asset could be exchanged, or a liability settled, between knowledgeable, willing parties in an arm's length transaction. If there is no market-based evidence, fair value can be estimated using an income or a depreciated replacement cost approach.

For estimating return on water assets, viable valuation bases include:

Current Replacement Cost – The cost to construct or replace the exact same asset today, regardless of the depreciation incurred.

Depreciated Replacement Cost – the current replacement cost, taking into account accumulated depreciation, generally a more reliable measure of the remaining economic benefits of the asset compared to current replacement cost.

Net Present Value (or value in use, discounted cash flow, internal rate of return) – the present value of future cash flows expected to be derived from an asset.

Market valuation is not always used, either because such valuation is not possible, or because it is considered inappropriate in the circumstances. In commercial accounting, either a Depreciated Replacement Cost or an income approach is generally used if market values are not available or are considered inappropriate.

Source: Adapted from Comisari et al. (2011).

Box 3.4 Applying a probabilistic cost–benefit analysis (CBA) to the Three Gorges Dam, China

Morimoto and Hope (2004) applied a comprehensive probabilistic CBA to the Three Gorges Dam in China. This CBA took project uncertainty into account and tried to deliver more robust and justifiable results than those produced by the more usual deterministic CBAs or multi-criteria analysis. Thus, the distribution of the net present value could be calculated and the most significant impacts identified. The results showed that, even though the reasonable and usual assumptions at the time of construction foresaw positive project impacts, these were highly sensitive to valuation methods, the choice of discount rates and project uncertainty. For example, costs of alternative renewable energy sources (such as solar) are now substantially less than at project design, making significant differences to projected hydropower costs and benefits. The authors also note that most previous studies focused only on each impact of the dam independently, and employed a mainly qualitative approach to both valuations of each impact and the comparison of values derived.

3.3.2 Assessing economic versus financial viability

It is important to recognize the differences between valuations based on economic or financial viability. *Financial viability* is the ability of an entity to continue to achieve its operating objectives, usually a defined financial rate of return, and fulfil its mission from a financial perspective over the long term. *Economic viability* assesses whether a project provides an overall positive net economic contribution to society after all costs and benefits have been accounted for, including social, environmental and financial costs and benefits to society (IHA, 2020). Therefore, a project that is financially viable is not necessarily economically viable, and vice versa. Despite this, many projects have been founded on financial valuations only, and even for those, cost recovery assumptions are hardly ever achieved in reality (World Commission on Dams, 2000).

That values can change over time highlights the value of flexible and adaptive strategies and 'no-regrets'-based decision-making

Current approaches for financing (Chapter 10) and the models employed do not encourage the required level of attention to the flexible, multi-purpose infrastructure that is needed for future water security. Moreover, despite the vast sums invested, the values and competing priorities of different affected stakeholders have not been adequately considered in past infrastructure financing (WWC/OECD, 2015). Water infrastructure investment needs to become more efficient to help properly maintain existing assets and also to "*avoid building future liabilities*" (WWC/OECD, 2015, p. III). Better valuing of water could contribute solutions to this challenge, including in the area of good water governance, where integrity and transparency will be paramount.

3.3.3 Factoring in capital and operational costs

A key question in valuation is whether large capital and operational and maintenance (O&M) costs are included in subsequent valuations of end uses. Full-cost charging for water services is the exception rather than the rule. In many countries, only part or all of the operational costs are recovered, and capital investments are covered by public funds (WWF, 2003). Large water infrastructure projects, and in particular large dams, often show a poor financial and economic performance. Usually, they fail to recover operation and maintenance costs, which suggests that even where it is an explicit objective, recovery of capital costs will be limited (World Commission on Dams, 2000). Many dams are multi-purpose, providing, for example, hydropower, irrigation, fisheries and flood control. Allocating costs to the various uses can be challenging. While valuation needs to somehow balance all benefits and costs of different water uses, it is artificial if capital and O&M costs are not factored in.

3.3.4 Recognizing that values can change

Values used to calculate the cost–benefit of projects can change. For example, the costs of renewable energy sources like solar or wind have gone significantly down over the past decade, a trend that is expected to continue (IEA, 2020). Hence, the original cost–benefit assumptions of hydropower dams may no longer hold true (an example is provided in Box 3.4). These reductions in renewable energy costs can also make water infrastructure more economically viable, such as in the case of desalination (Box 3.5; see Section 2.6.2).

Box 3.5 Valuing desalination

Where freshwater is scarce, its value is high. If coupled with water reuse for irrigation, desalination reduces freshwater abstraction and augments water supply. The environmental impacts of this procedure can be moderated if it is powered by renewable energy (Pistocchi et al., 2020). In Israel, desalination plants currently provide about a quarter of the potable water supply, and there are plans to expand this capacity. Water shortages have often caused economic losses affecting the entire Israeli economy. The economic value of desalinated seawater, determined in terms of the reduction in water shortages, is revealed to be about US$4 per m^3: much more than the direct costs of the desalination process (Palatnik, 2019).

In addition, the potential for future changes in societal values, such as increased values placed on the environment and recreation, can lead to calls for dam removal. For example, recovery of salmon stocks has been a major driver of dam removal in the USA (Whitelaw and McMullen, 2002). That values can change over time highlights the value of flexible and adaptive strategies and 'no-regrets'-based decision-making.

3.3.5 Water storage

The storage of water is an important objective of water infrastructure in order to deal with variations in the supply and availability of water, as well as in water demand. All parts of the hydrosphere, including oceans, lakes, soils, groundwater and the atmosphere act as reservoirs, as do human-built reservoirs that principally use dams. Despite the abundance of dams, by far the largest stores of freshwater are still contained in natural systems.

Trends in water storage

There are widespread declines in total water storage and associated freshwater availability that are primarily attributed to the intensive overextraction of groundwater and an increasing temperature-induced surface water loss (Liu et al., 2019). Impacts of climate change on land water storage trends exceed those of direct human intervention by about a factor of 2 (Scanlon et al., 2018). Globally, built reservoir capacity per person is decreasing (Figure 3.1), as reservoir expansion has not been able to keep pace with population growth, but also because storage capacity of existing reservoirs is decreasing chiefly due to sedimentation. Average annual storage volume losses equal about 1% of total built reservoir capacity, and the estimated costs for restoring these losses are approximately US$13 billion per year (George et al., 2017). An assessment of the value of storage capacity for enhancing water security in the world's 400 largest river basins identified water shortage risks in many parts of Africa, as well as in Australia, northern China, India, Spain and the western USA (Gaupp et al., 2015).

Figure 3.1
Global population growth and reservoir storage volume

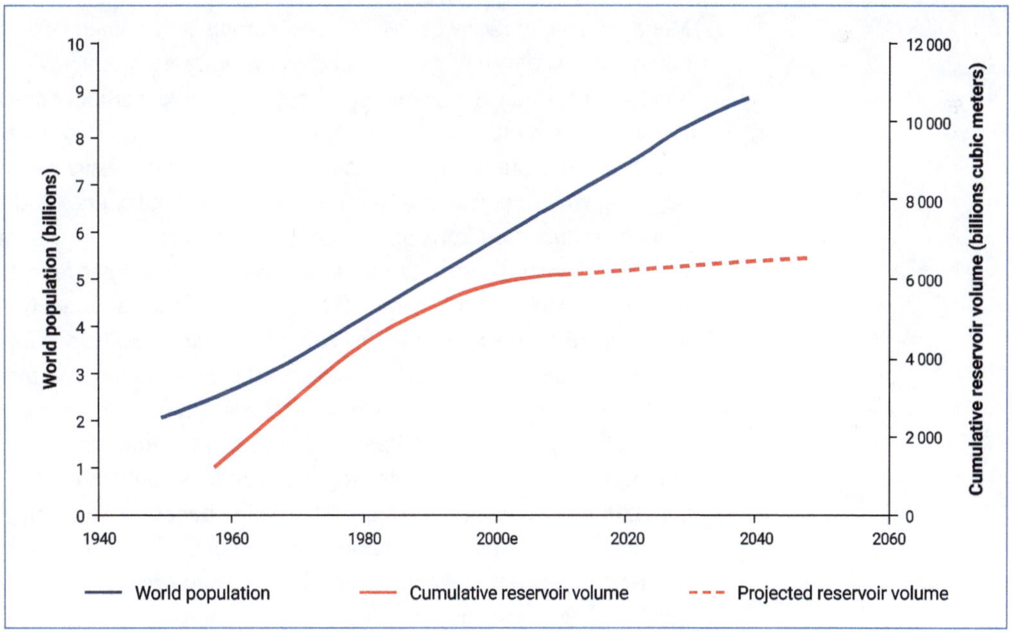

Source: Annandale et al. (2016, fig. 3.14, p. 41).

Losses in artificial reservoir storage due to sedimentation increase depreciation rates on investment capital and therefore returns on investment. They also increase the value of sediment abatement measures – implemented chiefly through nature-based solutions for improved catchment management (see WWAP/UN-Water, 2018).

Combined with the increasing need for storage, these trends question whether expansion of artificial reservoir capacity should be a central component of a sustainable water resources strategy (Wisser et al., 2013). There are viable alternatives such as: (i) recognizing the comparative value of storage in, or the conjunctive use of, natural systems, which is not only where most storage actually occurs but also where the main opportunities for sustainably increasing storage value can be found; (ii) recognizing the value of reducing demand; (iii) increasing supply through, for example, improved land management or water reuse; and (iv) using decentralized solutions.

There are significant non-use values associated with the way in which reservoirs store and release water

Evaporative losses

Artificial lakes and reservoirs suffer significant losses from increased evaporation as compared to the evaporation from the original river, estimated from AQUASTAT data at 346 km³/year globally (FAO, 2015), roughly 10% of total global water withdrawals. Losses can be expected to be proportionately higher than this average in hotter arid regions, which is also where water tends to be scarcer. These losses have a significant impact on valuations that are based on volumes of water used – suggesting that, on average, these volumes will be twice the amount measured directly. This highlights the value of the environment in storing water where evaporative losses can be lower. For example, groundwater dams deliver value by slowing groundwater flows, reducing evaporative losses and creating additional storage in the underground reservoir (aquifer) behind them (Onder and Yilmaz, 2005). Increasingly, aquifers and built surface storage are being managed together. Most conjunctive systems usually focus on managing demand by alternating reservoir versus aquifer use depending on seasons and demand. Aquifer recharge can be proactively increased through land management (Box 3.6).

Box 3.6 Managed aquifer recharge using green infrastructure: Valuing costs and benefits of water supply and other social, environmental and resilience services

Managed aquifer recharge (MAR) uses a broad set of green infrastructure solutions that harness the ecosystem services and natural infrastructure provided by well-functioning land and its subsurface. Such solutions, which belong to a broader category of Groundwater-Based Natural Infrastructure (GRIPP, n.d.), are increasingly incorporated as part of integrated water management solutions to increase water security and resilience and to sustain environmental services. While increasing water storage and availability are key drivers, MAR generally also reduces evaporation from, and reduces the land footprint of, alternative surface water storage. In terms of costs, most of the schemes using natural water for recharge are much cheaper than highly engineered schemes that use recycled water or apply wells for injecting new water, as indicated by a recent review of 28 long-standing MAR cases from around the world (Zheng et al., forthcoming). The same assessment indicates that investments in these solutions are practically always attractive, with benefit–cost ratios ranging from 1.3 to around 7 for a wide range of types of solutions. Benefits are calculated from estimated costs of the next-best alternative water source or the proportion of the value of production attributed to the recharged water. Ratios would be even higher if other co-benefits (which may be more difficult to assess) are included, such as water storage, socio-economic benefits, and positive impacts on health, biodiversity and environmental values. Further analysis of these benefits would provide additional evidence and incentive to guide policies and investment in MAR.

Contributed by Karen G. Villholth (IWMI).

Box 3.7 Valuing optimization of dam storage and release

Dam operators face pressures regarding the timing of water release. Direct users (e.g. for irrigation or domestic supply) may argue that water should be stored to minimize risks of shortages. However, this will reduce potential economic and environmental benefits downstream. Valuations are central to optimizing system performance.

Economic carryover storage value functions (COSVFs) are a means to calculate the value of storage and release to deal with risks and uncertainty in interannual inflow. For example, when applied to 30 reservoirs, 22 aquifers, and 51 urban and agricultural demand sites in the California Valley (USA), optimized interannual reservoir operation reduces the average annual scarcity volume and costs by 80% and 98%, respectively (Khadem et al., 2018). Coordination of multi-reservoir systems can enhance net benefits from irrigation and hydropower by 3–12%, with coordination benefits increasing with the water availability and inflow variability (Jeuland, 2020).

Built water infrastructure impacts the balance of services provided by a river and its flow regime. Mandatory minimum environmental releases do not account for the inherent and often complex trade-offs and synergies that must be considered in selecting a balance of ecosystem and engineered services. Using multiple performance metrics, covering the suite of ecosystem and engineered services in play, enables a better understanding of the interactions between natural and built assets. This helps in the identification of river basin interventions that deliver optimized value by appropriately trading off their services (Hurford et al., 2020).

Valuation of operational measures for dam storage and discharge

There are significant non-use values associated with the way in which reservoirs store and release water. Releasing too much water immediately can threaten future direct use supplies and costs, but not releasing enough creates immediate economic and environmental losses and hardship downstream. The timing of release of water from reservoirs can have large impacts on biological productivity and livelihoods downstream and therefore increase non-use values (Box 3.7).

3.4 Valuing risk and resilience

Water-related risk and resilience can have very high values. In a survey of 525 investors with US$96 trillion in assets, 45% reported exposure to substantive risks from water insecurity – risks that threaten their reputation and license to operate, the security of their supply chains, their financial stability, and their ability to grow. Among the companies reporting exposure, the combined business value at risk topped out at US$425 billion with about 40% of the risks anticipated to hit within the next 1–3 years (CDP, 2020).

Understanding the risk of multiple stressors and the importance of resource resilience in water infrastructure systems has always been essential, but its importance is especially pronounced in the face of climate change, which will have an impact on the risk factors. Managing water under increasing uncertainty and risk was the subject of the fourth *World Water Development Report* in 2012 (WWAP, 2012). Values associated with risk and resilience are often not adequately considered in strategies or assessments. Although engineers have well-established methodologies for assessing the risks of failure of individual constructed hydraulic structures, catastrophic failures of individual structures can occur. However, as opposed to failure of individual structures, there are bigger and more systemic risks. For example, those from natural and human-made disasters (e.g. flood, drought, desertification, water pollution incidents, etc.) or water system failures.

Resilience of water infrastructure refers to its capacity to avoid or recover quickly from difficulties, stresses or shocks. The ability of water infrastructure to continue to deliver its benefits in ordinary as well as extraordinary circumstances can be defined as resilience value. The value of resilience is reflected in the avoided costs of system failures or the speed of recovery from them.

There is a widespread assumption that built water infrastructure increases resilience and reduces risks. However, this is not always the case. For example, in India, 40% of thermal power plants are located in water-scarce areas, and between 2013 and 2016 the largest energy utilities in the country suffered losses of US$1.4 billion due to climate change when they were forced to temporarily shut down (Luo et al., 2018). The expansion of constructed reservoirs to improve resilience to water shortages is hotly debated in many places around the world. For example, Di Baldassarre et al. (2018) argue that there are two counterintuitive dynamics that should be considered in this debate: supply–demand cycles that describe instances where increasing water supply enables higher water demand, which can quickly offset the initial benefits of reservoirs; or where overreliance on reservoirs increases vulnerability and therefore the potential damage caused by droughts. It is well established that in some cases water infrastructure can significantly increase risks and their impacts. Valuation of ecosystem services in play can illuminate the hidden costs of water management infrastructure. For example, degradation of wetland values in the Mississippi Delta (USA) caused by sediment trapping behind dams contributed to increased impacts of Hurricane Katrina on New Orleans in 2005 (Batker et al., 2010). Worryingly, many of the world's population centres are located in river deltas with a similar history of infrastructure development upstream.

Water-related risk and resilience can have very high values

Using a spatial framework that quantifies multiple stressors and accounts for downstream impacts, Vörösmarty et al. (2010) drew attention to the pitfalls of development overly reliant on built infrastructure. They concluded that despite this infrastructure, nearly 80% of the world's population is exposed to high levels of threat to water security. Massive investment in water technology enables rich nations to offset high stressor levels without remedying their underlying causes, but leaves them vulnerable to climate-induced hydrological changes. At the same time, less wealthy nations remain vulnerable, but have options as to how to proceed. The authors conclude that a cumulative threat framework offers a tool for prioritizing policy and management responses to this crisis, underscoring the necessity of limiting threats at their source instead of through costly remediation of symptoms.

Risk assessments provide opportunities to incorporate system resilience and multiple stressors in the management of present and future socio-ecological values. While this is gradually being embraced by the water sector, the term resilience itself is not yet universally defined, nor has it become a standard part of water resources management (Makropoulos et al., 2018). More work is needed to evaluate climate change-related risks and their systematic uptake in water management (UNESCO/UN-Water, 2020). As with most strategies and plans, participation of the local population and the incorporation of local knowledge are key means to identify values in play (Box 3.8).

Box 3.8 Incorporating civil values and local knowledge in risk reduction strategies

Regarding the Great East Japan Earthquake in 2011, De Oliveira and Paleo (2016) noted that overreliance on technical information and on the opinion of experts occurred side by side with negligence of local knowledge and lack of effective public participation in decision-making, creating a sense of overconfidence regarding scientific knowledge and new infrastructure's abilities to withstand future disasters.

Imamura et al. (2016) found that, even in high-risk areas and subsequent to recent significant disasters, people who frequently visit the sea preferred ecosystem conservation and disliked seawall construction, whereas people strongly recognizing disaster risks preferred seawall construction. They also concluded that civil trust in scientific information affects civil preferences regarding coastal management.

Risk assessment methodologies are continually being improved (Box 3.9). Most centre on applying knowledge of the interdependencies of relevant social and ecological systems within the landscape, and assigning magnitudes and probabilities of hazards to evaluate the probable consequences of multiple stressors and/or future events. The outcomes inform trade-off considerations regarding the adaptive management of water resources to achieve sustainable outcomes (O'Brien et al., 2018). In all risk assessments, knowledge of the uncertainty in the predictions is critical and should always be considered alongside the risk outcomes.

Infrastructure value chains are proving a useful concept for connecting the concepts of resilience and value in the context of the infrastructure life cycle. The concept is familiar to most professionals working on the design, delivery and operation of infrastructure systems (Avello et al., 2019). Methodologies for assessing resilience value are constantly improving. For example, Makropoulos et al. (2018) describe a methodology for assessing resilience of urban water supplies using a stress test methodology that might also assist in the uptake and evolution of resilience thinking in strategic water infrastructure decision-making. The World Wide Fund for Nature (WWF) and the World Business Council for Sustainable Development (WBCSD) have jointly developed tools and approaches for assessing water-related risks and challenges for companies and investors (Morgan et al., 2020).

Attention to the values of green infrastructure in risk reduction has increased in recent times. For example, the values and benefits of healthy, resilient ecosystems have been considered in the context of the Sendai Framework for Disaster Risk Reduction (UNISDR, 2015) and recent guidance for implementation of nature-based flood protection (World Bank, 2017). As is the case with grey infrastructure, inappropriately designed or sited green infrastructure can also increase risks. For example, wetlands are widely reported to 'act like a sponge', reducing floods and preventing droughts, but some headwater wetlands can increase downstream flooding (Bullock and Acreman, 2003).

Box 3.9 Ecological risk assessments for dam development in Africa

Ecological risk assessments have been undertaken to evaluate the synergistic effects of multiple flow-, water quality- and habitat-altering stressors associated with dam development and operation in Africa. In the Nile, Niger and Orange-Vaal River basins, these tools have been implemented to establish environmental flows in the context of the synergist effects of non-flow variables, the resilience of ecosystems and the vulnerability of human communities to stressors associated with water resource developments. In the Orange-Vaal and part of the Nile basin, the risk that resources have already been over-allocated is high, demonstrating that use exceeds the resilience of the system to stressors and that continued developments will probably be unsustainable. In the Orange-Vaal case study, the South African government now financially compensates Lesotho for the value of ecosystem services if use exceeds ecosystem resilience. In other parts of the Nile and Niger River basin, however, there is opportunity for further sustainable development of the existing green infrastructure and for offsetting the use of threatened resources.

Sources: O'Brien et al. (2018); O'Brien et al. (forthcoming).

3.5 Ways forward

Valuation of water infrastructure involves various scales, from site-specific to system-wide, taking account of the type of project, as well as the hydrological, environmental and social conditions. Past experience with valuation of water infrastructure highlights the importance of effective participation of stakeholders, multidisciplinary approaches that reveal invisible costs and benefits, and the use of a variety of approaches to undertake economic, financial and social assessments. Impartiality is key. Politics should not affect such an analysis, nor should financiers. Of course, when deciding whether to proceed with an investment, they can decide whether the values in question are important to them. Approaches to considering multiple values, and reaching transparent and equitable decisions, are detailed further in Chapter 9. Better use needs to be made of the substantial existing guidance, methodologies and experience available, of which this report provides only a snapshot.

Valuation is only of use if the decision-making process in question is based on a fair assessment of values. Too many projects, particularly for high-profile water infrastructure such as dams, remain essentially vanity projects, politically motivated and/or potentially subject to corruption. Under such circumstances, values, if assessed, are opaque, selective, manipulated or ignored. No amount of guidance on valuation will change that. Fundamentally, valuation of water infrastructure is about good governance. At least the attempt to govern well must be in place for proper valuations to play their part.

Chapter 4

Valuing water supply, sanitation and hygiene (WASH) services in human settlements

UN-Habitat
Pireh Hezekiah and Lars Stordal

WWAP
Joshua Newton, Richard Connor and David Coates

With contributions from:
Guy Hutton (UNICEF); Virginia Newton-Lewis (WaterAid); Yasmine Zaki Abdelaziz, Gemma Arthurson and Antonio Torres (IOM); and Juliane Schillinger (WYPW)

4.1 Introduction

The role of water within households, schools, workplaces and health care facilities is so fundamental that it is, paradoxically, often overlooked or not assigned a value comparable with other uses. Water is a basic human need, required for drinking and to support sanitation and hygiene, sustaining life and health. In fact, both water and sanitation are human rights (UNGA, 2016). A direct extension of access to water, sanitation and hygiene (WASH) services not only improves educational opportunities and workforce productivity, but also contributes to a life of dignity and equality. WASH services also indirectly add value in the form of a healthier environment, as it allows for the proper management of wastewater, as well as climate change adaptation when infrastructure is built with these considerations in mind.

4.2 The value of WASH services

Analysing the interdependencies and values of sanitation and hygiene is key in determining the full value of WASH. Water is necessary for a variety of sanitation- and hygiene-related uses, which include use of safely managed sanitation, maintenance and operation of sanitation facilities, personal hygiene such as handwashing, and menstrual hygiene management (MHM). This is not only true for households, but also for institutions and public places, including schools, healthcare facilities and transport hubs. At the same time, safely managed sanitation and the management of all forms of waste (including toxic waste, MHM and sanitary waste, and faecal sludge and wastewater) are crucial to assuring water quality. An integrated approach to WASH can lead to better health gains for those left furthest behind. Safely managed sanitation interventions can only be fully effective if they ensure a universal reach, and include meeting the needs of women, girls, and individuals and groups in vulnerable situations.

Gains from improved sanitation include increased school attendance, greater privacy and safety – especially for women, children and older persons – and a greater sense of dignity for all (OECD, 2018).

A recent assessment of the impact of unsafe WASH on childhood diarrhoeal disease suggests that household connections to water supplies and higher levels of sanitation coverage in communities lower risks of diarrhoeal morbidity. The assessment found that point-of-use filter interventions with safe storage reduced diarrhoea risk by 61%, while piped water of higher quality and continuous availability to premises reduced diarrhoea risk by 75%, compared to a baseline of unimproved drinking water. Sanitation interventions reduced diarrhoeal risk by 25%, with evidence for greater reductions when high sanitation coverage is reached, while interventions promoting handwashing with soap reduced these risks by 30%, compared with no intervention (Wolf et al., 2018).

Household connections to water supplies and higher levels of sanitation coverage in communities lower risks of diarrhoeal morbidity

From an economic perspective, benefits from improved WASH include reduced health care costs for individuals and society, and greater productivity and involvement in the workplace (Hutton and Chase, 2017). The World Health Organization (WHO) estimated that the total economic losses associated with inadequate WASH services amount to US$260 billion annually in 136 low- and middle-income countries, which is roughly equivalent to an average annual loss of 1.5% of the aggregate Gross Domestic Product (GDP) of those countries (WHO, 2012).

It has been estimated that achieving universal access to safe drinking water, sanitation and hygiene (Sustainable Development Goals (SDG) Targets 6.1 and 6.2) in 140 low- and middle-income countries would cost approximately US$1.7 trillion from 2016 to 2030, or US$114 billion per year (Hutton and Varughese, 2016). The benefit–cost ratio (BCR) of such investments has been shown to provide a significant positive return in most regions (WHO, 2012; Hutton, 2018). Returns on hygiene are even higher, as they can greatly improve health outcomes in many cases with little need for additional expensive infrastructure (Black et al., 2016). While it has previously been reported that returns on investment in sanitation, based on the global averages, deliver over twice the return on investment compared to drinking water (WHO, 2012), new analysis by Hutton (2018), based on disaggregated data between rural and urban areas (Figure 4.1), suggest that current BCRs favour drinking water supply (with BCRs of 3.4 and 6.8 for urban and rural areas respectively) over sanitation (with 2.5 and 5.2. for urban and rural areas respectively). These differences in BCRs between the two services and the differences in BCRs for each service between urban and rural settings are possibly due to basic sanitation being generally more expensive to provide than basic water supply (Hutton and Varughese, 2016), while both are more costly in urban areas. This could partly explain why investments in drinking water have consistently been higher than those in sanitation (WHO, 2017).

Figure 4.1 Benefit–cost ratios for the supply of drinking water and basic sanitation services in rural and urban settings

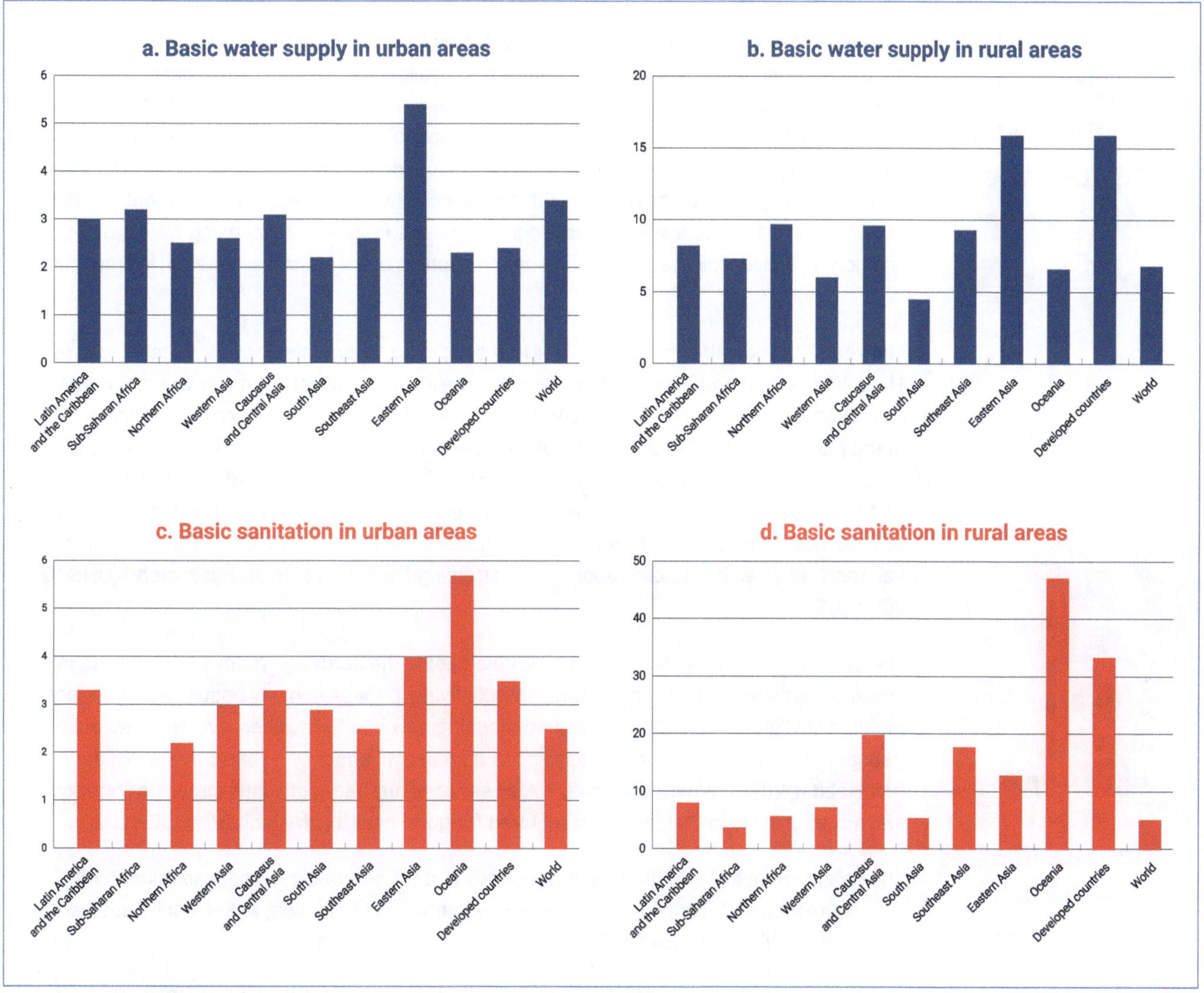

Note: A baseline 3% discount rate is used to calculate the present value of future costs.

Source: Based on data from Hutton (2018, Tables 23.9, 23.10, 23.11, and 23.12, pp. 434–436).

Similarly to WASH services, improved wastewater collection and treatment also improve health outcomes, while also reducing other impacts of environmental pollution. There are also benefits to be derived from wastewater reuse (see Sections 2.6.1 and 5.4.4), such as more water availability, energy production and use of by-products such as biosolids, which can be rich in phosphorus and nitrogen (WWAP, 2017). One study puts the value of wastewater at US$1.1 trillion, with that number expected to rise to US$2 trillion by 2050 according to a model focusing on water reuse, energy, nutrients and metals (Stacklin, 2012). In addition to the extra benefits mentioned above, wastewater reuse can reduce operating costs, thereby contributing to the sustainability of the plant and the operator (Rodriguez et al., 2020). This should incentivize governments at all levels to improve on wastewater collection and treatment.

Significant data gaps for wastewater remain. For example, reporting on SDG Indicator 6.3.1, the proportion of wastewater safely treated, shows that 59% of domestic wastewater flow is collected and safely treated, but this is based on data from only 79 countries, mostly high- and middle-income, and the data on industrial wastewater are insufficient (United Nations, 2018). It has been estimated that only 8% of industrial and municipal wastewater in low-income countries undergoes treatment of any kind (Sato et al., 2013).

4.3 Values and supplemental benefits of access to WASH services

The value of water and sanitation is well understood from a direct health perspective: reliable access to water supply, sanitation and improved hygiene reduces death, morbidity, malnutrition as well as illness from waterborne diseases. If a person is sick or malnourished, they are likely to be weaker and to have difficulty concentrating in school or in the workplace, which can also have dangerous repercussions. When people must go outside the home to defecate or collect water, they may be exposed to additional health challenges such as intense weather (monsoon rains, snow), infectious insects, wild animals, chronic muscle fatigue (from carrying water), and sexual and gender-based violence. The mental health impacts of these stresses are not insignificant.

4.3.1 Pandemics, including COVID-19

The year 2020 saw the rise of the COVID-19 pandemic, which threw the world into disarray. The health, social and economic impacts are likely to reverberate for many years to come. With an estimated 90% of all reported COVID-19 cases, urban areas have become the epicentres of the pandemic (UNSDG, 2020). Population densities and high levels of global and local interconnectivity make urban areas particularly vulnerable to the spread of the virus (Box 4.1). *"In the near term, for many cities, the COVID-19 health crisis has expanded to a crisis of urban access, urban equity, urban finance, safety, joblessness, public services, infrastructure and transport, all of which are disproportionally affecting the most vulnerable in society"* (UNSDG, 2020, p. 2).

Inadequate access to hand hygiene facilities causes an increased risk for the spread of COVID-19 and other infectious diseases

The pandemic hit the world's most vulnerable people the hardest – many of them living in informal settlements and urban slums. People living in these densely populated areas face multiple challenges including inadequate housing, few health facilities, overcrowded public transport, little or no waste management, and an overall absence of basic municipal services (UN-Habitat, 2020). Where available, WASH services are frequently intermittent, of poor quality, and not affordable in the quantities required for good health (UN-Habitat/UNICEF, 2020).

The health impact of COVID-19 also translates to days of work loss, reduced household income, reduced educational opportunities, potential (yet unknown) long-term health issues related to the virus, and loss of life.[4]

Hand hygiene is extremely important to prevent the spread of COVID-19 (WHO, 2020a). Globally, over three billion people and two out of five health care facilities lack adequate access to hand hygiene facilities. A lack of data on other aspects of hygiene in health care facilities prevents a more detailed analysis of the actual situation (WHO/UNICEF, 2019b). Inadequate access to hand hygiene facilities causes an increased risk for the spread of COVID-19 and other infectious diseases. The health, social and economic impacts of the COVID-19 pandemic, the surge of the purchase of hygiene products to mitigate the spread of the virus, and the environmental impact of these products, especially plastics, make the value of safely managed WASH, at all levels, much more visible than has been witnessed in recent memory.

[4] At the time of production of this report, the human and economic toll of the pandemic was yet to be assessed, but the scale and severity of its impacts are already widely known.

Box 4.1 Challenges to addressing COVID-19 in informal settlements and other poor or deprived communities

Most of the COVID-19 guidelines are almost impossible to implement in informal settlements and other poor or deprived communities. Overcrowding, housing design, and lack of access to water, sanitation and waste management facilities, make any form of physical/social distancing and simple interventions, such as regular handwashing, extremely difficult.

- In informal urban settlements, a large proportion of the population may have existing health conditions (respiratory infections, waterborne diseases and other chronic illnesses), aggravated by the harsh living conditions and, increasingly, some lifestyle diseases associated with poor nutrition and substance abuse. These communities also have limited access to, and ability to pay for, health care.
- Most households rely on day-to-day work to meet their living costs and do not have any savings or financial buffers to rely on to pay for basic services such as water, sanitation and hygiene (WASH). Balancing the need to control the public health emergency with the economic livelihood impacts on the poor, particularly women and children, will be critical to the success of any intervention strategy in the response and recovery phases.
- The lack of adequate data and information on informal settlements makes the planning and response to COVID-19 interventions difficult. The current use of city-wide data for access to WASH facilities masks the inequities present.
- The population profile in many informal settlements may not be the same as the rest of the urban agglomeration. Inequalities in access to basic WASH services also exist within this population. Access to such services can be less than 10% for many of the slum populations.
- Slums and informal settlements may be cut off from service provision in the event of quarantine without proper consultations. WASH services being essential, under no circumstances should they be discontinued.

Source: Adapted from UN-Habitat/UNICEF (2020, p. 2).

COVID-19 has brought to the fore the critical role of local governments and water and sanitation operators in ensuring continuity of WASH services during pandemics (UNSDG, 2020). A number of protocols and guidelines have emerged for local governments and water and sanitation operators to address the pandemic. According to the Global Water Operators Partnership Alliance (GWOPA), public utilities should work closely with local health officials and other relevant bodies to maximize access to safe drinking water and sanitation, especially for vulnerable communities. Furthermore, they should, where possible, ensure water service continuity, proper treatment, accessibility for all and affordability. For unserved areas, temporary measures may be taken to facilitate access to safe water or household water treatment (GWOPA, 2020).

Box 4.2 outlines the protocols and guidelines issued by the Government of Kenya on COVID-19 response to management of water and sanitation in Kenya.

4.3.2 WASH-related waterborne diseases

Each year, it is estimated that approximately 829,000 people die from diarrhoea as a result of unsafe drinking water, sanitation and hand hygiene. These causes represent 60% of all deaths due to diarrhoea globally, including nearly 300,000 children under the age of five, 5.3% of all deaths in this age group (Prüss-Üstün et al., 2019). This includes cholera, estimated to cause approximately 95,000 deaths each year (Ali et al., 2015). The cost of disease impact is measured in disability-adjusted life years (DALYs[5]), which means the loss of a 'healthy' life year. Inadequate WASH is responsible for 49.8 million DALYs, with Sub-Saharan Africa accounting for almost 28 million, and Southeast Asia for 13 million DALYs (Prüss-Üstün et al., 2019).

[5] Disability-adjusted life years (DALYs) is a measure of overall disease burden, expressed as the number of years lost due to ill health, disability or early death.

Box 4.2 Protocols and guidelines on the COVID-19 response on management of water supply in Kenya

Kenya's Protocols and Guidelines were issued to define specific actions and measures to ensure a continuous supply of water and adequate sanitation during the COVID-19 pandemic, with the objective of ensuring that people have adequate water for domestic use and handwashing. The Protocols and Guidelines are as follows:

That County Governments has:

1. Directed all the Water Service Providers (WSPs) to provide free water to informal settlements and vulnerable groups for three months, April–June 2020. Other consumers paid for water and sewerage services.
2. Ensured that all WSPs were fully operational without interruption and that essential personnel observed Health, Safety and Environment (HSE) regulations at all times.
3. Ensured that WSPs suspended disconnection of water for three months.
4. Ensured that in areas where water tracking was done to communities not connected to water supply, the communities receiving the service were sensitized on regular handwashing with soap, use of sanitizers and social distancing to avoid a rapid spread of the disease.
5. Ensured that WSPs enhanced information dissemination strategies on required measures to be observed through various platforms. Such messages were aligned to directives issued by Ministry of Health.
6. Ensured that handwashing points were accessible in strategic locations to serve needy communities.
7. Collaborated with the National Government to map out and prioritize areas, and to identify additional interventions necessary to ensure an adequate and safe water availability to the public.

Source: Ministry of Water & Sanitation and Irrigation, Republic of Kenya

This does not include the millions of non-fatal diarrhoeal episodes and the almost three million cases of cholera that occur (Ali et al., 2015). Most of these illnesses are preventable, but occur due to lack of water and sanitation services in homes, schools, health care facilities and the workplace. The value lost in human life, and in educational and economic potential, is a burden on society.

"In protracted conflicts, children younger than 15 are, on average, nearly three times more likely to die from diarrhoeal disease linked to unsafe water and sanitation than violence directly linked to conflict and war. For younger children, the impact of unsafe water, sanitation and hygiene is greater: Children under 5 are more than 20 times more likely to die from diarrhoeal disease linked to unsafe water and sanitation than violence in conflict" (UNICEF, 2019a, p. 3).

4.3.3 Neglected tropical diseases (NTDs)

Lack of access to WASH services in health care facilities and at home impacts the prevention of, and care for, neglected tropical diseases (Boisson et al., 2016), which every year affect more than one billion people worldwide (WHO, 2015). These include such diseases as trachoma, schistosomiasis and soil-transmitted helminthiases (STH: hookworms, whipworms and roundworms). Trachoma is the leading cause of infectious blindness in the world, responsible for the blindness or visual impairment of about 1.9 million people worldwide (WHO, 2020b). Schistosomiasis leads to liver and kidney failure. Depending on the species, STHs mostly impact school-age children, causing undernutrition and stunting, and maternal (foetal and female) health. In 2018, an estimated 229 million people required preventive treatment for schistosomiasis (WHO, 2020c). Approximately 1.5 billion people are infected with STHs, representing 24% of the world's population (WHO, 2020d).

STHs contribute to approximately 5.2 million DALYs, schistosomiasis to 3.3 million (GAHI, n.d.) and trachoma to between 4 and 39 million (Brooker, 2010). A value of access to WASH services therefore can be expressed in terms of to what extent interventions could help reduce the number of these diseases and lower the number of DALYs that people experience worldwide.

4.3.4 Nutrition

Poor sanitation and hygiene, as well as unsafe drinking water, cause diarrhoeal disease and environmental enteropathy, which inhibit nutrient absorption, resulting in undernutrition (Teague et al., 2014). Roughly 50% of all malnutrition is associated with repeated diarrhoea or intestinal worm infections as a direct result of inadequate WASH (Prüss-Üstün et al., 2008). Futures of children worldwide, but most notably in developing countries, are impaired by undernutrition. Infections that arise from poor access to WASH exacerbate undernutrition, which includes parasitic infections, diarrhoea and possibly environmental enteric dysfunction (EDD) – damage of gut lining caused by repeated infections. An estimated 45% of all deaths of children under the age of five is from undernutrition (United Nations, 2018). Stunting, which potentially prevents children from attaining their full height and cognitive ability, impacts 144 million children under five worldwide, 91% of them coming from low- and lower middle-income countries. Wasting also results from these infections, with 47 million affected globally, 92% from low- and lower-middle income countries (UNICEF/WHO/The World Bank Group, 2020). The economic cost of undernutrition is estimated to be up to US$2.1 trillion (FAO, 2013a).

4.3.5 Maternal health

Maternal health was codified in the Millennium Development Goals (MDG 5) and now in SDG Target 3.1. In 2017, approximately 295,000 women died during and following pregnancy and childbirth from preventable causes (WHO/UNICEF/UNFPA/World Bank/UN Population Division, 2019). Some of these causes are linked to a lack of access to WASH services. The connection between handwashing of birth attendants and reduced infection rates was established as early as 1795 (Gould, 2010). The impacts of poor sanitation and unsafe water supplies are not yet as clear, but there are a number of direct and indirect mechanisms through which poor sanitation and unsafe water have been shown to negatively impact the maternal health of women (Esteves-Mills and Cumming, 2016).

The connection between handwashing of birth attendants and reduced infection rates was established as early as 1795

At the global level, 11% of maternal deaths, mostly in low- and middle-income countries, are caused by infections linked to unhygienic conditions during labour and birth, at home or in facilities, and to poor hygiene practices in the six weeks after birth (WHO/UNICEF, 2019b). Infections associated with unclean births may account for more than one million deaths each year (WHO/UNICEF, 2019b). Basic hygiene practices during antenatal care, labour and birth, can reduce the risk of infections, sepsis and death of infants and mothers by up to 25% (PMNCH, 2014).

Poor sanitation can impact maternal health through hookworm, large roundworm, listeria and schistosomiasis. Unsafe water management affects maternal health through increased risks of malaria and dengue, arsenic or fluoride contamination, and exposure to metals in the water (Chitty and Esteves-Mills, 2015).

4.3.6 Menstrual hygiene management

Efforts to address MHM has in recent years gained momentum worldwide. Globally, more than 500 million women and girls do not have adequate access to MHM facilities, particularly in public places such as schools, health care facilities and in the workplace (World Bank, 2018). Women and girls are not able to manage menstrual hygiene with ease and dignity due to a combination of discriminatory social environments, inaccurate information, poor facilities and a limited choice of absorbent materials (UNICEF, 2019b). Health impacts of lacking MHM can be physical, potentially causing reproductive tract infections, or psychosocial, leading to embarrassment, fear of stigma, anxiety (Esteves-Mills and Cumming, 2016), shame and loss of dignity (UNICEF, 2019b). Ultimately, women and girls' contributions to society can be limited by the lack of MHM facilities.

4.3.7 Time

One of the most direct values of access to WASH services is the time gained for people, especially women and girls, who shoulder the burden of bringing drinking water closer to home. Around 230 million people, mostly women and girls, spent more than 30 minutes per trip collecting water from sources away from their home (WHO/UNICEF, 2017a). Across 61 countries, women and girls were responsible for carrying water in eight out of ten households. The United Nations Children's Fund (UNICEF) has calculated how much time women and girls spend carrying water every day, which equals 200 million hours, or 8.3 million days, or 22,800 years (UNICEF, 2016).

The World Bank (2015) showed that in Southeast Asia, walking times for sanitation practices also are significant (Table 4.1). Times differ based on setting, but as people usually make multiples trips per day, the assumption of 30 minutes per day globally (as was concluded by WHO, 2012 and Hutton, 2013) is not unreasonable.

Table 4.1 Estimated walking times (in minutes) for sanitation practices in selected countries of Southeast Asia

Country	Rural	Urban
Cambodia	10	3
Indonesia	3.5	7.5
Lao PDR	14	10
Philippines	20	9
Viet Nam	6	15
Yunnan (China)	6	3

Source: Based on data from World Bank (2015).

Access to WASH in schools and at home increases the access to quality education, resulting in better educational outcomes

4.3.8 Education

Water and sanitation also impact school attendance as well as livelihoods. If a person is sick, they cannot attend school or work and earn income. If the ill person is a young child or an older person, there is a high likelihood that someone else also misses school or forgoes income in order to provide the necessary care. The lack of MHM facilities in schools results in girls' lack of ability to manage their menstrual hygiene and thus increases absenteeism, which results in economic costs and reduced opportunities in their futures (World Bank, 2018).

The universal dimension of SDG Targets 6.1 and 6.2 implies all settings, which also translate to schools (WHO/UNICEF, 2017b). These targets codify the recent priority given to improving access to WASH services in schools. WHO/UNICEF (2018) showed that 69% of schoolchildren had access to drinking water (based on data from 92 countries), 66% to sanitation (in 101 countries) and 53% to hygiene (in 81 countries). This equates to 570 million children lacking drinking water in schools, 620 million lacking sanitation and 900 million lacking hygiene. UNDP (2006) reported that over 443 million school days are lost due to water-related illnesses.

The value to society of WASH in schools is clear. Access to WASH in schools and at home increases the access to quality education, resulting in better educational outcomes (United Nations, 2018). It enhances both students' and teachers' health, given their long hours in schools, and provides education on sanitation and hygiene, which can help develop healthy behaviours for life (UNICEF, 2012). For girls and young women, improving access to WASH in schools, especially MHM, can improve school attendance. Ensuring equitable access to WASH in schools for children with disabilities encourages equitable education and ensures that no child is left behind. Better education, in turn, leads to improved economic performance and growth, from the personal/household up to national levels.

4.3.9 Labour

An unhealthy workforce means a loss in staff productivity and a negative impact on livelihoods, which both translate into value lost for society. It has been shown that access to WASH services in the workplace is an important factor for a company's ability to function and prosper (WBCSD, 2018).

It is estimated that at least US$6.5 billion is lost per year in working days due to a lack of access to sanitation (WHO, 2012). In addition, almost 400,000 work-related deaths occur each year from communicable diseases, which have the main contributing factors being poor-quality drinking water, and poor sanitation and hygiene (WWAP, 2016).

It has been shown that access to WASH services in the workplace is an important factor for a company's ability to function and prosper

Access to WASH in the workplace is also an issue that impacts gender equality and women's workplace productivity. Not having a safe, private location, especially during a women's menstrual period, may lead to anxiety, stress and absenteeism, which results in lower productivity often translating to lower income. It was shown that in the Philippines and Viet Nam, in workplaces where WASH facilities were inadequate and assuming women would be absent for at least one day during their menstrual period for lack of such facilities, this would equate to 13.8 million and 1.5 million workday absences, respectively, and US$13 million and 1.28 million in economic losses (Sommer et al., 2016).

4.3.10 Gender-based violence

Lacking access to safe WASH facilities can expose people to increased levels of violence based on sexual orientation and gender identity (House et al., 2014). With women and girls shouldering the majority of the burden of carrying water from long distances to households, this puts them at additional risk of attack or rape. Open defecation, still practiced by almost 900 million people worldwide (United Nations, 2018), causes a feeling of shame among women and girls, and is therefore often practiced at night, when they face increased risk of harassment or attack. The use of sanitation facilities outside the home at night also carries a risk. Other scenarios where gender-based violence can be related to access to WASH services can occur in schools, during conflict situations, in situations where men hold power in WASH-related programmes, and in the home, among others. All of the occurrences mentioned can not only cause physical harm, but can have psychological repercussions as well, impacting health and well-being (House et al., 2014).

4.3.11 Human rights, quality of life and dignity

When the human right to water and sanitation was adopted in 2010, the United Nations Member States recognized it as "*essential for the full enjoyment of life and all human rights*" (UNGA, 2010). The Human Rights Council shortly thereafter added that it is "*inextricably related to the right to the highest attainable standard of physical and mental health, as well as the right to life and human dignity*" (HRC, 2010). In 2015, water and sanitation were recognized as separate rights given their specific challenges to implementation (UNGA, 2016). Without access to water and sanitation services, neither quality of life nor dignity can be attained. Human rights reflect the values of countries worldwide, and the implementation of the human rights to water and sanitation expresses how they also support all three pillars (economic, environmental, social) of sustainable development.

4.4 Accessing WASH: Subsidies and affordability

Because access to WASH is so fundamental to life and public health, in many countries WASH services are considered the realm of governments and therefore often subsidized, even in high-income countries. When governments in lower-income countries are unable to provide these services on their own, and cost recovery from the user cannot be achieved, they will often rely on donor assistance and charity to help fill in funding gaps. The reliance on public funding does not incentivize service improvement and obstructs conversations about the tariff structure, making it difficult even to keep pace with cost inflation.

4.4.1 Subsidies

Subsidies do not necessarily ensure that the poor are able to access basic services. Water subsidies can end up benefiting those with existing connections to sewerage or water networks, many of whom are non-poor (Nauges and Whittington, 2017). As a result, the poor do not benefit from the subsidy and the water service provider loses the tariff revenue it could have collected from wealthier households (WWAP, 2019). Value is lost in terms of revenue to the provider, while the negative impacts of not having access to WASH services, such as school and work absenteeism, are not mitigated.

Even so, part of the reason that WASH services are heavily subsidized is claimed to be that people living in poverty are unwilling or unable to pay for them. Often ignoring the potential negative influences of vested interests and corruption, this claim also fails to consider the amounts that such people already pay, which are generally higher than the non-poor, who benefit from the existing subsidized rates. According to research done across ten low- and middle-income countries, on average, 56% of subsidies end up in the pockets of the richest 20%, while only 6% of subsidies find their way to the poorest 20% (Andres et al., 2019). The 2019 *World Water Development Report* observed that people living in informal settlements often pay 10–20 times more for their water, which comes from suppliers such as water tankers (WWAP, 2019).

4.4.2 Affordability

Subsidies do not necessarily ensure that the poor are able to access basic services

The cost of access, including connection costs (fees, materials, labour, etc.), whether it is a monthly bill or an investment in household infrastructure, is sometimes the largest barrier to improved access. Even if household budgets allow for access to WASH services that meet the national minimum standard, they may still be far from the home, at risk of contamination, or not available in sufficient quantity.

However, little has been done to track WASH affordability at the global scale to date and the guiding texts in the human rights literature fail to define how economic accessibility can be measured or monitored. No indicators have yet been adopted that enable an understanding of the relationship between national policies, tariff policies and the actual costs faced by households. Until now, the main method to measure affordability has been to estimate the annual expenditure on water and wastewater as a proportion of annual income, and comparing this ratio with an 'affordability threshold' (Hutton, 2012). The weakness of measuring actual WASH costs, especially in low- and middle-income countries, is that for many households the expenditure surveys omit some major cost items, while the service level is below the national minimum standard. As a result, affordability assessments do not sufficiently show the service gap.

To understand affordability of WASH to a household, three key dimensions should be present: (i) what WASH costs to a household – whether actual or potential; (ii) the spending power of a household – which is a combination of wealth, assets and income; and (iii) spending needed to meet other 'essential' needs – which indicates the other needs for spending that WASH is competing with (UNICEF/WHO, 2021). Clearly, the most vulnerable households are those that are low-income, have high WASH costs and little support from the welfare state or other sources for their other essential needs. UNICEF/WHO (2021) concludes that affordability can be measured using different indicators, but that affordability assessments should compare actual costs faced by households to access their WASH service with the required cost to reach a given basic minimum, whether a national standard or the SDG definition.

Figure 4.2 Distribution of actual WASH expenditure share versus required WASH expenditure on operations and maintenance (O&M) for basic WASH services across major cut-offs, for Cambodia, Ghana, Mexico, Pakistan, Uganda and Zambia

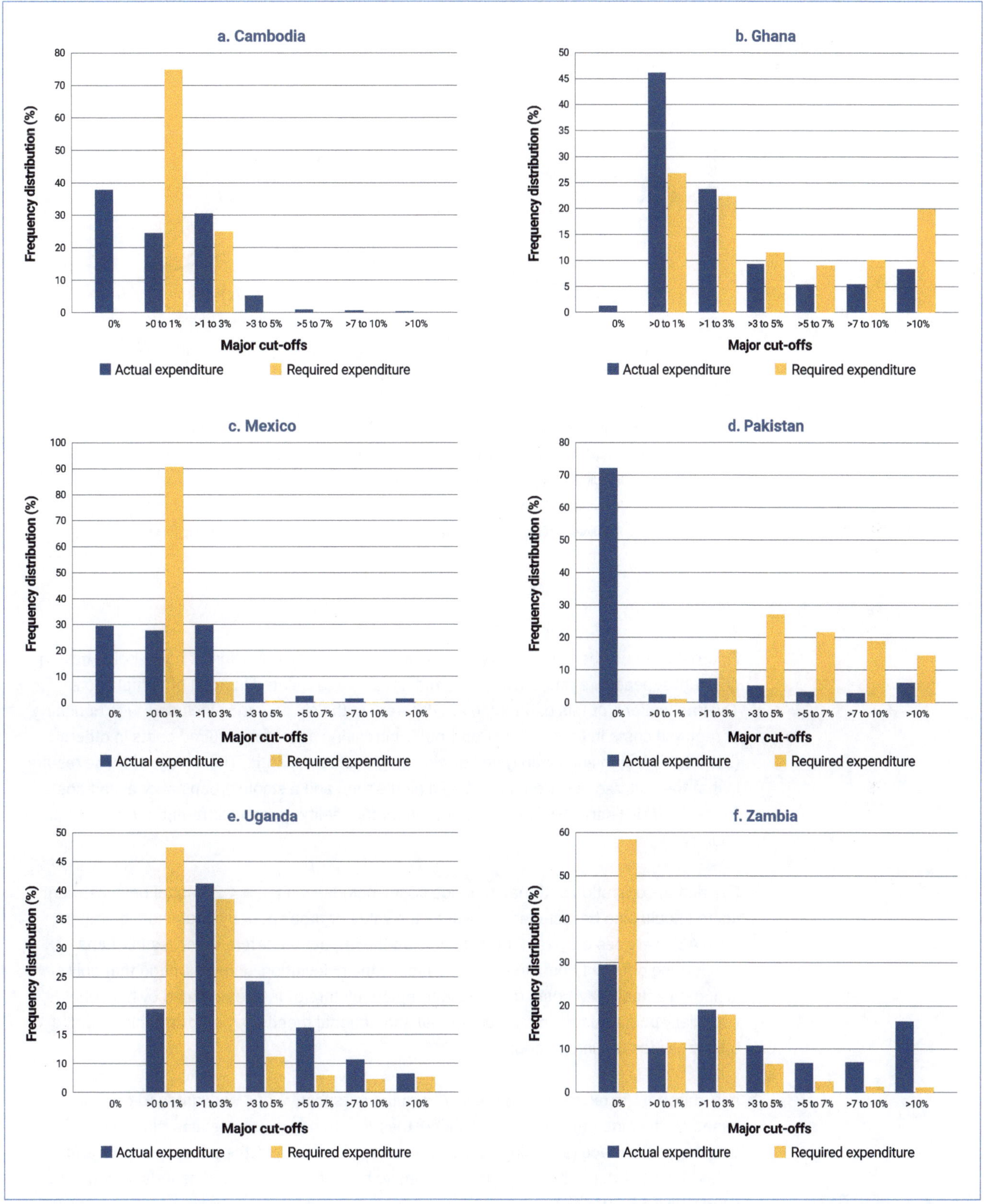

Note: The y-axis refers to the frequency distribution of households; the x-axis refers to the cut-offs of proportion of their total expenditure on water and sanitation.

Sources: Based on UNICEF/WHO (2021), Kingdom of Cambodia (2016) for Cambodia, GHS (2013) for Ghana, Instituto Nacional de Estadística y Geografía (2016) for Mexico, Pakistan Bureau of Statistics (n.d.) for Pakistan, Uganda Bureau of Statistics (2020) for Uganda and Republic of Zambia Central Statistical Office (2016) for Zambia.

Figure 4.3

Comparison of WASH costs as a percentage of total household expenditure under different indicators in Ghana, across deciles of total household expenditure

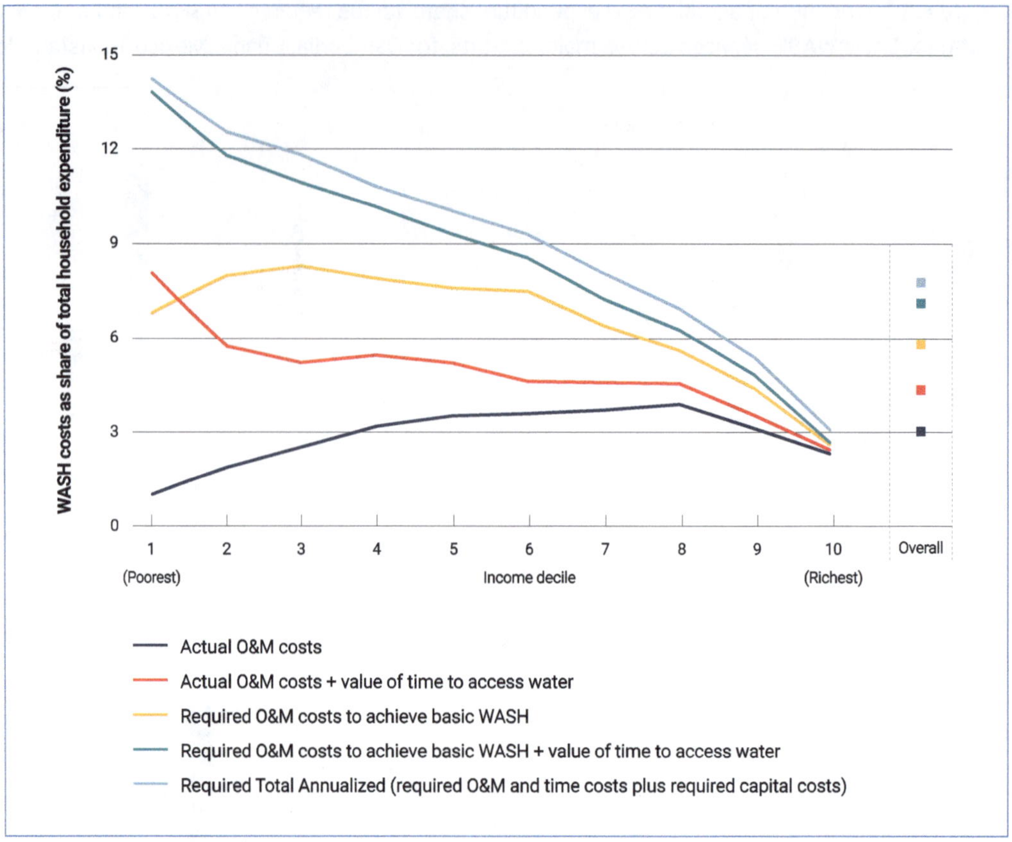

Sources: Based on data from UNICEF/WHO (2021) and GHS (2013).

Figure 4.2 shows the impact of WASH expenditure on the proportion of households having different expenditure ratios when required costs are calculated instead of actual costs. The implications of this estimation are different in the six countries included, with bunching[6] of required costs in Mexico and Cambodia, increasing costs for required costs in others (Zambia, Pakistan and Ghana) and diminishing costs in Uganda. The caveat of these results is that the required costs are based on a single rural and a single urban national unit cost for basic WASH services, which will not reflect the reality of many different contexts within a country.

Besides the operation and maintenance costs included in Figure 4.2, capital or investment costs should also be included, as well as the value of time spent by household members for WASH services off-plot. Figure 4.3 shows the impact on different deciles in Ghana of adopting different costs in the numerator of the calculation, demonstrating that only including actual O&M costs gives an incomplete picture of the costs faced by households, especially poor households. Future global and national monitoring of affordability should take these factors into account.

It is important to examine affordability from the perspective of disadvantaged groups, based on their income (poor, seasonality), their location (e.g. remoteness, slums) and the challenges they face (e.g. climate, water access). For example, the access to basic and safe drinking water and sanitation continues to be a challenge for indigenous communities (WHO/UNICEF, 2016).

---

6 Less higher and lower values (i.e. the values are more in the middle range).

Chapter 5

Food and agriculture

FAO
Marlos de Souza and Sasha Koo-Oshima

With contributions from:
Taher Kahil and Yoshihide Wada (IIASA); Manzoor Qadir (UNU-INWEH); Graham Jewitt (IHE Delft); Christophe Cudennec (IAHS); Stefan Uhlenbrook (IWMI); and Lulu Zhang (UNU-FLORES)

5.1 Introduction

Food security has long been a challenge for human societies and will become an increasingly pressing global issue over the coming decades (Fischer, 2018). Although global food production has kept pace with population growth, close to 750 million people (or 10% of the global population) were exposed to severe levels of food insecurity in 2019 (FAO/IFAD/UNICEF/WFP/WHO, 2020). Unfortunately, this number has increased even further over the course of 2020 due to the COVID-19 pandemic and its economic impacts worldwide. In the 2030 Agenda for Sustainable Development, Sustainable Development Goal (SDG) 2 aims to *"end hunger, achieve food security and improved nutrition and promote sustainable agriculture"* (UNGA, 2015). The food system is almost entirely supported by water, and agriculture uses the major share of global freshwater resources. However, water use for food production is being questioned continually as intersectoral competition for water intensifies and water scarcity increases. Additionally, in many regions of the world, water for food production is used inefficiently (D'Odorico et al., 2020). This is a major driver of environmental degradation, including depletion of aquifers, reduction of river flows, degradation of wildlife habitats, and pollution (Willett et al., 2019). A fundamental transformation of how water is being managed in the food system is therefore necessary if most of the SDG 2 targets are to be achieved by 2030, without further degradation of water resources to concurrently achieve SDG 6 to *"ensure availability and sustainable management of water and sanitation for all"* (IFPRI, 2019).

5.2 The multiple benefits of water for food production

Water is used for food production in various ways, including for agriculture, livestock and inland fishery production. Water use in agriculture ranges from essentially rainfed, relying on soil moisture from rainfall, to entirely irrigated. The global water footprint related to crop production in the period 1996–2005 was 7,404 km^3 per year, representing 92% of humanity's water footprint (Hoekstra and Mekonnen, 2012). Rainfed agriculture covers 80% of the world's cropland and accounts for the major part (60%) of food production (Rockström et al., 2007). Rainfed agriculture has a global water footprint of 5,173 km^3 per year (Mekonnen and Hoekstra, 2011a). Irrigated agriculture covers about 20% of cultivated lands, yet it accounts for 40% of food production (Molden et al., 2010) (Table 5.1), and has a global water footprint of 2,230 km^3 per year (Mekonnen and Hoekstra, 2011a). Water withdrawals from surface and groundwater resources for irrigation currently amount to 2,797 km^3 per year, which represents 70% of all water withdrawals in the world (Table 5.1). In many drier countries, it is not unusual for irrigation water use to account for more than 90% of total water withdrawals (FAO, 2012a). Water for livestock production is used for growing and producing livestock feed (which is included in rainfed and irrigation water demand), direct consumption by livestock, and livestock processing. While direct water consumption by livestock is very small in most countries, representing less than 1–2% of total water use, water availability and its quality are of utmost importance for livestock production (FAO, 2019c). Finally, inland fishery production relies fully on natural and modified water bodies (FAO, 2014a).

Efforts to value water for food production have advanced over the past 30 years (Young and Loomis, 2014). Existing water valuation studies often indicate that the value assigned to water in food production is low compared to its value in alternative water uses, such as domestic and industrial uses. They also indicate that the value of water could be very low (typically less than US$0.05/m^3) where water is used for irrigating food grains and fodder, while it could be high (of the same order of magnitude as values in domestic and industrial uses) where reliable supplies are needed for high-value crops such as vegetables, fruits and flowers (FAO, 2004). D'Odorico et al. (2020) indicate that the global mean values assigned to water in the production of the four major staple crops (wheat, maize, rice and soybean), representing about 60% of global food production, range between US$0.05 and 0.16 per m^3. Those values vary considerably within and among regions.

As exemplified in Box 1.3, there are multiple ways of expressing and calculating values of water used for food production. Variation also exists in terms of what is included in accounting, providing a wide range of results. However, estimates of values of water for food

Table 5.1 Land cultivated and equipped for irrigation, and total and agricultural water withdrawals, 2010

	Total cultivated land (million ha)	Land equipped for irrigation (million ha)	Land equipped for irrigation as % of total cultivated land	Total water withdrawal (km³/yr)	Agricultural water withdrawal (km³/yr)	Agricultural water withdrawal as % of total water withdrawal
Africa	259	15	6	226	183	81
Americas	365	52	14	854	412	48
Asia	562	227	40	2 584	2 103	81
Europe	291	25	9	322	88	27
Oceania	28	3	6	19	11	58
World	**1 505**	**322**	**21**	**4 005**	**2 797**	**70**

Note: Total cultivated land includes arable land and areas used for permanent crops, both rainfed and irrigated. Total water withdrawal includes water withdrawn for agricultural, industrial and municipal purposes. Agricultural water withdrawal consists of water withdrawn for irrigation.

Source: Based on data from FAOSTAT (land area) and AQUASTAT (water withdrawal).

production normally only consider the direct economically beneficial use of water (i.e. value to users of water), while many of the other direct and indirect benefits associated with water, which may be economic, sociocultural or environmental, remain unaccounted for or only partially quantified (Comprehensive Assessment of Water Management in Agriculture, 2007). Some of those benefits include achieving food security and improving nutrition, accommodating shifts in consumption patterns, generating employment and providing livelihood resilience especially for smallholder farmers, contributing to alleviating poverty and revitalizing rural economies, supporting climate change mitigation and adaptation, and providing multiple-use water services.

5.2.1 Food security

The food security value of water is high but rarely quantified – and it is often a political imperative irrespective of other values

Water is central to food security and nutrition. Making water available to agriculture helps boost crop yields, enables the expansion of the area under cultivation – as it allows for planting during the dry season and using areas where production was formerly unfeasible – and supports the production of more nutrient-dense fruits and vegetables (Hanjra and Qureshi, 2010; Domènech, 2015). The food security value of water is high but rarely quantified – and it is often a political imperative irrespective of other values. In two case studies in India, Rogers et al. (1998) estimated the food security value of water based on the avoided impact on consumers of increasing foodgrain prices – which could have resulted from water shortages and the subsequent reduction of food supply – and found that it is at least two times higher than the net value of crop output. Moreover, it has been shown that people who have better access to water tend to have lower levels of undernourishment, while lack of it can be a major cause of famine and undernourishment, especially in areas where people depend on local agriculture for food and income (FAO/WWC, 2015). Recently, disruptions of food supply and trading systems due to the COVID-19 pandemic had a negative impact on food security and nutrition in many countries that depend largely on food trade. This clearly adds to the often hidden value of water for local agriculture (FAO, 2020a).

In the coming decades, water for food production will be even more critical for food security. Global demand for food and other agricultural products is projected to increase by 50% between 2012 and 2050, driven by population growth (FAO, 2017b). Furthermore, rapidly rising incomes and urbanization in much of the developing world will encourage dietary changes towards increased consumption of livestock-based products, sugar and horticultural products, which all rely on crops with higher water requirements than traditional staple food diets (Ringler and Zhu, 2015). Food production is thus required to sustainably intensify and expand to keep up with food demand.

5.2.2 Poverty alleviation

Despite striking economic growth in the past, there are still 2.1 billion poor people, of whom 767 million people live in extreme poverty. Of all people living in poverty, 80% live in rural areas, where agriculture continues to be the mainstay of their livelihoods (World Bank, 2016b). In many of those areas, such as in Sub-Saharan Africa, insufficient and erratic water supplies constrain agricultural productivity and compromise income stability, with dramatic effects for the poorest households, who have limited assets and safety nets to cope with risks (WWAP, 2016). This limits rural inhabitants' capacities to accumulate the human capital and assets needed to sustainably lift themselves out of poverty (FAO, 2014b). In India, for example, a 30-year analysis shows that wages are highly sensitive to rainfall shocks (World Bank, 2007). Prolonged drought causes persistent unemployment, which often leads to migration from rural to urban areas, notably when off-farm employment is limited (WWAP, 2016). The impacts could be extremely large for women, who comprise about 43% of the agricultural labour force globally and half or more of the agricultural labour force in many African and Asian countries (FAO, n.d.a). Therefore, improving water security for food production in both rainfed and irrigated systems can contribute to reducing poverty and closing the gender gap directly and indirectly. Direct effects include higher yields, reduced risk of crop failure and increased diversity of cropping; higher wages from enhanced employment opportunities; and stabilized local food production and prices. Indirect effects include income and employment multipliers beyond the farm, and reduction of migration (Faurès and Santini, 2008). Enhanced and more stable incomes could help improve education and the skillsets of women, and thus foster their active participation in decision-making. Although increasing water productivity can have substantial positive impacts, care should be taken to account for possible perverse effects and implications for poverty alleviation (i.e. land grabbing and increasing inequality).

Water for food production can serve as a conduit of broader rural access to water resources

5.2.3 Multiple uses of water

Water for food production can serve as a conduit of broader rural access to water resources. Multiple uses of water involve the practice of using water from the same source or infrastructure for multiples uses and functions (FAO, 2013b). It may be used for different domestic purposes such as drinking, washing, bathing or hygiene, and for other productive purposes such as livestock rearing, aquaculture or supporting small businesses (Domènech, 2015). Water for food production could also indirectly support natural vegetation and simultaneously provide various cultural (e.g. recreation, tourism) and environmental services (e.g. groundwater recharge, water purification) (FAO, 2013b). Exploiting these opportunities is of paramount importance in order to make water use consistent with productivity, livelihoods, efficiency and environmental objectives, thus enabling direct contribution to various SDG targets.

The additional services that can be provided by water for food production result in improved environmental and human health, hygiene, and livelihood opportunities for the rural poor. The potential of multiple water uses is particularly high in irrigation, where the scheme irrigation efficiency (the proportion of water pumped or diverted through the scheme inlet that is used effectively by the crops) has been estimated at roughly 40–50% globally. This figure varies widely among regions and drops to 28% in Sub-Saharan Africa and 26% in Central America and the Caribbean (AQUASTAT, 2014). By allowing water to be used for different purposes, the value of water can be significantly amplified (FAO, n.d.b).

For example, in areas of northwest India where groundwater is saline, irrigation canals not only provide water for domestic and livestock uses, but seepage from these canals also recharges the groundwater table, thus enabling the pumping of high-quality water from handpumps and shallow tubewells. In the absence of this freshwater, use of saline groundwater by animals is reported to result in about 50% reduction of milk production. In this region, income from livestock accounts for a significant proportion of the income of poor households, particularly in the dry season. In addition to livestock, irrigation canals provide water for the environment. In some canals in southern India, canal drops are used for installation of small and mini hydropower plants (Rogers et al., 1998).

Promotion of multiple water use is particularly timely in the light of the spreading COVID-19. In response to the crisis, the Food and Agriculture Organization of the United Nations (FAO) highlights that inherent effects of the pandemic have grown beyond the well-defined spear of health risks and have shocked livelihoods and food security in several countries. Irrigation plays an important role in improving crop productivity and ensuring food security. However, expanding irrigation could impact the availability of water for sanitation and hygiene, which has a central role in slowing down the spread of the disease. Developing multiple water uses would certainly allow to fight the pandemic while ensuring the basic needs of food security in rural communities. A new initiative of the FAO's Land and Water Division, called SMART Irrigation – SMART WASH, offers corporate solutions to enhance irrigation and provide water, sanitation and hygiene (WASH) facilities to vulnerable communities, thus responding to their critical needs during the pandemic (FAO, 2020b).

5.3 Impacts and costs of inefficient use of water for food production

Despite the multiple benefits that water used for food production provides, its inefficient use has resulted in serious economic, social and environmental impacts (or negative values), such as the depletion of freshwater resources, deterioration of water quality, land degradation, increased vulnerability to climate shocks, and declines of biodiversity and ecosystem services (Willett et al., 2019).

5.3.1 Water scarcity

Water scarcity occurs when water supply is insufficient to meet water demand (FAO, 2012b). Continued increase in water use for food production over the last decades has exacerbated water scarcity conditions in many regions around the world (e.g. northeastern China, India, Pakistan, the Middle East and North Africa), where available surface water is limited due to lower precipitation and higher evaporation rates (Wada, 2016). In these regions, when the available surface water resources are insufficient for productive farming, groundwater resources serve as a main source for irrigation. Estimates based on comprehensive national and subnational data indicate that 40% of actually irrigated area in the world is serviced by groundwater sources (Siebert et al., 2010). In India, privately developed groundwater infrastructure now supports a larger area of irrigation than the area serviced by all surface irrigation investment (FAO, 2020c). However, excessive groundwater pumping often leads to overexploitation, causing groundwater depletion, which constrains sustainable food production (Giordano et al., 2017) and has devastating effects on groundwater-dependent ecosystems sustaining the livelihood of millions of people (Wada, 2016).

In the coming decades, many regions around the world are expected to face either absolute or seasonal water scarcity conditions, driven by increasing competition for water between agriculture and other sectors and a more variable water availability because of climate change (Greve et al., 2018). The World Bank (2016a) estimated that regions affected by water scarcity could see their growth rates decline by as much as 6% of Gross Domestic Product (GDP) by 2050 as a result of losses in agriculture, health, income and property – sending them into sustained negative growth.

5.3.2 Water quality degradation

Water scarcity is caused not only by the physical scarcity of the resource and lack of access to it, but also by the progressive deterioration of water quality in many countries, reducing the quantity of water that is safe to use (Van Vliet et al., 2017). Water use for food production is both the source and the receptor of water quality problems. During recent decades, food production became highly intensive in many developed and rapidly growing economies striving for food security. This intensification included high levels of agrochemicals use to maximize crop yields, as well as a significant increase in livestock production (Lu and Tian, 2017). This has resulted in high nutrient loads (mainly phosphorus and nitrogen), which are the main causes of the degradation of downstream water quality and the eutrophication of water bodies (Vilmin et al., 2018). There are numerous socio-economic costs associated with the deterioration of water quality, including costs related to water treatment and health; impacts on economic activities such as agriculture, fisheries, industrial manufacturing and tourism; degradation of ecosystem services; reduced property values; and opportunity costs of further development (WWAP, 2012). For example, the estimated total of annual cost of water pollution from diffuse sources (mainly agriculture) exceeds billions of American dollars in just the Member States of the Organisation for Economic Co-operation and Development (OECD). Algal blooms associated with excessive nutrients in freshwater systems cost Australia US$116–155 million annually, including through major disruptions of water supplies for livestock and urban areas, as well as fish kills (OECD, 2017a).

Water use for food production is both the source and the receptor of water quality problems

5.3.3 Increased vulnerability and ecosystem degradation

Over the past decades, intense irrigation has substantially affected local and downstream water flow in various regions of the world, including in Asia, southern Europe, and the western and central parts of the USA, which subsequently increased the magnitude and frequency of hydrological droughts in those regions (Wada et al., 2013). Additionally, irrigation was found to accentuate vulnerability to droughts. If farmers grow water-intensive crops, crop productivity suffers disproportionately during droughts as a result of their higher water needs (Damania et al., 2017). Irrigation has also caused environmental degradation of aquatic ecosystems that exceeds by far that of terrestrial and marine ecosystems (Arthington, 2012). Aquatic ecosystems, such as wetlands, provide a wide range of goods and services of significant value to society, including habitat for valuable species, flood control, carbon sequestration, pollution attenuation and recreational opportunities. The global economic value of the ecosystem services provided by wetlands only was estimated at US$26 trillion per year in 2011 (Costanza et al., 2014). However, much of the irrigation development worldwide that occurred in the last decades was considered a priority over environmental flows. If environmental flow requirements are being satisfied without improving irrigation efficiency, half of the globally irrigated cropland would face production losses of more than 10%, with losses reaching 20–30% of total production in some regions such as Central and South Asia (Jägermeyr et al., 2017).

5.4 Scalable solutions for valuing water for food production

Lack of valuation of water for food production has resulted in its inefficient use, which has hindered the progress towards global food security and poverty alleviation, and resulted in various negative socio-economic and environmental externalities. Therefore, valuing water in food production can play a key role in making the trade-offs explicit that are intrinsic to decision-making and priority-setting, especially when it concerns social needs such as food security, which is not revealed in the marketplace (Hellegers and Van Halsema, 2019). It also enables a better understanding of the causes of inefficient use of water in the food system and provides incentives to increase investments in the modernization of water infrastructure. This can in turn increase the efficiency and productivity of water use for food production, while avoiding the cascading negative impacts of inefficient water use (such as water scarcity and pollution) and ensuring that sufficient water remains for aquatic ecosystems to sustain their health, productivity and resilience to climate change.

Several management strategies that could maximize the multiple values of water for food production could be implemented, including improving water management in rainfed areas; transitioning to sustainable intensification; sourcing water for irrigated agriculture, especially from nature-based and non-conventional sources; improving water use efficiency; reducing demand for food and its consequent water use; and improving knowledge and understanding of water use for food production (FAO, 2011a; 2017b; 2018a; FAO/IFAD/UNICEF/WFP/WHO, 2020).

5.4.1 Improving water management in rainfed lands

Increasing water scarcity in many regions around the world leaves little room for further expansion of large-scale irrigation. Moreover, the large gaps between actual and attainable yields in rainfed agriculture in many regions suggest a large untapped potential for yield increases without irrigation (Rockström et al., 2010). For example, several African countries have yields that are at around 20% of their potential (FAO, 2011a). Closing this yield gap could substantially increase food production and reduce the need for irrigation. Some experts therefore indicate that rainfed agriculture will remain the major source of food production in the coming decades and argue that more investment should be directed toward improving water management in rainfed lands (Rockström et al., 2007). There are two broad water management strategies to improve yields and water productivities in rainfed agriculture: (i) capturing more water and allowing it to infiltrate into the root zone with water harvesting techniques such as surface microdams, subsurface tanks or some tree species, and with soil and water conservation practices such as runoff strips and terracing; and (ii) using the available water more efficiently by increasing the plants' water-uptake capacity and reducing non-productive soil evaporation with integrated soil, crop and water management strategies, such as conservation agriculture and improved crop varieties (Rockström et al., 2010). These management options are key to reducing yield losses in rainfed lands during dry spells, and play an important role in climate change adaptation. They allow farmers additional guarantees that may encourage them to invest in other inputs, such as fertilizers and high-yielding varieties, providing them with the opportunity to grow higher-value market crops, such as vegetables or fruits (Oweis, 2014). However, it is important to mention that water harvesting and other management practices to improve the infiltration and storage of rainwater in soils may result in water trade-offs with downstream users and ecosystems (Zhu et al., 2019).

Increasing water supply to irrigation must be coupled with options to improve water use efficiency (better management practices, technologies and regulatory measures)

5.4.2 Sustainable agricultural intensification

The transition of agricultural development towards sustainable intensification is a strategic avenue to use resources, including water, more efficiently (FAO, 2018a). Sustainable intensification refers to producing more from the same area of land while conserving resources, reducing negative impacts on the environment, and enhancing natural capital and the flow of ecosystem services (FAO, 2011b). Sustainable intensification includes production systems and practices such as agroforestry, conservation agriculture, integrated crop–livestock and aquaculture–crop systems, nutrition-sensitive agriculture, sustainable forest and fisheries management, and water-smart agriculture. Water-smart agricultural practices, for instance, aim at improving agricultural productivity while reducing vulnerability to increasing water scarcity (Lipper et al., 2014) (Box 5.1). Water-smart agricultural practices range from planting crops suited to higher temperatures and longer droughts, to adopting practices (such as alternate wetting and drying) that minimize energy and water use while improving crop yields. However, the adoption of these solutions tends to be slow in the absence of adequate incentives. For instance, a large share of the gains of approaches such as water-smart agriculture accrue to beneficiaries other than farmers, while the costs of technology adoption fall mainly on farmers. A wider uptake of such practices requires introducing incentives, including changes in subsidy regimes, public investments in infrastructure or extension services, selective forms of crop insurance, and increased access to credit (World Bank, 2016a). Moreover, "*achieving sustainable agricultural intensification requires a substantial paradigm shift to reconcile growing human needs with the need to strengthen the resilience and sustainability of landscapes and the biosphere. This calls for bold changes in the technological aspects of production systems to improve their ecological efficiency.*" (FAO, 2018a, p. 148).

5.4.3 Increasing water use efficiency in irrigation

Increasing water supply to irrigation must be coupled with options to improve water use efficiency (better management practices, technologies and regulatory measures) (Scheierling and Tréguer, 2018). Jägermeyr et al. (2015) showed that with proper water accounting and

Box 5.1 Systems of Rice Intensification (more productivity with less water)

Rice is a staple for nearly half the world's population. Irrigated, lowland rice cultivation, which covers about 56% of the total rice-cropped area, produces about 76% of the total amount of rice produced globally (Uphoff and Dazzo, 2016). The System of Rice Intensification (SRI) provides an example of a successful water-smart agricultural practice. SRI is a practice developed to increase the productivity of land, water and other resources in rice production systems, and is promoted in many rice-producing countries. It is based on the principle of developing healthy, large and deep root systems that can better resist drought, waterlogging and rainfall variability – all of which are potential impacts of climate change. SRI has proved particularly beneficial as it requires only intermittent water application, rather than continuous flood irrigation. The average increase in income from SRI compared to conventional practices in eight countries (Bangladesh, Cambodia, China, India, Indonesia, Nepal, Sri Lanka and Viet Nam) amounted to around 68%. Crop yields increased between 17 and 105%, while water requirements decreased between 24 and 50%. Additionally, SRI can possibly reduce methane emissions, as it reduces the amount of flooding required for irrigated rice cultivation (FAO, 2013c).

the enforcement of strict withdrawal regulations, the adoption of highly efficient irrigation systems could reduce non-beneficial water consumption at the river basin level with more than 70% while maintaining the current level of crop yields, enabling the reallocation of water to other uses, including environmental restoration. While irrigation losses may appear high, as globally on average only 40–50% of the water supplied to agriculture reaches the crops, it is now widely accepted that a large part of these losses return to the river basin in the form of return flow or aquifer recharge, and can be tapped by other users further downstream or serve important environmental functions (FAO, 2012b).

Efficiency measures to reduce irrigation losses upstream, such as the adoption of efficient on-farm-irrigation techniques (sprinkler and drip systems) or canal lining, while maintaining existing levels of withdrawal, often lead to intensification of water usage and even a net increase in water consumption (Box 5.2): the so-called rebound effect or irrigation efficiency paradox (Grafton et al., 2018). To avoid this rebound effect, some attempts have been made to introduce water consumption quotas or water extractions caps (Xie, 2009). Thus, measures to reduce irrigation water losses must be assessed at the basin level, and not only at individual farm level (Hsiao et al., 2007).

5.4.4 Sourcing water for irrigated agriculture

In order to have secure access to water for irrigation, people have always tried to control and store seasonal and irregular water flows (FAO, 2012b). Augmenting the supply of freshwater resources can be done by investing in built water supply infrastructure, such as water storage facilities, water transfer canals and groundwater wells, or through aquifer recharging and rainwater harvesting. Alternatively, nature-based solutions and improved land management offer promising possibilities to enhance the availability and quality of water for agriculture, while simultaneously preserving the integrity and intrinsic value of ecosystems and minimizing negative impacts for society (WWAP/UN-Water, 2018).

Water resources of lesser quality (e.g. domestic wastewater, drainage water, saline water) are now being valued, both for the resources they contain and for their associated benefits. Significant synergies for the wide adoption of non-conventional water supplies could be created through a transition to a circular economy, fostering sustainable agricultural water management with enhanced resource recovery (Voulvoulis, 2018). Drainage water can be reused either through loops in systems or by farmers pumping directly from drains. Use of these relatively saline waters poses agricultural and environmental risks, as it can cause soil salinization and affect water quality downstream. Therefore, salinity risk assessments and monitoring are required, as are actions to prevent the further salinization of land and water and to remediate saline or sodic soils. A successful example can be found in Egypt, which reuses over 10% of its annual freshwater withdrawals without deterioration of the salt balance (FAO, 2011a).

Box 5.2 Improved irrigation water use efficiency does not always lead to increased availability downstream

With the advent of pressurized irrigation, particularly from groundwater sources, governments worldwide have created subsidies for farmers who wish to transfer from flood irrigation to sprinkler and drip technologies, in the hope that improvements in irrigation efficiency at scheme level would reduce water withdrawals – whether from surface or groundwater sources. Documented examples have included China (Kendy et al., 2003), the United States of America (Ward and Pulido-Velazquez, 2008), Spain (Lopez-Gunn, 2012), Mexico (Carrillo-Guerrero et al., 2013), Chile (Scott et al., 2014), India (Birkenholtz, 2017), Morocco (Molle and Tanouti, 2017) and Australia (Grafton and Wheeler, 2018). Evidence from these countries indicates that any efficiency gains made through agricultural water use programmes, including the adoption of irrigation technology (subsidized or not), are internalized by farming units who tend to intensify crop production, expand areas under irrigation and thereby increase their evaporative consumption of water.

In the case of Australia, farmers were subsidized for adopting irrigation technology as an inducement to give up long-held water use rights in the Murray-Darling River basin and return the right to the Commonwealth in order to increase in-stream flows. After more than a decade of implementation, this recovery or 'buy-back' of water rights and the accompanying subsidy of irrigation technology has not resulted in any measurable impact on in-stream flows (Wheeler et al., 2020). This example highlights the relevance of implementing accompanying socio-economic and environmental policies, and of carefully selecting compliance instruments, including the operation of water markets (Seidl et al., 2020b). At the very least, technical 'fixes' to water scarcity problems need accurate measurement of the resulting surface and groundwater flows and a stronger approach to regulatory compliance and water accounting. What might be apparent on paper (the return of water entitlements) does not necessarily translate to reductions in agricultural water withdrawals.

The conclusion reached is that water productivity can be increased through efficiency programmes in agriculture, but that there is little or no evidence for water being 'freed up' for other uses, including environmental flows. Compliance at the point of withdrawal is essential, but has to go hand-in-hand with the capacity to measure and account for return flows and the environmental outcomes downstream of irrigated areas.

The use of treated wastewater is becoming particularly appealing for agriculture in peri-urban and urban settings

The use of treated wastewater (see Section 2.6.1) is becoming particularly appealing for agriculture in peri-urban and urban settings (Box 5.3). It is estimated that 380 km^3 of wastewater is produced annually across the world, which equals about 15% of agricultural water withdrawals. The irrigation potential of this volume of wastewater stands at 42 million ha (Qadir et al., 2020). With urbanization, more and more wastewater will be available in the coming years, revealing an opportunity to address water scarcity in dry areas through the collection, treatment and fit-for-purpose use of wastewater in agriculture and other sectors. Wastewater is also a source of nutrients for agricultural production systems. The full nutrient recovery from wastewater would offset more than 13% of the global demand for these nutrients in agriculture. The recovery of these nutrients could result in a revenue generation of US$13.6 billion globally (Qadir et al., 2020). Beyond the economic gains of reusing wastewater to maintain or improve agricultural productivity, there are critical human health and environmental benefits (FAO, 2010a).

Desalination (see Section 2.6.2 and Box 3.5) is one of the technological options that can provide an additional source of freshwater for irrigation, especially in water-stressed coastal areas. One challenge with its large-scale implementation is that most desalination technologies entail considerable upfront investment costs and energy requirements. However, investment costs for the main commercial desalination technologies, along with energy requirements, have been decreasing since the first projects were implemented (Mayor, 2020). The supply of desalinated water for agriculture is most likely to be cost-effective in a tightly controlled environment, using agricultural practices with the most efficient water use, crops with high productivity, and renewable energies (Barron et al., 2015). Such conditions are often associated with greenhouses, vertical farming and the production of high-value crops in urban and peri-urban areas, where the cost of water is small compared to the infrastructure investment. In recent years, the use of desalination powered by renewable energies for irrigating high-value crops in remote areas became a more viable option (Burn et al., 2015).

Box 5.3 The use of treated wastewater to address agricultural water scarcity

Treated municipal wastewater is increasingly recognized as an important source of water for agriculture. Despite such recognition, the potential of wastewater irrigation remains underexploited. The *Real Acequia de Moncada* is a centuries-old irrigation system in Valencia (Spain) that successfully uses treated wastewater for irrigation. The *Real Acequia de Moncada* uses treated wastewater obtained from the closest wastewater treatment plant (WWTP) and shows clear benefits for both farmers and WWTP managers. Benefits for agriculture include additional regularity in the water supply for farmers, especially during the dry summers when the crop water requirements are higher and water is scarce. At the same time, using treated wastewater in agriculture avoids its pumping into the sea, providing wastewater treatment with an additional value proposition while protecting aquatic environments. Several factors fostered the use of treated wastewater in the traditional irrigation systems of Valencia. First, the high level of water scarcity and recurring droughts reduced freshwater availability for irrigation. Second, traditional irrigation systems in Valencia have always used wastewater (even untreated) for irrigation. Lastly, the treated wastewater was supplied to farmers at no additional cost, as all the costs involved in treating the wastewater were financed by the sanitation fees.

Source: Hagenvoort et al. (2019).

5.4.5 Water pricing and incentives for efficiency gains

Water pricing can be used to improve water use efficiency in agriculture and to make users aware of the value of water. Different pricing instruments (e.g. volumetric pricing, non-volumetric pricing, tradeable permits) can be implemented to achieve different objectives (e.g. cost recovery, efficient use, reallocating water use) (Davidson et al., 2019). Although water pricing to reduce the demand from the domestic and industrial water sectors has been met with varying levels of success, for agriculture, zero or very low water prices are common, and in some areas even the energy for pumping is subsidized. This situation may persist because of vested interests, political problems associated with price reform, practical difficulties in measuring and monitoring water use, and social norms (e.g. the perception of water as a free good and access to water as a basic right) (FAO, 2004). These low prices can have an adverse bearing on the effectiveness of irrigation systems and water use. They result in poor maintenance and consequent inefficient operation of existing irrigation systems, limited capacity for improvements or investment in new infrastructure, and waste of water at the farm level. It is, however, well documented that irrigation demand is highly inelastic when prices are in a low range. The price levels that can induce substantial conservation or recover the costs of providing sustainable irrigation services would have to be very high to be feasible (Zhu et al., 2019). Such high prices would impose disproportionate costs for farmers, leading to land fallowing while hindering food security and poverty alleviation (Cornish et al., 2004). Two-tiered water pricing, setting a low price for subsistence needs while charging a price equal to marginal cost, including environmental cost, for discretionary uses, has been alternatively suggested (Ward and Pulido-Velazquez, 2009). This pricing arrangement can promote efficient and sustainable water use patterns, while meeting subsistence needs of poor households and supporting the provision of ecosystem services. An alternative instrument to implement water pricing would be to pay farmers to save water and improve its quality (e.g. subsidies for investing in efficient irrigation systems) (Ringler and Zhu, 2015). However, it is claimed that those payments tend to favour the wealthy and thereby exacerbate inequalities in resource access and wealth distribution in rural areas (FAO, 2004).

Although water pricing to reduce the demand from the domestic and industrial water sectors has been met with varying levels of success, for agriculture, zero or very low water prices are common, and in some areas even the energy for pumping is subsidized

5.4.6 Reducing food loss and waste and adopting sustainable diets

Lifestyle changes, such as reducing food loss and waste (FLW) and adopting sustainable diets, when aggregated at a larger scale, could have a considerable impact on water use for food production (Jalava et al., 2016). Reduction of FLW could increase food availability without the need for extra food production and the associated resource needs. Updated estimates of food losses, prepared by FAO, indicate that globally around 14%, in terms of economic value, of the food produced is lost from post-harvest up to, but not including, the retail level (FAO, 2019c).

Kummu et al. (2012) found that the global production of lost and wasted food crops accounts for 24% of total freshwater resources used in food crop production. However, efforts to reduce FLW must overcome the challenge posed by the fact that losses occur mostly in small percentages at different stages of the food chain. Reducing these losses requires shared commitments, strong quantitative goals, careful measurement and persistent action. Additionally, public interventions (i.e. policies and infrastructure investments) should create an enabling environment that allows private actors to invest in the reduction of FLW (FAO, 2019a).

Shifts towards sustainable diets could also reduce the use of water for food production by about 20% compared to current diets

Shifts towards sustainable diets could also reduce the use of water for food production by about 20% compared to current diets (Springmann et al., 2018). Sustainable diets are defined as those that are healthy, have a low environmental impact, are affordable and culturally acceptable (FAO, 2010b). Such diets involve a limited consumption of meat, added sugars and highly processed foods, and eating a diversity of plant-based foods (Tilman and Clark, 2014). Several measures could be implemented to encourage shifts towards sustainable diets. One of the biggest challenges for these shifts is the current cost and affordability of sustainable diets. To address this challenge, agricultural priorities must be reoriented towards sustainable food and agricultural production. This requires an increase in public expenditure to raise productivity, encourage diversification in food production and ensure that sustainable healthy foods are made abundantly available. Policies that penalize food and agricultural production (through direct and indirect taxation) should be avoided, as they tend to have adverse effects on the production of sustainable healthy foods (FAO/IFAD/UNICEF/WFP/WHO, 2020). At the consumption level, it is necessary to raise the awareness of the general public on the importance of sustainable consumption through education, public information and promotional campaigns (e.g. meat-free days), and food labelling (Capacci et al., 2012).

5.4.7 Improving knowledge on water use for food production

Lastly, robust water monitoring, modelling and accounting collectively constitute the foundation for water valuation, and a necessary step towards sustainable management of water resources (Garrick et al., 2017). However, only limited knowledge and data are available about freshwater resources and how they are being used for food production at the global scale. The FAOSTAT and AQUASTAT databases are unique sources on agriculture and water, containing data for over 200 countries and grouped by region, from 1961 to the most recent year available.[7] New digital technologies are creating unprecedented opportunities to leverage data and analytics in order to improve the assessment and management of water use (IWA, 2019). As an example, the FAO Water Productivity Open Access Portal (WAPOR) (Box 5.4) can be used to interactively map, monitor and report on agricultural water productivity in near-real time, using data generated with remote sensing technologies.

[7] See www.fao.org/faostat/en/; www.fao.org/aquastat/en/.

Box 5.4 Water Productivity Open Access Portal (WaPOR)

Water productivity, which is expressed as the quantity of biomass produced in relation to the total volume of water consumed in that year (actual evapotranspiration) can be retrieved from the FAO Water Productivity Open Access Portal (WaPOR). These data can be assessed at the continental, national, river basin and sub-basin/irrigation scheme scales (FAO, n.d.c). Water productivity gaps can be identified this way, facilitating proposed solutions to reduce them, and contributing to a sustainable increase of agricultural production, while taking valued ecosystems and equitable use of water resources into account (FAO, 2020d). Eventually these steps should lead to reduced overall water stress. Many of the new digital technology interventions are already in use on large-scale commercial farms (e.g. in Europe), but knowledge transfer to small-scale farms using simple agricultural methods (e.g. in Africa or Asia) is limited and needs to be further enhanced.

Illustration of mapping with the WaPOR system

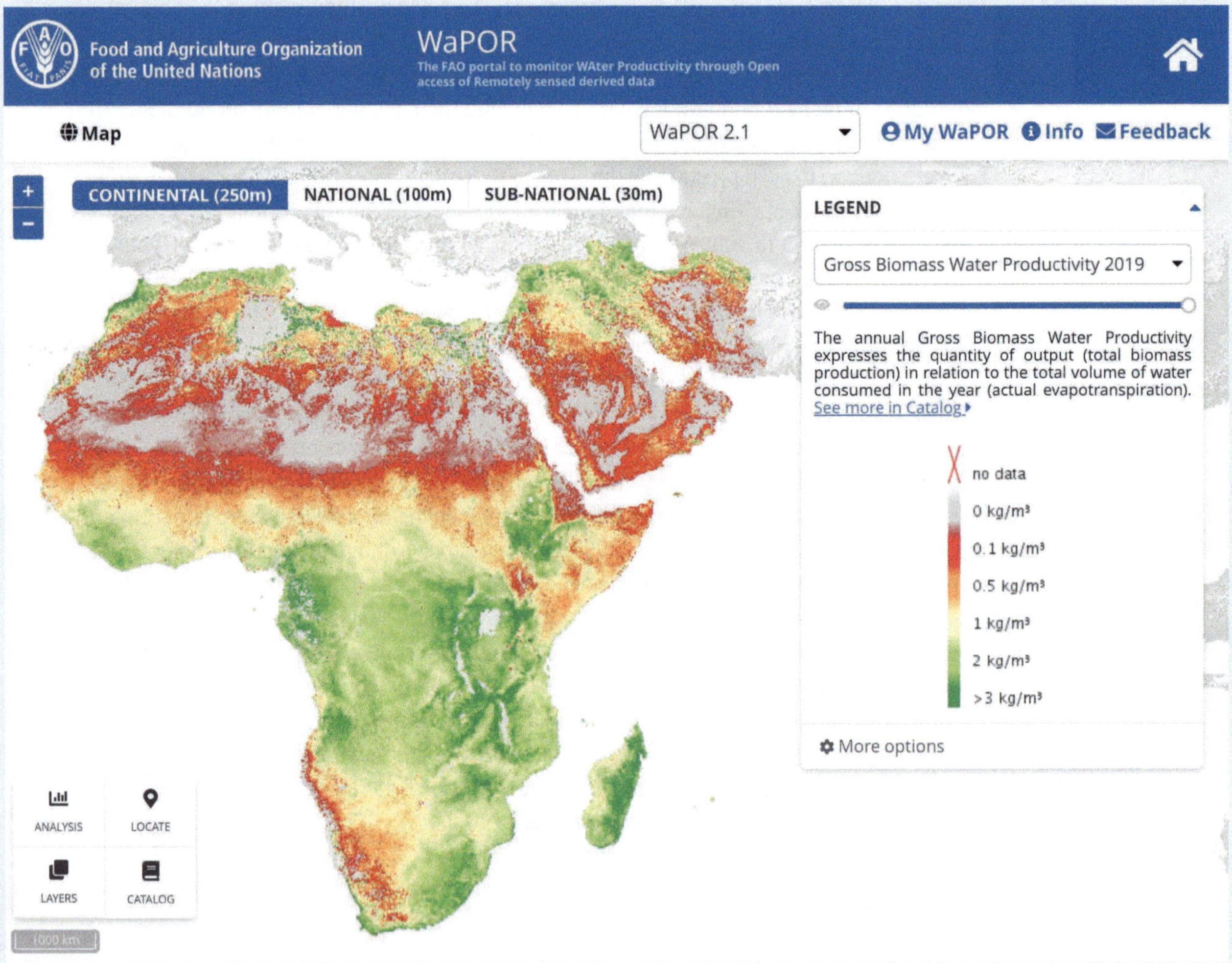

Source: FAO WaPOR.

Chapter 6

Energy, industry and business

UNIDO
John Payne

With contributions from:
Tom Williams (WBCSD);
Rebecca Welling and
James Dalton (IUCN)

6.1 Context

There is a contradictory relationship between the energy, industry and business (EIB) sector[8] and water. On the one hand, water is essential for the EIB[9] sector's operations, which would be impossible without such a resource, as there is no substitute. On the other hand, the reality in most business-as-usual cases is that water is expected to be cheap (even free), clean and plentiful. The needs from the EIB sector may come in competition with, or at the expense of, other users, many of whom regard water from completely different perspectives. The EIB sector's demand for water may also impact the environment and ecosystems in a variety of ways. Clearly, for the sustainable and equitable use of water resources, this sectoral view and situation need to change, while at the same time the EIB sector needs to continue providing the goods and services demanded from it. The value of water in its many uses and facets is a common denominator. The good news is that for the EIB sector, the process of appreciating the varied values of water is under way, yet the multidimensional challenges are many.

6.2 Water use

The importance of water to successful operations in the EIB sector is reflected in the quantity it requires. Industry and energy combined withdraw 19% of the world's freshwater, ranging from 2% in South-East Asia to 74% in western Europe in 2010 (AQUASTAT, 2016). These amounts relate only to self-supplied water, as opposed to municipally supplied water, and do not include hydropower. As a result, the actual percentage used by EIB is even higher, though no figure is available. Another perspective suggests that companies in seven sectors (food, textile, energy, industry, chemicals, pharmaceuticals and mining) *"account for and wield influence over 70% of the world's freshwater use and pollution"* (CDP, 2018, p. 11).

The International Energy Agency (IEA) estimates that energy (primary energy and power production) in 2014 was responsible for approximately 10% of total water withdrawals, of which about 3% was consumed (IEA, 2016). The IEA also estimates that a similar amount (about 10% of global water withdrawals) was used by the other industries. These numbers combined are in general agreement with AQUASTAT's 19%.

Projected global water demand between 2000 and 2050 shows a 400% increase for manufacturing and a 140% increase for thermal power generation (OECD, 2012). Another study (2030 WRG, 2009) foresees almost a doubling of industrial water withdrawals to 2030, reaching a percentage of 22% globally. At the same time, the IEA foresees that by 2040, withdrawals of water for energy are expected to increase by less than 2%, while water consumption[10] is estimated to increase by close to 60% (IEA, 2016). Moreover, in the last four years, even though the number of companies reporting water reduction targets to the CDP (formerly the Carbon Disclosure Project) has close to doubled, there is a nearly 50% increase in companies reporting higher water withdrawals with expanding production, particularly in Asia and Latin America (CDP, 2018).

Clearly, EIB is a major user of water and will continue to be so. With increasing water scarcity, the significance of value[11] will increase and, by extension, influence the interaction with other users and stakeholders.

---

[8] The terms industry and business are frequently interchanged: for the purposes of this chapter the terms are used as in the references cited. Business is a broad term that includes manufacturing, heavy and resource industries, and also commerce, services etc. as used by the World Business Council on Sustainable Development (WBCSD), the Business Alliance for Water and Climate (BAFWAC), and the United Nations Guiding Principles on Business and Human Rights. Energy, while also an industry, is identified separately.

[9] For convenience in the chapter, EIB will be used as an abbreviation.

[10] Water consumed is water that is not returned to a source after being withdrawn.

[11] The Paradox of Value or the Diamond–Water Paradox, where price is determined by scarcity and not by utility, states that scarce diamonds fetch a higher price than abundant water, even though water is more useful. Increasing water scarcity may well change this, as water's marginal utility becomes more valuable.

6.3 The case for water valuation in the EIB sector

The call for EIB to adequately incorporate the value of water into their business models has been increasing in recent years, particularly as water has been generally undervalued, leading to severe consequences – "*Inadequate valuation and ineffective pricing of water for energy generation, industrial and agricultural activities and domestic uses has led to inefficient water use, high discharges of pollutants, and degraded marine and freshwater systems; all leading to high levels of water stress due too little, too much, or too dirty water*" (SIWI, 2018, p. 3).

The World Business Council for Sustainable Development (WBCSD) makes the case that there are drivers that push and drivers that pull businesses into valuing water (WBCSD, 2013). The former are trends, both global and regulatory, involving natural capital accounting, water valuation and better water pricing. The latter is the growing business case and prospective benefits (summarized in Figure 6.1), with important points being better decision-making, higher revenues, lower costs, improved risk management and a better reputation (Box 6.1). A review of business water valuation studies (WBCSD, 2012) found many benefits, which are also often interrelated. Risk management, for instance, can reduce costs. The report provides more rationale and detail on mounting the case for valuing water, and calls for businesses to consider their externalities and manage their use of natural resources in relation to societies and economies.

Figure 6.1

The business case for valuing water

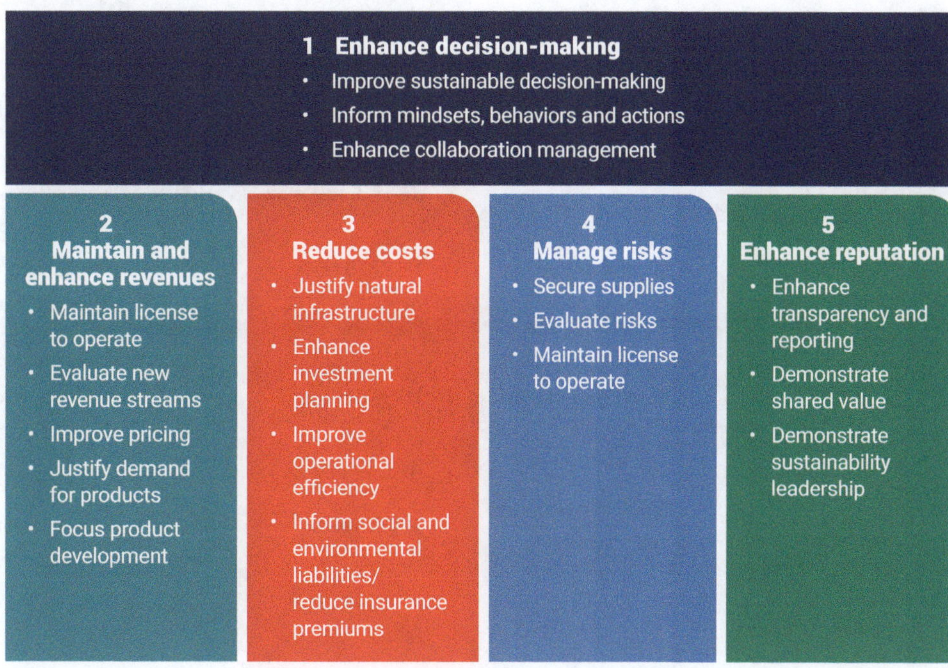

Source: WBCSD (2013, fig. 3, p. 10).

The higher costs, lower earnings and financial losses related to water risks are significant. According to the CDP, the top five water risk drivers are increased water scarcity, flooding, drought, increased water stress and climate change (CDP, 2017). The ensuing top five risks were higher operating costs, supply chain disruption, water supply disruption, constraint to growth and brand damage. From another perspective, 76% of the water-related risks were physical, while regulatory risks constituted 16%, and reputation and markets 6% of these risks (CDP, 2018). When risk to EIB is considered financially through valuation, there is a stronger case for good stewardship (WWF/IFC, 2015). Water-related financial company losses of US$38.5 billion were noted in 2018, with the largest impacts relating to two companies in mineral extraction and power generation (Table 6.1). These numbers may be larger, as at least 50 companies could not provide figures (CDP, 2018). In 2019, the combined risk to business value was US$425 billion (CDP, 2020). Figure 6.2 illustrates how water risk relates to financial consequences.

Box 6.1 Water efficiency, mitigating risks and water value

Sustainable access to water is essential to all of Unilever's operations, 40% of which take place in water-stressed areas. In such locations, the cost of buying water is often low and does not reflect its availability, or its true value, to the company's business or to local communities. Consequently, where the business case for many water efficiency measures is made solely on the basis of the purchase price of water, they may not meet the standard investment criteria.

The company's Clean Technology Fund for sustainable capital expenditure has different allocation criteria for water saving projects at water-stressed sites. First, the payback period is increased from three to five years, increasing also the number of projects that can receive funding and changing the investment mindset. Second, a water stress factor is applied as water saved in water-stressed sites could be five times more valuable than where water is in abundance. In 2019, the amount of water abstracted by Unilever's factories was cut by 46.8% per tonne of production, as compared to 2008. The cumulative costs avoided through direct water savings driven by water efficiency improvements are over €122 million since 2008. In addition, sites are encouraged to explore the energy, chemical and labour cost savings/costs avoided through the water efficiency measures (the true costs of water), which have shown very attractive payback periods of 1.3 years.

Source: Based on internal information from Unilever, provided to WBSCD.

Table 6.1
Sectors with the largest water-related financial impacts

	Financial impacts reported	Most common impacts
Mineral extraction	US$20.5 billion	• Increased operating costs • Reduction/disruption in production capacity • Fines, penalties or enforcement orders
Power generation	US$9.6 billion	• Increased operating costs • Impact on company assets • Increased compliance costs
Biotech, health care and pharma	US$3.5 billion	• Reduction/disruption in production capacity • Constraint to growth • Increased operating costs

Source: Adapted from CDP (2018, p.12).

6.4 Approaches to water valuation

As with other sectors and stakeholders noted in this report, the EIB sector has its own perspective on the value of water. Water is seen as both a resource with withdrawal and consumption costs determined by prices, and as a liability involving treatment costs and regulatory penalties, leading to a perception that water is a cost or risk to sales and compliance (WWF/IFC, 2015). A series of case studies brought together by the World Wide Fund for Nature (WWF) and the International Finance Corporation (IFC) led to the conclusion that business tends to focus on operational savings and short-term revenue impacts, and tends to pay less attention to water value in administrative costs, natural capital, financial risk, future growth and operations, and innovation.

The WBCSD has argued that *"it is not always possible or desirable to express all values in monetary terms"*. In fact, qualitative valuation (descriptive, high, medium, low) should be the starting point (WBCSD, 2013, p. 3). Then follows quantitative valuation using 'indicators' or metrics of value (cubic metres, people affected). Finally, the monetary value is calculated. This hierarchy is shown in Figure 6.3.

Figure 6.2
Water risk and financial consequences

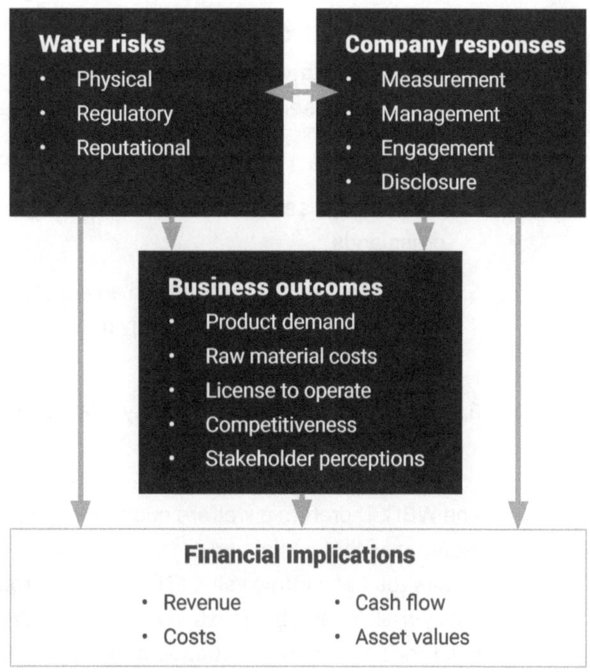

Source: Adapted from Ceres (2012, fig. 1.3, p.19).

Figure 6.3
Hierarchy of water valuation approaches

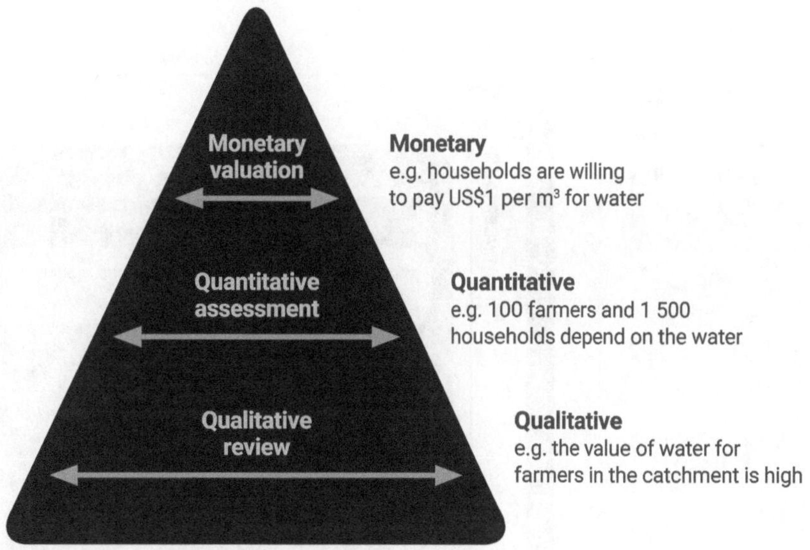

Source: WBCSD (2013, fig. 2, p. 5).

It is also important to determine what to quantify. The WBCSD points out that water valuation strictly means *"the worth of water to different stakeholders under a set of specific circumstances"* (WBCSD, 2013, p. 2). However, for the WBCSD it also encompasses *"water-related valuation"*, which *"means assessing the worth of all benefits and costs associated with water."*[12] (p. 8). Their report looks at six possible categories of water-related value for water valuation studies noting that the *"coverage depends on the objective and context of the assessment"* (p. 3):

---

12 The WBCSD adds that *"a technical definition of what is covered by water valuation is assessing values (as well as prices and costs), whether qualitatively, quantitatively or monetarily, associated with: water use; changes in the quantity and/or quality of water in situ; hydrological services; non-water impacts, and extreme water-related events."* (WBCSD, 2013, p. 8).

1. Off-stream – abstraction for surface or groundwater and the costs of using such water, such as the costs associated with decontamination.
2. In-stream – the value of services provided by water remaining in a waterbody, such as hydrological services, fishing, biodiversity, and recreation and environmental flows.
3. Groundwater – the value from services such as storage and filtration.
4. Hydrological services – the value of benefits from non-aquatic habitats such as forests and grasslands.
5. Non-water impacts – common environmental costs such as greenhouse gas (GHG) emissions related to the energy used for pumping or for desalination. Carbon sequestration is a positive impact.
6. Extreme events – costs usually related to the effects of drought or flooding now made worse by climate change.

The WBCSD prefers a welfare economics approach based on human well-being, and therefore recognizes that social and environmental aspects also should be considered. To address this, it uses total economic value (TEV),[13] an approach it argues is more attractive to international policy-makers and business. By contrast, WWF and IFC advocate for the importance of water risk (uncertainty) in valuation and for risk mitigation by stewardship (WWF/IFC, 2015). They also point to how time and space play into this view (Figure 6.4). However, any approach would benefit from including what is not currently being valued, looking at any changes in values over time, and scalable solutions for valuing water.

Figure 6.4

How valuation is affected by uncertainty

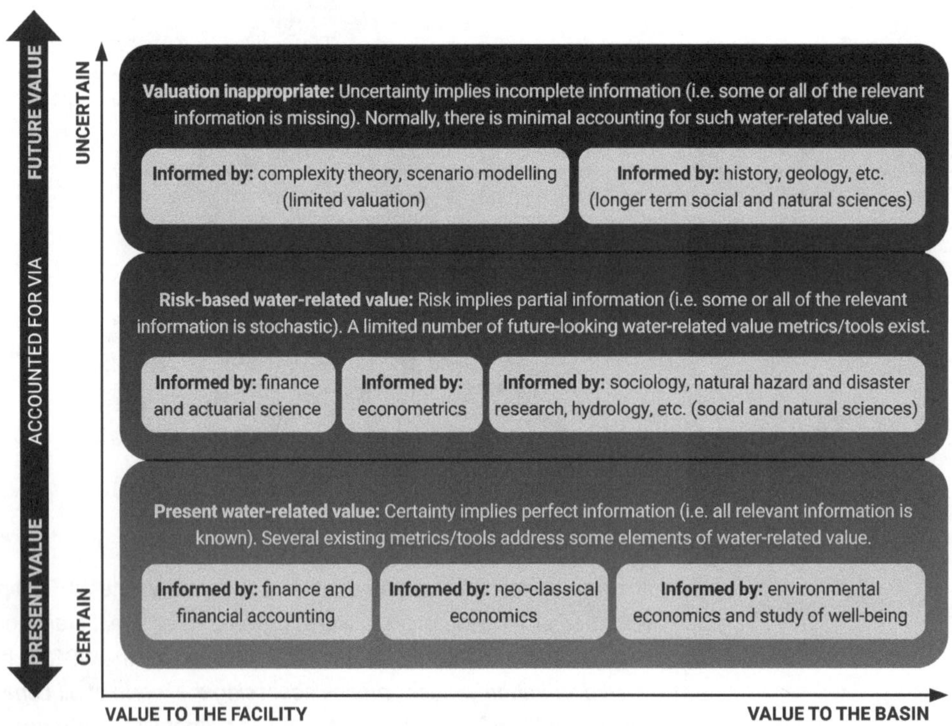

Source: WWF/IFC (2015, fig. B, p.2).

[13] *"Using the TEV approach, monetary values can be estimated for human-related environmental and social benefits that are additive. In effect, this converts environmental and social values into economic (i.e., societal or public) values to enable a total or net human welfare value to be derived through the use of BCA [Benefit Cost Analyses]."* (WBCSD, 2013, p. 16).

The WBCSD, WWF and IFC provide valuation tools, but before an evaluation can done, the EIB sector needs to determine its water risks. A number of risk tools are available (the WWF Water Risk Filter, for instance), essentially mapping tools using average weighted scores of unrelated indicators (WWF/IFC, 2015). They indicate areas in which companies are likely to face water risks, but they do not address value.

6.5 The monetization of water

Due to its character, the EIB sector is highly focused on monetization (monetary value). This provides a predisposition to certain aspects of value (e.g. price of a cubic metre of water) and sometimes an indifference to others (e.g. the tangible and intangible value of water to other stakeholders).

6.5.1 Measurement

The most straightforward monetary valuation is volumetric – price per cubic metre, multiplied by the volume of water used, plus the cost to treat and dispose of wastewater. These items may be nuanced by considerations of consumed or recycled water. In Canada, a detailed industrial water survey is conducted every two years and for 2015 the total water costs[14] of manufacturing were almost CA$1.4 billion (Statistics Canada, 2020a). However, inefficient use of water is promoted by subsidies that artificially lower prices (McKinsey & Company, 2011). Prices of between US$0.03 and US$1.50 per cubic metre for industrial water have been noted in Member States of the Organisation for Economic Co-operation and Development (OECD), with subsidies ranging from 5 to 90% (McKinsey & Company, 2011). It is also noted that prices have been increasing as abstraction and treatment and their associated energy and transport costs have also risen. For a realistic picture of evaluation, the EIB sector needs to factor in the real costs of undervaluing the water it uses.

The most straightforward monetary valuation is volumetric – price per cubic metre, multiplied by the volume of water used, plus the cost to treat and dispose of wastewater

The metrics for the commercial performance of water use in EIB are relatively simple. They include water productivity, defined as profit or value of production per volume ($\$/m^3$); water use intensity, defined as volume to produce a unit of value added ($m^3/\$$); water use efficiency, defined as value added per volume ($\$/m^3$); and the change in water use efficiency over time, for Sustainable Development Goal (SDG) Indicator 6.4.1. It is telling with respect to valuing water that current data for these indices are not readily available, patchy, or not clearly disaggregated into energy and industry, as opposed to data on the overall economy. However, a yardstick is provided by the Canadian physical flow account for water use in 2015, which reports *"industrial water use intensity was 18.3 cubic metres per $1,000 of real GDP"* (Statistics Canada, 2018).

6.5.2 Economic growth

The overall economic productivity of water (GDP/m^3) in the EIB sector also leads at local, regional and national levels to various co-benefits, such as job creation and new enterprises. These are not easy to quantify, as many factors come into play, of which water is only one. The influence of water on value added and industrial jobs was noted in a Swedish study on water-intensive industries (EEA, 2012). In areas where water use was decoupled from economic output, water abstraction remained the same or went down in tandem with a large increase in value added. Where water withdrawal increased, there was only a small increase in value added. As the number of jobs remained constant in each situation, the value of water to jobs would change. A corollary to this could be the rebound effect (Ercin and Hoekstra, 2012), where reducing a water footprint by efficiency is negated by increased production. In this case, the same amount of water would produce more value as opposed to less water producing the same value.

---

[14] Acquisition, intake treatment, recirculation and discharge treatment.

A market value of gross value added[15] per cubic metre of water (AU$/m^3) used in production in Australia shows much higher economic values for mining and manufacturing (>100AU$/m^3) than agriculture (<10AU$/m^3) (Australian Bureau of Statistics, 2010). However, this measure should be viewed with caution, as water often represents a small cost that may not limit production (Prosser, 2011). It also does not include capital costs or price changes related to production. The report suggests that the increase in marginal profit for each extra unit of water used may be a better economic value measure of changes in water use, and more efficient users may therefore buy more water.

Access to water and water infrastructure are not included in the World Bank's Ease of Doing Business Index, because it is *"often taken for granted"* (Damania et al., 2017). Based on a large survey of firms, Damania et al. (2017) showed that water shortages affect smaller firms and low- or middle-income countries the most. Formal firms see an 8.7% average loss in sales for one extra water outage per month. However, for informal firms – more often associated with developing countries – this number rises to 34.8%. Moreover, repeated power outages show a positive correlation with repeated water outages and in countries with frequent water outages, bribery is sometimes used by firms to have access to it, which also plays into the value of water (Damania et al., 2017).

6.5.3 Water footprints and virtual water

A water footprint is a gauge of the value of water in an EIB product. It measures how much water is used to produce a product over its entire supply chain (Water Footprint Network, n.d.). It includes direct and indirect use as well as consumption and pollution. It can also be scaled to a national level. The metrics are usually cubic metres of water per a variety of units such as tonne of production, currency etc. For industrial products, a global average water footprint of 43 m^3 per US$1,000 value added has been calculated between 1996 and 2005, with a wide range of values, such as 1,350 m^3 in Viet Nam and 5.56 m^3 in Germany, to illustrate two countries with different economic structures (Mekonnen and Hoekstra, 2011b).

Water-scarce countries can virtually import water through water-intensive products from countries with adequate water resources

A closely related measure is virtual water, which is *"the volume of water required to produce a commodity or service"* (Hoekstra and Chapagain, 2007, p. 36). It has an international economic connotation as it is a measure of water exported from one country to another, expressed as an embedded volume in that export. Thus, water-scarce countries can virtually import water through water-intensive products from countries with adequate water resources. This clearly has a bearing on the value of water between the trading partners. Globally, for industrial products the average virtual water content[16] is 80L/US$ (Hoekstra and Chapagain, 2007), with a wide range between countries. For example, in the USA it is 100L/US$, whereas in China and India it is between 20 and 25L/US$.

6.5.4 Water quality, wastewater and pollution impacts

In the EIB sector, meeting water quality standards is customarily seen as a cost, either to treat wastewater or to pay fines: indeed, in some countries it is cheaper to do the latter than the former (WWAP, 2015). Data regarding the amount of industrial wastewater generated are sparse, as is information regarding treatment costs. This is emphasized in the European Union's data, where of the 34,000 facilities reporting to the European Pollutant Release and Transfer Register (E-PRTR) only 2,500 industrial facilities reported emissions into water (EEA, 2018). Facilities emitting below thresholds do not have to report and the data suggest that smaller point sources of industrial pollution may have bigger effects than the regulated larger installations. Significantly, as pollutant releases generally declined between 2007 and 2017, industry's gross value added increased by 11% (EEA, 2019).

---

15 Wholesale value minus operating cost of production (input goods and labour).

16 *"the ratio of the industrial water withdrawal (m^3/yr) in a country to the total added value of the industrial sector (US$/yr), which is a component of the Gross Domestic Product."* (Hoekstra and Chapagain, 2007, p. 38).

Box 6.2 Costs and ramifications of pollution

In March 2018, two pipeline leakages occurred at Anglo American's mine in the State of Minas Gerais, Brazil. 1,686 tonnes of iron ore slurry were discharged, 492 of which flowed directly into the Santo Antônio stream. The water supply to the Santo Antônio do Grama community was interrupted and operations were suspended until December 2018. The incident resulted in a substantive impact of US$0.6 billion on the group's earnings before interest, taxes, depreciations and amortization (EBITDA). This included the cost of 280 days of lost production; immediate risk mitigation, including river clean-up and community compensation (approximately US$7.5 million); the inspection and repair of the pipeline (US$20 million); and eight non-compliance notices (US$50 million). Remedial action included provision of potable water to the community; immediate clearing of iron ore sediment on affected land and in the river; and recovery and restoration of areas directly affected and over eight miles beyond.

Source: Excerpt from CDP (2020, p. 14).

In its report on 2019, the CDP focused on water pollution (CDP, 2020). The results show that less than half of their respondents *"regularly meter and monitor the quality of their discharges"* (CDP, 2020, p. 2) and a very low percentage have targets for reduction in water pollution. Pollution can have large financial consequences for companies and investors (Box 6.2).

The relationship balance between water pollution and economic cost has been further explored in a World Bank study (Damania et al., 2019a) (see Box 2.3). Assuming that upstream pollution lowers downstream economic growth, using a large database and biological oxygen demand (BOD) as a proxy for other contaminants, it found that growth of Gross Domestic Product (GDP) is lowered by a third in heavily polluted surface water (BOD > 8 mg/L).[17] This indicates a relationship between productivity upstream and reduced growth downstream. The report also challenges the environmental Kuznets curve that suggests that pollution declines with increasing prosperity.[18] Indeed, it argues that economic growth brings a greater number of pollutants, pointing out that in the USA there are notifications for the release of over 1,000 new chemicals per year. In those cases where the curve does hold true, it is not for economic reasons but attributable to environmental groups and major investments in infrastructure.

Wastewater treatment is a direct cost to the EIB sector. Worldwide, there is a lack of data on this topic, but detailed data are available in Canada where, in 2015, the cost for manufacturing treatment and discharge was CA$506 million, representing 36% of all water costs in the manufacturing sector (Statistics Canada, 2020a). By contrast, the thermal power sector spent only CA$12 million or 5% of their total costs on water (Statistics Canada, 2020b).

If wastewater is considered as a resource (WWAP, 2017), such costs can be mitigated by wastewater use and recycling (see Sections 2.6.1 and 5.4.4). Cooling, heating and process water, either treated or untreated, can be reused for a variety of purposes, maybe many times. This has a double payback, as it reduces the costs of both freshwater demand and wastewater discharges. Obstacles can include the availability of wastewater, the cost–benefit ratio and an increased energy use. Impediments may be overcome by industrial symbiosis, where facilities exchange wastewater for their mutual benefit. The next step is the formation of eco-industrial parks where a number of industries work together to share wastewater and the cost of its

---

17 For middle-income countries where BOD is more prevalent, GDP growth was reduced by close to a half.

18 *"In the early 1990s, it was famously claimed by economists Gene Grossman and Alan Krueger that pollution would follow an inverted-U pattern with development. As countries grow and industrialize, pollution will increase. At some point, outrage from citizens or sufficient affluence would result in policies and cleaner technologies that cause the trend to reverse, with growth leading to a cleaner environment. This hypothesis, known as the environmental Kuznets curve, implies that growth is the best means to environmental improvement"* (Damania et al., 2019a, p. 2).

Box 6.3 Fostering eco-industrial parks in Viet Nam

This five-year project of the United Nations Industrial Development Organization (UNIDO), completed in 2019, aimed to increase the transfer, deployment and diffusion of clean and low-carbon technologies, to minimize emissions of greenhouse gases (GHGs), persistent organic pollutants (POPs) and water pollutants, and to improve water efficiency and the sound management of chemicals. The project promoted and supported the gradual transformation of industrial zones into eco-industrial parks. If all 18 opportunities that were identified are implemented, 885,333 m^3 of freshwater is expected to be saved every year, along with Resource Efficient and Cleaner Production (RECP) options saving 488,653 m^3 of water per year. The water reductions contribute to overall financial savings that often have short payback periods: in the order of months.

Source: Adapted from UNIDO (n.d.).

treatment, as well as energy supply. This then becomes a part of Resource Efficient and Cleaner Production (RECP) and Green Industry (Box 6.3), moving toward a circular economy (UNESCO/UN-Water, 2020).

In addition to the direct costs of poor water quality, such as the costs of treatment, there are external socio-economic costs, such as impacts on drinking water, ecosystems, public health, tourism and fisheries. These impacts are difficult to disaggregate and quantify in relation to EIB, as other factors are involved, such as diffuse agricultural pollution. Mining tailings dam failures that directly affect river systems with heavily polluted water do provide a specific cause. The cost of the human and environmental impacts, plus the fines and loss in production can be huge, not to mention the immeasurable cost of the fatalities.

Another World Bank study assessed the effects of water quality on land prices and property values (amenity value) as indicators of economic prosperity. Using data from Brazil, Argentina and Mexico, it showed that a 100% decrease in BOD increased house prices between 6.9 and 13.7%, while property values would increase 5.3 to 6.0% if a uniform standard for BOD was adopted (Damania et al., 2019b).

6.5.5 Bookkeeping for energy

The energy industry differs from other industries in that it either needs enormous amounts of water for thermal cooling or hydropower, or virtually none at all for other renewables like solar or wind power. Biofuels are an in-between resource, which, if rainfed, do not put extraordinary demands on local water resources, but, if irrigated, can make a large demand on supply. However, out of the approximately 10% of global water withdrawals attributable to energy, 58% is used for fossil fuel-based power generation (Figure 6.5), whereas primary energy, including biofuels, represent only 12% (IEA, 2016).[19]

The large amounts of water necessary for electricity generation in thermal power, nuclear power and hydropower is often withdrawn from lakes and rivers for free, though much is returned after use (e.g. cooling) through dam gates and spillways. In New Zealand, the asset value of the water for hydroelectricity in 2015 was estimated at NZ$9.8 billion, with a return from use of NZ$586 million (Stats NZ, 2017). The value of this 'free' water can only be seen when it becomes unavailable. For example, in the drought that struck California (USA)

[19] In terms of water intensity (L/MWh), electricity generation ranges from about 10 (solar photovoltaic) to 100,000 (nuclear) L/MWh. For primary energy, fossil fuels range from approximately 1 to 10,000 L/toe (tonnes of oil equivalent) and biofuels (irrigated water) about 1,000 to 5 million L/toe (IEA 2016, figures 3 and 4).

Figure 6.5
Water withdrawals in the energy sector, 2014

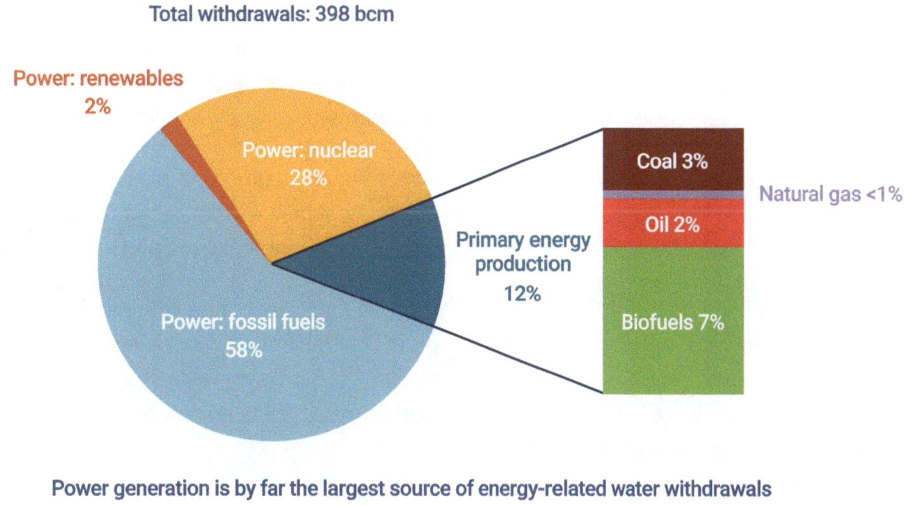

Notes: Renewables include solar photovoltaic, Concentrated Solar Power (CSP), wind, geothermal and bioenergy. Water requirements are quantified for 'source-to-carrier' primary energy production (oil, gas, coal), a definition that includes extraction, processing and transport. Water withdrawals and consumption for biofuels account for the irrigation of dedicated feedstock and water use for processing. For electricity generation, freshwater requirements are for the operational phase, including cleaning, cooling and other process-related needs; water used for the production of input fuels is excluded. Hydropower is excluded.

Source: IEA (2016, fig. 2, p. 14).

between 2007 and 2009, hydropower generation dropped and was offset by using US$1.7 billion worth of natural gas, which besides the financial cost, also significantly increased CO_2 emissions (Christian-Smith et al., 2011).

It has been argued that for thermal plants in the USA, cooling water use is not reduced as a function of the price of water (Stillwell, 2019). Currently, water is so cheap that water prices would have to be significantly greater than average USA prices to make investing in improved thermodynamic efficiency to reduce the use of cooling water worthwhile in the long run. The situation is exacerbated as most plants self-supply their water and thus only have small costs for pumping and possibly treatment. In the short run, if cooling water becomes scarce, once water costs become too high in relation to electricity generation, a plant will shut down at minimum power output. Kablouti (2015) has put forward that water availability and regulations mainly drive investment, not the price of water use. He argues that investment should be based on the total value of water, rather than technological options. In a similar vein, the true economic value of water in electricity generation can be viewed through life cycle analysis. Meldrum et al. (2013) revealed that, though water in thermal plants is mainly used for cooling, renewable technologies needed substantial amounts of water for their manufacture and construction. The lowest total life cycle water use was in photovoltaics and wind energy, and the highest for coal and nuclear energy.

Hydropower, in multipurpose situations, leads to a hybrid value of water, as electricity is being produced while there are, or can be, environmental and economic costs and benefits to other water users (see Chapter 3). Opperman et al. (2015) have proposed that, particularly given the worldwide growth of hydropower, there is an opportunity for a balanced approach for sustainable energy and healthy rivers using *"Hydropower by Design"*. This avoids bad siting of hydroelectric power plants, minimizes impacts and offsets others by investment in mitigation. An example of energy water valuation by a power company involving other stakeholders is given in Box 6.4.

Box 6.4 Energy water valuation

The Serre-Ponçon multipurpose dam and reservoir in southeast France produces 6.5 billion kWh of renewable electricity, supplies drinking and industrial water, irrigates over 150,000 hectares of farmland and regulates flood control. It also provides many water-related recreation and tourism activities with an average turnover of about €150–200 million a year.

At times, climate change is affecting the availability of water for different uses. The water must be managed in accordance with the European Union's Water Framework Directive to balance water needs between environmental objectives and economic development, taking into consideration different economic uses and values of the water.

The Electricité de France (EDF) Group signed a Water Saving Convention with two main irrigators, who were remunerated by EDF for using less water, which means using water more efficiently. This left more water in the reservoir to cope with drought and provided more flexibility for power generation. EDF used its own in-house software water valuation tool (PARSIFAL) to manage and optimize the allocation of water resources, to enhance environmental and social aspects, and to assess the amount of compensation for the irrigators.

Two scenarios were evaluated: one based on saving 32 Mm^3/year of water from being withdrawn by the irrigators, and the other saving 100Mm^3/year. A sensitivity analysis was also performed using three different sets of weather conditions: a dry year, a normal year and a wet year. The valuation focused on the value of each m^3 of water saved.

The EDF software can be used for short- and long-term planning and management of hydropower reservoirs by the hour, taking into account a range of alternative simulated operating conditions. Multipurpose uses of the water are taken into account, including the economic valuation for the supply of a discharge or volume of water.

Using water values allocated to the volumes of water stored as a function of date, the software compares the revenue or savings between present and future releases of a given volume of water. The valuation reflects a 'change in productivity', as the value of water is based on the value of energy that can be derived from each m^3 of water at a particular time. The overall calculations are based on €/m^3 of water saved under the two scenarios. This value is effectively the financial cost of energy (€/KWh) (based on current and future energy prices in France) linked to the energy productivity (m^3/KWh) and volume of water used (m^3) by the hydropower plant.

The valuation revealed how much additional value in terms of energy prices could be generated through the water saving initiatives, and that within the range of 32–100 Mm^3/year of water saved, the economic gain is linear and proportional to the volume of water saved. This determined the level of remuneration for the irrigators for their reduced water consumption. Agricultural consumption of water was reduced from 310 million to 201 million m^3 in six years. In addition, the environment benefited, as around 84% of the water savings were used for ecological purposes. The timing of the water savings was key as more electricity could be generated during peak demand periods when prices were higher. The results were used as a starting point for negotiations with the irrigators to determine how much money they will receive from EDF for saving water. The next step is to extend this idea to other stakeholders in the basin for long-term water savings.

Source: Based on internal information from EDF, provided to WBSCD.

Desalinization is receiving increased attention, particularly in areas of water stress (see Sections 2.6.2 and 5.4.4). However, its energy use is significantly higher, as much as 23 times, than conventional water sources, which results in a cost of four to five times that of treated surface water (World Bank, 2016a). This makes it too expensive for many uses. Although the cost is falling,[20] the impacts of the brine, the impacts of water intake, as well as the GHG emissions need resolution. However, the use of saline water for energy crops and energy generation provides a value for marginal-quality water.

---

[20] According to a recent study, decarbonizing desalination using renewable energy "*will result in global average levelised cost of water decreasing from about 2.4 €/m³ in 2015, considering unsubsidised fossil fuel costs, to approximately 1.05 €/m³ by 2050*" (Caldera and Breyer, 2020, p. 1).

6.6 Accounting for the environment

Incorporation of the value of the environment in water resources management has been discussed in Chapter 2. The EIB sector has an increasingly recognized and important role through its activities and coordination with other stakeholders in sharing and contributing to this value equitably. Decisions by EIB regarding how to allocate, price and invest in water are usually made by a comparison between the economic returns of different water demands, and the economic costs of supplying water – as described in the sections above. Yet on both demand and supply sides, ecosystems form an important – but often ignored – component of these calculations and business management decisions. It is now recognized that ecosystems, through their demand for water, provide a wide range of goods and services for human production and consumption, and therefore for EIB (Emerton and Bos, 2004; Green et al., 2015; Cohen-Shacham et al., 2016).

6.6.1 Natural capital accounting

Natural capital accounting is a useful tool to inform the private sector about the services nature provides as well as the relationship between these services and businesses. The EIB sector interacts with natural capital whether directly or indirectly, in the form of production inputs (raw materials, water, energy) or in the form of dependency to the services nature provides (regulatory services such as pollination, supportive services such as the nutrient cycle, cultural services such as recreation and, importantly, waste assimilation and water quality – see Chapter 2). Natural capital accounting can help determine the extent to which businesses may be impacted, positively or negatively, by these natural services in their daily operations in terms of monetary value (see Section 2.4.3). Tangible information on ecosystem services value could enable the EIB sector to understand these impacts and values and to take more conscious decisions. Businesses that recognize the importance of natural capital for their operations can make more reliable and informed investments and can better assess risks and opportunities. A useful document in this respect is the *Natural Capital Protocol*, intended to provide businesses with a standardized framework for including natural capital in decision-making (Natural Capital Coalition, 2016).

Decisions by EIB of how to allocate, price and invest in water are usually made by a comparison between the economic returns of different water demands, and the economic costs of supplying water

6.6.2 Nature-based solutions

Nature-based solutions (see Section 2.5.1) can be used in combination with others types of interventions, which makes them more accessible to the EIB sector, where mixed built and natural assets can deliver optimal results for food supply chains as well as energy production (Cohen-Shacham et al., 2016). For example, investing in natural infrastructure within a river basin to support existing built water infrastructure systems can result in lower costs and more resilient services, as dams benefit from forests that stabilize soils and hold back erosion upstream.

6.6.3 Environmental flows

Where EIB activities rely heavily on existing water regimes, changes in flow patterns can affect production and costs. Equally, environmental flows (see Section 2.5.2) can be critically impacted by water or fragmented by dams that store water and regulate water flows[21] (Grill et al., 2019) to maximize hydropower generation. Water accounting is a useful tool as it can provide evidence-based information for decision-making and policy development around water supply (quantity and quality), the demand of different water users and uses, as well as the current level of consumptive water use and whether or not it is sustainable. However, the limited or lacking considerations regarding environmental flows, in particular the seasonal timing of flows, limits the water accounting approach in being able to encompass the full value of ecosystem

[21] Only 37% of rivers longer than 1,000 km still flows freely over their entire length, and only 23% flows uninterrupted to the ocean (Grill et al., 2019).

services in water provision over an extended period. The focus on primarily water volumes, similar to other methods such as the Volumetric Water Benefit Accounting (VWBA) approach (Reig et al., 2019), means that social and environmental water benefits are not included in the water balance. For EIB, this difference between valuing water volumes and water benefits needs to be clarified, since the measurement of water saved may or may not generate appropriate information by which to assess companies' performance (Newborne and Dalton, 2019). Complementary indicators to measure non-volumetric outputs, as well as elements of effective water stewardship activities that increase the likelihood of generating social, economic and environmental benefits to solve shared water challenges in river basins, are critical for decision-making (Reig et al., 2019; Newborne and Dalton, 2019).

6.7 Stakeholders, corporate social responsibility (CSR) and stewardship

In response to water security concerns and increasing awareness of both pollution of watercourses and the impacts of climate change on precipitation, companies have become more aware of their risks from changes in hydrology. Moreover, as companies increasingly recognize the value of water to their operations, they expand from CSR to stewardship (see Section 2.5.3).

A better understanding of the motivations behind corporate interests in water management should align with those of water management agencies pursuing Integrated Water Resources Management (IWRM) planning approaches.

A significant challenge to overcome the transition from being a corporate water user to becoming a good steward, is the realization that individuality does not resonate in water management. Stewardship and the 'collective action' needed across a range of actors requires a greater recognition of public goods generated from good water management, and a reorientation in thinking from 'my water supply' to 'our water basin' (Box 6.5). This also includes taking into account gender equality, in order to meet human rights-related responsibilities and sustainable development in general.

Box 6.5 Valuing 'Every Drop'

As water, more specifically high-quality water, comprises 95% of beer, it is as valuable as it is essential to brewing. In the last decade, beer producer Heineken has reduced its water use by almost a third. Recognizing that water is precious and undervalued, it has committed itself to water protection for communities in the water-stressed areas where it operates. Its Every Drop 2030 Water Ambition in support of the United Nations Sustainable Development Goal 6 is dedicated to this end. In water-stressed areas, Heineken commits to fully balance within the local watershed every litre of water used in its products, to maximize water circularity, and to reduce water usage from 3.2 of water per hectolitre of beer to an average of 2.8 hl/hl. In addition, it has invested in reforestation, landscape restoration, desalination and water capture, working closely together with other water users. For example, in Indonesia, as a consequence of working alongside the United Nations Industrial Development Organization (UNIDO), Heineken is part of a water alliance ('Aliansi Air'), in which government, businesses, non-governmental organizations (NGOs) and local community groups work together on water conservation and pollution reduction in the Brantas river basin.

Source: Adapted from Heineken (2019a; 2019b).

6.8 Future value for EIB – Succeeding and surviving

In concert with all sectors and stakeholders, EIB enterprises, in order to succeed and survive commercially and to play their necessary part in overall water management and stewardship in the face of climate change, will need to improve their understanding of value and valuation of water: some potential avenues are outlined below.

6.8.1 Internal pricing

In a similar way as companies have developed internal prices for carbon, there is increasing momentum to do this for water. Such an internal price is one "*used in economic analysis, when market price is felt to be a poor estimate of 'real' economic value*" (Emerton and Bos, 2004, p. 86), and attempts to account for future uncertainty around price (WWF/IFC, 2015). In 2017, of the companies reporting to CDP, 53 (7%) were accommodating environmental and social costs by performing internal pricing of water (CDP, 2017). For example, using a tool that quantifies hidden costs like pre-treatment and wastewater treatment, Colgate Palmolive discovered that their true cost of water was 2.5 times what they paid for it. Limitations to shadow pricing include the assumptions required and changes to the value of money over time: it works for procurement, but most impacts are caused by other factors, such as operational interruption (WWF, 2019a).

Blockchain technology could offer a transparent way to manage water and trade water rights in real time between parties, including industry and energy

6.8.2 Industry 4.0

The fourth industrial revolution[22] is anticipated to lead to increased productivity and growth, with up to 30% faster production and 25% increases in efficiency (Rüßmann et al., 2015). It blends digital and physical technology into cyberphysical systems using nine technology pillars.[23] Such systems will be connected along the value chain (Box 6.6), collecting data and optimizing production. Clearly, as water's true value is increasingly recognized in EIB, water efficiency will be an integral part of such developments. In Industry 4.0, water efficiency will also be connected with increasing energy efficiency and with the uptake of renewable clean energy sources (UNIDO, 2017).

Box 6.6 'Supply chain' versus 'value chain'

A '**supply chain**' refers to the system and resources required to move a product or service from supplier to customer. The **supply chain (or indirect) water footprint** of a business is the volume of freshwater consumed or polluted to produce all the goods and services that form the input of production of a business.

The '**value chain**' concept builds on this, but also considers the manner in which value is added along the chain, both to the product/service and the actors involved. From a sustainability perspective, 'value chain' has more appeal, since it explicitly references internal and external stakeholders in the value creation process. It also encourages a full-lifecycle perspective and not just a focus on the (upstream) procurement of inputs. Value is generally used in a narrow economic sense, but it can be interpreted to encompass 'values', i.e. ethical and moral concerns as well as other non-monetary utility values such as the closing of material loops, the provision of ecosystem services and added customer value.

Sources: Extracted and adapted from Hoekstra et al. (2011, p. 192) and University of Cambridge (n.d.).

---

[22] The fourth industrial revolution was preceded by three others, two of which had strong connections with water. The first focused on water power and the steam engine. The second centred on electricity, which has a strong nexus with water. The third was driven by computers and automation.

[23] Autonomous robots, simulation, horizontal and vertical system integration, the industrial internet of things, cybersecurity, the cloud, additive manufacturing, augmented reality, and big data and analytics.

Outside the factory fence, Industry 4.0 has a great potential to combat water insecurity – not only in the EIB sector but also in agriculture, municipal water supply and wastewater treatment. A report by the World Economic Forum (2018) suggests new ways for Industry 4.0 to address five urgent water issues (Figure 6.6). The use of satellite imagery could lead to significant improvements in information on supply and demand, and can also be extended to groundwater. As such, the water intensity of supply chains could be optimized. Blockchain technology could offer a transparent way to manage water and trade water rights in real time between parties, including industry and energy. Moreover, water quality could be monitored through a network of sensors to find contamination and its sources. Using blockchain linked to smart contracts, fines could automatically be levied for infringements of standards (Damania et al., 2019a). The possibilities are numerous but investment financing will be necessary, as well as an enabling environment for an innovation ecosystem to actively promote new ideas and technology. Furthermore, multi-stakeholder governance should include both the public and private sectors (World Economic Forum, 2018).

The circular economy will value water to the extent that each litre is reused again and again, making water itself almost become part of the infrastructure rather than a consumable resource

6.8.3 Beyond stewardship

The value of water is so broadly based in so many aspects of EIB that numerous methods and approaches will be required under an overall strategy to realize its true economic worth. In many respects, the attention EIB will have to pay to the true value of water is similar to the major and dramatic shift in corporate operations and thinking that will be required to meet the water-related challenges of climate change as outlined in the *2020 World Water Development Report* (UNESCO/UN-Water, 2020). At present, only a small proportion of large corporations are responding to the challenge. CDP reports that "*[i]n 2019, companies representing a quarter of global market capitalization disclosed water security information*" (CDP, 2020, p. 2). This report covered 2,433 companies, noting that more than 2,500 did not meet "*investor or customer requests for data*" (CDP, 2020; p. 6). To put this in perspective, according to an OECD publication there are approximately 41,000 listed companies worldwide (De La Cruz et al., 2019). These numbers do not include the countless Small and Medium-sized Enterprises (SMEs) worldwide,[24] many of which may have water and wastewater low on their list of priorities, either because of poor regulation and enforcement or because they barely survive, especially given the COVID-19 pandemic.

As has often been stated, business-as-usual is not going to provide a solution for the water-related challenges that the EIB sector will face in the future. A recalibration of corporate thinking about water, combined with better all-round management, will be required in the context of a different and new global economy (CDP, 2018). Production and consumption must be further decoupled from the use of water resources to allow water value to establish a realistic level based on other drivers. The circular economy will value water to the extent that each litre is reused again and again, making water itself almost become part of the infrastructure rather than a consumable resource.

The investment and financing necessary will need to transcend the 'quarterly capitalism' (Barton, 2011) view of shareholder value, which expects short-term returns on investment. Instead, it should move to much longer time-frames. A current trend is inclusive capitalism, which, by engaging all sectors, seeks to open "*the opportunities*

[24] It is estimated that there are approximately 400 million SMEs, accounting for 95% of firms and 60 to 70% of employment worldwide (National Action Plan on Business and Human Rights, n.d.)

Figure 6.6 Development level of Fourth Industrial Revolution technology applications that address water and sanitation challenges

	Obtaining a complete, current and accessible picture of water supply and demand	Providing access to and quality of water, sanitation and hygiene (WASH) services	Managing growing water demand	Ensuring water quality	Building resilience to climate change
3D printing					
Advanced materials				●	
Advanced sensor platforms	●	●	●	●	
Artificial intelligence	●	●	●	●	●
Bio-technologies					
Blockchain		●	●	●	●
Drones and autonomous vehicles	●	●			
The Internet of Things (IoT)	●	●	●	●	●
Robotics					
Virtual, augmented and mixed realities					
New computing technologies	●	●	●	●	●

Source: World Economic Forum (2018, fig. 1, p. 9).

and benefits of our economic system to everyone" (Coalition for Inclusive Capitalism, n.d.). Sustainable capitalism complements this. An aspect that became significant recently is impact investing by asset managers, such as BlackRock, allocating capital to companies with good environmental, social and governance (ESG) records. This is still mainly aimed at climate change, but water and its value, including under conditions of scarcity and desertification, will be a factor when adaptation is considered. Certainly, there is the start of a movement in the USA to redefine the purpose and responsibilities of companies to focus on their broader sphere of influence and to include all stakeholders, with commitments to customers, employees (fostering "*diversity and inclusion, dignity and respect*"), suppliers and communities, not just shareholder value (Business Roundtable, 2019). In so doing, as water tightly links all these parties and is central to them, its value will be a paramount consideration moving forward.

Chapter 7

Culture and the values of water

UNESCO-IHP
Alexander Otte

WWAP
David Coates and Richard Connor

With contributions from:
Giulia Roder (UNU-IAS); David Hebart-Coleman,* Martina Klimes and Elizabeth Yaari (SIWI);** Maria Teresa Gutierrez (ILO); Nigel Crawhall (UNESCO); Rémy Kinna (UNECE); Marlos de Souza (FAO); Eva Mach (IOM); Barbara Van Koppen (IWMI South Africa); and Nicole Webley (UNESCO-IHP)

* On behalf of the UNDP-SIWI Water Governance Facility, hosted by SIWI.

** On behalf of the International Centre for Water Cooperation, hosted by SIWI.

7.1 Introduction

Culture directly influences how the values of water are perceived, derived and used. The United Nations Educational, Scientific and Cultural Organization (UNESCO) defines culture as *"the set of distinctive spiritual, material, intellectual and emotional features of society or a social group ... it encompasses, in addition to art and literature, lifestyles, ways of living together, value systems, traditions and beliefs"* (UNESCO, 2002, p. 62). Every society, group or individual exists in their own cultural setting that is moulded by a varying mix of heritage, tradition, history, education, life experience, exposure to information and media, social status, and gender, among many other factors.

Culture is multifaceted, and each culture usually comprises a set of subcultures. Besides, scientists working in many different parts of the world also share some kind of 'scientific culture', which is often a dominant factor in the way in which values are generated and used, and is pivotal in the development of global science (Wang, 2018). But different disciplines within science, such as hydrology, economics, engineering or sociology, have their own subcultures that influence what elements each of them portrays as important. Some scientific cultures may disregard, or even be hostile to, alternative approaches, such as the value of indigenous and local knowledge. The societies within which these cultures operate choose the weight they place on science and the outcomes are far from uniform. Take, for example, the diversity in societal acceptance of anthropogenic climate change or scientific knowledge associated with the COVID-19 pandemic (Lewis, 2020). Science tends to favour valuations based on data and information, whereas most other people value water without using data and information at all. Thorough assessment and discussion of these cultural influences on the values of water is beyond the scope of this report. The key point is that, for any values, it is important to understand the cultural background under which they arise and how culture influences how they are used.

Culture directly influences how the values of water are perceived, derived and used

Some cultures can hold values that are difficult to quantify or indeed, in some cases, articulate. Water can appeal to people for spiritual reasons, or through scenic beauty, because of its importance for wildlife or recreation, among others, or combinations of these. *"Cultural practices reflect and constitute cultural values and are a discernible way that culture can be said to manifest itself, both at particular moments in time (e.g. recreational activity) and as part of a broad cultural realm of lived experience (e.g. a whole 'way of life')"* (Fish et al., 2016a, p. 213).

Water-related values may harbour profound emotional dimensions, and are often anchored in the collective social imaginary, expressed in narratives and artistic works (see, for example, COMEST, 2018; Fish et al., 2016b). These values can be problematic to compare with values derived through other formal means, such as economics, and are therefore often excluded from value assessments that favour those.

Culture changes and evolves over time, sometimes rapidly. For example, Chapter 3 provides examples of how increasing values attributed to the environment can drive dam decommissioning and how climate change has elevated values associated with water-related risks. Chapter 4 cites the case of how COVID-19 has reminded societies of the value of safe water, sanitation and hygiene (WASH) services. Global history and geopolitics have often imposed one culture's values on another, for instance through colonization (Box 7.1). However, cultural values of water are also frequently shared and appreciated by several different societies, outside the group where the values and their expressions emerged.

Contradictions between water-related values exist, and research is increasingly interested in understanding how and why diverse groups within and among societies regard a seemingly identical substance very differently. A juxtaposition of the social and cultural background of values of water can help to understand the origin, complexity and drivers of value systems. This process can inform ethics and foster learning in harmony with the living world, increasingly considered indispensable (COMEST, 2018; HLPW, 2018).

Box 7.1 The legacy of colonial value systems on water resources law in Africa

Statutory water permit systems prevail in most African countries and are designed to override customary water law. This is a colonial legacy where colonial authorities vested water resources in their overseas monarchs and granted permits to settlers only. This state ownership concept transferred to post-independence and extended permit requirements to the millions of small-scale water users. However, implementation appears logistically impossible. As such, a large number of micro-users, often the most vulnerable, are unable to obtain a permit, leaving them in a state of legal limbo. Meanwhile, national or international high-impact users, often more proficient with administrative and legal matters, continue to benefit from the strongest, sometimes even tradable, entitlements (Burchi, 2012). New hybrid forms of water law should target and enforce permits to regulate these relatively few high-impact users and finally recognize customary water rights at equal legal standing (Schreiner and Van Koppen, 2018).

7.2 Methods of categorization, assessment and analysis of cultural values

Recent research seeks to create an analytical framework for cultural values. For example, many of the cultural values related to water can be assessed and expressed by considering them as cultural ecosystem services. Fish et al. (2016b) have suggested that, to aid analysis and assessments, these cultural services can be categorized according to:

- Environmental spaces – the places, localities, landscapes and seascapes in which people interact with each other and with the natural environment;
- Cultural practices – expressive, symbolic and interpretive interactions between people and the natural environment;
- Cultural benefits – dimensions of human well-being that can be associated with these interactions between people and the natural environment; and
- Cultural goods – the interactions between values, services and benefits, potentially amenable to market transactions, creating cultural goods that can be exchanged, sometimes but not always, in monetary terms.

These distinctions can be placed in a framework of dynamic feedback loops for cultural ecosystem services, in order to obtain a general theoretical viewpoint that can be applied to water (Figure 7.1). This can help us understand cultural ecosystem services and how these contribute to a wider set of cultural values. Economic valuation methodologies, including for estimating monetary and non-monetary values, can be applied to many of these individual cultural services, enabling a comparison between them and other ecosystem service categories (see Chapter 2 for further details).

However, using ecosystem services frameworks is no panacea for holistic valuation. Even where applied, the approach can still lead to bias towards direct and indirect use values, that are easier to quantify and therefore under-represent more intangible values such as bequest or existence value. There can be dramatic inconsistencies when economic, social and cultural values are not reconciled (Box 7.2).

7.3 Faith-based values

Across faith-based traditions worldwide, water can symbolize elements as diverse as life, purity, renewal and reconciliation, but also chaos and destruction (Oestigaard, 2005). In some, water is seen as a gift for humans to care for, whilst others embrace a view that accentuates water's importance for the environment and wildlife.

There is a close relationship between religion, or faith, and ethics. The World Commission on the Ethics of Scientific Knowledge and Technology proposed ethical principles that seek to integrate human concerns with those of the various ecosystems affected by the global water cycle (COMEST, 2018). Contexts of values can influence their representations. For example, narratives originating from regions characterized by water scarcity often feature illustrations of lawful and morally correct living beings, often as characterized by the local religion, rewarded

Figure 7.1

A conceptual framework for cultural ecosystem services

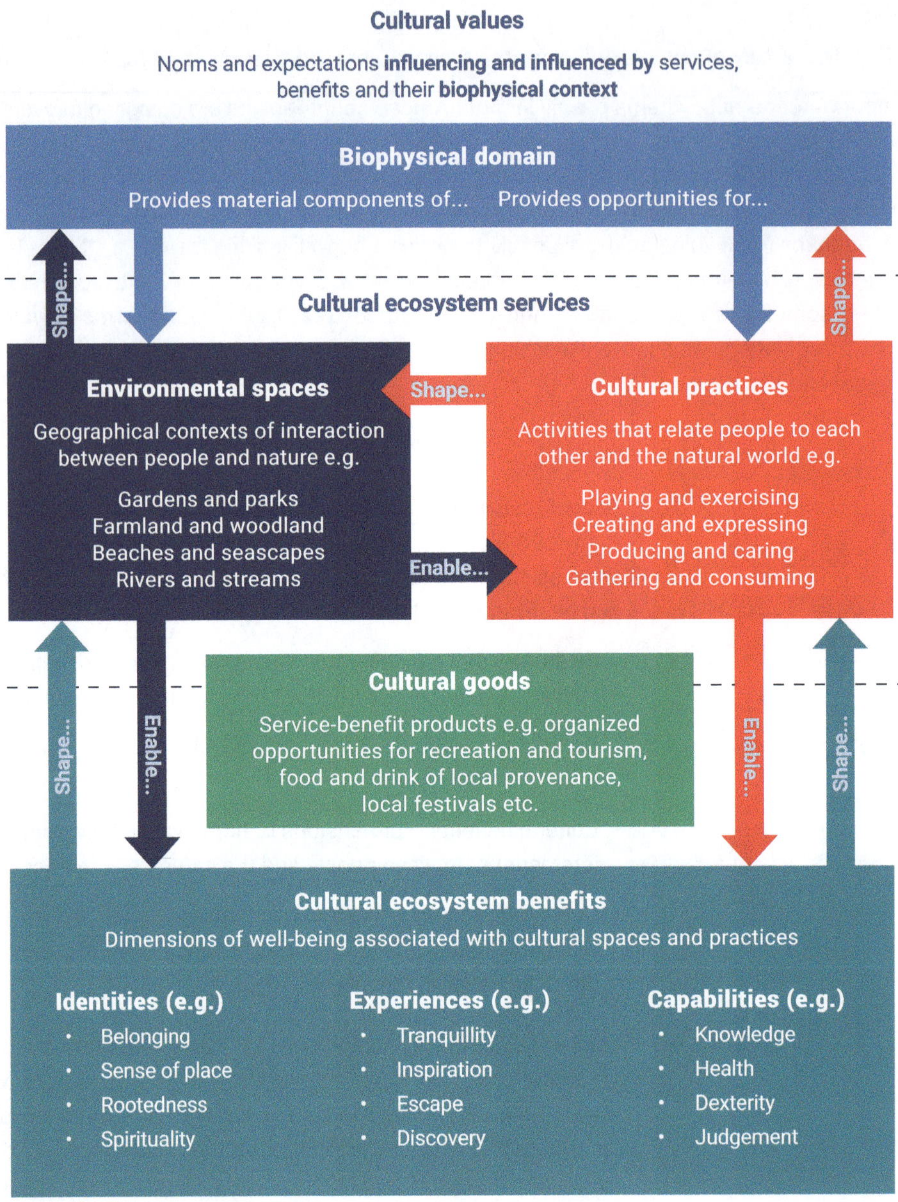

Source: Fish et al. (2016a, fig. 1, p. 331).

with rainfall and access to water. By contrast, the modern economic conception of water can be characterized by its abstraction from social, cultural and religious contexts (Anderson et al., 2019). Water in the global economic development context is often considered a resource at the disposal of society and is therefore distinct from water as it may be recognized by religions or the belief systems of many indigenous peoples, creating quite diverse, and potentially contradictory, perspectives of values (Jiménez et al., 2014).

7.4 Indigenous peoples' values systems, place-based water stewardship and customary laws

As pointed out earlier, culture is integral to all societies. The values and value systems of indigenous peoples are frequently used as examples of 'cultural values', embodying societies that see themselves as part of the living world. Certainly, indigenous worldviews are not homogeneous. At the same time, the Intergovernmental Science-Policy Platform on Biodiversity and Ecosystem Services (IPBES) has demonstrated that indigenous peoples bring technical, governance and complementary capacity to the management of natural resources (IPBES, n.d.). The High-Level Panel on Water recognizes the role of indigenous knowledge as part of concerted action and institutional coherence through generating ideas and realizing the various values of water (HLPW, 2018). The legally binding Convention on Biological Diversity (1992)

Box 7.2 Trying to understand cultural values through investigating mass fish kills in the Menindee region, Australia

A mass fish kill in the Menindee region of New South Wales over the summer of 2018–2019 was investigated by the Australian Academy of Sciences. Two conceptual frameworks for ecosystem services (that of the Millennium Ecosystem Assessment and the concept of Total Economic Value, see Chapter 2) were concluded to be potentially controversial and problematic. Using standard techniques, there is more certainty in determining direct and indirect uses of water resources than there is in determining option, bequest and existence values, as well as other cultural values.

In Australian indigenous societies, cultural affiliations with landscapes and water features are expressed through social etiquette, place-based knowledge, narratives, beliefs and daily practices. Some challenges to applying economic methods to indigenous values include:

- income disparities: price-based valuation techniques give greater voice to richer people than to the preferences of the poor;
- (in)separability: direct and indirect benefits are frequently interdependent and overlap, hence it is difficult to value them collectively;
- value and culture: monetary valuation methods are often inappropriate and offensive in the indigenous context; and
- community-held values: individual values are easier to assess than community-held values.

Testimonials of representatives of the Aboriginal communities emphasized that the river is a living being to many, and fundamental for ongoing survival. The investigation concluded that alternative approaches, such as the life satisfaction approach, subjective scaling, cognitive mapping, storytelling and benchmarking can be more suitable in valuation contexts.

Source: Australian Academy of Science (2019).

was one of the first global instruments to require State Parties to work with indigenous and local peoples to promote, preserve and maintain their local knowledge and traditional systems[25] (broadly applicable to water due to the intimate relationship between biodiversity and water on the one, and water as an ecosystem service on the other hand). The United Nations Declaration on the Rights of Indigenous Peoples (UNGA, 2007, Article 25) elaborated these principles in a broader context: *"indigenous peoples have the right to maintain and strengthen their distinctive spiritual relationship with their traditionally owned or otherwise occupied and used lands, territories, waters and coastal seas and other resources and to uphold their responsibilities to future generations in this regard."* Despite these global commitments and aspirations, the recognition of indigenous rights in practice, the incorporation of their values and knowledge, and their full and effective participation in decision-making is far from universal.

The connection between water and place, often categorized as 'relational values' (see Chapter 1), can be strong in many indigenous cultures. Water is a central element in the cultures of certain indigenous peoples in the Arctic, for example, where knowledge and values around water, ice and snow are carefully entwined into the cultural life of the group and water plays the lead role in knowledge mapping, functions as a teaching tool and provides directional sense, amongst many other roles (Hayman, 2018). Originating in such settings, values-led management as a participatory, scalable approach that can be learned collectively has the objective of sustaining the collective community-desired state of their relationship with a given place (Artelle et al., 2018).

Water, as a whole, may be seen as a sentient being by certain cultural groups. For example, recognition of the importance of relational values led to the granting of legal personhood and protection of the Whanganui River, under the custodianship of the local Maori People, in New Zealand (Box 7.3).

---

[25] Article 8j: *"[Each Contracting Party shall] Subject to its national legislation, respect, preserve and maintain knowledge, innovations and practices of indigenous and local communities embodying traditional lifestyles relevant for the conservation and sustainable use of biological diversity and promote their wider application with the approval and involvement of the holders of such knowledge, innovations and practices and encourage the equitable sharing of the benefits arising from the utilization of such knowledge, innovations and practices."*

Traditional value systems can be expressed through customary water law. Most Africans, for example, rely on customary rights for their access to water (Ramazzotti, 1996), with significant legal and social impacts. Individuals and groups in rural communities have invested in water infrastructure to develop surface and groundwater sources for basic livelihoods such as for domestic, livestock, irrigation and other uses. In some cases, self-supply is an indispensable complement to government water schemes. Water tends to be seen as a shared resource, or, in cosmological terms, as provided by higher powers – and thus simultaneously of spiritual and physical, life-sustaining value (Box 7.4).

7.5 Collective normative values

There are several examples of how the global community has come together to reach consensus on values and principles regarding water that reflect a world ethic or 'culture'. For example, the rights to safe and clean drinking water and sanitation have been recognized to be fundamental to the realization of all human rights and to human dignity (UNGA, 2010). The Special Rapporteur on the human rights to safe drinking water and sanitation of the United Nations has documented at the intergovernmental level how human rights are directly impacted by ill-considered water management projects, water uses or activities deteriorating water around the world (UNGA, 2019). The Special Rapporteur also stressed the need to respect local cultural values and the free, prior and informed consent of indigenous groups.

The 2030 Agenda for Sustainable Development, defining the Sustainable Development Goals (SDGs), is perhaps the broadest and most integrated international framework. It recognizes the importance of water in its SDG 6 ("*Ensure availability and sustainable management of water and sanitation for all*"), with the various dimensions of the values of water reflected through its six targets covering drinking water, sanitation, water quality, water use efficiency, Integrated Water Resources Management (IWRM), and ecosystems, as well as cooperation and capacity-building, and the participation of local communities in improving water and sanitation management. Water also has transversal value across all the SDGs (Figure 7.2).

Agreements on shared values are also manifest in many other forms at the global, national and subnational level – for example, in transboundary water agreements that incorporate provisions for sharing water and its benefits (see Chapter 8 for examples).

Box 7.3 Place-based value systems, stewardship and legal personhood of the Whanganui River, New Zealand

The Maori Peoples generally recognize an indivisible whole, rather than breaking environmental complexities into its constituent components, such as riverbeds. This holistic approach avoids dividing water into sociocultural, economic and ecological values. From this perspective, a river, for example, is a living basin that carries its own meaning, life and character, built up over time and embodying both tangible and intangible components, many of which defy measurement and therefore assessment in terms of identifying trade-offs. In 2017, the Parliament of New Zealand conferred the Whanganui River legal personhood, settling an ancient dispute over the ownership of the river, the water and the land (Waitangi Tribunal, 1999; Parliament of New Zealand, 2017). Representatives of the local Maori community administer a fund for environmental enhancement and are responsible for keeping the intrinsic values that represent the essence of the river intact (Te Aho, 2018). The success of the Maori approach to stewardship is still subject to debate (e.g. Eckstein, 2018), but the legal personhood of the river reflects the community value system and its recognition by the national government.

Box 7.4 Value aspects of customary water law: Views from Africa

The Borana people of Ethiopia value water as either a source that you 'share in' as a member of a descent-based collective, or something to be 'shared out' to signify respect (Dahl and Megerssa, 1990). Customary principles of basic human needs are in line with human rights values, not only safeguarding the right to drinking water, but also often the right to water for irrigation, which supports family food security (Hellum et al., 2015). Customary socioterritorial principles see water as belonging to land and customary land tenure. Those who constructed and maintain water infrastructure exert claims to water stored or conveyed ('hydraulic property rights creation'), providing additional value components (economic and otherwise) to the previous ones. These principles are further shaped by first-come-first-served claims, by transfers that are based on kinship (marriage, inheritance), or by sharing with or without monetary compensation, and/or by force and violence.

Figure 7.2

Water connecting across the SDGs

Source: Adapted from PBL Netherlands Environmental Assessment Agency (2018, p. 13).

7.6 The values of water for peace, security and transboundary cooperation

The values of water in the context of conflict, peace and security are paradoxical. Whilst much has been written about the positive value of water in promoting peace, in many cases it was water itself that was a contributing factor to the conflict in the first place. Water, therefore, can at times act as a conflict indicator, as the source of contention, and/or as connector to support conflict resolution and peacebuilding. Growing threats to peace and security due to increasing environmental challenges and water insecurity are well documented today (Mach et al., 2019).

The need for transboundary water agreements often stems from water having high inter-state value and, therefore, being a potential source of conflict. International water cooperation initiatives have existed for millennia, the first document occurrence being the two Sumerian city-states of Lagash and Umma crafting an agreement to end a water dispute along the Tigris River in 2500 BCE – an agreement that is thought to be the first recorded treaty of any kind (Priscoli and Wolf, 2009). More than 3,600 treaties related to international water resources have been concluded between CE 805 and 1984 alone (FAO, 1984). *"Despite the complexity of the problems, records show that water disputes can be handled diplomatically. The last 50 years have seen only 37 acute disputes involving violence, compared to 150 treaties that have been signed. Nations value these agreements because they make international relations over water more stable and predictable"* (UNDESA, n.d.a).

It has been argued that a spirit of dialogue helps to transform water-related conflicts into cooperation (Wolf, 2017). One example of such dialogue-based cooperation is the Lake Chad region, where Cameroon, the Central African Republic, Chad, Libya, Niger and Nigeria cooperate in the Lake Chad Basin Commission, with the Democratic Republic of Congo, Egypt, the Republic of Congo and Sudan having observer status, to jointly improve the state of this shared water body and co-develop its resources to the benefit of the riparian population.[26] Although initially established to address water- and environment-related issues, the Commission has a broad mandate and has ventured into military cooperation to support peace (Assanvo et al., 2016).

Whilst much has been written about the positive value of water in promoting peace, in many cases it was water itself that was a contributing factor to the conflict in the first place

The value of water for peace can be further augmented by encouraging inclusive multi-track water diplomacy processes and evidence-informed political decision-making (Klimes and Yaari, 2019). Many initiatives support cooperative water management through value-based approaches. The Shared Waters Partnership of the Stockholm International Water Institute (SIWI) and the United Nations Development Programme (UNDP), for example, advances peace, security and environmental protection, while opening new opportunities for riparian states to sustainably develop their water resources.[27] Various tools help with conflict resolution, including the global and regional tools developed in the framework of the Water, Peace and Security (WPS) partnership that help predict conflicts in advance and seek to take action to improve cooperation among parties.[28] Fostering a better mutual understanding among countries to reconcile differences over shared waters is an underpinning of the UNESCO-led initiatives From Potential Conflict to Cooperation Potential (PCCP)[29] and Internationally Shared Aquifer Resource Management (ISARM).[30] For the SDG Indicator 6.5.2 (*"Proportion of transboundary basin area with an operational arrangement for water cooperation"*), as at December 2020, 130 countries responded positively in the second reporting exercise, out of 153 countries sharing water resources, testifying to the important value of transboundary water cooperation in the global development context. However, in the first reporting exercise in 2017–2018, only 17 countries reported that all their transboundary basins were covered by such arrangements (UNESCO/UNECE/UN-Water, 2018).

Further details on valuing water in the transboundary context, and on the role of transboundary watercourse agreements and the United Nations global water conventions, can be found in Section 8.2.2.

Water has also had a high value as a weapon since ancient times (Del Giacco et al., 2017). It was used as a strategic weapon during the Second World War (Lary, 2001), can be used selectively to favour or disfavour ethnic or social groups (Cleaver, 1995), and has seen a resurgence as a weapon in recent times (Von Lossow, 2016).

---

26 www.cblt.org/en.

27 www.watergovernance.org/programmes/shared-waters-partnership/#:~:text=The%20Shared%20Waters%20Partnership%20(SWP,sustainably%20develop%20their%20water%20resources.

28 waterpeacesecurity.org.

29 groundwaterportal.net/project/pccp

30 isarm.org/.

7.7 The values of water for mental health and life satisfaction

The values of water to human well-being extend well beyond its role in supporting direct physical life-sustaining functions, and include mental health, spiritual well-being, emotional balance and happiness. According to the *Constitution of the World Health Organization* (International Health Conference, 1946), *"health is a state of complete physical, mental and social well-being and not merely the absence of disease or infirmity."*[31]

The broader values of access to safe WASH, such as improving access to education and employment and enhancing security and dignity, and the disproportionate importance of these to women and girls, are covered in Chapter 4. In some cultures, water can have a more systemic role, so that access to it defines the wealth of the family/individual and hence social status. This increases the burdens of shame for those with limited access to water, who by consequence can only live up to lower hygienic standards and may be unable to fulfil normative expectations of hospitality, such as offering drinking water to guests. This can become a factor of discrimination (Stevenson et al., 2012). Distress and conflict can also be generated when water allocation, distribution and/or regulation are applied unequally and/or in contradiction to commonly held values in a given context (WWAP, 2019).

Water in landscapes has aesthetic values that contribute to mental health (Völker and Kistemann, 2011). Unsurprisingly, life satisfaction and happiness depend to a great extent on water (Guardiola et al., 2013). For example, access to water infrastructures was directly related to household life satisfaction in Bolivia (Guardiola et al., 2014), Pakistan (Nadeem et al., 2018) and the United Kingdom (Chenoweth et al., 2016). The expansion of piped water lines has been found to increase people's happiness regarding both monetary (Mahasuweerachai and Pangjai, 2018) and non-monetary outcomes (Devoto et al., 2012).

These, and other, values of water in the context of mental health, life satisfaction and happiness are much more than anecdotal. There is increasing attention to measuring well-being beyond traditional economic indicators. It is well known that Gross Domestic Product (GDP) is not a measure of well-being, sustainability or inequality (Hoekstra, 2019). Literally hundreds of 'beyond-GDP' alternatives are being explored based on the goal of creating a society that enhances broader aspects of well-being and is able to sustain a 'good life'. For example, in 2019 the New Zealand government presented the first budget with priorities explicitly based on well-being (Government of New Zealand, 2019). The first *World Happiness Report* was prepared to support a United Nations High-Level Meeting on 'Well-Being and Happiness: Defining a New Economic Paradigm' held at the UN in 2012. The latest report for 2020 (Helliwell et al., 2020) notes how blue spaces and local water quality are used as metrics for measuring subjective well-being, and that SDG 6 positively correlates with subjective well-being in all regions.

7.8 Integrating cultural values into decision-making

After understanding, categorizing or codifying cultural values, there is a need to identify ways and means of incorporating these values into decision-making. Examples of integrative methods to understand and integrate cultural values would include: adapted Environmental Flow Assessments that include cultural values (Tipa and Nelson, 2012); Social and Cultural Impact Assessments (Croal et al., 2012), and Cultural Heritage Management Plans, which are increasingly promoted worldwide (ICOMOS, 2019). These tools can help to better understand cultural values of water, reconcile antagonistic values, and build resilience with regard to current and future challenges, such as climate change. A fundamental need is the full and effective gender-sensitive participation of all stakeholders in decision-making, allowing everyone to express their own values in their own way.

---

[31] The definition has not been amended since 1948.

Certain tools, such as cultural mapping, have been recognized by UNESCO as crucial to preserving the world's intangible and tangible cultural assets (UNESCO Bangkok Office, 2017). Cultural mapping can help articulate the holistic values of local and indigenous peoples to decision- and policy-makers, who may favour economic values over the health and well-being of waterscapes. Cultural mapping can be integrated in and used to inform environmental flow assessments, for instance to record the cultural significance and social function of certain water bodies, and to rank their associated values for water management schemes (Tipa and Nelson, 2012).

Further ways and means to accommodate multiple values and value systems for water are covered in Chapter 9.

7.9 Heritage and water values

Water is often a prominent component of heritage values through both tangible and intangible benefits that can be categorized by: the acquisition, management and control of water; the various types of water use; the management of constraints and the control of natural water; water and health; water quality and the associated representations; water-related knowledge, knowhow, myths and symbols; and cultural landscapes of water (ICOMOS, 2015).

Given the role of water in all societies, sites whose heritage value is associated with water abound on the UNESCO World Heritage List. The 39 sites on the List that represent both natural and cultural values are water-related (Willems and Van Schaik, 2015; UNESCO, 2011). The same holds true for water-related heritage that is not listed as a World Heritage property (Hein, 2020). The importance of protecting water heritage in order to achieve SDG 6, especially in relation to SDG Target 6.6 on the protection and restoration of water-related ecosystems, has been noted.[32]

7.10 Creating wider space for cultural values

A truly holistic understanding/approach to IWRM can help integrate different stakeholder values, if applied cognizant of the diversity of meanings and values of water, and the relationships they create within and between societies (Krause and Strang, 2016). However, while IWRM can assume the paradigm of control over nature and be a resource-centric, utilitarian approach, it also remains a theoretically open and adaptive approach that can very well include nature conservation as a positive outcome, and that the river basin or lake is supported to be able to reach their fullest purpose. Better recognition of this dimension holds potential for more holistic approaches to water management and sustainable development in which local, indigenous and traditional values and knowledge can contribute to addressing contemporary water resources challenges.

Social learning, individual and collective psychology and emotions play a crucial role in interiorizing values. Values influence human behaviour and are learned and expressed in interaction with others. UNESCO's Education for Sustainable Development (ESD)[33] aims to empower learners to take informed decisions and responsible actions for environmental integrity, economic viability and a just society, for present and future generations, while respecting cultural diversity, including as related to water. Community initiatives, water museums, local interpretation centres and their networks[34] can be complementary tools to formal education in this endeavour, as is harnessing the power of engaging youth (UNPFA, 2014) in valuing water holistically.

---

[32] For example, participants' understanding of the importance of protecting water heritage in order to achieve the SDG Target 6.6 has been pursued during the session on water and heritage of the UNESCO International Water Conference held in May 2019. For further information, see en.unesco.org/waterconference/programme.

[33] en.unesco.org/themes/education-sustainable-development.

[34] Such as the Global Network of Water Museums (WAMU-NET), www.watermuseums.net/.

Chapter 8

Regional perspectives

8.1 **UNESCO Office in Nairobi**
Jayakumar Ramasamy and Samuel Partey

8.2 **UNECE**
Rémy Kinna, Sonja Koeppel, Diane Guerrier and Chantal Demilecamps

8.3 **UNECLAC**
Silvia Saravia Matus and Marina Gil Sevilla

8.4 **UNESCAP**
Solene Le Doze
With contributions from:
Yumiko Asayama (Asia-Pacific Water Forum)

8.5 **UNESCWA**
Ziad Khayat and Carol Chouchani Cherfane

8.1 Sub-Saharan Africa

8.1.1 Water resources and challenges

Africa's freshwater resources are estimated to be nearly 9% of the world's total (Gonzalez Sanchez et al., 2020). However, these resources are unevenly distributed, with the six most water-rich countries in Central and Western Africa holding 54% of the continent's total resources and the 27 most water-poor countries holding only 7% (UNESCO Regional Office for Eastern Africa, 2020). Large rivers include the Congo, Nile, Zambezi and Niger. Lake Victoria (spreading across Kenya, Tanzania and Uganda) is the second-largest freshwater lake in the world by surface area, while Lake Tanganyika (shared among Burundi, the Democratic Republic of the Congo, Tanzania and Zambia) is the second-largest by volume, as well as the second-deepest freshwater lake in the world. This notwithstanding, Africa is the second-driest continent in the world, after Australia. Arid and semi-arid areas cover about two thirds of the continent. About 73% of the total population of Sub-Saharan Africa did not use safely managed drinking water services in 2017 (WHO/UNICEF, 2019a). An estimated 14% of Africa's population (about 160 million people) currently live under conditions of water scarcity (Hasan et al., 2019), due in part to the uneven distribution of water resources as well as inequalities in the access to clean and potable water services (UNEP, 2002).

Willingness to pay for improved water provision services was found to be especially high among rural households

The *Africa Water Vision 2025* (UNECA/AU/AfDB, 2003, p. 2), which calls for "A*n Africa where there is an equitable and sustainable use and management of water resources for poverty alleviation, socio-economic development, regional cooperation, and the environment*", offers a context within which water security and sustainable management of water resources could be achieved. However, rapid population growth, inappropriate water governance and institutional arrangements, depletion of water resources through pollution, environmental degradation, deforestation, and low and unsustainable financing of investments in water supply and sanitation are some of the main challenges to the achievement of Agenda 2063[35] and the Sustainable Development Goal (SDG) 6 on the continent (NASAC, 2014).

8.1.2 Adopted methodologies for valuing water

In Sub-Saharan Africa, valuing water has been a challenging task for many researchers and development experts, due at least in part to limited baseline historical data. Researchers studying the value of water have focused mainly on using the actual price paid or the willingness to pay (WTP) from the consumer's point of view by adopting the contingent valuation (CV) method (Markantonis et al., 2018). For example, Kaliba et al. (2003) used the CV method to estimate the WTP to improve domestic water supply in rural areas of central Tanzania, while Bogale and Urgessa (2012) used the CV method to study the willingness of rural households in the Haramaya District in eastern Ethiopia to pay for improved water service provision, and the determinants of water value. Similar studies, such as Markantonis et al. (2018) and Arouna and Dabbert (2012), have used the CV method to estimate WTP in the West African countries of Burkina Faso, Benin and Niger. In South Africa, Yokwe (2009) used a mixed approach by applying the residual valuation method (RVM), WTP and cost-based approaches (CBA) (i.e. accounting costs of operation and maintenance) to evaluate water productivity and values per crop, per farm and by scheme.

8.1.3 Valuing water in Sub-Saharan Africa: Important cases and results

Studies valuing water in Sub-Saharan Africa have mostly focused on domestic water use. Below are the results of selected cases of water valuation on the continent.

West Africa

In West Africa, Markantonis et al. (2018) used the CV method to investigate a household's WTP for domestic water in the transboundary Mékrou River basin in Burkina Faso, Benin and Niger, and also explored the payment for domestic water provision in relation to poverty. The

---

[35] Agenda 2063 is Africa's blueprint and master plan for transforming Africa into the global powerhouse of the future. au.int/en/agenda2063/overview.

study revealed that depending on the state of wealth, households in the Mékrou River basin were, on average, willing to pay €2.81 per month for a domestic water provision network. The survey estimated that the average maximum WTP per household and per month is CFA2089 (€3.18), whereas the average minimum WTP is CFA1532 (€2.34). The maximum and minimum WTP amounts were found to be almost 10% higher in Burkina Faso and around 5% lower in Niger. Meanwhile, the results on daily household domestic water consumption and expenses revealed that the residents of Niger had the highest expenses for domestic water (mean value = CFA109.55), which was more than 30% higher than the basin-wide average. In contrast, Benin was the country with the lowest mean annual expenses (CFA72) (Markantonis et al., 2018).

East Africa

Kaliba et al. (2003) estimated the WTP to improve community-based rural water utilities in the Dodoma and Singida Regions of Tanzania. With surveys covering 30 villages in the two regions, the study revealed *"respondents who wanted to increase water supply in Dodoma Region were willing to pay 32 Tsh above the existing tariff of 20 Tsh/bucket. In the Singida Region, the analogous amount was 91 Tsh per household per year above the existing user fee of 508 Tsh per household per year. If the tariff or user fees have to be increased, the estimated average potential revenue for the surveyed villages was 252 million Tsh/year (US$265 263) in the Dodoma Region, and 5.2 million Tsh/year (US$5474) in the Singida Region." (p. 119)*

Similarly, Bogale and Urgessa (2017) studied the willingness of rural households in the Haramaya district in eastern Ethiopia to pay for improved water service provision, and the determinants of water value. On the basis of primary data obtained from a survey conducted on randomly selected rural households, the study revealed that the mean WTP of households equalled US$0.273 per 20-litre jerrycan. Using a bivariate probit model, the study concluded that WTP for improved water service provision was also determined by factors such as household income, education, sex, time spent to fetch water, water treatment practice, quality of water and expenditure on water.

Southern Africa

Yokwe (2009) applied the residual valuation method (RVM), WTP and CBA (i.e. accounting costs of operation and maintenance) to evaluate water productivity and values under two irrigation schemes (Zanyokwe and Thabina) in South Africa. The study revealed that in the Zanyokwe scheme, the WTP per m^3 among active farmers was, with ZAR0.03, lower than the gross margin of output (ZAR0.69), while the accounting cost per m^3 of water (ZAR0.084) was less than the gross margin. In the Thabina scheme, active farmers were willing to pay ZAR0.19 per m^3 of water, which is three times the proposed costs of operations and maintenance (O&M – ZAR0.062) per m^3 of water used. The study showed that both the accounting cost and WTP were less than the gross margin per m^3 of water in the Zanyokwe scheme.

Farolfi et al. (2007) assessed which factors determined the household-level WTP for an improvement in water quantity and quality in Eswatini, using the CV method. A Tobit model was applied to a survey among 374 households. As could have been expected, WTP was shown to be significantly influenced by household income, but the distance of water sources (in both rural and urban environments), and the household's head's age, level of education and gender were also important factors. Furthermore, it was found that current water consumption negatively impacted WTP, in other words: the more water a household consumed, the less it was willing to pay to increase its quantity – but that same household turned out to be willing to pay more to improve the water's quality. WTP for improved water provision services was found to be especially high among rural households.

8.2 The Pan-European region

8.2.1 Valuing water in the Pan-European region

Valuing water is a challenging task within any single jurisdiction, hence doing so across borders presents even greater challenges. Within the Pan-European region as defined by the United Nations Economic Commission for Europe (UNECE), the development of overarching frameworks such as the 2000 European Union Water Framework Directive (European Parliament/Council of the European Union, 2000) demonstrates the increasing significance that is being placed on valuing water. Nonetheless, efforts to value water, especially in a transboundary context, remain limited in scope and often use different approaches. Shared water management between states is very advanced within the UNECE Pan-European region (United Nations/UNESCO, 2018), supported by the Convention on the Protection and Use of Transboundary Watercourses and International Lakes (Water Convention) (UNECE, 1992). Hence, this section focuses on efforts and approaches at valuing water in transboundary contexts rather than any national examples.

8.2.2 Valuing water within transboundary basins: Case studies and benefits of cooperation

The Pan-European region contains few basin agreements and river basin organizations (RBOs) that include an explicit methodology on the quantitative valuation of water in their legal and institutional frameworks. Rather, the discernable approaches to valuing water quantitatively in the transboundary context are more targeted on specific aspects of managing transboundary water resources, such as flood management, disaster risk reduction (DRR), early-warning systems (EWS) and ecosystem services.

The Kura River basin shared by Azerbaijan and Georgia has been the focus of several iterations of frameworks for valuing water (OECD, 2015a). The initial phase aimed at conducting an inventory of the benefits and related values of cooperative management of the Kura River for both basin states. This was based on a framework developed in 2013–2015 under the Water Convention (see Table 8.1 below), whose aim it is to support transboundary cooperation.

As a second step, "*a methodology for assessing the net benefits of trans-boundary cooperation under different scenarios was developed, which included both the assessment of the gross benefits and costs of coordinated action*" (OECD, 2015a, p. 48). This methodology was tested using two Kura River basin case studies: water quantity in the transboundary Jandari Lake and flooding issues along the Kura River. Lastly, mechanisms were suggested on how to realize these benefits.

In summary, while "*a thorough assessment of the costs and benefits of trans-boundary cooperation in the two case studies was not possible, due to a lack of basic, quantitative data on water use and of economic information and data*" (OECD, 2015a, p. 48), it was determined that the collective economic benefits for both basin states outweighed the collective investment costs by more than 15 times, in comparison to a scenario of not acting on flood management within the basin. As a result, the installation of a joint EWS was recommended. Several general conclusions relevant to valuing water in a transboundary context also emerged. Firstly, "*economics should inform the decision-making process from the very beginning, hand-in-hand with environmental data*" (OECD, 2015a, pp. 48–49). Hence, investment in data collection systems is recognized as being of vital importance and while it comes at an additional cost, that cost can be compensated by the benefits of effective cooperation. Moreover, the inclusion of economic thinking in transboundary water management in this context is constrained by the lack of an appropriate legal framework on regional use of water resources. Thus, the two basin countries could, for example, establish a bilateral commission, based on a bilateral agreement (OECD, 2015a).

Another example is the Elbe River, shared between the Czech Republic and Germany. In 2002, heavy rainfall caused disastrous floods, which led to significant economic damage, costed within Germany at around €9 billion (Teichmann and Berghöfer, 2010). After this event, an extended CBA was conducted on the value of developing a more integrated approach to flood risk management. Three possible options were assessed: "*a. to relocate selected dykes, thereby permanently enlarging the river bed; b. to establish flood polders, specially designated flood retention areas which can be opened for flooding upon demand; c. a combination of a) and b)*" (Teichmann and Berghöfer, 2010, p.1). The CBA framework that was developed allowed for the comparison of policy options as regards to: "*(i) their maintenance costs, (ii) the annually avoided flood damage (based on previous flood incidences), (iii) their biodiversity value and (iv) their nutrient retention value*" (Teichmann and Berghöfer, 2010, p.1). Importantly, this CBA framework to assess the value of integrated flood risk management not only accounted for monetary costs and benefits, but also included two other wider ecosystem service benefits in the calculation and assessment, namely: the water purification function performed by biological decomposition in natural floodplains, and the restoration of riparian biodiversity and habitats. Ultimately, the CBA of several ecosystem services revealed "*polder flood retention areas to provide cost-effective protection against flood damage, with additional ecological benefits*" (Teichmann and Berghöfer, 2010, p.1).

Investment in data collection systems is recognized as being of vital importance and while it comes at an additional cost, that cost can be compensated by the benefits of effective cooperation

At a broader regional scale, the 2017 joint Adelphi and Regional Environmental Centre for Central Asia (CAREC) study on Central Asia sought to assess the general value of water cooperation via a calculation of the costs of inaction compared to the interrelated benefits of transboundary management. The aim of the study was to develop "*a comprehensive analysis and a monetary value of both the direct and indirect impacts of inadequate transboundary cooperation on water management in the region*" (Adelphi/CAREC, 2017, p. I). 'Inaction' in this regard was defined not as a complete lack of action, but rather as measuring the gap between existing limited cooperation activities and the benefits that would result for the future development of the region from full cooperation over transboundary water resources. Using existing frameworks and regional stakeholder engagement, this study identified 11 types of costs that stemmed from suboptimal water management (Figure 8.1).

The study recognized that a full quantification across all 11 types of costs of inaction would be difficult, particularly if attempting to integrate significant indirect costs that cannot be directly attributed to transboundary water governance (Adelphi/CAREC, 2017). Despite this inherent difficulty, the study noted that "*it is important not to neglect these indirect costs of suboptimal water management because they demonstrate that the true value of water cooperation is far greater than the direct economic benefits that can be derived from better water management*" (Adelphi/CAREC, 2017, p. VII).

In order to reach an approximate valuation, the project subsequently drew on three previous studies (UNDP, 2005; World Bank, 2016c; Shokhrukh-Mirzo et al. 2015) that calculated monetary values of proxies for three cost categories: agricultural losses, inefficient electricity trade and lack of access to finance due to non-cooperation. In sum, total costs for insufficient cooperation were calculated at more than US$4.5 billion per year, yet this calculation was subsequently qualified as not reflecting the true costs, given that certain elements were deemed to be systematically undervalued. Overall, it was posited that "*the **quality** of water governance will have an enormous impact on future economic development* [emphasis added]" (Adelphi/CAREC, 2017, p. VIII) in the region. The study then mapped out how cooperation at different levels can transform a 'business-as-usual' approach to transboundary cooperation. In addition, several entry points for mutually beneficial solutions were proposed to address existing inaction on the premise that "*the scale of these costs contains significant opportunities as better water management and closer cooperation can lower these costs substantially*" (Adelphi/CAREC, 2017, p. III).

Figure 8.1

Type of costs resulting from limited cooperation

Source: Adelphi/CAREC (2017, p. VI).

Many, but not all, benefits can undergo a quantitative assessment. Only in some cases can the monetary value of the benefits be assessed

In terms of available tools, the Water Convention has developed two specific approaches with the objective of identifying a range of benefits of transboundary water cooperation, to increase the value of shared water management in transboundary contexts. The first approach focuses on the identification, assessment and communication of the benefits of transboundary water cooperation, in order to assist countries in reaping the numerous benefits of joint action (Table 8.1). It provides step-by-step guidance on how to carry out a benefit assessment exercise as well as how the assessment of benefits can be integrated into policy processes to foster and strengthen transboundary water cooperation (UNECE, 2015). Many, but not all, benefits can undergo a quantitative assessment. Only in some cases can the monetary value of the benefits be assessed.

The second, related approach is the Water–Food–Energy–Ecosystem Nexus approach. The Transboundary Basin Nexus Assessment (TBNA) methodology aims to jointly identify intersectoral issues in the respective transboundary basins and to address them through concrete policy and technical solutions to be applied at regional, basin, national and local levels. One such dialogue, underpinned by an analysis, that combined both approaches to valuing transboundary water cooperation was conducted in 2016–2017 in the Drina River basin mainly shared by Bosnia and Herzegovina, Montenegro and Serbia (UNECE, 2017). The assessment concluded that coordinating the operation of the existing dams in the basin would not only allow for better flood management, but would also improve national energy security, increase electricity export opportunities and reduce annual greenhouse gas (GHG) emissions in the long term.

What is clear from this brief examination of the few available selected case studies within UNECE's Pan-European region is that: a) no single unified approach exists to quantitatively valuing water; b) within transboundary contexts, quantitatively valuing water is significantly

Table 8.1
Typology of the potential benefits of transboundary water cooperation

Origin of benefits	Benefits for economic activities	Benefits beyond economic activities
Improved water management	**Economic benefits** Expanded activity and productivity in different economic sectors (aquaculture, irrigated agriculture, mining, energy generation, industrial production, nature-based tourism) Reduced cost of carrying out productive activities Reduced economic impacts of water-related hazards (floods, droughts) Increased value of property	**Social and environmental benefits** Health impacts from improved water quality and reduced risk of water-related disasters Employment and reduced poverty impacts of the economic benefits Improved access to services (such as electricity and water supply) Improved satisfaction due to preservation of cultural resources or access to recreational opportunities Increased ecological integrity and reduced habitat degradation and biodiversity loss Strengthened scientific knowledge on water status
Enhanced trust	**Regional economic cooperation benefits** Development of regional markets for goods, services and labour Increase in cross-border investments Development of transnational infrastructure networks	**Peace and security benefits** Strengthening of international law Increased geopolitical stability and strengthened diplomatic relations New opportunities from increased trust (joint initiative and investments) Reduced risk and avoided cost of conflict and savings from reduced military spending Creation of shared basin identity

Source: UNECE (2015, Table 2, p. 19).

more challenging as the data that are required to base calculations upon are often lacking, while the countries that share a water resource often put different emphases on values, needs and priorities attached to water-related sectors; c) almost all elements that can be valued at all, are valued on the basis of approximations and thus inherently undervalued, especially due to the lack of data and the inability to quantify indirect benefits; and d) considering that transboundary water cooperation in the UNECE Pan-European region is among the most advanced worldwide, it can be assumed that countries significantly value transboundary cooperation and are therefore eagerly engaging in it (United Nations/UNESCO, 2018). Notwithstanding these general conclusions, several broad-based approaches exist for identifying the intersectoral benefits of transboundary water cooperation on a case-by-case basis. These benefits, when strengthened, can consequently help increase the value of transboundary water management by reducing the economic and other costs of 'inaction' or insufficient cooperation in shared basins.

8.3 Latin America and the Caribbean

Latin America and the Caribbean (LAC) are a water-abundant region. According to the latest regional estimations, it possesses an average water endowment per inhabitant of close to 28,000 cubic metres per year, which is more than four times the world average of 6,000 m^3/inhabitant/year (FAO, 2016). Similarly, it holds the largest wetland in the world, the Pantanal, with an area of 200 thousand square kilometres, which regulates the hydrology of large areas of the continent (UNEP-WCMC, 2016), while the Amazon River has the largest discharge in the world: it contains much more water than the Nile, the Yangtze and the Mississippi combined. These facts often feed a misperception that water in the LAC region is easily and equally available to all citizens. This is far from the truth.

Despite comprising a third of the renewable resources of freshwater in the world, this endowment is very unequally distributed. Water is found mainly in rural and natural Amazonian areas, while expanding urban areas in arid or semi-desert zones (such as Lima, Santiago or Buenos Aires) or those located at high altitudes with smaller water catchment areas (such as Bogotá, Mexico City and Quito) face greater challenges in securing a stable access to water. The same is true for the small island states of the Caribbean (UNECLAC, forthcoming).

If the levels of stress due to water scarcity (FAO, 2018b) are analysed not at the national level, but disaggregated at the level of river basins or specific territories, localized scenarios of high water pressure in LAC are again identified in the most populated areas, which at the same time are centres of economic activity. The most relevant cases are those of the Central Valley in Chile, the Cuyo region in Argentina, the coastline of Peru and southern Ecuador, the Cauca and Magdalena Valleys in Colombia, the Bolivian *altiplano*, the Brazilian Northeast, the Pacific coast of Central America, and much of northern Mexico (FAO, 2016). All these areas report water stress levels above 80% (which is considered extremely high) for periods ranging from 3 to 12 months per year (Mekonnen et al., 2015). According to Manson et al. (2013), in Mexico per capita water available is currently 64% lower than it was in the middle of the last century, due to population growth. In the Andes mountain range of South America, there has also been substantial loss of glaciers, estimated at 22.9 Gt per year between March 2000 and April 2018 (Dussaillant et al., 2019), the equivalent of nine million Olympic swimming pools per year.

Water stress in the LAC region has fuelled a number of conflicts, as various sectors, including agriculture, hydroelectricity, mining and even drinking water and sanitation, are competing over scarce resources

Water stress in the region has fuelled a number of conflicts, as various sectors, including agriculture, hydroelectricity, mining and even drinking water and sanitation, are competing over scarce resources. While the agricultural sector is the largest water user with up to 71% of all water withdrawals, followed by 17% used as drinking water and for sanitation, and only 12% for industrial purposes (FAO, 2016), the use of water in mining is frequently associated with a high potential for conflict with the local population. This is because mining is concentrated in high-altitude areas with little water and with the capacity to contaminate springs of water sources (head basins or 'headwater') or in arid or semi-arid areas where reservoirs are located (UNECLAC, forthcoming). In the case of hydroelectric dams, whose use is not accounted for in withdrawals (although evaporation is currently recognized as a relevant source of water loss), conflicts often emerge in the contexts of pass-through plants with little or no previous storage, thus leaving long sections of channels without water, which could generate downstream conflicts (Embid and Martín, 2017).

Water usage allocation, whether in the form of concessions (the most widespread mechanism used in the region) or water rights (as in the case in Chile), has not been very effective in reducing conflicts nor in controlling overexploitation and pollution of water bodies throughout the region. In fact, about a quarter of the river stretches in the region are affected by severe pathogenic contamination, with monthly concentrations of faecal coliform bacteria in excess of 10,000cfu/L (which increased by almost two thirds from 1990 to 2010). The main source of this kind of pollution is domestic sewage (UNEP, 2016).

Some of the major obstacles in securing effective allocation processes are connected to poor regulation, missing incentives and/or lack of investment. All these factors ultimately reflect the low value that is largely attributed to water resources in the region. For instance, in LAC, the average proportion of wastewater that is safely treated is just below 40%. The proportions of wastewater properly treated in 2018 were 22% in Argentina, 23% in Colombia, 34% in Brazil, 39% in Peru, 43% in Ecuador, 51% in Mexico and 72% in Chile (UNDESA, n.d.b). The costs of water use or maintenance (once the concession or right of use is granted), are usually nill or insignificant for hydroelectric plants, mining companies and even farmers; and sometimes these costs are not even included in their economic balances (Embid and Martín, 2017). The latter represents an implicit subsidy that does not reflect the strategic value of water in the multiple production processes and under a context of climate change. This becomes particularly problematic when water becomes scarce as conflicts for multiple uses increase and there are frequently no pricing mechanism in place to establish adequate signalling that may lead to economizing or restricting usage. Lastly, most countries in the region have not assigned sufficient funds for proper law enforcement in cases of pollution or overexploitation.

Despite the many examples of water evidently not being adequately valued for the varied and irreplaceable economic, social and environmental benefits it provides, there have been some promising attitudes and innovative initiatives in LAC.

Regarding access to drinking water, a World Bank study using CV to reveal preferences indicated that the poorest urban households in Central America were willing to pay much more per cubic metre for a piped service (Walker et al., 2000). A more recent study for Guatemala registered an increase of over 200% in the WTP for reliable supplies of safe drinking water (Vásquez and Espaillat, 2016). Also, in rural areas of El Salvador a very high WTP for drinking water and sanitation was evident (Perez-Pineda and Quintanilla-Armijo, 2013). These findings suggest that there is great need among this vulnerable segment to access water and sanitation services.

Some of the major obstacles in securing effective allocation processes are connected to poor regulation, missing incentives and/or lack of investment

The payment for ecosystem services (PES) approach, related specifically to water, has been a positive experience in recognizing the role and value of ecosystems in flow regulation, protection against storms, and the provision of water from basins in terms of both quality and quantity. Since these services are often dependent on sufficient forest cover, payments are aligned to forest conservation and regeneration. Payments for hydrological services and forests have been implemented in Colombia, Costa Rica, Ecuador and Mexico (Sánchez, 2015). Beltrán (2013) documents the case of PROBOSQUE, a decentralized body of the Ministry of the Environment of the government of Mexico. Between 2003 and 2011, PROBOSQUE has invested US$16.3 million in 142,087 hectares, belonging to 219,218 beneficiaries, to ensure that forests were able to provide hydrological services. Another positive experience of PES related to water is found in Costa Rica´s FONAFIFO. FONAFIFO, or *Fondo Nacional de Financiamiento Forestal*, is a decentralized body of the Ministry of Environment and Energy of Costa Rica. The programme is funded by a fixed tax on hydrocarbons and between 2003 and 2011, about 9% of the national surface, equivalent to 51,000 square kilometres or 17.4% of all forested areas, was under this scheme of PES (Manson et al., 2013). Most of these hectares were previously used for cattle grazing, so that the scheme has also contributed to reducing GHG emissions in the country over the last decades (Saravia-Matus et al., 2019).

Lastly, an innovative approach that aims at better valuing and protecting the environmental benefits of water is found in Colombia. In 2017, the Constitutional Court recognized the Atrato River in the province of Chocó as a subject of law. The rights of the river include its protection, conservation, maintenance and, in this specific case, restoration. The court ordered the State to set up a commission of guardians and to implement a protection plan against over-proliferation of mining activity in the area (Benöhr and González, 2017).

Departing from the value of water bodies per se, the *Constitution of Ecuador* (Constitución de la República de Ecuador, 2008) also brings another interesting example of the valuing of the environment. In its 7th Chapter, Article 71, it expresses that nature or *Pacha Mama* has rights to ensure its reproduction. Ecuador became the first country in the world to formally recognize the rights of nature and establish a biocentric Constitution. Yet, others have followed, such as Bolivia, which in 2010 proclaimed the Law of the Rights of Mother Earth (*Ley de Derechos de la Madre Tierra*) (Benöhr and González, 2017).

While these legal precepts are of extreme relevance, it is necessary, as with any other law or grant of rights, to secure proper enforcement and policing. In this respect, regulation and monitoring as well as well-aligned incentives are essential in the region to not only ensure a better appreciation of the role and value of water but also to prevent its overexploitation and pollution, particularly in a context of increasing climate instability.

8.4 Asia and the Pacific

8.4.1 Context

The Asia and the Pacific region is home to 60% of the world's population but has only 36% of the world's water resources, causing its per capita water availability to be the lowest in the world (APWF, 2009).

Due to population growth, urbanization and increased industrialization, water competition among sectors has become more severe in the region, threatening agricultural production and food security while also affecting water quality. Unsustainable water withdrawals are a major concern in the region, as some countries withdraw unsustainable proportions of their freshwater supply – exceeding half of the total water availability – and seven of the world's 15 biggest abstractors of groundwater are in Asia and the Pacific (UNESCAP/UNESCO/ILO/UN Environment, 2018). Research suggests that groundwater use will increase 30% by 2050 (UNESCAP/UNESCO/ILO/UN Environment, 2018; ADB, 2016). Severe water stress due to the demands from irrigation is observed in the North China Plain and northwest India, which are known to be the major food baskets of the region (Shah, 2005). Water is therefore a relatively scarce and valuable resource in the region, and water scarcity is likely to worsen due to the negative impacts of climate change. In addition to the low levels of per capita water availability, high levels of water pollution are observed in the region, with more than 80% of the wastewater generated in the region's developing countries not being treated (Corcoran et al., 2010).

Wastewater remains an underutilized resource in the region. There is therefore an urgent need in Asia and the Pacific to tap into wastewater, as well as to tackle water pollution and promote water efficiency, including from the industrial sector (UNESCAP, 2019). This is particularly urgent in the region's least developed countries, on islands and in countries where water resources are particularly scarce.

The region has seen diverse positive water-valuing initiatives that leverage new financial, governance and partnership models. In China, water stewardships schemes are being developed, including with the support of the Alliance for Water Stewardship's projects in Kunshan (Alliance for Water Stewardship, 2018). These schemes are defined as *"the use of water that is socially and culturally equitable, environmentally sustainable and economically beneficial, achieved through a stakeholder-inclusive process that involves site and catchment-based actions"* (Alliance for Water Stewardship, n.d.). In Malaysia, an evaluation of the aquatic ecosystem services of the Putrajaya lake and wetland was carried out as part of the Malaysia UNESCO Cooperation Programme (MUCP), aiming to inform decision-making in terms of management and to ensure public understanding and support for decisions made (Ghani, 2016). In the Murray–Darling Basin in Australia, a cap-and-trade agricultural water market has been implemented based on secure tradable water rights, recognizing the value of water to current and future generations by restricting total consumptive water use to an administratively determined environmentally sustainable level (Australian Water Partnership, 2016).

8.4.2 Case study: Valuing groundwater in the city of Kumamoto, Japan

Kumamoto is located in a volcanic region, with groundwater aquifers on which over one million people depend for drinking water and industrial use (Kumamoto City, 2020a). Scientific research has established that paddy fields and rice farming in the middle Shira River watershed area contribute up to one third of the groundwater recharge. Consequently, the reduction of paddy fields due to the building of residential areas and crop conversion has resulted in a decrease of the groundwater resources in Kumamoto (Japanese Ministry of Environment, 2015).[36]

---

[36] Without taking any action, groundwater was projected to decrease to 563 million m^3 by 2024, down from roughly 600 million m^3 in 2007. The Kumamoto region aims to conserve the amount of groundwater recharge by 6.36 million m^3 in 2024 (Kumamoto City, 2020b).

To reverse this trend, in 2004, the city government has provided subsidies to farmers in the form of a PES scheme (Japanese Ministry of Environment, 2010). The aim was to incentivize them to flood their crop-rotated paddy fields with water from the nearby Shira River during the fallow period (between May and October) as a part of their farming practice (United Nations, 2013). The payments cover management and preparation costs based on a per hectare basis and period, as presented in Table 8.2. Both public and private sector parties joined the initiative, incentivized by the public ordinance to annually report on quantities of groundwater extraction and recharged, as well as financial support and provision of workers.

As a result, quantities of groundwater recharge have increased since 2004, with, in 2018, 12.2 million m^3 of groundwater recharged (Kumamoto City, 2020c).[37] Groundwater extraction has also been reduced, to a total of 104.7 million m^3. Converted into the rates at which consumers are charged for water in this region, the amount of water recharged would have a value equivalent to US$27,145,300.[38] A total financial contribution of US$6.46 million was provided from 2004 to 2018[39] to ensure more water security for people, the economy and the environment of the Kumamoto region.

Table 8.2

PES of the groundwater recharge project of rice paddy fields in Kumamoto, Japan

Period of recharge	Subsidy per m^3 recharged
0.5 month (more than 15 days and less than 25 days)	JP¥8.25 (US$0.078)
1 month (more than 25 days and less than 40 days)	JP¥11 (US$0.12)
1.5 months (more than 40 days and less than 55 days)	JP¥13.75 (US$0.13)
2 months (more than 55 days and less than 70 days)	JP¥16.5 (US$0.16)
2.5 months (more than 70 days and less than 85 days)	JP¥19.25 (US$0.18)
3 months (more than 85 days and less than 100 days)	JP¥22 (US$0.21)
3.5 months (more than 100 days and less than 115 days)	JP¥24.75 (US$0.24)
4 months (more than 115 days and less than 120 days)	JP¥27.5 (US$0.26)

Source: Kumamoto City (2020d).

Valuing groundwater also institutionalized the multi-stakeholder partnership between the water and the agro-forestry sectors in 11 municipalities. For instance, the establishment of the Kumamoto Groundwater Foundation in 2012 supplemented the existing programmes implemented by the City of Kumamoto: another groundwater recharge project in the fallow fields during the winter season and a water offset programme (Japanese Ministry of Environment, 2015).

The adoption of the PES approach for groundwater conservation in Kumamoto has also had an additional positive effect on the private sectors' water management practices, including the enhancement of companies' corporate social responsibility policies for water sustainability through water stewardship certificates in their factories.

---

37 78,155,820 m^3 for tapped water, 10,577,233 m^3 for agriculture and aquaculture, and 15,960,929 m^3 for industries, buildings, households, etc. Data from an internal document of Water Conservation Section of Kumamoto City.

38 Data from an internal document of Water Conservation Section of Kumamoto City. The water bill rate of Kumamoto City is available from www.kumamoto-waterworks.jp/waterworks_article/11113/. The calculation method is available from Kumamoto Groundwater Foundation, kumamotogwf.or.jp/File/doc/donation/bessi.pdf.

39 Data from an internal document of the Water Conservation Section of Kumamoto City.

8.5 The Arab region

8.5.1 Regional setting

Few other regions value water as much as the water-scarce Arab region. For thousands of years, the identity, lives and livelihoods of peoples in the region have been closely tied to the ability to access and benefit from water. Civilizations flourished along the Nile and between the Tigris and Euphrates river systems, based on irrigated agriculture while navigation allowed their economies to prosper. Communities extended along coastlines thanks to coastal aquifers. Nomads survived because of *wadis*, oases and intermittent streams that speckled the desert landscape and provided an anchor for modern cities. Ingenious indigenous methods were developed, such as the *aflaj* canalization system in Oman, which ensured water was valued and shared at the community level and which in 2006 was included as a unique system of water management in the UNESCO World Heritage List.

In the Arab region, nearly 86% of the population, or nearly 362 million people, live under conditions of water scarcity or absolute water scarcity (UNESCWA, 2019a). Fourteen countries in the region use more than 100% of their available freshwater resources, which strains efforts to achieve SDG Target 6.4 that aims to reduce the number of people facing water stress, as shown in Figure 8.2. This scarcity has increased dependency on transboundary waters, non-renewable groundwater resources and non-conventional water resources. The quantity of freshwater that can be abstracted in a sustainable way would probably even be lower if water quality considerations were included.

Figure 8.2

Level of water stress in the Arab region, as per SDG Indicator 6.4.2

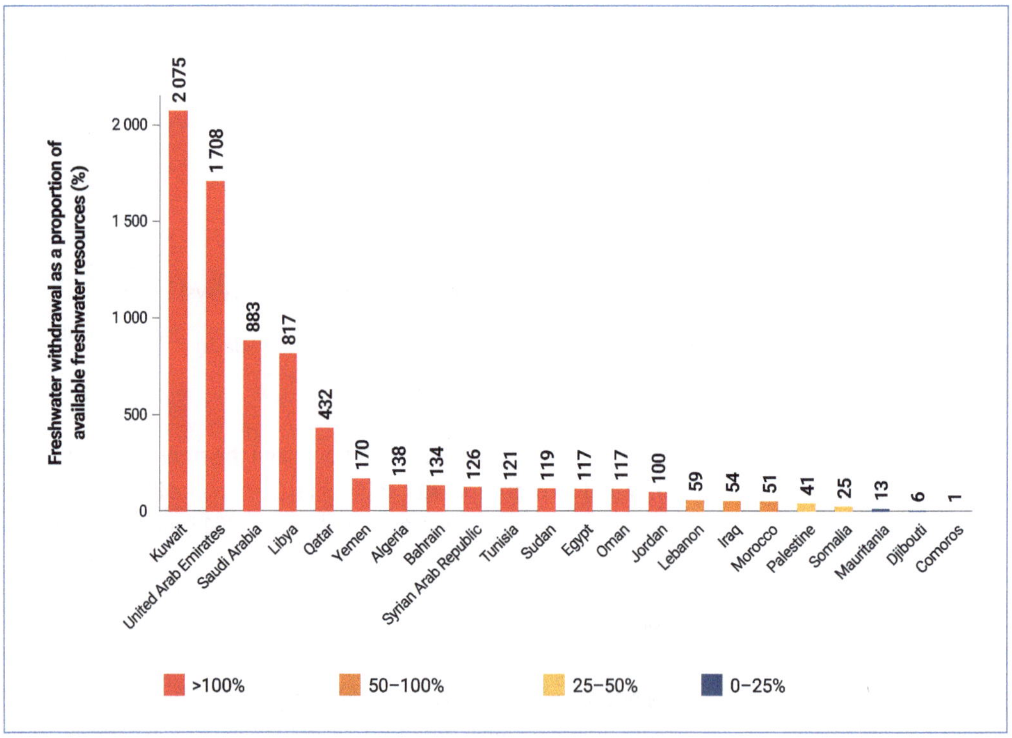

Note: All country data are for the year 2017, except for Mauritania, the Syrian Arab Republic and Yemen where data are for 2014, Somalia for 2012, Kuwait for 2011, and Comoros and Djibouti for 2009.

Source: Based on data from UNDESA (n.d.b).

8.5.2 Regional challenges and opportunities

Freshwater scarcity is aggravated by several challenges, including high population growth, water pollution, high dependency on transboundary water resources, water infrastructure damage due to conflict and occupation, and inefficient use of water especially in the agricultural sector. This is further worsened by climate change impacts due to a projected rise in temperature and generally decreasing precipitation trends (UNESCWA et al., 2017).

Water is so highly valued in the region that it is considered a topic of security in bilateral and multilateral discussions among states. This is amplified by the fact that over two thirds of freshwater resources available in Arab states cross one or more international boundaries. The Arab Ministerial Water Council has prioritized cooperation on shared water resources management since it adopted the Arab Strategy for Water Security in the *Arab Region to Meet the Challenges and Future Needs for Sustainable Development 2010–2030* (AMWC, 2012). However, joint methodologies for the economic valuation of transboundary waters have not yet been incorporated into cooperation arrangements, and funding to inform joint management efforts remains limited (UNESCWA, 2019b). Furthermore, national security considerations and a water rights perspective tend to dominate the discourse among riparian states, although nascent initiatives exist to value transboundary water cooperation, such as efforts to scope the benefits of transboundary water cooperation on the North Western Sahara Aquifer System which is shared between Algeria, Libya and Tunisia (UNECE, 2019), and analysis focused on climate security and risk mitigation in transboundary water contexts in the Middle East and North Africa (Schaar, 2019).

In terms of conventional water resources, countries have increasingly drawn upon renewable and non-renewable groundwater to support cities, industry and agriculture in areas where surface water is limited or not available. However, this has come at the cost of depleting groundwater reserves and lowering the groundwater levels in several countries, threatening the future socio-economic development benefits from the use of this groundwater. It has also introduced trade-offs where the value of water and energy are contrasted when brackish water is pumped into the ground to help extract oil and gas. Over-abstraction of groundwater and especially of non-renewable groundwater is a major concern, especially in the Member States of the Gulf Cooperation Council (GCC – Figure 8.3). Recognizing the value of groundwater for water security and for reversing the trend of declining groundwater levels, several GCC States, including Qatar and Saudi Arabia, have recently invested in managed aquifer recharge projects with the majority depending on treated wastewater as the recharge source.

Figure 8.3
Over-abstraction of groundwater resources in the Gulf Cooperation Council States

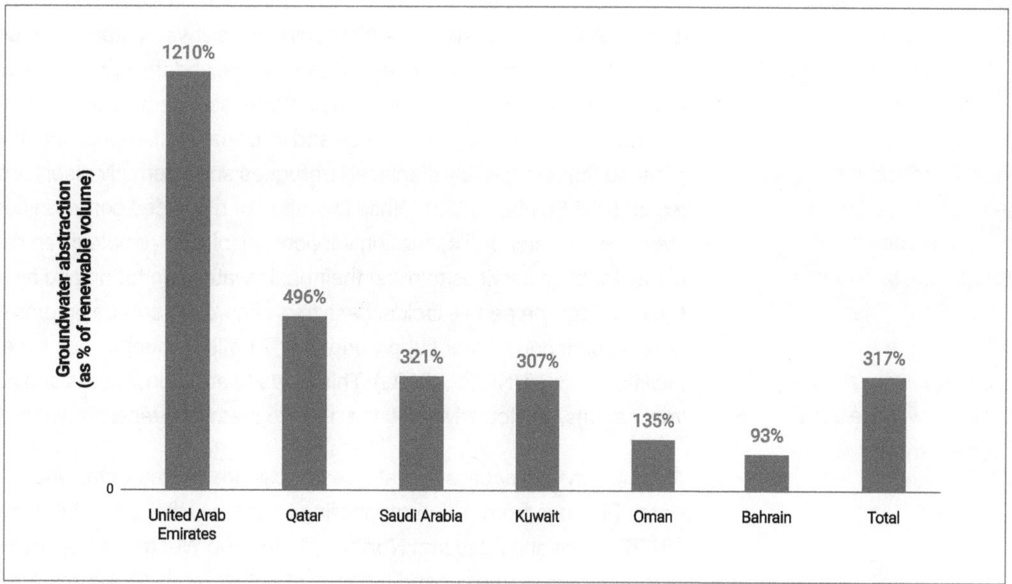

Source: Based on data from Al-Zubari et al. (2017, Table 2, p. 3).

The Arab region has also expanded its dependency on non-conventional sources of water to meet its growing water needs. Desalination and the use of treated wastewater have significantly expanded as the cost of production has decreased. Over half of the world's desalination capacity is in the Arab region, and mostly in GCC States (UN Environment, 2019). The use of desalinated water is needed to meet the rising water demand, particularly in urban areas, albeit more and more desalination plants are being used to supply water for agriculture as well. An example is the recently commissioned desalination plant in Agadir, Morocco (see Box 8.1). Although the cost of desalination has dropped greatly in recent years, several countries are investing in new technologies and renewable energy to further lower the cost of desalination and avail more sustainable options. Saudi Arabia has constructed a photovoltaic desalination plant in Khafji using nanotechnology, with an expected full capacity of 60,000 cubic metres per day (Harrington, 2015).

Box 8.1 Agadir Desalination Plant, Morocco

The construction of Africa's largest desalination plant is underway in Agadir, Morocco. The plant will initially produce an average of 275,000 cubic metres of desalinated water per day, with a maximum capacity of 450,000 cubic metres per day. As such, the plant would supply drinking water to 2.3 million people living in the region of Souss-Massa, with a second phase supplying desalinated water to irrigate an area of some 15,000 hectares. The project's cost is over €370 million. As farmers in the region realize the value of water for their livelihoods, they contribute in exchange for a discounted price on future desalinated water (Novo, 2019). Energy from a wind farm and a pressure exchanger will help lower the cost of desalination in future phases (Mandela, 2020).

The use of treated wastewater in the region has been spreading considerably. More than two thirds of collected wastewater in the Arab region is safely treated at the secondary or tertiary level. Nevertheless, only a quarter of this volume is used for agriculture and groundwater recharge. In most countries of the Arabian Penninsula, treated wastewater is used for greenbelts and nature reserves, and to combat land degradation. Jordan leads the Arab region in the use of treated wastewater, with 100% of treated wastewater reportedly used in 2013 (UNESCWA, 2017). Nevertheless, there is a significant potential for the expansion of the use and value of safely treated wastewater in other parts of the Arab region and specifically for the agricultural sector.

While agriculture represents only 7% of the regional Gross Domestic Product (GDP), the sector consumes 84% of all freshwater withdrawals in the region (UNESCWA, 2019a). Although the value of this water is not well reflected in the pricing and export of agricultural commodities, the sector employs approximately 38% of the region's population and produces 23% of GDP in Arab Least Developed Countries (UNESCWA, 2020a). This renders water for crops and livestock essential for sustaining rural livelihoods, income and food security in some of the most vulnerable parts of the region. The value of water in this water-scarce region, however, is well understood given the range of efforts underway to enhance water use efficiency and productivity in the agricultural sector at the intergovernmental, national and farm levels, as regularly addressed by the High-Level Joint Committee of Arab Ministers of Agriculture and Water. Improvements in water use efficiency and productivity in the Arab region have been valued at about 0.5% of regional GDP (Rosegrant et al., 2008), where the average irrigation efficiency is below 46% (AFED, 2015).

The region is relatively urbanized, with more than 58% of its population now living in cities (UNESCWA, 2020a). The disparity in coverage between urban and rural areas, the intermittent supply, the high amounts of non-revenue water, and the low cost recovery render it difficult to value water effectively in cities as well. Water service providers are under increasing pressure to meet the needs of growing cities and informal settlements, including around 26 million of those that are forcibly displaced (refugees and internally displaced people) in the Arab region (UNESCWA, 2020b). While the influx of displaced communities adds to the growing pressure on water and sanitation services, displaced people often do not have the means to pay for such services to meet their basic water, sanitation and hygiene (WASH) needs. Nearly 87 million people lack access to an improved source on premises, 70 million do not have a continuous water supply and over 74 million people lack access to basic handwashing facilities (WHO/UNICEF, 2019a). This leads to additional costs and has many health implications, particularly given the need to stem the transmission of COVID-19.

Affordability and access to water resources are fundamental when considering the value of water. Findings from SDG 6 monitoring under the WHO/UNICEF Joint Monitoring Programme (JMP) have highlighted that Northern Africa and Western Asia, which largely overlaps with the Arab region, have the second-highest rate of water expenditures. Nearly 20% of the population spent more than 2 to 3% of their household expenditures on WASH services (United Nations, 2018). Vulnerable communities, which are most often not connected to water supply and sanitation networks, end up paying much more for water-related services than their connected counterparts. The health cost is no less, as in 2016 there were nearly 30,000 deaths in the region attributed to unsafe water, unsafe sanitation and lack of hygiene (SDG Indicator 3.9.2 – WHO, n.d.).

For the full value of water to be captured and considered by all to be a human right, there is a need for considerable investment in infrastructure, appropriate technologies and the use of non-conventional water resources to improve productivity, sustainability and access for all.

Chapter 9

Enabling multi-value approaches in water governance

UNDP

Marianne Kjellén

GWP

Ranu Sinha

With contributions from:

David Hebart-Coleman* and Elizabeth Yaari** (SIWI); Enrico Muratore (WSSCC); Amanda Loeffen (Human Right 2 Water/WaterLex); Lesley Pories (Water.org); Jerome Delli Priscoli (GWP Global Technical Committee); Dustin Garrick (GWP Global Technical Committee, University of Oxford); Gina Gilson (University of Oxford); Colin Herron (GWP); Edeltraud Guenther (UNU-FLORES); Ambika Jindal (VWI); Sebastien Willemart (WYPW); Nicole Webley (UNESCO-IHP); and Rémy Kinna (UNECE).

* On behalf of the UNDP-SIWI Water Governance Facility, hosted by SIWI.

** On behalf of the International Centre for Water Cooperation, hosted by SIWI.

9.1 The increasing emphasis on bringing multiple perspectives into water governance

The 2030 Agenda for Sustainable Development emphasizes the integrated nature of development and the need to balance economic, social, and environmental considerations. This would require institutional reforms and innovative governance approaches that mitigate the trade-offs and maximize the synergies between the Sustainable Development Goals (SDGs) and their policy domains (Breuer et al., 2019; OECD, 2017c). There is an evolving understanding that a diverse set of values drives the economic and financial considerations in water-related decision-making (Schulz et al., 2018; Pahl-Wostl et al., 2020). Taking a much broader stance on values than what was advocated under the Dublin principles (ICWE, 1992); the High-Level Panel on Water (HLPW, 2018) encourages countries to "*Recognize and Embrace Water's Multiple Values*" (the related Bellagio Principles are outlined in Box 1.6). Coupled with a recognition of water's multiple values, there is also a call for more robust measurement and valuation methods to help resolve trade-offs (Garrick et al., 2017). This is broadly what this Chapter refers to as a transition to *multi-value approaches to water governance*.

The use of multi-value approaches to water governance entails acknowledging the role of values in driving key water resources management decisions as well as a call for active participation of a more diverse set of actors, thereby also incorporating a varied set of values into water governance. Incorporating the intrinsic or relational values of diverse groups to better inform and legitimize water and related land resources management decisions entails the direct participation of groups or interests that are often excluded from water-related decision-making. It may bring greater emphasis on ecological and environmental processes and refocus efforts on sharing water resource benefits – for present and future generations – rather than allocating water quantities for highest-value economic priorities.

9.2 Challenges in bringing multiple values to bear on water governance

This section points to a set of challenges in transitioning to a system of water governance that recognizes multiple values and the active participation of a varied set of actors. The first challenge relates to acknowledging that the governance of water is driven by a set of implicit or explicit values (Schulz et al., 2018). This entails recognizing that different interests and diverging perspectives inherent to the social, cultural, environmental, ecological and economic values integral to water drive diverse resource-related decisions. This does not only relate to 'who is at the governance table,' but also explicitly recognizes the worth of water to different groups in society. The second challenge relates to water valuation: the assessment or description of the value or worth of using water in different ways. However, water valuation is fraught not only with measurement issues, but also with a whole array of issues relating to what can – and should – be measured at all, and by whom. This then leads to the third challenge, which relates to the common disconnect between public decision-making processes and actions on the ground, including the risk of agendas being controlled by vested interests.

9.2.1 Bringing diverse voices and values into the discussion – The challenges of meaningful participation

The effective participation of a more diverse set of actors can greatly influence the outcome of water governance, including the generation and sharing of a greater set of benefits from the use of water. Despite the fact that participatory approaches are not new to the water sector (e.g. the Dublin Principles suggest "*full public consultation and involvement of users in the planning and implementation of water projects*" (ICWE, 1992, Principle 2)), the Agenda 2030 calls for renewed efforts to *inform* decision-making, and to *recognize* and *manage* trade-offs and potential conflicts between policy priorities in participatory and inclusive ways (OECD, 2016). In reality, individuals or groups from indigenous communities, women, and youth groups are often not included; not considered 'relevant', or for other reasons impeded from participating in relevant decision-making processes (Pahl-Wostl, 2020). Resolving the challenges of exclusion has been underscored in the HLPW *Outcome Document,* which calls for a transition with respect to the identification of, and roles for, 'relevant' stakeholders, including to "*identify and take into account the multiple and diverse values of water to different groups and interests in all decisions affecting water*" (HLPW, 2018, p. 17).

Despite the best intentions to involve a diverse set of actors, it should be stressed that participation takes time. This time investment, which is a must for governance processes, might be incompatible with specific projects, policies, or national and local political timelines. Dialogue mechanisms need to already be established for any strategic 'co-governance' of a multiple values-based approach to water use and protection, if it is to go beyond donor-driven project lifecycles and actually enable longer-term 'governance' of projects and water uses, in specific locations and with specific stakeholders. On the other hand, projects are a means to finance development, and 'governance processes' may not provide the type of return that would motivate investment. Hence, participation – or governance for that matter – cannot be treated as a 'magic bullet' or quick solution. It does require both time and funding in order to take place.

Despite the best intentions to involve a diverse set of actors, it should be stressed that participation takes time

Another obstacle for participation is that it must be continuously reinvented. Even though a successful consultation in one location can lend its 'approach' as a lesson learned to other locations, the potential training of stakeholders or facilitators, or the time needed for officials or managers to visit different sites and participate in processes, cannot be reduced, even if a certain approach has already been carried out successfully in other locations. Hence, there are few opportunities for economies of scale. In addition, participation – understood as 'co-ownership' or real influence – can challenge the status quo, in which vested interests can be important. There may be reasons to rush projects in ways to forgo discussion and full vetting of all parties, as participation might lead to projects not going ahead, even if the required financing is available.

Finally, it is important to mention that 'more' or 'better' participation with 'more actors' may still not resolve the complex array of challenges and competing interests inherent to water governance processes. Stakeholders with the best of intentions at moments can be deeply dissatisfied with the outcomes of multi-stakeholder processes to activate the necessary reforms, or when ideas proposed by vested interests may prevent lasting change. This implies that 'more participation' alone may not resolve the challenges described in this Chapter but must be embedded within a country's water policy, along with a wider basket of interventions that seek to strengthen multi-value governance processes in water resources management.

9.2.2 Balancing trade-offs when you cannot measure what you really treasure

Water valuation exercises have come to predominantly focus on quantifying a monetary value of water-related goods and services. Hellegers and Van Halsema (2019, p. 522) argue that "*as wider scopes and concerns on how water affects the well-being of society entered the fray of valorisation, it has become increasingly clear that decision-making should be more concerned with weighing* [and reconciling] *the trade-offs among the diverse values of water, rather than establishing one commensurate value. Valuation then should no longer be solely targeted at 'economic' value determination ..., but more towards offering a structured and transparent mechanism that supports a multi-stakeholder process*" to recognize, balance and address the trade-offs among diverse types of values. Water decision-making appears at the nexus of ethics, public policy, nature, values, beliefs and rationality (Priscoli, 2012).

Garrick et al. (2017) emphasize the importance of valuing water by going beyond what can be easily measured. Valuing water is difficult and contentious not only due to measurement issues but also because of what it represents: "*Disputes may arise regardless of the validity and precision of valuation methods, reflecting the inevitable trade-offs underlying water governance*" (p. 1004). The contribution of valuation or measurement for such inherent political deliberations can be seen to lie principally in how it can expose the diverse values attached to water, and the different ways such values may – or may not – be captured. This can also enable decision-makers to explicitly acknowledge which values are driving water governance decisions. This makes clear the need for multi-stakeholder participatory processes as an institutional strategy to support the recognition and inclusion of values and to activate governance mechanisms that manage water according to a broader set of values (e.g. representing social, cultural, economic and ecological values), which can facilitate inclusive and value-based water decision-making. As Hellegers and Van Halsema (2019, p. 521) point out, multi-stakeholder processes (as outlined in

Section 9.3.1) can seek to include multiple values *"to jointly reach a certain level of agreement on the management of water resources within the set priorities of [a country's] development strategy"*. However, beyond the relevance of multi-stakeholder processes, a key challenge is how to consider or measure diverse sets of values, often without a common denominator or metric (see Boxes 1.1 and 1.2, and Figure 1.3, where different types of 'values' are defined).

Different communities (professional and non-professional, indigenous and non-indigenous groups, etc.) have diverse knowledge and value systems. Moreover, different stakeholders relate differently to water bodies, nature, the environment, as well as to other groups in society.

Some sets of values are less tangible and notably difficult to quantify or translate into monetary terms – which is a common methodology for comparing different sets of values. For example, indigenous peoples' worldviews and values related to the environment can go beyond instrumental or intrinsic values.[40] Figure 9.1 below captures this as 'relational' [or place-based] values in relation to nature. Such moral and emotional links to water challenge the worldviews embedded in most standard approaches to measurement and valuation of water resources management.

Figure 9.1

Illustrating instrumental, intrinsic and relational values with respect to nature

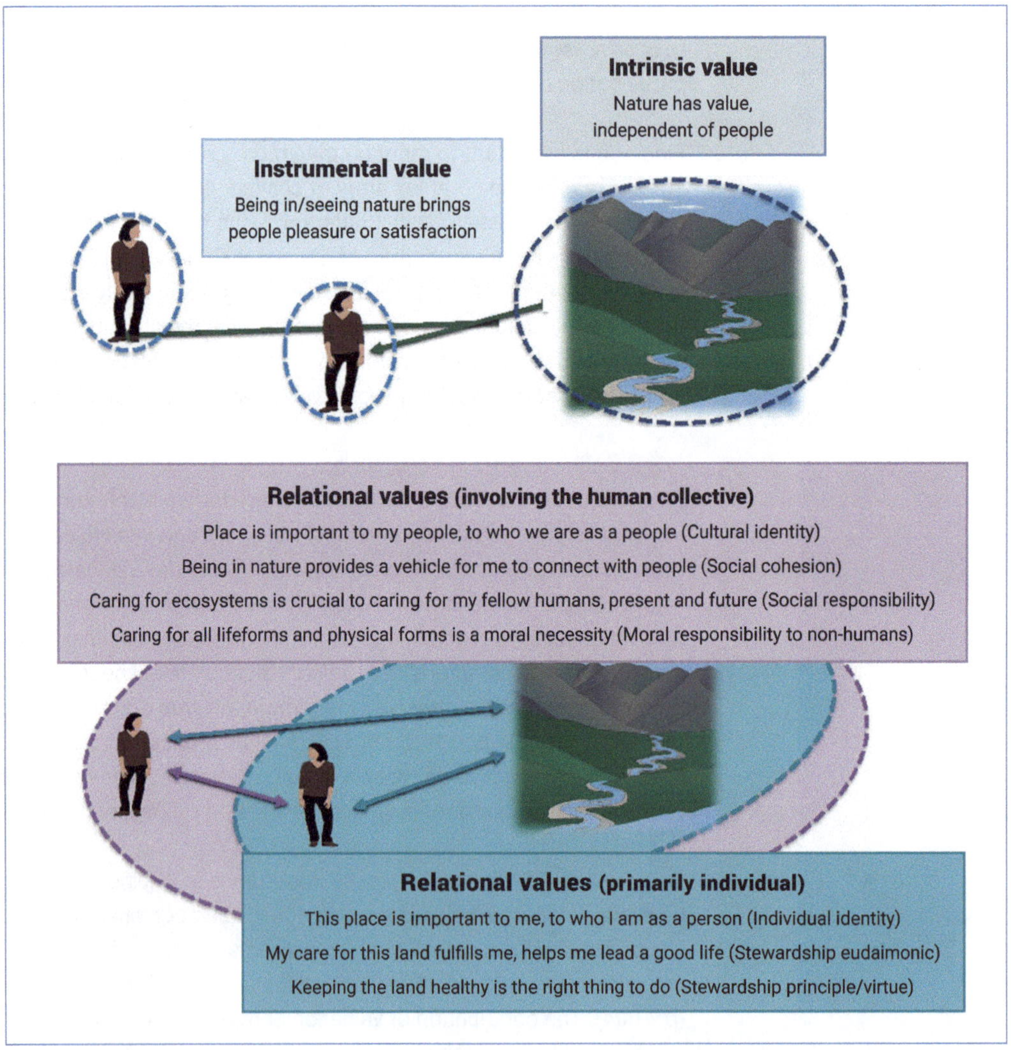

Source: Chan et al. (2016, fig. 1, p. 1462). The Attribution Share-Alike 3.0 IGO (CC BY-SA 3.0 IGO) licence does not apply to this figure.

[40] Instrumental values refer to a matter that is important/has value because of the service or utility it provides, e.g. a washbasin for convenient handwashing. For instance, art or music can be instrumentally valuable because their value is dependent on and derives from the responses they evoke. Intrinsic values, on the other hand, refer to a matter that is important/has value or is valued by others for its own sake, regardless of whether it provides services or utility. Handwashing may be intrinsically valuable if it makes a person feel good, regardless of being healthy or clean. It may even have an intrinsic value for moral reasons – being the right thing to do. Further, intrinsic and instrumental values are fundamental in moral theory as well as conservation biology (see e.g. Justus et al., 2009)

Other examples of these deeper attachments and long-standing relationships expressed as values can be found through ethics of care or stewardship that contribute to human well-being (Bennett et al., 2018; Jax et al., 2018). There are several definitions of relational values, but most capture *"the importance attributed to meaningful relations and responsibilities between humans and between humans and nature"* (Arias-Arévalo et al., 2017). As observed in Chan et al. (2016), relational values are not present in things but derivative of relationships and responsibilities to them. The recognition and use of 'relational values' are important for fostering pluralistic approaches that help bridge differing worldviews in relation to water bodies (Parsons and Fisher, 2019).

Balancing the representation of instrumental economic growth priorities with relational and/or intrinsic values may reinvigorate the national and subnational political dynamics

Balancing the representation of instrumental economic growth priorities with relational and/or intrinsic values may reinvigorate the national and subnational political dynamics. In practice, this is very complex, as there is no 'optimal' water allocation strategy that encompasses all the multiple values associated with water, as different value systems intersect and overlap (Hellegers and Leflaive, 2015). Indeed, the essence of water governance is about resolving trade-offs and conflicts in ways that create the most possible benefits and synergies, as such methodologies for grappling with multiple values and uncertainty are maturing (LeRoy Poff et al., 2015; see also Section 9.3 on pathways below).

Beyond challenges related to measurement methodologies, as described above; the next challenge resides in the implementation of an open, inclusive and balanced process for decision-making, which is discussed in the next section.

9.2.3 From theory to practice: Navigating hidden agendas and vested interests

The third set of challenges involves some of the many obstacles in enabling and sustaining multi-value governance processes. If decision-makers fail to take people's views into account – meaning to not only listen, but to actually reframe questions and answers – they have only wasted people's time, and therefore the consultation loses credibility. In the worst case, consultation can turn into an unjust exercise that depoliticizes local development, or is 'captured' by economic or political elites (Cooke and Kothari, 2001; Gaynor, 2014; OECD, 2015b). An experience of India's Swachh Bharat Mission highlights the need for robust consultation measures to include diverse groups and the potential hierarchies between them (Mukherjee, 2020).

The implementation process also risks running into problems of bureaucratic inertia. Disinterest, excessive regulation or rigid conformity to rules may compound with corruption. The Water Integrity Network (2016, p. 23) suggests that *"corruption and a lack of integrity threaten every area of life where power, money and prestige are at stake."* Apart from derailing policy implementation, corruption also reinforces existing inequalities (Søreide, 2016) between broader groups in society, and the resources available to women and men (UNDP/Huairou Commission, 2012). As suggested in the section below, transparency and the equal involvement of people of different gender identities and backgrounds may help break up networks of vested interests and hidden agendas.

As a result of these and other challenges, a multi-values driven governance approach does not only relate to water, but aims to engage with the whole social, cultural, economic and wider political system. Water governance needs to navigate explicit priority-setting at the political level along with the implicit prioritizations (values) carried out in practical policy implementation. This does not only involve public servants, but the whole society, including the private sector, civil society and other groups.

9.3 Pathways towards multi-value water governance processes

This section highlights some potential pathways for how nations can transition into multi-value governance. These pathways build on existing approaches such as Integrated Water Resources Management (IWRM). IWRM represents a plan-led, multi-scale catchment-based approach that integrates interests of diverse stakeholder groups operating at various political levels and policy sectors (Lubell and Edelenbos, 2013), which would be open or inclusive of any nexus or set of issues. IWRM is most often represented as cutting across water for people, food, nature, industry and other uses, and aims to encompass all social, economic and environmental considerations.[41]

The different pathways or approaches presented below aim to respond to many of the challenges highlighted in the previous section.

9.3.1 Strengthen multi-stakeholder processes that recognize and reconcile a comprehensive mix of values in water governance

The process of enabling a multi-value approach to water governance means recognizing that values ultimately drive water governance decisions, and actively incorporating a balance of cultural, spiritual, economic, environmental or social values into water resources management decisions within a specific policy context (Hellegers and Van Halsema, 2019). This may be achieved by activating decision-making processes that enable a wide array of stakeholders to express their values, with a view to reaching a certain level of agreement. Such processes can be considered to 'co-create' water management (see Hermans et al., 2006). Above all, strengthening [multi-stakeholder] water governance includes *"giving 'voice' to communities that are historically underrepresented or ignored in decision-making processes"* (Garrick et al. 2017, p. 1005). This section provides examples of where underrepresented groups or additional values are brought into water governance processes at different levels.

Since the early 2000s, there is a growing will and effort to make up for the historic exclusion of indigenous peoples' interests in water and environmental management. This has led to the integration of perspectives and knowledge of indigenous peoples in water governance, most notably at the global level (IWGIA, 2019; Makey and Awatere, 2018). Incorporating the knowledge and beliefs of indigenous peoples into water governance implies foundational changes in the valuation of water, involving different cultural and social identities and institutions, separate from the mainstream or dominant society or culture (Awume et al., 2020). For instance, in New Zealand, the Integrated Kaipara Harbour Management Group connects Maori values alongside principles of ecosystem-based management. This involves values related to sustainable resource management (*kaitiakitanga*), respect (*manaakitanga*) and relationships (*whanaungatanga)* (Harmsworth et al., 2016). Box 9.1 illustrates another example of how governments are actively seeking to embed values of water from the perspective of indigenous communities into water governance processes.

In addition to indigenous communities, there are many groups whose voices are often not effectively incorporated into water management decisions. For instance, women usually provide most of the labour for securing household water needs but remain underrepresented in structures of formal water management (Thakar, 2019; World Bank, 2019). Efficiency gains can be realized by bringing women into water governance bodies at various levels (Mommen et al., 2017; Trivedi, 2018).[42] A diversification of genders in governing bodies may also have knock-on effects like the opening-up of close-knit management communities and shine light on hidden agendas. Such additional transparency brought on by broader participation and mix among decision-makers can reduce corruption and mismanagement.

---

[41] IWRM has been defined as *"a process which promotes the coordinated development and management of water, land and related resources in order to maximise economic and social welfare in an equitable manner without compromising the sustainability of vital ecosystems"* (GWP, 2000, p. 22).

[42] This 'efficiency argument' speaks for the *instrumental* value of involving women more equally in water management. Yet, there is also an *intrinsic* value relating to the moral imperative of equal involvement or influence of women and men in decision-making.

Box 9.1 The National Water Initiative in Australia

In Australia, Commonwealth and State government agencies have aimed to move beyond a resource exploitation focus and towards acknowledging different values and interests in water governance. This is of importance to indigenous Australians whose interests in water were only formally recognized in 2004 with The National Water Initiative (National Water Commission, 2004; Bark et al., 2012).

The National Water Initiative directs all signatories to provide for indigenous access to water resources by: (i) ensuring inclusion of indigenous representation in water planning where possible; (ii) taking account of existing Native Title rights to water in the catchment area; (iii) allocating water to Native Title holders.[1] As long as the indigenous interests are 'non-consumptive' and 'non-commercial', they do not require a water allocation (see Maclean et al., 2014).

Indigenous Australians have developed governance activities to blend their knowledge with their contemporary conservation and land management knowledge and training, enabling them to engage in water planning and management on their traditional lands (Maclean et al., 2014). Further, partnerships between Aboriginal groups and social researchers to document their water values, knowledge and interests has been shown to have multiple benefits. First, these partnerships record valuable traditional ecological knowledge and related values. Second, they can also articulate indigenous interests in ways that make them accessible to scientists and planners, while most importantly, remaining true to the relevant worldview. Indigenous groups can use social research tools to directly communicate their water knowledge, values and interests to government agencies and to build the necessary relationships to maintain a meaningful dialogue.

Source: Based on Maclean et al. (2015, pp. 142–144).

[1] Native Title is *"a right to access and take water for the purposes of satisfying personal, domestic, social, cultural, religious, spiritual or non commercial communal needs, including the observance of traditional laws and customs, including a right to teach the physical and spiritual attributes of places and areas of importance on or in the land and waters"* (O'Donnell, 2011, p. 11; see also Jackson and Langton, 2012).

Next, mobilizing youth networks into water governance can be construed as a way of integrating future generations' rights into water governance. The vibrant youth movement 'Fridays for Future' has had a major influence on environmental policy through massive and consistent mobilizations, constituting a critical force for global change (Braw, 2019). Youth movements have also been engaged in the management of water scarcity in the Mediterranean (Pedrero et al., 2018). Such voices and perspectives greatly influence the values – and the time perspective – that are considered in water decision-making.

At the international level, the challenge is to bring states, international agencies, bodies of the United Nations (UN), civil society and academia together. The Global High-Level Panel on Water and Peace (2017) urges states to adhere to and implement International Water Law, and thus calls for wide accession by states to the 1997 Watercourses Convention and the 1992 Water Convention hosted by the United Nations Economic Commission for Europe (UNECE). The panel also recommends intensified work on supplemental instruments to these two United Nations global water conventions, including 'soft law instruments' such as guidelines and procedures that facilitate water cooperation. The Working Group on Integrated Water Resources Management promotes technical and political dialogues on water governance, e.g. with respect to water allocation, hydropower development and irrigation. Such work draws on the values and benefits outlined in Table 9.1.

Finally, the integration of human rights principles represents an attempt to broaden stakeholder processes, through yet another angle, towards more equitable water governance processes and outcomes. The human rights-based approach (HRBA) focuses on those who are the most marginalized, excluded or discriminated against, but not with an eye to the 'basic needs' of 'beneficiaries,' but rather to 'fulfil the rights' of people (UNFPA, n.d.). The human rights to water and sanitation do not only refer to the contents of universal and adequate access to water and sanitation, but also to the procedural right of influencing the ways in which these services are being provided.

Table 9.1
The benefits of transboundary water management

Benefit type	Related values	Description of benefits
Type 1: the benefits from improved water availability	Consumptive direct use values	Benefits arising from cooperation can address water scarcity issues and result in improved water security and efficient water allocation among sectors (supply augmentation – demand management)
Type 2: the benefits from improved water quality	All use values depending on water quality	Improved quality for outdoor recreation, avoided treatment costs, avoided sedimentation costs, avoided health risks
Type 3: the benefits from watershed or the quality of water ecosystems	Indirect use values, option values, non-use values	Improved biodiversity, improved flood control, improved storm protection, avoided or reduced costs of desertification, improved groundwater recharge, etc.
Type 4: the benefits from improved regional security and integration	Secondary benefits	Avoided or reduced costs resulting from conflicts, improved trade relations and regional integration

Source: OECD (2015a, Table 3, p. 9), based on Sadoff and Grey (2003).

9.3.2 Include benefit-sharing into water governance decisions

In water resources management, explicit benefit-sharing to enhance the productivity of shared water resources has been advocated as an alternative to water allocation by water volume (Sadoff and Grey, 2003; 2005). Sadoff and Grey (2003) argued that by refocusing from the sharing of *water* (quantities) to the sharing of *benefits* that may be derived from the use of water, a zero-sum game of water-sharing is being replaced by a positive-sum game. "[F]*ocusing on the benefits derived from the use of water in a river basin, rather than the physical water itself, is another way to broaden the perspective of basin planners*" (p. 396). Benefit-sharing yields far greater scope for mutually beneficial and sustainable arrangements among different stakeholders (Yu, 2008). The goods and services (benefits to which values may be attached) include hydropower, flood regulation, irrigated agriculture or improved navigation. Benefits may be non-economic, like improved environmental stewardship, regional integration or even political gains, and go well beyond monetary compensations. As highlighted in the previous section, Table 9.1, benefits also extend to regional integration, trade and reduced conflict. The case of the Senegal River basin (Box 9.2) offers insights into how benefit-sharing approaches have been tried on a transboundary scale in Africa.

Benefit-sharing can also enable enhanced poverty reduction. Yet, as discussed in the box above, in order to realize such gains, the mix of actors that benefit and those involved in determining the benefit-sharing is critical. As benefits can be measured through values, benefit-sharing is an example how to integrate a diverse set of values into water governance within and between nations.

Although most discussions on benefit-sharing relate to the transboundary scale (see Section 8.2.2), the original concept offers a framework to resolve the rising competition for water between urban and rural, domestic, industrial, and agricultural uses (Garrick et al., 2019). Benefit-sharing may even be seen as an application of the systems perspective – going well beyond the water liquid itself – and the need to grapple with different interests, represented by the various benefits (and their values) accruing to different actors or stakeholders.

9.3.3 Focus on systems to go beyond narrow sectoral interventions

A systems-based approach to water involves multi-scale policy and planning to integrate water allocation incentives into wider sectoral processes of institutional reform and infrastructure development. This requires an understanding of behavioural responses, which can amplify or undermine such actions (Garrick et al., 2020b). Therefore, priorities for water governance and the appropriate level of management depend greatly on the scale at which the problem appears (Kjellén, 2018). Water governance processes may gain from 'breaking siloes' to address global, regional and/or local issues.

A systems approach that integrates multiple values across multiple scales into water governance calls for: (i) understanding the *interconnections* between hydrological, administrative, economic, political, social, and ecological/environmental systems and the underlying values embedded within these systems; (ii) identifying the *risks*, shocks or stressors faced by people and/or the ecosystem or production systems; (iii) developing *scenarios* or *models* to understand trends, responses, issues and impacts (involving actors from various sectors as described in Section 9.3.1); (iv) co-designing the type and mix of *actions* to be taken based on agreement among representatives of a diverse set of values; and (v) testing, learning

Box 9.2 Benefit-sharing and cost allocation in the Senegal River basin

The Senegal River, the second longest river in western Africa, flows through Guinea, Mali, Senegal and Mauritania to the Atlantic Ocean. Between the 1960s and the 1980s, the basin area suffered severe aridity, leading to famine and severe degradation of the natural resources base, enormous losses in agriculture and ecology, and problems of groundwater recession and saltwater intrusion. It was in this context, in 1972, that the Organisation pour la mise en valeur du fleuve Sénégal (OMVS), the Senegal River Basin Organization, was established comprising Mali, Mauritania, and Senegal. The OMVS hoped to a) promote food self-sufficiency in the basin, b) reduce economic vulnerability to climatic fluctuations and external factors, c) accelerate economic development, and d) secure and improve the incomes of basin populations through benefits-sharing and cooperation among the three riparian countries.

In order to govern and manage the Senegal River, a framework was needed to allocate benefits and costs in a way that would be satisfactory to all member states, so a methodology was developed to allocate joint costs across services (hydropower, navigation, and irrigation) and member states. In a traditional single-country multi-purpose investment, cost allocation is typically accomplished by comparing the benefits to the costs of the various project services. Multi-country approaches are far more complex as the benefits to be gained from the river differ from country to country. For Mali, gaining navigable access to the Atlantic Ocean and power production were of primary interest. For Mauritania and Senegal, developing irrigation and to a lesser degree power production (except for the cities) was of primary interest.

Thus, to estimate the hydropower, irrigation and navigation benefits derived from two reservoirs that were to be built on the Senegal river, a cost allocation was made based on the benefits that member states could gain from irrigation, power generation and shipping, allocating cost percentages for Mali, Mauritania and Senegal as 35.3%, 22.6% and 42.1%, respectively.

In the early 1970s, this was a unique and innovative approach for river basin projects. At that time, preparing a comprehensive environmental and social assessment for a major project was not common practice.

The experience of the OMVS stands out compared to other river basins around the world where the dialogue among riparian members is often entrenched in discussions over water allocations, instead of focusing on the benefits derived from diverse uses of the river among various members. This vision of benefit-sharing was integral to the discussions among the nations of Mali, Mauritania and Senegal, and helped to reaffirm that *"regional cooperation was an absolute necessity since all would benefit in ways that none could accomplish alone"*. The commitment among the three countries to these principles of benefits sharing was codified through the establishment of legal conventions and a remarkable degree of supra-national executive authority vested in the OMVS. Moreover, the greatest demonstration of solidarity on benefit-sharing is espoused in the early OMVS goals, which state that *"the benefits and aims for development would supersede political boundaries and be intended for all of society living in the Senegal River Basin"*.

Source: Adapted from Yu (2008, pp. 12–26).

Box 9.3 Nexus approaches

The conceptual framework articulated as Integrated Water Resources Management (IWRM) arguably pursues the integrated and coordinated management of water and land as a means of balancing different water uses, while meeting social and ecological needs and promoting economic development. However, by explicitly focusing on water, there is a risk of overfocus on water-related development goals, thereby reinforcing traditional sectoral approaches.

A common nexus approach to water considers the different dimensions of water, energy, food and the environment and recognizes the interdependencies of different resource uses to develop sustainably in order to strike a balance between the different goals, interests and needs of people and the environment. It explicitly addresses complex interactions and feedback between human and natural systems. Nexus interactions are about how resource systems are used and managed, describing interdependencies (depending on each other), constraints (imposing conditions or trade-offs) and synergies (mutually reinforcing or having shared benefits).

Going beyond many IWRM approaches, a nexus approach considers interactions taking place within the context of globally relevant drivers, such as demographic changes, urbanization, industrial development, agricultural modernization, international and regional trade, markets and prices, technological advancements, diversification and changes of diets, and climate change, as well as more context-specific drivers, like governance structures and processes, and cultural and societal beliefs and behaviours. These drivers often have a strong impact on the resource base, causing environmental degradation and resource scarcity, but they also affect and are affected by different social, economic and environmental goals and interests.

A recurring criticism of the nexus approach is that it adds relatively little to already existing integrated approaches to resources management such as IWRM, if IWRM is implemented properly and holistically.

Source: Adapted from FAO (2014c, pp. 6–9).

and *adapting.*[43] As pointed out by Garrick et al. (2019), periodic reviews should be built into the process to avoid crisis-driven responses. The importance of such analyses to take cognizance of systemic linkages of water decisions across sectors have been emphasized in the Dutch-supported Valuing Water Initiative (VWI), which builds coalitions to foster dialogue with diverse groups around trade-offs and competing interests in Colombia, Ethiopia, the Netherlands, Peru, and Zambia (VWI, 2020).[44]

Although IWRM is seen as a 'systems approach' to water management designed to enable a sequenced, inclusive and institutional approach that responds to contextual realities in order to achieve water security (GWP 2009; Schenk et al., 2009; Villarroel Walker et al., 2012), in practice it has been criticized as 'too water-centric' in its approach to managing water resources (Giordano and Shah, 2014). IWRM has often not fully considered important social, economic and environmental linkages across other sectors of an economy (Hoff, 2011; Roidt and Avellán, 2019). For this reason, different 'nexus' approaches have emerged as complementary frameworks, aiming to more explicitly account for certain interdependencies and linkages beyond the water sector (see Box 9.3).

Among these complementary 'nexus' approaches one may include nexuses of 'water and health,' 'source-to-sea'/'ridge-to-reef', or for example, 'ecosystem-based approaches' (EBA). EBA and the greater consideration of ecological interdependencies have been brought forward along with the increasing recognition of the global crises of climate change and the crossing of 'planetary boundaries' (UNDP, 2020).

---

43 Put differently, a systems approach that integrates multiple values into water governance may consider the following elements: a) define the boundaries of the system; b) stress the system; c) model the scenarios, d) co-design the approach, and; e) learn, test and adapt the approach.

44 For more information on the VWI, see: www.government.nl/topics/water-management/valuing-water-initiative.

9.3.4 Integrating ecological and environmental values into climate-resilient water management

In recent calls for enhancing climate resilience in water governance and management, it is suggested to systematically consider uncertainty and risk, and to build resilience into water-related decision-making (Timboe et al., 2019). One of the major issues is to identify what values (and for whom) are associated with climate change (the risks and costs of diverse climatological shocks to societies, economies, as well as ecological health) and whether underrepresented ecological and environmental values can be better integrated into water governance to enable climate resilient water management.

In recent calls for enhancing climate resilience in water governance and management, it is suggested to systematically consider uncertainty and risk and build resilience into water-related decision-making

The European Union (EU) has pioneered ways to embed ecological and environmental values into water management, as an EBA has been integrated into the EU's biodiversity strategy, the EU's 7th Environment Action Programme and the EU's Water Framework Directive (WFD). The WFD focuses on the ecological perspective, having as its main objective to attain a good ecological status of water resources (European Parliament/Council of the European Union, 2000). To achieve this objective, the EU supports the following: a) implementation mechanisms that focus on the assessment of water resources and of pressures, b) participatory processes, and cost–benefit considerations in support of watershed decision-making, c) the development of River Basin Management Plans (European Commission, 2019a; Grizzetti et al., 2016), and d), mapping, assessment and accounting of ecosystems and their services, both in biophysical and monetary terms (Maes et al., 2018).

Next, ecosystem frameworks may be a viable approach to identify and integrate ecosystem and environmental values into water governance (see Chapter 2). These policies are contributing to preserving and restoring Europe's natural capital by integrating ecosystems and their services into decision-making (European Commission, 2019b). Outside Europe, the use of ecosystem services-based approaches highlighting the multiple values of water-dependent ecosystems have gained momentum also in Costa Rica, Ecuador and Mexico (Engels et al., 2008).

More broadly, a climate-resilient water management approach would go beyond IWRM, as it would not only aim to manage natural resources by adapting to global climate-driven changes, but also ensure to go beyond 'business-as-usual'; include redundancy,[45] flexibility, and adaptability; and specifically aim to reduce the vulnerability of poor communities (James et al., 2018).

9.4 Conclusions

This chapter has highlighted both challenges and pathways for transitioning towards multi-value and multi-stakeholder water governance processes. Such governance approaches emphasize the multiple perspectives that need to be incorporated into decision-making processes, and not only for the sake of improving decisions and outcomes. The inclusion of multiple values and perspectives is also a moral imperative that provides legitimacy to decision-making and subsequent policy implementation.

Water management processes tend to include only a limited number of stakeholders, and to focus narrowly on exploitation of water resources to prioritize economic objectives. Such technocratic or narrow water management approaches have been critiqued on both social and environmental grounds. Water managers and decision-makers need to reach out beyond 'the water sector' not only to reach those sectors and industries that implicitly decide over land and

---

[45] *"Redundancy refers to spare capacity purposely created within systems so that they can accommodate disruption, extreme pressures or surges in demand"* (The Rockefeller Foundation/Arup, 2014, p. 5). It is achieved when multiple functions, elements or components provide the *"same, similar, or backup functions"* (Ahern, 2011, p. 342), providing resilience by way of *"saving from failure."*

water use in the course of running their businesses, but also to include communities that have historically been excluded from natural resource governance and water management. This broadening of interests to incorporate multiple values into a decision-making process adds complexity to the formal process. It may also run into resistance from vested interests as conflicting demands or worldviews relating to how water and land should be used or protected are brought to the table.

The most important way to achieve the multi-value approach remains participation to allow new and underrepresented groups into the process

Opportunities for overcoming these differences and attempts to find mutually supportive solutions to highly complex water management decisions include the active incorporation of a values lens into governance processes. The most important way to achieve the multi-value approach remains participation, as highlighted above, to allow new and underrepresented groups into the process. The HRBAs to development affirm the imperative of involving all concerned in an effective way. But beyond this, the way in which the issues are framed can make a great difference: foremost, by broadening the perspective from the water as such, and seeing resources as a means to achieve many other things. Such 'benefit-sharing' approaches can lead to a more rational and mutually beneficial sharing and use of water, as a means to higher-level goals.

Also, it is imperative that all stakeholders see and understand the interlinkages. The approaches and pathways discussed in this chapter all build on a systems perspective – including ecosystems-based, nexus and climate-resilient approaches to water management. Again, this may help stakeholders find new and mutually beneficial ways to cooperate on preserving or developing values even with a broader time horizon, i.e. longer-term sustainability.

While the chapter has provided a glimpse into the benefits associated with multi-value water governance approaches, there are also great challenges. Active transitions towards inclusive, multi-values approaches to water management that balance ecological, social, economic/financial and other key concerns (many of which are often underrepresented in major water-related decisions) also break with vested interests and the status quo. Even if decision-making can achieve an equitable and inclusive process, it is imperative that financing and policy implementation follow suit. Governments, the private sector and civil society can gain by engaging from a values perspective in future development projects and governance processes. By balancing environmental, social, cultural, economic and other priorities, and systematically integrating the interdependencies and trade-offs between goals and decisions, inclusive multi-value and multi-stakeholder approaches stand to improve water governance.

Chapter 10

Financing and funding water services: Challenges and opportunities for valuing water

World Bank
Jason Russ

With contributions from:
Neil Dhot (AquaFed), Winston Yu (World Bank)
and Valentina Abete (WWAP)

10.1 Introduction

A fundamental challenge with managing and valuing water is that water encompasses the qualities and benefits of many different types of goods.[46] At its source, it is usually treated as a public good, an open access resource, or a common-pool resource, available for the public to use without exclusion (Anisfeld, 2011). With open access, common-pool resources, users get all the benefits from their own use, but costs are distributed – often unequally – amongst users (e.g. resource depletion or quality degradation), potentially subjecting it to overuse, exploitation and degradation. In order to provide benefits to cities, farms and households, costly investments in infrastructure like dams, pipes and treatment systems are needed. In the case of water supply and sanitation infrastructure, these services are generally private goods (i.e. the services are both excludable and rivalrous), which means that the poor can be excluded if the price is too high. Other services, like flood protection provided by dams and levees, are public goods, where no one can be excluded, nor can user fees be easily collected. Water can also simultaneously be an economic good – a critical input for nearly all forms of economic production – as well as a merit good – a commodity which should be made available based on need rather than willingness to pay, as it is vital for life and human health.

Any costs not recovered through tariffs must be covered through a combination of taxes and transfers

In order to maximize the benefits of water, several different valuation criteria must be simultaneously considered. First, given water's status as a merit good and a declared human right in Resolution 64/292 of the United Nations General Assembly (UNGA, 2010), access to safely managed drinking water at an affordable price needs to be extended to all. At the same time, in order to prevent tragedy-of-the-commons situations, where water is used without care for the sustainability of the resource, a price or 'tariff' is often needed to constrain profligacy. However, the price of water, its cost of delivery and its value are not synonymous, and price is merely one tool for aligning water's use with its values (see Chapter 1). Finally, the vital infrastructure needed for service delivery has operational, maintenance and construction costs that must be recouped to ensure access and network expansion. Where these funds come from can play an important role in determining who gets access, how service is expanded, and ultimately to whom service providers are responsive.

There are three major means for funding water investments: tariffs, taxes and transfers. Tariffs are user-paid fees and typically increase with the use amount of service used.[47] Cost-recovery tariffs may be estimated in order to cover the total costs of service provision (i.e. including the depreciation and the profitability of the total capital employed) or some selected portions of these. Any costs not recovered through tariffs must be covered through a combination of taxes and transfers (Andres et al., 2019). A recent survey of 16 countries shows just how countries can vary in their sources of funding of hygiene projects (Figure 10.1).

---

[46] The taxonomy of goods presented in this chapter is the one extensively debated in the economic literature since the 1950s. Goods are classified in four types on the basis of two attributes: rivalry in and excludability from consumption. Rivalry refers to the attribute for which the consumption of a good (or a service) by a person reduces the ability or prevents another person in consuming simultaneously the same good (or service), while excludability refers to the feasibility of excluding other people from accessing and consuming a good (or a service). The goods can be classified in: private goods (excludable and rivalrous); public goods (non-excludable and non-rivalrous); and mixed goods as common goods or common-pool resources (non-excludible and rivalrous); and club goods (excludible and non-rivalrous). The nature of goods – if private or public – does not depend on and is not related to who provides them, whether they be private companies or public entities. The use of 'public' and 'private' throughout the entire chapter relates to the meanings as provided in this footnote, and does not refer to categories of funding sources or ownership (private vs. public funding/ownership).

[47] Domestic or industrial tariffs typically have a fixed portion, as well as a variable portion that increases based on usage (see Section 10.4). Irrigation water tariffs may also include volumetric charges, but are often based on the size of the area under irrigation (number of hectares) and/or the crops that are being produced (see, for instance, Berbel et al. 2019 for a discussion on irrigation tariffs in Europe).

Figure 10.1 Global Analysis and Assessment of Sanitation and Drinking-Water (GLAAS) 2018/19 country survey on hygiene expenditures

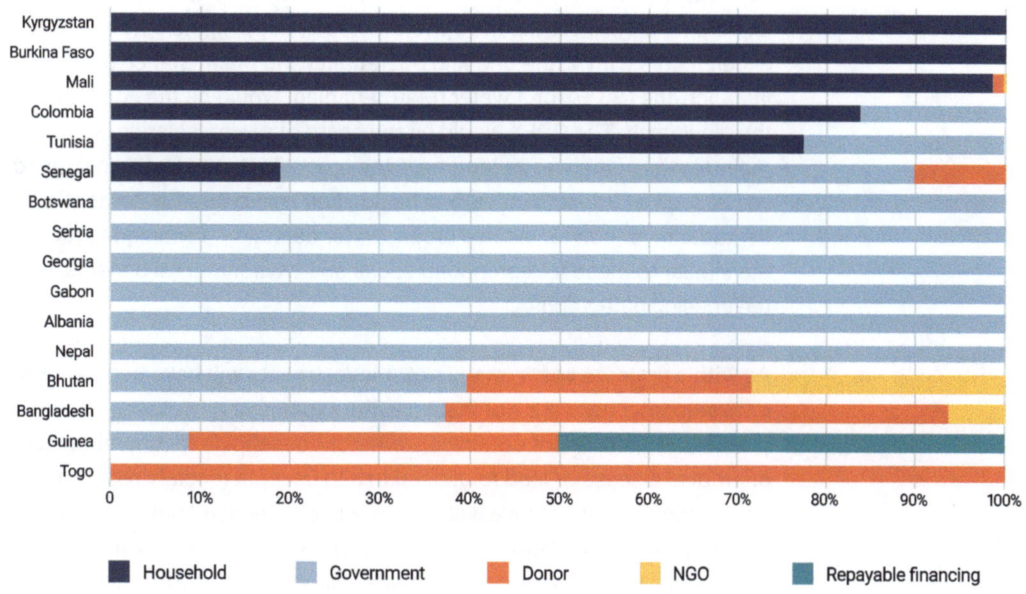

Source: WHO (2020e, fig. 5 p. 12).

When decisions on whether to finance a water infrastructure project are made, several criteria must be considered. Whereas an investment bank seeking to invest in a business might only take into consideration its financial prospects, investments in water sector infrastructure must consider that and more. This is because many of the benefits of water infrastructure are non-pecuniary – i.e. they do not result in a financial return – but still benefit society in meaningful ways. And yet, decisions on whether to finance an investment and how that investment will be funded are often interrelated, as the source of funding can determine the overall benefits of the project. It is in this context that this chapter discusses methods to value investments in the water sector, the challenges and importance of financing and funding infrastructure, and ways to maximize the benefits that they provide.

10.2 Valuation of infrastructure investments and financing decisions

Different types of water infrastructure will have different economic and financial return profiles. Generalization is difficult given the diversity of infrastructure types. Some water infrastructure will generate largely private economic benefits (e.g. drinking and irrigation services) while some will generate largely public economic benefits (e.g. flood protection, storm water drainage). Some infrastructure, like multi-purpose dams, may provide both. There may also be infrastructure that provides, under certain conditions, common-pool and club economic goods as well. Some water infrastructure will also have greater opportunities to generate cash flow through user fees (i.e. higher financial returns), while other water infrastructure will be justified largely on economic grounds (funded through taxes and other sources). Understanding these different economic benefits and financial returns is important to identify the funding mechanism over the full life cycle (planning, appraisal, implementation, operation, maintenance and replacement). Nevertheless, all water infrastructure needs to undergo a financial and economic cost–benefit analysis (CBA) to determine whether scarce funding resources are best allocated to this infrastructure in comparison to other potential investments in other sectors. Water services-related infrastructure (e.g. water supply, wastewater, irrigation, hydropower) can potentially draw upon a wider range of financing modalities, from both governments and commercial sources.

A cost–benefit analysis compares the costs of the project with the benefits, to determine if the project is economically viable and worthwhile. Given scarce government and donor budgets, it is critical that those funds finance only the projects that return the greatest net benefits. An ideal analysis will include in the cost side of the analysis both capital expenditures (CAPEX; i.e. the upfront costs of building the infrastructure) and operational expenditures (OPEX; the ongoing operational and maintenance costs of the project). For instance, the CAPEX of a water treatment plant would be the costs of designing and building the plant itself. The OPEX would be the costs of paying salaries and materials to operate and maintain the plant over its lifetime. Other costs that are ideally accounted for include social costs, such as impacts on human health, and environmental costs like land conversation/degradation or non-renewable groundwater depletion. Techniques for estimating these costs are similar to those for estimating social and environmental benefits, and are discussed in the ensuing paragraphs.

As with a project's costs, many water investments will have economic, social and environmental benefits. For instance, the expansion of water and sanitation infrastructure will reduce the costs of obtaining water for households (economic); reduce illnesses such as diarrhoeal disease or lead to general health benefits (social); reduce time needed to fetch water (social); and improve water quality due to reduced nutrient effluence and bacterial contamination (environmental). Aggregating these types of benefits can be difficult, as they are not all easily converted into monetary amounts. Nevertheless, economists have tools for monetizing some of these benefits (see Box 10.1). In cases where benefits cannot be monetized, other valuation tools can be used, such as cost–effectiveness analyses, which compare costs with non-pecuniary outcomes such as lives saved, people served or environmental metrics achieved.

Box 10.1 Tools for monetizing non-monetary costs and benefits of water projects

The field of environmental economics provides several different ways to value non-monetary benefits. The most common methods include:

- **Contingent valuation:** This approach asks people directly about their willingness to pay (WTP) for a certain good or service, or what they would be willing to accept (WTA) to give up a good or service. For instance, the construction of a wastewater treatment plant could improve water quality in a nearby river. This may not financially benefit nearby residents, but it may give them more recreational opportunities, and improve nearby environmental quality and therefore ambiance. By aggregating the residents' WTP for this water quality improvement, the evaluator can get a sense of how much residents value a cleaner river, and factor that in when assessing the benefits provided by the wastewater treatment plant (Alberini and Cooper, 2000).
- **Hedonic pricing:** This approach typically relies on measuring how benefits are capitalized within housing or property prices. A hedonic pricing model attempts to estimate how different factors affect the price of a home. Using the example from above, the model will estimate how housing prices will change when the construction of a wastewater treatment plant improves nearby river water quality. To do so, it compares the prices of houses in areas with poor water quality with similar houses in areas with better water quality, while controlling for other confounding factors. The difference in housing prices or rents is the value that the public places on the water quality improvement.
- **Travel costs method:** The underlying assumption of the travel cost method is that if an individual is willing to pay the cost of visiting a recreational site, then they should value that site at least as much as what they paid to visit it. The underpinning of this approach is that the effect of increasing travel cost is considered the same as increasing the price of admission. Since many natural areas have either low or no admission prices, this approach uses travel cost as a proxy for estimating consumer surplus (Bolt et al., 2005). If individuals are willing to pay more to travel to a lake or river with cleaner water, that difference in the travel cost can be used as a lower bound for the value that individuals attach to the water quality improvement.

For further details see Chapters 1 and 2.

A critical factor for determining economic benefits of a project is comparing it to what would happen if the project were not undertaken. For instance, an expanded water supply system that connects households to water utilities greatly reduces the cost of fetching water. Nevertheless, water is a basic human need, and in the absence of this water connection, households will find alternative means for water collection. In addition, there may be alternative, lower-cost options for providing improved water to households, such as a community tap. The costs and benefits of the proposed investment should therefore be compared to the baseline (i.e. the status quo) as well as to these alternative projects, in order to determine the true net benefits of the investment. By going through this process, one can determine if the proposed investment is truly the best use of scarce funds, or if viable alternatives exist.

10.3 Accounting for the scarcity value of water

In order to properly value water when planning and designing infrastructure projects, it is vital that economic analyses factor in all externalities generated by the project. An externality is a positive or negative side effect of an activity that is imposed on other parties. A project that aims to expand a water supply piped network to new residents, for instance, will generate significant externalities. Some will be positive, such as health benefits to the community due to reduced spread of communicable diseases; and some can be negative, for instance if the water comes from a non-renewable groundwater supply. The proper way to include the value of water into the economic analysis, and thus account for water depletion, is through the use of a shadow price of water.[48] By accounting for the shadow price of scarce water resources, an economic analysis can internalize the wider economic and ecological impacts of the project and lead to better decision-making. Put simply, when water is very scarce and has many competing uses, it will have a higher shadow price, and will impact the estimated net benefits of a water investment.

Determining the true shadow price of water is non-trivial and requires a lot of information or assumptions. The standard way to calculate the shadow price of water is through an optimal control technique that aims to maximize a series of benefits over time. As this needs to occur in a way that is economically credible and adequately rigorous, it requires a lot of information about the future use of water. To calculate water's shadow price, one must know information (or make assumptions) about a whole host of future economic conditions, such as population size, industry composition, domestic and international markets, as well as future hydrological conditions. Adding to the complexity is the fact that the shadow price of water will vary by location, as water availability and quality can fluctuate significantly from one basin to the next, and thus must be estimated separately for each potential investment project.

Because of the difficulty in deriving a shadow price for water, it is often excluded from economic analyses of water investments; however, less rigorous solutions do exist. One such technique is the replacement cost method (see Box 1.4). Here, one estimates the costs to the economy of needing to replace the water that is being used through either a reduction in use by other sectors, or a switch from the current water source to another source such as an inter-basin transfer or desalination. Both methods give an estimate of the value of a particular water source to the broader economy (Box 10.2). Nevertheless, it must be noted that the replacement cost method is an imperfect substitute for the optimal control problem, as it will not factor in all significant externalities. Thus, the result may be above or below the net present value of the true shadow price.

---

48 **Shadow price**: The value used in economic analysis when the market price is in some way an inadequate measure of economic value (Young, 1996).

Box 10.2 Using the replacement cost method to address falling groundwater tables in Dhaka, Bangladesh

The city of Dhaka relies heavily on groundwater sources for its industrial and municipal water use. However, due to over-extraction, the groundwater table is declining dramatically, in some areas by up to 2 metres per year. A major reason for this is rapid industrialization and urbanization, poor planning, and the lack of a tariff that signals the growing scarcity of water. In an ideal world, the value of groundwater could be estimated using optimal control methods, and that shadow price can be used to inform a redesign of the tariff structure or new investments/policies. However, for many of the reasons described above this is not feasible.

In an analysis commissioned by the 2030 Water Resources Group, Gulland et al. (2020) employed the replacement cost method to assess the cost of declining groundwater. To do so, they examined the textile industry, an industry that is both economically critical for the country and also very water-intensive. They estimated the increased costs to the industry of switching to two alternative water sources – surface water and rainwater harvesting – as well as the cost of reducing water demand by improving water efficiency. The results show that, depending on the availability of surface water as a viable substitute for groundwater, the total value of groundwater availability is between 5 and 46% of the textile industry's net profit, annually. This equates to BDT108–964 million (US$1.2–11.3 million) per year, for the use of 17 million m^3 of water per year. This information can then be used to inform the shadow price of water, and help the city of Dhaka make better decisions on its water use strategy.

10.4 Financial viability of water infrastructure investments

The above discussion surrounds the economic viability of a water sector investment; however, water sector services such as water supply, sanitation, irrigation, flood protection and water treatment have financial costs that must be paid for. When evaluating whether to make a water sector investment, one must take into consideration whether and how it will be funded. This is a critical component to the valuation analysis, as a project which does not have a means for funding will eventually see a service disruption when operations and maintenance are unfunded and capital costs cannot be repaid (UNICEF/WHO, 2021). Similarly, the dynamics of the funding type will impact the net benefits of the investment itself, and who receives them, as will be discussed in this section. This is particularly a challenge when it comes to water supply, sanitation and irrigation services, as these services offer private goods (as opposed to flood protection or wastewater treatment, which are largely public goods). This section therefore focuses on the water supply and sanitation subsectors.

For investments in water supply, sanitation or irrigation services, designing an appropriate water tariff structure is a challenge as there are multiple, often competing, policy goals that need to be taken into consideration. Water is simultaneously a basic human right, a vital economic input and a renewable (but depletable) resource, and it requires significant investments to get it from source to tap. Valuing water resources and services as a whole, and maximizing the benefits of these services requires prudent management of often competing goals of environmental sustainability, fairness and equity, cost recovery, and economic efficiency. These services must be supplied while taking care to ensure affordability for the poor, expansion to the widest number of individuals, and funding to ensure reliability and network improvements. The water tariff (i.e. price) must be carefully designed to accomplish as many of these goals as possible. In addition, there are other issues to be considered in the design of tariffs, including climate change, public acceptability, simplicity and transparency (Box 10.3).

A tariff structure that appropriately considers all of these different goals is unlikely to be found. For instance, increasing access to water services may involve lowering water tariffs. However, this would encourage profligacy, unsustainable withdrawals and inefficient use of water. It will also leave water services underfunded, reducing their quality and limiting their expansion. On the other hand, while higher prices may reduce waste and increase efficiency, they restrict access to the wealthy. In some cases, even a single objective may require multiple policy interventions. Experience suggests that motivating farmers to change irrigation practices requires more than just price incentives. Higher prices may need to be combined with other interventions such as extension services, water rights allocations, education and improved access to markets (Frija et al., 2012; Levidow et al., 2014).

Box 10.3 Innovative mechanisms to ensure affordability of water tariffs in France

The Organisation for Economic Co-operation and Development (OECD, 2020) found in a study that water expenditures in the lowest household income decile in France was on average 1.17% between 2011 and 2015. Since helping those who are unable to pay is preferable over lowering tariffs for all (WWAP, 2015), local private water operators have innovated the following mechanisms to ensure access and affordability, and better deliver against the Human Rights to Water and Sanitation:

- In 1995, public and private bodies have together co-created the 'Multi-Services Points of Information' (PIMMS), involving the State of France and several cities (Assemblée nationale, 2016). By 2020, 67 PIMMS were in operation throughout the territory, with an estimated one million people assisted, including on water and sanitation aspects.[1]
- In 2000, the Federation of Private Water Operators (FP2E) spearheaded an idea to erase unpaid bills for households in difficult financial situations, within the framework of the Housing Solidarity Fund (FSL) (République française, 2015, Article L115-3). This measure currently covers 75% of the French territory (Da Costa et al., 2015).
- In 2010, 'water vouchers' were created by French private operators to alleviate the pressure on the least favoured households, benefiting 20,000 households per year (BIPE-BDO/FP2E, 2019).
- Finally, social tariffs were tested in several cities, involving FP2E members. Based on the positive returns (Comité national de l'eau, 2019), France adopted in 2019 a law allowing their introduction throughout the country (République française, 2019).

Contributed by AquaFed.

1 For further information, see www.pimms.org/.

Although pricing can be an effective tool to reduce profligacy, the prevailing price of water in most locations is far too low to discourage overuse. Several recent studies from the USA have used statistical approaches to demonstrate how water markets and pricing can increase water use efficiency and lead to significant economic gains (Debaere and Li, 2020; Hagerty, 2019). Broader literature exists on the responsiveness of demand for municipal water to its price (see for reviews Arbués et al., 2003; Dalhuisen et al., 2003; Espey et al., 1997; Nauges and Whittington, 2010; Worthington and Hoffman, 2008). The overall finding is that demand for piped water is price-inelastic (i.e. it does not respond significantly to changes in price), and that usage increases slightly with income. This has important implications for demand management and suggests that a significant increase in effective prices will be needed if users are to be induced to consume less water. As noted above, if water is overused and becomes scarce, its shadow price will be high, reducing the net benefits of network expansions.

The increasing block tariff (IBT) is widely believed to be the solution to balance access/affordability with the need for funding and sustainability, particularly in the case of domestic and industrial systems. With an IBT, the tariff rate starts low and increases with use, so that the 1st cubic metre of water is cheaper than the 100th. The popularity of IBTs is based on the assumption that the poor consume less water than the rich. Accordingly, by reducing prices for the lower brackets of consumption, the service is rendered more affordable for the poor. Thus, those consuming larger amounts of water implicitly subsidize water use for those consuming lesser amounts of water. In addition, profligacy can be disincentivized if the higher volumetric blocks are costly enough to limit overuse of water.

IBTs have become by far the most popular form of water tariff in the world. While there is no complete database available to determine the kinds of tariff structures in use globally, several comprehensive sources can be used as sources of information: the International

Benchmarking Network for Water and Sanitation Utilities (IBNet) Tariff database[49] and a survey of utilities conducted by Global Water Intelligence (GWI).[50] Together, these sources indicate that about half of global utilities covered in these databases use IBTs (Figure 10.2). They are especially popular in Latin America (70% of the utilities), the Middle East and North Africa (74%), and East Asia and the Pacific (78%). The uniform volumetric tariff is the next most common water tariff, and used in many developed countries (44%). It is the dominant practice in Europe and Central Asia (85%) (IBNet Tariffs database, 2018). A contrasting variant of the IBT is a decreasing block tariff (DBT), where higher volumes consumed are charged at lower rates. This system is used by about 7% of utilities in parts of North America, Western Europe and Africa. Such a tariff structure neither generates incentives to save water, nor does it appear to meet any presumed equity goals.

Figure 10.2

Summary of tariff structures implemented by utilities, by region

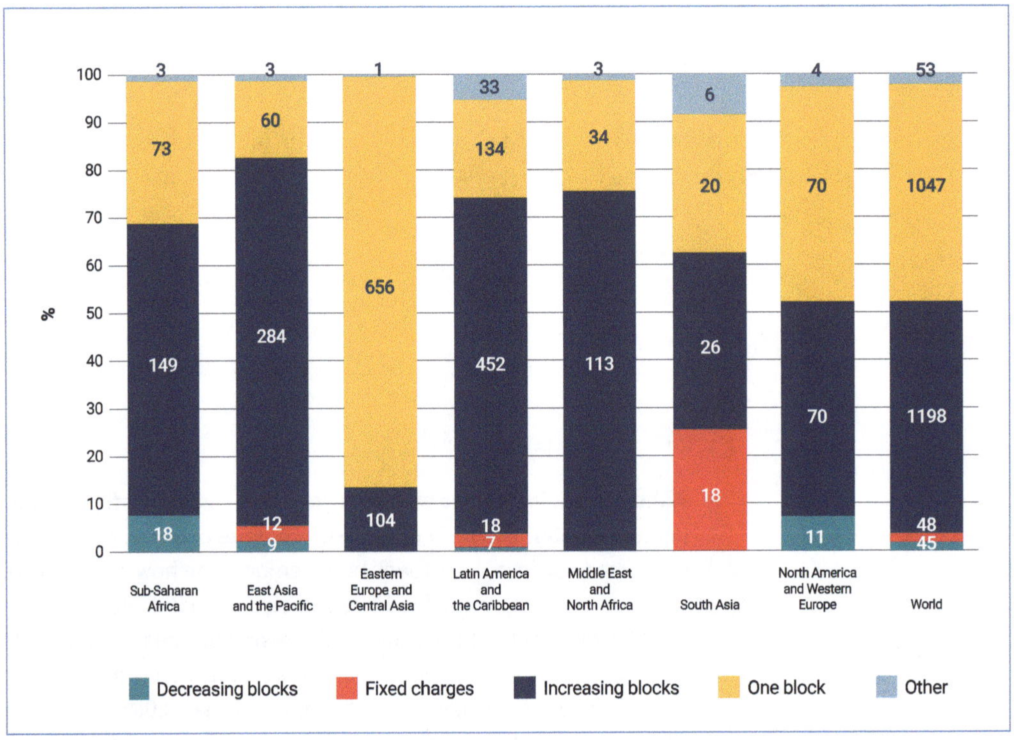

Source: Based on data from IBNet Tariffs database (2018). Data for North America and Western Europe come from the Global Water Intelligence (GWI).

Despite their popularity and perceived benefits, IBTs are no panacea for managing and valuing water. Previous studies have found that IBTs are not effective tariff designs if the stated goal is to subsidize low-income households or limit overuse (Foster et al., 2000; Walker et al., 2000; Banerjee et al., 2010; Angel-Urdinola and Wodon, 2012; Barde and Lehmann, 2014; Whittington et al., 2015). Indeed, the outcomes of the use of IBTs have been found to be rather disappointing. To explain this, at least five factors have been identified in the literature:

1. **Errors of exclusion**: IBTs determine the water bills for those connected to the piped network. But especially in low-income countries, the poorest households do not have water connections. Thus, they are not eligible to receive the 'lifeline' (i.e. cheapest) rate of water, and they miss out on the subsidies implicit in IBTs.

---

[49] tariffs.ib-net.org/.

[50] The annual tariff survey conducted by Global Water Intelligence does not contain a representative sample of utilities across the globe, in particular regions or in particular countries. The IBNet database is not representative either, but it is larger and more focused on developing countries.

2. **Shared connections**: Poorer households tend to share connections, as they may have multiple families living in one residence, or may have a communal tap. Thus, the IBT has a perverse effect – the more households share the primary customer's connection, the more water is billed through the primary connection, and the more water is sold at the prices in the higher blocks of the IBT. As a result, the poorer may end up paying higher tariff rates.
3. **Low income elasticity of demand for water**: The IBT is based on the assumption that the correlation between household water use and income is high, so that poor households who use little water fall into the lower blocks, and rich households that use more water fall into the upper blocks. However, it turns out that the correlation between water use and income is low. As a consequence, any subsidies delivered through the lower blocks are poorly targeted.
4. **Low average costs**: Around the world, and especially in developing countries, the volumetric prices of all the blocks in the IBT are quite low, and below total average cost of delivery. Using an IBT that prices all water below total average cost means that customers do not receive an economic signal about the scarcity value[51] of the raw water resource, or about the marginal costs imposed on the utility by increased water use (see Box 10.4).
5. **Customers respond to average, not marginal prices**: In order for an IBT to achieve the objective of reducing water use, customers must respond to marginal, not average, prices. This is because the marginal price (i.e. the price of the next unit of water consumed) is what is targeted by the IBT. There is little empirical evidence to suggest that households respond to marginal prices. It seems more plausible that households respond to average prices (i.e. the total bill) because many IBT tariff structures are complex and hard to understand, and because tariffs in most low- and middle-income countries are so low.

10.5 Subsidizing water, sanitation and hygiene (WASH) services

Subsidies in the WASH sector are pervasive across the world, in nearly all regions, income groups and settings. A recent World Bank study found that only 35% of utilities can cover operation and maintenance costs through revenues generated by tariffs, and only 14% can cover all economic costs related to service provision (Andres et al., 2019). Even fewer of these utilities can cover the original capital costs, which is often on par or higher than operation and maintenance costs (for instance, capital costs amount to an average of 49% of total costs for water utilities in the United Kingdom (Kingdom et al., 2018)). The remainder of expenses are either covered by subsidies, which can be explicit (such as direct cash transfers to water utilities), implicit (through discounted inputs such as energy needed for pumping and water purification), or 'resolved' by deferring maintenance, and allowing services to crumble.

Large subsidies for WASH service provision are justifiable from an economic as well as a social and moral standpoint; however, they are often poorly targeted, resulting in poor outcomes. As discussed above, water is a merit good and a declared human right. Thus, it is vital that access is ensured for all, and subsidies are an important means for achieving this goal. Nevertheless, as found by Andres et al. (2019), upwards of 56% of subsidies in the WASH sector benefit the wealthiest quintile of the population, while a paltry 6% go to the poorest quintile. This is largely driven by two factors. First, subsidies tend to focus on networked services, whereas poorer neighbourhoods are typically not serviced by piped networks. Second, there are many households that have the potential to connect to networks, but that do not because they cannot afford the connection costs or the volumetric charges. Thus, the subsidy recipient pool is dominated by wealthier households, which capture the bulk of the subsidies.

[51] Scarcity value is an economic factor describing the increase in an item's relative price by an artificially low supply.

Box 10.4 Day Zero events and scarcity signalling in South Africa

The struggle of Cape Town with the approach of 'Day Zero' during 2017 and 2018, the day when the city's water supplies were estimated to run out, illustrates the importance of consumption efficiency. As Day Zero approached, Cape Town's water utility was saddled with a complex Increasing Block Tariff (IBT), which failed to send customers a clear price signal that Day Zero was approaching and that everyone needed to conserve water. Even when the forecasts indicated that Day Zero was just a few months away, most customers in Cape Town were still receiving price signals that water was cheap and plentiful, and the average tariff was far below the cost of incremental water supplies (Booysen et al., 2019).

The lessons learned are not only applicable to Cape Town. Anywhere in the world, as the demand for water rises with urbanization and affluence, the cost of water provision rises with the exhaustion of cheaper options. Price signals that fail to convey the scarcity value of water artificially inflate the demand for water and create path dependence that increases vulnerability to drought.

Large, untargeted WASH subsidies can be counterproductive, reducing the benefits of water services, and thus the valuations of WASH investments

Large, untargeted WASH subsidies can be counterproductive, reducing the benefits of water services, and thus the valuations of WASH investments. Indeed, in countries where piped water is deemed to be very low-cost or free, the poor are often unserved or underserved, and are compelled to pay a much higher price for their water than the rich (World Bank, 2016a). This is because large subsidies leave the utilities beholden to the provider of those subsidies – often local or national governments – rather than the customers themselves. Water connections tend to go hand-in-hand with political connections, leaving the poor dependent on informal means like water tankers, which can be significantly more expensive than water from the formal, piped system. In addition, when funding relies on subsidies, then future funding may be uncertain if government budgets tighten or priorities shift, thus adding uncertainty to economic valuations.

Resolving these unintended outcomes would require a change in how investments are funded. Subsidies, rather than reductions of per unit costs, should fund investments in lower-income communities, and make it more affordable for poorer households to connect to networks. In addition, rather than an IBT that provides subsidies based on water use, households in need of subsidies can be targeted through administrative selection, such as means-testing, or observable factors like household location. This will better ensure that the subsidy reaches the poor, and that the utility is beholden to its customers.

10.6 Conclusions

In sum, the needs for investments in the water sector are numerous, whereas public funds are scarce. Maximizing the value of water in investment decisions requires careful valuation of the costs and benefits that a project provides. For this, all benefits need to be taken into account, including those that are economic, social or environmental. Many of the unintended consequences of these investments, both negative and positive, must also be considered. Only then can we prioritize projects that will bring the most benefits to the most people.

Chapter 11

Knowledge, research and capacity development as enabling conditions

IHE Delft
Yong Jiang

WWAP
David Coates and Richard Connor

With contributions from:
Juliane Schillinger and Waqar Ahmed Pahore (WYPW); Graham Jewitt and Marloes Mul (IHE Delft); David Hebart-Coleman (SIWI); Marianne Kjellén (UNDP); Angelos Findikakis (IAHR); Christophe Cudennec (IAHS); and Lesha Witmer (WfWP)

11.1 Introduction

'Water data' are the physical, environmental, ecological, social, economic, cultural and political parameters of water use, availability and accessibility (Laituri and Sternlieb, 2014). 'Data' are *"facts and statistics collected together for reference or analysis"*, whereas 'information' is a broader concept and includes *"facts provided or learned about something or someone and/or what is conveyed or represented by a particular arrangement or sequence of things"* (Oxford English Dictionary). Data are always discrete and computable, whereas information can be much broader and include quantified, qualitative or unmeasured knowledge. Data are not usually useful as information until assessed or presented in a context. Often, the same data can be used to present different knowledge, like there are variations in how statistics can be interpreted. This is apparent in a number of places in this *World Water Development Report* where different stakeholders use the same data to portray different information or interpretations of value, place the same data in different contexts, and/or apply different assumptions and methods to interpret them. In addition, a key factor in valuations is that some stakeholders can deliberately exclude data in order to strengthen their case. This implies that whilst data as such are important, the way in which they are used to create messages is equally influential.

There are some belief systems that value water without data, or indeed knowledge, such as those based on faith, religion or cultural beliefs. Homeopathy, for example, is based on the scientifically unfounded belief that 'water has memory' (Baran et al., 2014). Yet, as interpreted by millions of 'believers', these beliefs can ultimately influence value judgements, regardless of the full spectrum of scientifically accepted data and knowledge. For example, Chapter 2 points out that some cultural or faith-based concepts of value can override any valuations based on science and data.

The *World Water Development Report* Series has consistently highlighted the shortcomings in data and information availability to underpin the sustainable management of water. This Chapter explores this issue with regards to data and information as enabling conditions for supporting and promoting valuing water broadly, consistent with the Bellagio principles (see Chapter 1). The focus is on requirements for improving data and knowledge regarding the valuation of the multiple benefits of water. However, as pointed out in all previous chapters, current methodologies for valuation, where they exist, as well as different value and belief systems, result in a wide variety of values and opinions on their relative importance.

11.2 Knowledge building and sharing

11.2.1 Valuing data, access and use

As a core component of knowledge building and sharing, water-related data and information are central to understanding and valuing the resource, including with regards to human and environmental needs, to inform decision-making. Many aspects of water resources cannot be valued or managed unless some data and information are available concerning its location, quantity and quality, and how these vary over time (Stewart, 2015). But data and information on these hydrological aspects of water do not, by themselves, inform values that relate to the benefits that water delivers. Therefore, data and information relating to social, economic and environmental demands and uses for water are needed to complete the picture for potential value generation from water. Hydrology is driven by climate and weather, which can be difficult to accurately predict. While data from hydrological networks collected over many decades offer insights into the dynamics of the water cycle (Tetzlaff et al., 2017), serving as the basis for hydrological modelling and several other purposes (Box 11.1), lack of data and information remains a challenge for water resources management (Alida et al., 2018). In addition, the rise of climate change means that previous hydrological records no longer accurately predict future conditions.

The need for, and the value of, hydrological data are likely to further expand in the future due to the global changes related to a growing population, processes of urbanization and economic developments. While those changes will increase the demand for and competition over water,

Box 11.1 Use and value of hydrological data

Hydrological data have been widely used to support water management to meet societal needs. Examples of applications include: i) multipurpose water management systems planning, design, operation and maintenance; ii) the preparation and distribution of flood forecasts and warnings aimed at protecting lives and property; iii) the design of spillways, highways, bridges and culverts; iv) floodplain mapping; v) determining and monitoring environmental or ecological flows; vi) managing water rights and transboundary water issues; vii) education and research; and viii) protecting water quality and regulating pollutant discharges (Stewart, 2015; Hester et al., 2006). A literature review of economic studies assessing the returns on investment from hydrological monitoring programmes found that a dollar of investment in public water data systems generates at the median four dollars in social benefits (Gardner et al., 2017), which highlights the socio-economic and management value of hydrological data.

climate change will make the spatiotemporal distribution of water resources more variable and increasingly difficult to predict, threatening the reliability of water supply (IPCC, 2018). To address these challenges, improved, adaptive water management is needed. This in turn requires hydrological data with a higher density (more parameters measured at higher spatial and temporal resolution), better continuity over longer periods, and improved availability (i.e. discoverability, access machine readability), to account for the changing hydrological conditions and their impacts on biophysical, social, economic and environmental conditions (Cho et al., 2017).

Despite their great societal value, hydrological data, including for groundwater, are still deficient across the globe. Although the increasing competition for water and the projected impacts of climate change further broaden the need for and value of hydrological data, the levels of publicly reported data are well below established benchmarks for station coverage. The reported data in three of the most widely available and globally comprehensive public water datasets show a growing gap, with particularly the developing countries of Africa, Asia and South America lagging behind (Cho et al., 2017) (Table 11.1). There has also been an overall decline in in-situ monitoring systems across the world, including a diminishing number of precipitation gauges (Stokstad, 1999; Sun et al., 2018), water quality monitoring systems

Table 11.1 Illustration of the hydrological data gap between actual reporting and recommended coverage

Water data	Source	Station Reporting	Country Reporting	Reporting Gap*
Streamflow	Global Runoff Data Center (GRDC)	By 2010, the number of stations has declined 40% since peak reporting in 1979.	Declined from 142 countries in 1979 to less than 40 after 2010.	Gap of 30,938 to 52,057 in current global database.
Precipitation	National Oceanic and Atmospheric Administration (NOAA)	By 2010, the number of stations has declined 31% since peak reporting in early 1980s.	Over 180 countries reporting since the mid-1800s.	Gap of 6,416 to 14,773 in current aggregated database.
Water quality	Global Environmental Monitoring System (GEMS)	By 2010, the number of stations has declined41% since peak reporting in 1993.	Total of 83 countries reporting since 1965, but only 16 after 2010.	Not calculated as no targets by parameter.

*Reporting gaps are defined as the number of stations as recommended by the World Meteorological Organization (WMO), minus the number of reported stations in the specific database since 2010.

Source: Adapted from Cho et al. (2017, Table 3, p. 8). Reproduced with permission from Xylem Inc.

(Zhulidov et al., 2000) and river discharge sensors (Fekete et al., 2012). Finally, despite Sustainable Development Goal (SDG) Target 6.5, promoting transboundary cooperation for integrated water resources management, there is no single global hydrological monitoring system, but rather a proliferation of networks designed and operated by their respective owners for specific uses and at different spatial scales, covering different parameters and data types (Cho et al., 2017).

The situation is even worse when it comes to water-related socio-economic and environmental data. These are critical to revealing the different values of water and to driving or influencing decision-making regarding planning, policy and management. Data related to societal use of and demands for water, including in relation to environmental water needs and constraints and their relative values, remain scattered, fragmented or simply unavailable. For example, gender-disaggregated data on topics such as access to water supply, sanitation and hygiene (WASH) or water resources management tend to be lacking and where they do exist they are very limited or not reported due to the methodologies and high aggregation levels used (Chapter 4). Gender- and age-disaggregated data on participation in water management and decision-making are also deficient. The result is that gender-sensitive analysis is hardly ever done in real time despite its critical importance to policy formulation. The *Toolkit on Sex-Disaggregated Water Data* developed by the UNESCO World Water Assessment Programme (WWAP) taskforce on gender,[52] and the inventory of available policies and tools developed in the frame of the International Waters Learning Exchange and Resource Network (IW:LEARN)[53] can provide valuable assistance here. Women tend to have different preferences to men when it comes to solutions, and are more prone to take issues like environmental considerations into account (OECD, 2014).

Further efforts and investments are needed to sustain the supply chain of data from its collection, analysis, sharing and application in support of the management needs across sectors and scales

There is also a need to standardize the compiling, storing and disseminating of data and information relating to the economic values of water under its diversity of uses. Especially social, cultural and other intrinsic values are hardly standardized. Further efforts and investments are needed to sustain the supply chain of data from its collection, analysis, sharing and application in support of the management needs across sectors and scales.

11.2.2 Knowledge and data sharing tools

With the modern advancements in earth observation as well as information and communication technology (ICT), both the sources and tools for collecting and sharing water data have been expanding. Water-related data and information are derived from seven main sources (Table 11.2). These include measurements through monitoring networks specially operated by governments directly, model estimation, and administrative collection (e.g. regulation data such as permits or census data) (Bureau of Meteorology, 2017). Water-related data and information can also be generated by other sources such as earth observations, sensor networks and citizen data, including on social media. The development of earth observation has progressed to include a plethora of sensing opportunities afforded by CubeSats, uncrewed aerial vehicles and smartphone technologies, enabling new means of measurement, such as real-time high-definition videos of storm cell development, flood propagation and precipitation monitoring, among others (McCabe et al., 2017). These expanded data sources complement each other, increase the knowledge base for management decision-making (e.g. Hadj-Hammou et al., 2017), and improve data and information for understanding the values of water (Table 11.2).

---

52 The 2019 edition of the UNESCO WWAP *Toolkit on Sex-Disaggregated Water Data* can be found here: www.unesco.org/new/en/natural-sciences/environment/water/wwap/water-and-gender.

53 See www.iwlearn.net/gender for further information about IW:LEARN's gender subcomponent.

Table 11.2 Comparisons of sources of water data

Data source	Mechanism	Characteristics
Direct official measurement	Measurements by meteorological, hydrologic and other measurement instruments in monitoring networks, usually with scientifically designed sampling programmes and strategies	• Covers mostly physical, chemical and biological parameters of water; • Usually yields the most accurate and reliable data; • Essential part of water data strategy; • Most costly (in terms of instruments, installation and lab analysis); • Limited size and density of monitoring networks, limited intensity and longevity of sampling programmes due to budget constraints; • Limited coverage of water data in space and time.
Model estimation	Estimates from hydrological/biophysical models validated and calibrated with monitored data from direct measurement	• Used when direct measurement is inadequate, unaffordable or problematic; • Fills gaps in the spatial coverage of monitoring networks; • Fills gaps in continuous data records; • Provides predictions/forecasting of future conditions; • Synthesizes large amounts of complex information for understanding/ decision-making; • Requires model design, development, programming tools and data input; • Based on assumptions of similar conditions and real world observations.
Administrative collection	Data from administratively maintained records, documents, information and reports captured by management agencies as part of business processes, or from household and business surveys by statistical agencies and researchers	• Used for data types that are not amenable to direct measurement or model estimation; • Usually covers socio-economic, management-related water data, such as infrastructure inventories, water abstraction permits, etc.; • Vital contextual information for the development and evaluation of water management strategies and policy.
Earth observations	Inference from imagery of passive (e.g. radiometers and spectrometers) or active (e.g. radars and lidars) remote-sensing instruments/sensors mounted on satellites, aircrafts and drones	• Cover mainly physical water parameters such as soil moisture content, rainfall rate, evaporation, temperature and environmental conditions; • Require careful calibration using direct measurement; • Provide opportunities for low-cost measurements over extensive areas with continuous spatial coverage; • Provide temporally regular data; • Relatively coarse spatial resolution due to the long distance from Earth; • Require significant information technology infrastructure to handle large datasets and complex image-processing tasks to make data suitable for use.
Spatial data infrastructure	A framework of spatial data, metadata, tools and user communities interactively connected to allow for the efficient and flexible use of spatial data (e.g. national hydrography datasets, watershed boundary datasets, national elevation datasets)	• Large in size, cost and number of interactors; • Requires defined standards and coordination among actors for proper functioning.
Commercial/ business data	Data managed and maintained by private-sector firms for individual business purposes (e.g. accounting/ financial data, mobile phone records)	• Privately owned with little or limited public access; • Dispersed, distributed.
Citizen-generated data	Data generated passively or purposefully by citizens or via social media or crowdsourcing	• Local in situ observations; • Human engagement, perceived observations; • Relatively low cost; • Provides opportunities for public engagement, learning and awareness-raising.

Source: Based on information from Fritz et al. (2019) and Bureau of Meteorology (2017).

These rich sets of data streams need to be converted into value-related information products and tools that inform policy and management. Important aspects herein include: i) coordination and communication between data providers and users to help ensure that the data and tools created are useful and to avoid mismatches between data needs and availability; ii) strategies or methods to unlock private data and to stimulate data sharing among stakeholders; and iii) common standards to allow data aggregation and integration (Grossman et al., 2015). Functioning water observation networks producing fit-for-purpose data and information, and their sharing with all stakeholders, are essential for minimizing uncertainties and informing water resources management (WMO, 2009).

The World Wide Fund for Nature (WWF) has compiled a database listing tools, processes and methods that have emerged over the past 15 years related to water and environmental risks, impacts and values (WWF, 2019b). The database allows for comparisons between the various approaches to valuing water in a broad sense that have been adopted in practice by different stakeholders, or that target different audiences and management needs with varying outputs and levels of accessibility.

Some standards and protocols, such as the *International Water Stewardship Standard* (Alliance for Water Stewardship, 2019) and the *Hydropower Sustainability Assessment Protocol* (HSAC, 2018), are increasingly incorporating criteria and assessments of stakeholder involvement and social inclusion, including indigenous peoples' rights and women's participation, as well as ecosystem protection.

11.3 Local and indigenous knowledge

To promote inclusive and transformative change in valuing water, it is strategically important to recognize the unique role of local and indigenous knowledge (LIK), in addition to the mainstream or traditional scientific or academic knowledge. LIK refers to the understandings, skills and philosophies developed by societies over long histories of interaction with their natural surroundings that inform decision-making about fundamental aspects of day-to-day life (UNESCO, n.d.). It provides sociocultural information necessary for community survival and for flourishing within local environmental, geographical and cultural contexts, while facilitating communication and decision-making within a community (Tharakan, 2015). Until recently, water resources management and policy have not appropriately included LIK that reflects and carries the local values of water, despite its relevance to sustainability (e.g. Escott et al., 2015). Connecting LIK and mainstream science can allow for the creation of new spaces for collaborative approaches to value and manage water resources (Box 11.2). Scientific studies

Box 11.2 The Great Canoe Journey

Indigenous knowledge can raise awareness of the perspectives on values that people prescribe to water. The Great Canoe Journey, a learning tool developed by the Canadian organization Waterlution, is an example of such a project. The programme combines cultural and water education and is targeted at Canadian students aged 7–18. Educational activities include local indigenous canoe builders who teach students about the traditional boats and the local waters, alongside indigenous and non-indigenous youth advisors who specialize in other areas related to the local environment, drawing from scientific research. The programme utilizes local knowledge to sensitize students to their local cultures, waterways and other natural resources. It also challenges students to reflect on their own relation to water, based on the different indigenous and non-indigenous perspectives and value systems presented to them. Between 2018 and 2020, the Great Canoe Journey events reached more than 4,200 youth in Canada.

Source: Waterlution (2020).

have identified, shown or justified the unique value of LIK in various water-related contexts and applications including, for example, climate change adaptation (Makondo and Thomas, 2018; Son et al., 2019), coastal resilience enhancement (Chowdhooree, 2019), water and river management (Parsons et al., 2019; Borthakur and Singh, 2020), environmental management (Boiral et al., 2020), and disaster risk reduction (Cuaton and Su, 2020). Examples or practices of LIK regarding water management prevail across cultures and regions in the world (UNESCO, n.d.), and provide inspirational and locally adapted solutions, illustrating how water is valued and can be effectively managed at the local level (Box 11.3).

Box 11.3 Local and Indigenous Knowledge (LIK) in managing water scarcity with value generation

The small streams, called *oueds*, in the vicinity of Tiznit, Morocco, flow rarely and erratically. Local communities created long underground tunnels called *foggara* or *khettara* to exploit groundwater in a sustainable way, recognizing its important future and scarcity values. After the infrequent rains, the *oueds* can also be exploited by barriers that are maintained by users, which allows for water storage for irrigation when required. The 'water master' (*abbar*) distributes water according to pre-established value-based rules so that each user knows exactly when and for how long they are entitled to water their crops. Hence, LIK is included and applied in value-based thinking to smartly manage water.

Source: Civiltà dell'Acqua Centro Internazionale (n.d.).

11.4 Transdisciplinary and participatory research

Estimates of water-related values are often incomplete, approximate and conflicting (Garrick et al., 2017). Some can be addressed through transdisciplinary and participatory research, which can help identify, understand and incorporate the diverse values of water by engaging multiple disciplines and stakeholders to identify effective, acceptable solutions to common problems.

Part of the solution is to expand citizen science. Citizen science often pre-dates formal science – citizens have been involved with collecting meteorological data for centuries (Buytaert, et al., 2014). Local communities, including women, youth and indigenous people organizations, are usually well informed about local conditions and practices and have a vested interest in contributing to improved management (Box 11.4). One of the constraints to expanding citizen science can be resistance from formally trained academics. In order to improve uptake of citizen science, ten principles for its use have been developed by the European Citizen Science Association (ECSA, 2015) (Box 11.5). Although access to internet has been a constraint to using mobile apps, particularly in least developed countries, the digital divide continues to narrow (UNESCO, 2017). In areas where ICT approaches to disseminating knowledge are lacking, radio, printed information and storytelling can be important means to transfer knowledge.

The involvement of representative local stakeholders in ground-truthing data and information is important. However, for example, women are often not invited or able to go to meetings where information is collected or disseminated.

Citizen science not only facilitates data and knowledge generation but also inclusive, participatory decision-making, local leadership, awareness-raising and capacity development (Liebenberg et al., 2017; McKinley et al., 2017). It can, therefore, create better-informed policy through a bottom-up inclusive approach to understanding and valuing water, while building a foundation for a more sustainable community in the long term (Hugh, 2019).

11.5 Capacity development

Capacity development is the process through which individuals, organizations and societies obtain, strengthen and maintain the capabilities to set and achieve their own development objectives over time. Within the context of valuing water, capacity development concerns the establishment of know-how to inclusively and properly value water and to effectively manage it on the basis of those values, applied at different levels and under diverse conditions leading to variable outcomes. As a key enabling condition, capacity development seeks to establish a strong knowledge base, awareness of its necessity, understanding of valuing water, and the ability to utilize, apply and improve this knowledge (Wehn de Montalvo and Alaerts, 2013). Particular attention is required to:

- increase the collection and coverage of water data, particularly socio-economic data, from all traditional and non-traditional sources, in multiple metrics reflecting diverse values;
- develop and strengthen effective mechanisms to integrate water data and to use them to inform policy and management;
- enhance knowledge and data sharing mechanisms, within and beyond the water sector, to broaden participation in the knowledge production process, facilitating closer stakeholder collaboration and creating mutual trust in contested situations, and to stimulate and support innovation; and
- recognize and include local and indigenous knowledge in scientific research, including in setting the research agenda and in policy and management decision-making, so as to integrate a deeper understanding of local values, human–water interactions and locally adapted/proven solutions, as well as to increase equity.

Innovation in education is much needed to keep pace with the increasing complexity and new developments in the water sector

With the achievement of the Bellagio principles on valuing water as the overall goal, specific goals can be established for capacity development in the short, intermediate and long terms (Table 11.3). Immediate goals centre on the metrics and methodologies for measuring and analysing water values, including coverage and quality of water data. The intermediate- to long-term goals centre more on institutions and the enabling environment at the societal level, including water literacy regarding social norms and the cultural aspects of valuing water.

Innovation in education is much needed to keep pace with the increasing complexity and new developments in the water sector. There are gaps in professional education programmes related to water. Yet, there is limited, if any, educational and training support to meet the societal needs, which are very significant considering that climate change elevates water resilience, risk and security as goals. There is a need for more investment to support these, and other, needs and to develop more integrated education programmes between the various water-related disciplines.

Table 11.3

Capacity development for valuing water strategies

Overall goal: achievement of Bellagio principles on valuing water	***Intermediate- to long-term goal:*** improving institutions and enabling environment for valuing water	***Immediate goal:*** improving data and methodology for measuring and analysing water's importance and value, improving the quality and coverage of water data and statistics
• Recognize water's multiple values • Reconcile values and build trust • Protect sources • Educate to empower • Invest and innovate	• Improve value assessment using more reliable and consistent data and statistics and based on improved methodology • Improve analytic skills to evaluate risk and value impact of water or related policies • Introduce new methods and tools for monitoring and evaluating the value impact of policies and programmes • Improve understanding of trade-offs and costs of different policy instruments and policies	• Improve quality, consistence, reliability and coverage of data and statistics surrounding water availability, variability, quality, use and needs, and gender relevance • Improve the metrics, indicators and methodology of value measurement and a system of administrative statistics for enhanced monitoring and policy-oriented analytic work • Generate consensus on the taxonomy of values, characteristics and indicators • Publicize and disseminate data to other sectors/agencies within the government • Guarantee open access to data • Promote participation and dialogue on values, interests and equality

Source: Partially based on World Bank (2003, Table 1, p.16).

Box 11.4 Citizen science helps fill hydrological data and information gaps in Zambia

People in the Kafue River basin use *FreshWater Watch* to meet Ministry objectives to improve monitoring in this large river. The Zambian Water Resources Management Authority (WARMA), together with the World Wide Fund for Nature (WWF) Zambia and Earthwatch Europe, initiated this citizen science activity in 2018 to meet Ministerial and local objectives to improve catchment management and national reporting responsibilities. Data are collected through the programme app and passed to WARMA.

Photo: © Enock Mwangilwa, Unite4Climate and Conservation.

Source: Excerpt from Earthwatch Institute (n.d.)

Box 11.5 Ten principles for citizen science

1. Citizen science projects actively involve citizens in scientific endeavours that generate new knowledge or understanding.
2. Citizen science projects have a genuine science outcome.
3. Both the professional scientists and the citizen scientists benefit from taking part.
4. Citizen scientists may, if they wish, participate in multiple stages of the scientific process.
5. Citizen scientists receive feedback from the project.
6. Citizen science is considered a research approach like any other, with limitations and biases that should be considered and controlled for.
7. Citizen science project data and metadata are made publicly available and, where possible, results are published in an open access format.
8. Citizen scientists are acknowledged in project results and publications.
9. Citizen science programmes are evaluated for their scientific output, data quality, participant experience and wider societal or policy impact.
10. The leaders of citizen science projects take into consideration legal and ethical issues surrounding copyright, intellectual property, data sharing agreements, confidentiality, attribution and the environmental impact of any activities.

Source: ECSA (2015).

Chapter 12

Conclusions

WWAP

Richard Connor and David Coates

12.1 What is the value of water... *to whom?*

Water is a unique and non-substitutable resource. As the foundation of life, societies and economies, it carries multiple values and benefits. But unlike most other natural resources, it has proven extremely difficult to determine its 'true' value. As such, the overall importance of this vital resource has not been appropriately reflected in political attention and financial investment in many parts of the world. This not only leads to inequalities in access to water resources and water-related services, but also to inefficient and unsustainable use and degradation of water supplies themselves, affecting the fulfilment of nearly all the Sustainable Development Goals (SDGs), as well as basic human rights.

Approaches to valuing water vary widely across – and even within – different user dimensions and perspectives. Whereas criteria for valuing water resources and the environment (Chapter 2) focus mainly on quantifying the economic impacts and benefits of water provision, purification and other ecosystem services, valuing water infrastructure (Chapters 3 and 10) lends itself more to a cost–benefit type of analysis. Valuing water supply and sanitation (Chapter 4) is closely related to the benefits these services bring to people and communities, including improved health and living conditions. The value of water for agriculture (Chapter 5), industry and energy (Chapter 6) is easiest assessed though an input–output economic perspective, which can include quantifying economic returns and other benefits, such as employment, as value delivered per unit of water. Finally, the often intangible nature of some sociocultural values attributed to water (Chapter 7) regularly defies any attempt at quantification but, nevertheless, can be regarded amongst the highest values.

These are, of course, oversimplifications. The reality, as described throughout this report, is much more complicated. For example, attempts to value water are likely to suffer from some level of bias, even where unintentional, on the part of those directly involved in valuation processes, as the perception of the values attributed to water and its related benefits can be highly subjective. The fundamental question about value is, then, value to whom? Valuations often tend to target specific beneficiaries, while other stakeholders may benefit less or even be negatively impacted.

12.2 Recognizing and overcoming complexities

Consolidating the different approaches and methods for valuing water across multiple dimensions and perspectives will likely remain challenging. As exemplified in Box 1.3, even within a specific water use sector (in this case agriculture), different approaches can lead to strikingly different valuations. Trying to reconcile valuations across sectors would normally increase the overall level of difficulty, as would taking account of some of the more intangible values attributed to water in different sociocultural contexts. While there may be scope to reduce complexities and standardize metrics in some circumstances, the reality is the need for better means to recognize, maintain and accommodate different values.

Currently, although tools and methodologies exist for valuing water, even if imperfect, they are often poorly utilized. Economics is perhaps the discipline that logically has the greatest utility in valuations and its application has improved in some approaches, notably for the environment (Chapter 2). To be more effective, economics must have the broadest of scopes, not be limited to monetary-based valuations or market-based approaches, and include analyses of all costs and benefits in play, including those that are hidden or invisible. Even so, it must be recognized that there are values that can override those based on economics.

Yet as complex as valuing water may be, it remains an absolutely necessary step in addressing water-related challenges worldwide. Otherwise, water will remain poorly accounted for and, thus, routes to its better management harder to identify. Making all the different values of water more explicit gives recognition and a voice to dimensions that are otherwise easily overlooked, poorly understood or ill-defined, which can lead to inequitable sharing of benefits, inadequate reconciliation of negative impacts and costs, unsustainable solutions, unintended consequences, risks, and weakly performing policies and institutions.

One critical step lies in a better understanding of the concept of 'value' itself. As described throughout this report, 'price', 'cost' and 'value' are by no means synonymous. Whereas the first two are easily quantifiable from a primarily economic monetary-based perspective, the notion of 'value' encompasses a much broader set of often intangible benefits. While monetary valuation is arguably easier than most other approaches, and has the important advantage of using a common metric whereby values of different uses can be quantitatively compared, it can lead to the undervaluation or exclusion of benefits that are more difficult to monetize.

Another issue involves recognizing the shortcomings of current approaches to valuation in order to improve their application and performance. For example, as alluded to in Chapters 3, 4 and 10, capital costs are often not considered when valuing water infrastructure, which in turn leads to a skewed analysis. Consideration of the impacts of subsidies, whether directly related to water infrastructure or major water use sectors like agriculture and industry, is generally lacking in most water valuation schemes. Including the costs of capital or subsidies can change the benefit–cost analysis from positive to negative. Although subsidies, including for capital, may be justified in some circumstances, if not transparent they lead to illusory values.

Approaches to valuing water vary widely across – and even within – different user dimensions and perspectives

The importance of knowledge (Chapter 11) is also critical. There is a need across the board to improve data and information, and to incorporate them better into decision-making. However, better data will not necessarily lead to better management outcomes. Many policy, management and investment decisions regarding water deliberately ignore relevant data and information. No improvement in the data will be able to correct such decisions. Examples include decisions driven by vested interests or corruption (see Chapters 3 and 9). Therefore, issues go well beyond the extent, relevance and reliability of the data and information. Equally important are the ways in which data and information are used.

The idea that 'valuing water' would necessarily translate into local water savings needs to be reconsidered. Chapters 5 and 6 clearly point to the fact that, in some cases, improving water productivity and use efficiency can not only fail to reduce demand, it can also lead to conflicting trade-offs, notably with respect to poverty alleviation. This is not to say that efforts to reduce water use should not be pursued vigorously across all sectors, but rather that the full range of potential socio-economic impacts need to be taken into consideration. Valuing water also has an important role in identifying the value of investments in its management; for example, the incremental value of improved water use efficiency in agriculture is delivered, not necessarily through higher-value crops, but by making more water available for other higher- value uses. This begs the important question of how incentives are transferred from higher- to lower-value uses. For example, most would consider food security to be a priority, but food itself is a low value use of water. So how can the promotion of higher-value uses for industrial, domestic or environmental purposes provide the incentives for improved crop water productivity?

Intangible values are not limited to 'water for peace' or to the various sociocultural perceptions and realities described in Chapter 7. For example, the value of water for food security is arguably incalculable, yet water is often undervalued (or even shown to have a negative value) in agriculture (Chapter 1). This illustrates a certain disconnect between water and other sectoral policies where the value of water remains hidden or ignored. Similarly, while water is essential for electricity production, its value usually remains hidden until generation is undermined by water scarcity.

A significant gap is where valuations fail to factor in the potential costs associated with risks and uncertainties, or the benefits of reducing them. Extreme water-related events, the catastrophic failure of water supply systems or sudden changes in price assumptions made, among other sources of risk and uncertainty, can drastically affect valuations. In a world of increasing risks and uncertainties due to climate change, this is a surprising omission.

12.3 Addressing conflicting views

Addressing conflicting views and managing potential trade-offs remains one of the greatest challenges to water management. Various water use sectors, from water supply, sanitation and hygiene, to agriculture, energy, industry and the environment, stand to benefit over the longer term from an improved integration of the values of water across the full development cycle, from planning through to improved efficiencies, adaptive management and monitoring. But in the near term, there will be trade-offs and a need for adjustments, through a set of controls and incentives for certain sectors to use water more efficiently in particular instances. The initial phases of water resources planning and infrastructure design present considerable, but underused opportunities for introducing various aspects of water's value. Once identified through stakeholder processes of engagement and empowerment, acknowledging the various aspects of water's value can help ensure their equitable treatment in subsequent stages of water management. Similar opportunities to further address trade-offs exist in later stages of decision-making. In the short term, not all sectors will benefit every time, and some sectors, if not all, will need to adapt in response to the different values of water.

The risks of undervaluing water are far too great to ignore

As described in Chapter 9, stakeholder engagement and empowerment by means of multi-stakeholder platforms, dialogues, and vision and objective-setting processes tailored to water development all provide entry points for ensuring full consideration of the multiple values of water. Institutionalizing ethics into all water decisions and water behaviours could contribute a complementary set of behavioural guidance to that of the laws, policies and regulations concerning water. Political will to consider all value sets for water, and to then act on that basis, is critical, necessitating the transformation of political processes and a redistribution of power and voice, through the building of public awareness and pressure for change.

Finally, the demand for valuing water needs to be created. Water is universally underpriced and undervalued. Very few governments, businesses or citizens are demanding that water is valued. Moreover, where citizens perceive water as a human right, and therefore a free or public good, valuations can be resisted.

12.4 Coda

Even though it is not always recognized by all, water clearly has value. In some perspectives the value of water is infinite, since life does not exist without it and there is no replacement for it. This is perhaps best exemplified by the efforts and investments made in the search for extra-terrestrial water and the recent elation in finding it on the Moon and Mars. It is a shame that all too often, it is taken for granted here on Earth. The risks of undervaluing water are far too great to ignore.

References

A

2030 WRG (2030 Water Resources Group). 2009. *Charting Our Water Future: Economic Frameworks to Inform Decision-Making. Executive Summary*. www.mckinsey.com/business-functions/sustainability/our-insights/charting-our-water-future.

Abell, R., Asquith, N., Boccaletti, G., Bremer, L., Chapin, E., Erickson-Quiroz, A., Higgins, J., Johnson, J., Kang, S., Karres, N., Lehner, B., Mcdonald, R., Raepple, J., Shemie, D., Simmons, E., Sridhar, A., Vigerstøl, K., Vogl, A., Wood, S. 2017. *Beyond the Source: The Environmental, Economic and Community Benefits of Source Water*. Arlington, Va., The Nature Conservancy. www.nature.org/content/dam/tnc/nature/en/documents/Beyond_The_Source_Full_Report_FinalV4.pdf.

Acuña, V., Díez, J. R., Flores, L., Meleason, M. and Elosegi, A. 2013. Does it make economic sense to restore rivers for their ecosystem services? *Journal of Applied Ecology*, Vol. 50, No. 4, pp. 988–997. doi.org/10.1111/1365-2664.12107.

ADB (Asian Development Bank). 2016. *Asia Water Development Outlook 2016: Strengthening Water Security in Asia and the Pacific*. Manila, ADB. www.adb.org/sites/default/files/publication/189411/awdo-2016.pdf.

ADB/APWF (Asian Development Bank/Asia-Pacific Water Forum). 2013. *Asian Water Development Outlook 2013: Measuring Water Security in Asia and the Pacific*. Mandaluyong City, Philippines, ADB. www.adb.org/sites/default/files/publication/30190/asian-water-development-outlook-2013.pdf.

Adelphi/CAREC (Central Asia Regional Economic Program). 2017. *Rethinking Water in Central Asia: The Costs of Inaction and Benefits of Water Cooperation*. Berlin, Adelphi. www.adelphi.de/en/system/files/mediathek/bilder/Rethinking%20Water%20in%20Central%20Asia%20-%20adelphi%20carec%20ENG.pdf.

Adikari, Y. and Yoshitani, J. 2009. *Global Trends in Water-Related Disasters: An Insight for Policymakers*. United Nations World Water Assessment Programme (UNESCO), Insights Side Publication series. Paris, UNESCO. unesdoc.unesco.org/ark:/48223/pf0000181793.

AFED (Arab Forum for Economic Development). 2015. *Sustainable Consumption for Better Resource Management in Arab Countries. Annual Report of the Arab Forum for Environment & Development*. AFED.

Ahern, J. 2011. From fail-safe to safe-to-fail: Sustainability and resilience in the new urban world. *Landscape and Urban Planning*, Vol. 100, No. 4, pp. 341–343. doi.org/10.1016/j.landurbplan.2011.02.021.

Alberini, A. and Cooper, J. 2000. *Applications of the Contingent Valuation Method in Developing Countries: A Survey*. FAO Economic and Social Development Paper No. 146. Rome, The Food and Agriculture Organization of the United Nations (FAO). www.fao.org/3/X8955E/x8955e00.htm.

Ali, M., Nelson, A., Lopez, A. and Sack, D. 2015. Updated global burden of cholera in endemic countries. *PLoS Neglected Tropical Diseases*, Vol. 9, No. 6. doi.org/10.1371/journal.pntd.0003832.

Alida, C., Kiparsky, M., Kennedy, R., Hubbard, S., Bales, R., Pecharroman, L. C., Guivetchi, K., McCready, C. and Darling, G. 2018. *Data for Water Decision Making: Informing the Implementation of California's Open and Transparent Water Data Act through Research and Engagement*. Berkeley, Calif., Center for Law, Energy & the Environment, Berkeley School of Law, University of California. doi.org/10.15779/J28H01.

Alliance for Water Stewardship. 2018. *First Municipal Incentive for AWS Certification*. Alliance for Water Partnership website. a4ws.org/updates/first-municipal-incentive-for-aws-certification/.

____. 2019. *The International Water Stewardship Standard – Version 2.0*. North Berwick, UK, Alliance for Water Stewardship. a4ws.org/the-aws-standard-2-0/.

____. n.d. Alliance for Water Stwardship website. a4ws.org. (Accessed August 2020).

Al-Zubari, W., Al-Turbak, A., Zahid, W., Al-Ruwis, K., Al-Tkhais, A. Al-Muataz, I. AbdelWahab, A., Murad, A., Al-Harbi, M. and Al-Sulaymani, Z. 2017. An overview of the GCC Unified Water Strategy (2016–2035). *Desalination and Water Treatment*, Vol. 81, pp. 1–18. doi.org/10.5004/dwt.2017.20864.

AMWC (Arab Ministerial Water Council). 2012. Arab Strategy for Water Security in the Arab Region to Meet the Challenges and Future Needs for Sustainable Development 2010–2030. AMWC.

ANA (Agéncia Nacional de Água). 2011. *ANA abre seleção para projetos de conservação de água e solo* [ANA calls for projects on water and soil conservation]. ANA website. www2.ana.gov.br/Paginas/imprensa/noticia.aspx?id_noticia=9304. (In Portuguese.)

Anderson, E. P., Jackson, S., Tharme, R. E., Douglas, M., Flotemersch, J. E., Zwarteveen, M., Lokgariwar, C., Montoya, M., Wali, A., Tipa, G. T., Jardine, T. D., Olden, J. D., Cheng, L., Conallin, J., Cosens, B., Dickens, C., Garrick, D., Groenfeldt, D., Kabogo, J., Roux, D. J., Ruhi, A. and Arthington, A. H. 2019. Understanding rivers and their social relations: A critical step to advance environmental water management. *WIREs Water*, Vol. 6, No. 6, e1381. doi.org/10.1002/wat2.1381.

Andres, L. A., Thibert, M., Lombana Cordoba, C., Danilenko, A. V., Joseph, G. and Borja-Vega, C. 2019. *Doing More with Less: Smarter Subsidies for Water Supply and Sanitation*. Washington, DC, World Bank. © World Bank. openknowledge.worldbank.org/handle/10986/32277. License: CC BY 3.0 IGO.

Angel-Urdinola, D. F. and Wodon, Q. 2012. Does increasing access to infrastructure services improve the targeting performance of water subsidies? *Journal of International Development*, Vol. 24, No. 1, pp. 88–101. doi.org/10.1002/jid.1668.

Anisfeld, S. C. 2011. *Water Resources*. Washington, DC, Island Press.

Annandale, G. W., Morris, G. L. and Karki, P. 2016. *Extending the Life of Reservoirs: Sustainable Sediment Management for Dams and Run-of-River Hydropower*. Directions in Development – Energy and Mining. Washington, DC, World Bank. openknowledge.worldbank.org/handle/10986/25085. License: CC BY 3.0 IGO.

APWF (Asia-Pacific Water Forum). 2009. *Regional Document: Asia Pacific*. Istanbul, Turkey, 5th World Water Forum Secretariat. apwf.org/documents/ap_regional_document_final.pdf.

AQUASTAT. 2010. *Global Water Withdrawal*. AQUASTAT website. Rome, Food and Agriculture Organization of the United Nations (FAO). www.fao.org/nr/water/aquastat/water_use/image/WithTimeNoEvap_eng.pdf.

_____. 2014. *Did you know...? Facts and Figures about*. Rome, Food and Agriculture Organization of the United Nations (FAO). www.fao.org/nr/water/aquastat/didyouknow/print3.stm.

_____. 2016. *Water Withdrawal by Sector, around 2010*. Rome, Food and Agriculture Organization of the United Nations (FAO). www.fao.org/aquastat/en/overview/methodology/water-use.

_____. n.d. *AQUASTAT – FAO's Global Information System on Water and Agriculture*. Rome, Food and Agriculture Organization of the United Nations (FAO). www.fao.org/aquastat/en/.

Arbués, F., García-Valiñas, M. A. and Martínez-Espiñeira, R. 2003. Estimation of residential water demand: A state-of-the-art review. *Journal of Socio-Economics*. Vol. 32, No. 1, pp. 81–102. doi.org/10.1016/S1053-5357(03)00005-2.

Arias-Arévalo, P., Martín-López, B. and Gómez-Baggethun, E. 2017. Exploring intrinsic, instrumental, and relational values for sustainable management of social-ecological systems. *Ecology and Society*, Vol. 22, No. 4, Art. 43. doi.org/10.5751/ES-09812-220443.

Arouna, A. and Dabbert, S. 2012. Estimating rural households' willingness to pay for water supply improvements: A Benin case study using a semi-nonparametric bivariate probit approach. *Water International*, Vol. 37, No. 3, pp. 293–304. doi.org/10.1080/02508060.2012.687507.

Artelle, K. A., Stephenson, J., Bragg, C., Housty, J. A., Housty, W. G., Kawharu, M. and Turner, N. J. 2018. Values-led management: The guidance of place-based values in environmental relationships of the past, present, and future. *Ecology and Society*, Vol. 23, No. 3, Art. 35. doi.org/10.5751/ES-10357-230335.

Arthington, A. H. 2012. *Environmental Flows: Saving Rivers in the Third Millennium*. Berkeley, Calif., University of California Press.

Arthington, A. H., Bhaduri, A., Bunn, S. E., Jackson, S. E., Tharme, R. E., Tickner, D., Young, B., Acreman, M., Baker, N., Capon, S., Horne, A. C., Kendy, E., McClain, M. E., Poff, N. L., Richter, B. D and Ward, S. 2018. The Brisbane Declaration and Global Action Agenda on environmental flows (2018). *Frontiers in Environmental Science*, Vol. 6, No. 45, Art. 45. doi.org/10.3389/fenvs.2018.00045.

Assanvo, W., Abatan, J. E. and Sawadogo, W. A. 2016. *Assessing the Multinational Joint Task Force against Boko Haram*. ISS West Africa Report, No. 19. Institute for Security Studies (ISS).

Assemblée nationale. 2016. Rapport d'Information sur l'évaluation des politiques publiques en faveur de l'accès aux droits sociaux [Information report assessing public policies on the access to social rights], N° 4158. Enregistré à la Présidence de l'Assemblée nationale le 26 octobre 2016. www.assemblee-nationale.fr/14/rap-info/i4158.asp. (In French.)

Australian Academy of Science. 2019. *Investigation of the Causes of Mass Fish Kills in the Menindee Region NSW over the Summer of 2018–2019*. Canberra, Australian Academy of Science. www.science.org.au/supporting-science/science-policy-and-sector-analysis/reports-and-publications/fish-kills-report.

Australian Bureau of Statistics. 2010. *Water Account, Australia, 2008–09*. ABS Cat. No. 4610.0. Canberra, Australian Bureau of Statistics. www.abs.gov.au/AUSSTATS/abs@.nsf/DetailsPage/4610.02008-09?OpenDocument.

Australian Water Partnership. 2016. *Valuing Water: A Framing Paper for the High-Level Panel on Water*. Canberra, Australian Water Partnership. waterpartnership.org.au/wp-content/uploads/2016/08/HLPW-Valuing-Water.pdf.

Avello, P., Beane, G., Birtill, K., Bristow, J., Bruce, A., Bruebach, K., Ellis, L., Fisher, S., Fletcher, M., Karmann, C., Giné, R., Jiménez, A., Leten, J., Pharr, K., Romano, O., Ruiz-Apilánez, I., Saikia, P., Shouler, M., Simkins, P., Sobey, M. and Svidran, R. 2019. *City Water Resilience Assessment – Methodology*. The Rockefeller Foundation/The Resilience Shift/Stockholm International Water Institute (SIWI)/ARUP. www.arup.com/perspectives/publications/research/section/city-water-resilience-assessment-methodology.

Awume, O., Patrick, R. and Baijius, W. 2020. Indigenous perspectives on water security in Saskatchewan, Canada. *Water*, Vol. 12, No. 3, Art. 810. doi.org/10.3390/w12030810.

Bakker, K. 2012. Water: Political, biopolitical, material. *Social Studies of Science*, Vol. 42, No. 4, pp. 616–623. doi.org/10.1177/0306312712441396.

Banerjee, S. G., Foster, V., Skilling, H. and Wodon, Q. 2010. *Cost Recovery, Equity, and Efficiency in Water Tariffs: Evidence from African Utilities*. Policy Research Working Paper No. WPS 5384. Washington, DC, World Bank. openknowledge.worldbank.org/handle/10986/3868. License: CC BY 3.0 IGO.

Baran, G. R., Kiana, M. F., and Samuel, S. P. 2014. Science, pseudoscience, and not science: How do they differ? G. R. Baran, M. F. Kiani and S. P. Samuel, *Healthcare and Biomedical Technology in the 21st Century*. New York, Springer. doi.org/10.1007/978-1-4614-8541-4_2.

Barde, J. A. and Lehmann, P. 2014. Distributional effects of water tariff reforms – An empirical study for Lima, Peru. *Water Resources and Economics*, Vol. 6, pp. 30–57. doi.org/10.1016/j.wre.2014.05.003.

Bark, R., Garrick, D., Robinson, C. J. and Jackson, S. 2012. Adaptive basin governance and the prospects for meeting Indigenous water claims. *Environmental Science & Policy*, Vol. 19–20, pp. 169–177. doi.org/10.1016/j.envsci.2012.03.005.

Bark, R., Hatton MacDonald, D., Connor, J., Crossmann, N. and Jackson S. 2011. Water values. I. Prosser (ed.), *Water: Science and Solutions for Australia*. Collingwood, Australia, CSIRO Publishing. www.publish.csiro.au/book/6557.

Barredo, I. J., Ambrušová, L., Nuijten, D., Viszlai, I. and Vysna, V. 2019. *Valuation and Payments for Forest Ecosystem Services in the pan-European region*. Final Report of the FOREST EUROPE Expert Group on Valuation and Payments for Forest Ecosystem Services. Bratislava, Ministerial Conference on the Protection of Forests in Europe, Liaison Unit Bratislava. foresteurope.org/wp-content/uploads/2016/08/PES_Final_report.pdf.

Barron, O., Riasat, A., Hodgson, G., Smith, D., Qureshi, E., McFarlane, D., Campos, E. and Zarzo, D. 2015. Feasibility assessment of desalination application in Australian traditional agriculture. *Desalination*, Vol. 364, pp. 33–45. doi.org/10.1016/j.desal.2014.07.024.

Barton, D. 2011. Capitalism for the long term. *Harvard Business Review*, March 2011. hbr.org/2011/03/capitalism-for-the-long-term.

Bate, R. N. and Dubourg, W. R. 1997. A net-back analysis of irrigated water demand in East Anglia. *Journal of Environmental Management*, Vol. 49, No. 3, pp. 311–322. doi.org/10.1006/jema.1996.9986.

Batker, D., De la Torre, I., Costanza, R., Swedeen, P., Day, J., Boumans, R. and Bagstad, K. 2010. *Gaining Ground: Wetlands, Hurricanes and the Economy: The Value of Restoring the Mississippi River Delta*. Tacoma, Wash., Earth Economics.

Beltrán, S. A. 2013. Pago por servicios ambientales hidrológicos en el estado de México [Payment for hidrological environmental services in the State of Mexico]. A. Lara, P. Laterra, R. Manson and G. Barrantes (eds.), *Servicios ecosistémicos hídricos: estudios de caso en América Latina y el Caribe* [Water ecosystem services: Case studies from Latin America and the Caribbean]. Valdivia, Chile, Red ProAgua CYTED Imprenta América. (In Spanish.)

Bennett, N. J., Whitty, T. S., Finkbeiner, E., Pittman, J., Bassett, H., Gelcich, S. and Allison, E. H. 2018. Environmental stewardship: A conceptual review and analytical framework. *Environmental Management*, Vol. 61, pp. 597–614. doi.org/10.1007/s00267-017-0993-2.

Benöhr, J. and González, T. 2017. *Los derechos de los ríos* [The rights of rivers]. rebelion.org/los-derechos-de-los-rios/. (In Spanish.)

Berbel, J., Borrego-Marin, M., Exposito, A., Giannoccaro, G., Montilla-Lopez, N. M. and Roseta-Palma, C. 2019. Analysis of irrigation water tariffs and taxes in Europe. *Water Policy*, Vol. 21, No. 4, pp. 806–825. doi.org/10.2166/wp.2019.197.

Bester, R., Blignaut, J. N., Van Niekerk, P. H. 2020. The cost-effectiveness of water augmentation and management: Assessing the Unit Reference Value. *Journal of the South African Institution of Civil Engineering*, Vol. 62, No. 2. doi.org/10.17159/2309-8775/2020/v62n2a5.

BIPE-BDO/FP2E (Fédération professionnelle des entreprises de l'eau). 2019. *Public Water and Wastewater Services in France, Social, Economic and Environmental Data*. BIPE/FP2E Report (7th edition). Paris, BIPE-BDO/FP2E. www.eureau.org/resources/publications/member-publications/5299-public-water-and-waste-water-services-in-france/file.

Birkenholtz, T. 2017. Assessing India's drip-irrigation boom: Efficiency, climate change and groundwater policy. *Water International*, Vol. 42, No. 6, pp. 663–677. doi.org/10.1080/02508060.2017.1351910.

Black, R., Laxminarayan, R., Temmerman, M. and Walker, N. 2016. *Reproductive, Maternal, Newborn, and Child Health*. Disease Control Priorities, Third Edition, Vol. 2. Washington, DC, World Bank. openknowledge.worldbank.org/handle/10986/23833. License: CC BY 3.0 IGO

Bogale, A. and Urgessa, B. 2012. Households' willingness to pay for improved rural water service provision: Application of contingent valuation method in Eastern Ethiopia. *Journal of Human Ecology*, Vol. 38, No. 2, pp. 145–154. doi.org/10.1080/09709274.2012.11906483.

Boiral, O., Heras-Saizarbitoria, I. and Brotherton, M. C. 2020. Improving environmental management through indigenous people's involvement. *Environmental Science & Policy*, Vol. 103, pp. 10–20. doi.org/10.1016/j.envsci.2019.10.006.

Boisson, S., Engels, D., Gordon, B. A., Medlicott, K. O., Neira, M. P., Montresor, A., Solomon, A. W. and Velleman, Y. 2016. Water, sanitation and hygiene for accelerating and sustaining progress on neglected tropical diseases: A new Global Strategy 2015–20. *International Health*, Vol. 8, Suppl. 1, pp. i19–i21. doi.org/10.1093/inthealth/ihv073.

Bolong, N., Ismail, A. F., Salim, M. R. and Matsuura, T. 2009. A review of the effects of emerging contaminants in wastewater and options for their removal. *Desalination*, Vol. 239, No. 1–3, pp. 229–246. doi.org/10.1016/j.desal.2008.03.020.

Bolt, K., Ruta, G. and Sarraf, M. 2005. *Estimating the Cost of Environmental Degradation: A Training Manual in English, French and Arabic*. Environment working paper series, No. 106. Washington, DC, World Bank Group. documents.worldbank.org/curated/en/652751468138260264/Estimating-the-cost-of-environmental-degradation-a-training-manual-in-English-French-and-Arabic.

Booysen, M. J., Visser, M. and Burger, R. 2019. Temporal case study of household behavioural response to Cape Town's "Day Zero" using smart meter data. *Water Research*, Vol. 149, pp. 414–420. doi.org/10.1016/j.watres.2018.11.035.

Borthakur, A. and Singh, P. 2020. Indigenous knowledge systems in sustainable water conservation and management. P. Singh, Y. Milshina, K. Tian, D. Gusain and J. P. Bassin (eds.), *Water Conservation and Wastewater Treatment in BRICS Nations*. Amsterdam/Oxford, UK/Cambridge, Mass., Elsevier, pp. 321–328. doi.org/10.1016/C2018-0-03850-5.

Braw, E. 2019. 2020 for the Future. *Foreign Policy*, 30 December 2019. foreignpolicy.com/2019/12/30/fridays-for-future-foreign-policy-bureacrats-officials-2019-greta-thunberg/.

Bresnihan, P. 2017. *Valuing Nature: Perspectives and Issues*. NESC Research Series Paper No. 11. Dublin, National Economic and Social Council (NESC). www.nesc.ie/publications/valuing-nature/.

Breuer, A., Leininger, J. and Tosun, J. 2019. *Integrated Policymaking: Choosing an Institutional Design for Implementing the Sustainable Development Goals (SDGs)*. Discussion Paper 2019. Bonn, Germany, German Development Institute. doi.org/10.23661/dp14.2019.

Brooker, S. 2010. Estimating the global distribution and disease burden of intestinal nematode infections: Adding up the numbers – A Review. *International Journal for Parasitology*, Vol. 40, No. 10, pp. 1137–1144. doi.org/10.1016/j.ijpara.2010.04.004.

Bullock, A. and Acreman, M. C. 2003. The role of wetlands in the hydrological cycle. *Hydrology and Earth System Sciences*, Vol. 7, No. 3, pp. 358–389. doi.org/10.5194/hess-7-358-2003.

Burchi, S. 2012. A comparative review of contemporary water resources legislation: Trends, developments and an agenda for reform. *Water International*, Vol 37, No. 6, pp. 613–627. doi.org/10.1080/02508060.2012.694800.

Bureau of Meteorology. 2017. *Good Practice Guidelines for Water Data Management Policy: World Water Data Initiative*. Melbourne, Australia, Bureau of Meteorology. public.wmo.int/en/resources/library/good-practice-guidelines-water-data-management-policy.

Burek, P., Satoh, Y., Fischer, G., Kahil, M. T., Scherzer, A., Tramberend, S., Nava, L. F., Wada, Y., Eisner, S., Flörke, M., Hanasaki, N., Magnuszewski, P., Cosgrove, B. and Wiberg, D. 2016. *Water Futures and Solution: Fast Track Initiative (Final Report)*. IIASA Working Paper. Laxenburg, Austria, International Institute for Applied Systems Analysis (IIASA). pure.iiasa.ac.at/id/eprint/13008/.

Burn, S., Hoang, M., Zarzo, D., Olewniak, F., Campos, E., Bolto, B. and Barron, O. 2015. Desalination techniques – A review of the opportunities for desalination in agriculture. *Desalination*, Vol. 364, pp. 2–16. doi.org/10.1016/j.desal.2015.01.041.

Business Roundtable. 2019. *Business Roundtable Redefines the Purpose of a Corporation to Promote 'An Economy That Serves All Americans'*. Business Roundtable website. www.businessroundtable.org/business-roundtable-redefines-the-purpose-of-a-corporation-to-promote-an-economy-that-serves-all-americans.

Buytaert, W., Zulkafli, Z., Grainger, S., Acosta, L., Alemie, T. C., Bastiaensen, J., De Bièvre, B., Bhusal, J., Clark, J., Dewulf, A., Foggin, M., Hannah, D. M., Hergarten, C., Isaeva, A., Karpouzoglou, T., Pandeya, B., Paudel, D., Sharma, K., Steenhuis, T., Tilahun, S., Van Hecken, G. and Zhumanova, M. 2014. Citizen science in hydrology and water resources: Opportunities for knowledge generation, ecosystem service management, and sustainable development. *Frontiers in Earth Science*, Vol. 2, No. 26. doi.org/10.3389/feart.2014.00026.

C

Caldera, U. and Breyer, C. 2020. Strengthening the global water supply through a decarbonised global desalination sector and improved irrigation systems. *Energy*, Vol. 200, Art. 117507. doi.org/10.1016/j.energy.2020.117507.

Capacci, S., Mazzocchi, M., Shankar, B., Brambila Macia, J., Verbeke, W., Pérez-Cueto, F. J. A., Koziol-Kozakowska, A., Piórecka, B., Niedzwiedzka, B., D'Adessa, D., Saba, A., Turrini, A., Aschemann-Witzel, J., Bech-Larsen, T., Strand, M., Smillie, L., Wills, J. and Traill, B. W. 2012. Policies to promote healthy eating in Europe: A structured review of policies and their effectiveness. *Nutrition Reviews*, Vol. 70, No. 3, pp. 188–200. doi.org/10.1111/j.1753-4887.2011.00442.x.

Carey, J. M. and Sunding, D. L. 2001. Emerging markets in water: A comparative institutional analysis of the Central Valley and the Colorado-Big Thompson projects. *Natural Resources Journal*, Vol. 41, No. 2, pp. 283–328.

Carrillo-Guerrero, Y., Glenn, E. P. and Hinojosa-Huerta, O. 2013. Water budget for agricultural and aquatic ecosystems in the delta of the Colorado River, Mexico: Implications for obtaining water for the environment. *Ecological Engineering*, Vol. 59, pp. 41–51. doi.org/10.1016/j.ecoleng.2013.04.047.

CDP. 2017. *A Turning Tide: Tracking Corporate Action on Water Security*. CDP Global Water Report 2017. London, CDP. www.cdp.net/en/research/global-reports/global-water-report-2017.

_____. 2018. *Treading Water: Corporate Responses to Rising Water Challenges*. CDP Global Water Report 2018. London, CDP. www.cdp.net/en/research/global-reports/global-water-report-2018.

_____. 2020. *Cleaning Up Their Act: Are Companies Responding to the Risks and Opportunities posed by Water Pollution?* CDP Global Water Report 2019. London, CDP. www.cdp.net/en/research/global-reports/cleaning-up-their-act.

Ceres. 2012. *The Ceres Aqua Gauge: A Framework for 21st Century Water Risk Management*. Boston, Mass., Ceres. www.ceres.org/sites/default/files/reports/2017-03/Ceres_AquaGauge_All_101113.pdf.

Chan, K. M. A., Balvanera, P., Benessaiah, K., Chapman, M., Díaz, S., Gómez-Baggethun, E., Gould, R., Hannahs, N., Jaxi, K., Klain, S., Luck, G. W., Martín-Lópezk, B., Barbara Muraca, B., Norton, B., Ott, K., Pascual, U., Satterfield, T., Tadaki, M., Taggart, J. and Turner, N. 2016. Why protect nature? Rethinking values and the environment. *Proceedings of the National Academy of Sciences of the United States of America*, Vol. 113, No. 6, pp. 1462–1465. doi.org/10.1073/pnas.1525002113.

Chan, K. M. A., Gould, R. K. and Pascual, U. 2018. Editorial overview: Relational values: what are they, and what's the fuss about? *Current Opinion in Environmental Sustainability*, Vol. 35, pp. A1–A7. doi.org/10.1016/j.cosust.2018.11.003.

Chenoweth, J., López-Avilés, A., Morse, S. and Druckman, A. 2016. Water consumption and subjective wellbeing: An analysis of British households. *Ecological Economics*, Vol. 130, pp. 186–194. doi.org/10.1016/j.ecolecon.2016.07.006.

Chitty, A. and Esteves-Mills, J. 2015. *WASH and Maternal and Newborn Health: Time to Act*. Policy Brief. London, London School of Hygiene and Tropical Medicine. www.lshtm.ac.uk/sites/default/files/2017-07/Policy%20Brief%20-%20WASH%20%26%20MNH.pdf.

Cho, A., Fischer, A., Doyle, M., Levy, M., Kim-Blanco, P. and Webb, R. 2017. *The Value of Water Information: Overcoming the Global Data Drought*. White Paper. New York, Xylem Inc., Rye Brook. xylem.com/waterdata.

Chowdhooree, I., 2019. Indigenous knowledge for enhancing community resilience: An experience from the south-western coastal region of Bangladesh. *International Journal of Disaster Risk Reduction*, Vol. 40, Art. 101259. doi.org/10.1016/j.ijdrr.2019.101259.

Christian-Smith, J., Levy, M. C. and Gleick, P. H. 2011. *Impacts of the California Drought from 2007 to 2009*. Executive Summary. Oakland, Calif., Pacific Institute. pacinst.org/publication/impacts-of-the-drought-2007-2009/.

Civiltà dell'Acqua Centro Internazionale. n.d. *Water and Traditional Knowledge: Learn from the Past for a Sustainable Future*. Paris, UNESCO. www.unesco.org/new/fileadmin/MULTIMEDIA/FIELD/Venice/pdf/special_events/bozza_scheda_DOW_6_1.0.pdf.

Cleaver, F. 1995. Water as a weapon: The history of water supply development in Nkayi District, Zimbabwe. *Environment and History*, Vol. 1, No. 3, pp. 313–333. doi.org/10.3197/096734095779522564.

Coalition for Inclusive Capitalism. n.d. Coalition for Inclusive Capitalism website. www.inc-cap.com/.

Cohen-Shacham, E., Walters, G., Janzen, C. and Maginnis, S. (eds.). 2016. *Nature-Based Solutions to Address Global Societal Challenges*. Gland, Switzerland, International Union for Conservation of nature (IUCN). doi.org/10.2305/IUCN.CH.2016.13.en.

COMEST (World Commission on the Ethics of Scientific Knowledge and Technology). 2018. *Report of COMEST on: "Water Ethics: Ocean, Freshwater, Coastal Areas"*. Paris, UNESCO. unesdoc.unesco.org/ark:/48223/pf0000265449.

Comisari, P., Feng, L. and Freeman, B. 2011. *Valuation of Water Resources and Water Infrastructure Assets*. Australian Bureau of Statistics. unstats.un.org/unsd/envaccounting/londongroup/meeting17/LG17_12.pdf.

Comité national de l'eau. 2019. *Rapport d'analyse de l'expérimentation pour une tarification sociale de l'eau* [Analysis report of experimentation with a social water tariff]. Direction de l'eau et de la biodiversité/Direction générale des collectivités locales, Ministère de la Transition écologique/Ministère de la Cohésion des territoires et des Relations avec les collectivités territoriales. www.ecologie.gouv.fr/sites/default/files/Rapport_experimentation_eau_loi-Brottes_2019_0.pdf. (In French.)

Comprehensive Assessment of Water Management in Agriculture. 2007. *Water for Food, Water for Life: A Comprehensive Assessment of Water Management in Agriculture*. London/Colombo, Earthscan/International Water Management Institute (IWMI).

Conniff, R. 2012. What's wrong with putting a price on nature? *YaleEnvironment360*, 18 October 2012. e360.yale.edu/features/ecosystem_services_whats_wrong_with_putting_a_price_on_nature.

Constitución de la República de Ecuador [Constitution of the Republic of Ecuador]. 2008. Last update: 13 July 2011. www.oas.org/juridico/pdfs/mesicic4_ecu_const.pdf. (In Spanish.)

Convention on Biological Diversity. 1992. Rio de Janeiro, 5 June 1992. treaties.un.org/pages/ViewDetails.aspx?src=TREATY&mtdsg_no=XXVII-8&chapter=27.

Cooke, B. and Kothari, U. (eds.). 2001. *Participation. The New Tyranny?* London, Zed Books.

Corcoran, E., Nellemann, C., Baker, E., Bos, R., Osborn, D. and Savelli, H. 2010. *Sick Water? The Central Role of Wastewater Management in Sustainable Development: A Rapid Response Assessment*. Nairobi/Arendal, Norway, UNEP/UN-Habitat/GRID-Arendal (United Nations Environment Programme/United Nations Human Settlements Programme). wedocs.unep.org/handle/20.500.11822/9156.

Cornish, G., Bosworth, B., Perry, C. and Burke, J. 2004. *Water Charging in Irrigated Agriculture: An Analysis of International Experience*. FAO Water Report No. 28. Rome, Food and Agriculture Organization of the United Nations (FAO). www.fao.org/3/y5690e/y5690e00.htm.

Costanza, R., D'Arge, R., De Groot, R., Farber, S., Grasso, M., Hannon, B., Naeem, S., Limburg, K., Paruelo, J., O'Neill, R.V., Raskin, R., Sutton, P. and Van den Belt, M. 1997. The value of the world's ecosystem services and natural capital. *Nature*, Vol. 387, pp. 253–260.

Costanza, R., De Groot, R., Sutton, P., Van der Ploeg, S., Anderson, S. J., Kubiszewski, I., Farber, S. and Turner, R. K. 2014. Changes in the global value of ecosystem services. *Global Environmental Change*, Vol. 26, pp. 152–158. doi.org/10.1016/j.gloenvcha.2014.04.002.

CRED (Centre for Research on the Epidemiology of Disasters). 2020. *Natural Disasters 2019: Now is the Time to not give up*. Brussels, CRED. www.emdat.be/natural-disasters-2019-now-time-not-give.

Croal, P., Tetreault, C. and members of the IAIA IP section. 2012. *Respecting Indigenous Peoples and Traditional Knowledge*. Fargo, ND, International Association of Impact Assessments. www.iaia.org/uploads/pdf/SP9_Indigenous_Peoples_Traditional_Knowledge.pdf.

Cuaton, G. P. and Su, Y. 2020. Local-indigenous knowledge on disaster risk reduction: Insights from the Mamanwa indigenous peoples in Basey, Samar after Typhoon Haiyan in the Philippines. *International Journal of Disaster Risk Reduction*, Vol. 48, Art. 101596. doi.org/10.1016/j.ijdrr.2020.101596.

D

Da Costa, V., Jobard, E., Marquay, J., Ollagnon, M., Plat, B. and Radureau, S. 2015. *Public Water and Wastewater Services in France: Economic, Social, and Environmental Data*. Paris, BIPE/Fédération professionnelle des entreprises de l'eau (FP2E). www.fp2e.org/userfiles/files/publication/RAPPORT_BIPE_GB_ENTIER.pdf.

Dahl, G. and Megerssa, G. 1990. The sources of life: Boran concepts of wells and water. G. Pálsson (ed.), *From Water to World-Making. African Models and Arid Lands*. Uppsala, the Scandinavia Institute of African Studies, pp. 21-37.

Dalhuisen, J. M., Florax, R. J. G. M., De Groot, H. L. F. and Nijkamp, P. 2003. Price and income elasticities of residential water demand: A meta-analysis. *Land Economics*, Vol. 79, No. 2, pp. 292–308. doi.org/10.2307/3146872.

Damania. R., Desbureaux, S., Hyland, M., Islam, A., Moore, S., Rodella, A., Russ, J. and Zaveri, E. 2017. *Uncharted Waters: The New Economics of Water Scarcity and Variability*. Volume 2. Technical Background Papers. Washington, DC, World Bank. openknowledge.worldbank.org/handle/10986/28096. License: CC BY 3.0 IGO.

Damania, R., Desbureaux, S., Rodella, A. S., Russ, J. and Zaveri, E. 2019a. *Quality Unknown: The Invisible Water Crisis*. Washington, DC, The World Bank. openknowledge.worldbank.org/handle/10986/32245. License: CC BY 3.0 IGO

_____. 2019b. *Quality Unknown: Technical Appendixes*. Washington, DC, World Bank. openknowledge.worldbank.org/bitstream/handle/10986/32245/211459App.pdf?sequence=5&isAllowed=y. License: Creative Commons Attribution CC BY 3.0 IGO.

Davidson, B., Hellegers, P. and Namara, R. E. 2019. Why irrigation water pricing is not widely used. *Current Opinion in Environmental Sustainability*, Vol. 40, pp. 1–6. doi.org/10.1016/j.cosust.2019.06.001.

Debaere, P. and Li, T. 2020. The effects of water markets: Evidence from Rio Grande. *Advances in Water Resources*, Vol. 145, Art. 103700. doi.org/10.1016/j.advwatres.2020.103700.

De Groot, R., Brander, L., Van der Ploeg, S., Costanza, R., Bernard, F., Braat, L., Christie, M., Crossman, N., Ghermandi, A., Hein, L., Hussain, S., Kumar, P., McVittie, A., Portela, R., Rodriguez, L. C., Ten Brink, P. and Van Beukering, P. 2012. Global estimates of the value of ecosystems and their services in monetary units. *Ecosystem Services*, Vol. 1, No. 1, pp. 50–61. doi.org/10.1016/j.ecoser.2012.07.005.

De Groot, R. S., Stuip, M. A. M., Finlayson, C. M. and Davidson, N. 2006. *Valuing Wetlands: Guidance for Valuing the Benefits derived from Wetland Ecosystem Services*. Ramsar Technical Report No. 3/CBD Technical Series No. 27. Gland, Switzerland/Montreal, PQ, Ramsar Convention Secretariat/Secretariat of the Convention on Biological Diversity (CBD). www.cbd.int/doc/publications/cbd-ts-27.pdf.

De la Cruz, A., Medina A. and Tang, Y. 2019. *Owners of the World's Listed Companies*. OECD Capital Market Series. Paris, Organisation for Economic Co-operation and Development (OECD). www.oecd.org/corporate/Owners-of-the-Worlds-Listed-Companies.pdf.

Del Giacco, L. J., Drusiani, R., Lucentini, L. and Murtas, S. 2017. Water as a weapon in ancient times: Considerations of technical and ethical aspects. *Water Supply*, Vol. 17, No. 5, pp. 1490–1498. doi.org/10.2166/ws.2017.043.

De Oliveira, J. A. P. and Paleo, U. F. 2016. Lost in participation: How local knowledge was overlooked in land use planning and risk governance in Tōhoku, Japan. *Land Use Policy*, Vol. 52, pp. 543–551. doi.org/10.1016/j.landusepol.2014.09.023.

Devoto, F., Duflo, E., Dupas, P., Parienté, W. and Pons, V. 2012. Happiness on tap: Piped water adoption in urban Morocco. *American Economic Journal: Economic Policy*, Vol. 4, No. 4, pp.68–99. doi.org/10.1257/pol.4.4.68.

Diao, X. and Roe, T. 2000. The win-win effect of joint water market and trade reform on interest groups in irrigated agriculture in Morocco. A. Dinar (ed.), *The Political Economy of Water Pricing Reforms*. New York, Oxford University Press. documents1.worldbank.org/curated/en/199301468771050868/pdf/multi-page.pdf.

Di Baldassarre, G. Wanders, N., AghaKouchak, A., Kuil, L., Rangecroft, S., Veldkamp, T. I. E., Garcia, M., Van Oel, P., Breinl, K. and Van Loon, A. 2018. Water shortages worsened by reservoir effects. *Nature Sustainability*, Vol. 1, pp. 617–622. doi.org/10.1038/s41893-018-0159-0.

D'Odorico, P., Chiarelli, D. D., Rosa, L., Bini, A., Zilberman, D. and Rulli, M. C. 2020. The global value of water in agriculture. *Proceedings of the National Academy of Sciences of the United States of America*, Vol. 117, No. 36, pp. 21985–21993. doi.org/10.1073/pnas.2005835117.

Domènech, L. 2015. Improving irrigation access to combat food insecurity and undernutrition: A review. *Global Food Security*, Vol. 6, pp. 24–33. doi.org/10.1016/j.gfs.2015.09.001.

Dussaillant, I., Berthier, E., Brun, F., Masiokas, M., Hugonnet, R., Favier, V., Rabatel, A., Pitte, P. and Ruiz, L. 2019. Two decades of glacier mass loss along the Andes. *Nature Geoscience*, Vol. 12, pp. 802–808. doi.org/10.1038/s41561-019-0432-5.

Earthwatch Institute. n.d. *Citizen Science*. Freshwater Watch. Earthwatch Europe website. freshwaterwatch.thewaterhub.org/our-data/citizen-science.

EASAC (European Academies' Science Advisory Council). 2018. *Extreme Weather Events in Europe: Preparing for Climate Change Adaptation: An Update on EASAC's 2013 Study*. Halle, Germany, EASAC. easac.eu/publications/details/extreme-weather-events-in-europe/.

Eckstein, G., D'Andrea, A., Marshall, V., O'Donnell, E., Talbot-Jones, J., Curran, D. and O'Bryan, K. 2018. Conferring legal personality on the world's rivers: A brief intellectual assessment. *Water International*, Vol. 44, No. 6–7, pp. 804–829. doi.org/10.1080/02508060.2019.1631558.

ECSA (European Citizen Science Association). 2015. *Ten Principles of Citizen Science*. ecsa.citizen-science.net/documents/.

EEA (European Environmental Agency). 2012. *Towards Efficient Use of Water Resources in Europe*. Report No. 1/2012. Copenhagen, EEA. www.eea.europa.eu/publications/towards-efficient-use-of-water.

_____. 2018. *Industrial Waste Water Treatment – Pressures on Europe's Environment*. EEA Report No 23/2018. Luxembourg, Publications Office of the European Union. www.eea.europa.eu/publications/industrial-waste-water-treatment-pressures.

_____. 2019. *Industrial Pollution in Europe*. Indicator Assessment. EEA website. www.eea.europa.eu/data-and-maps/indicators/industrial-pollution-in-europe-3/assessment.

Embid, A. and Martín, L. 2017. *El Nexo entre el agua, la energía y la alimentación en América Latina y el Caribe: planificación, marco normativo e identificación de interconexiones prioritarias* [The Nexus between water, energy and food in Latin America and the Caribbean: Planning, normative framework and identification of priority connections]. Série Recursos Naturales e Infraestructura No. 179 (LC/TS.2017/16). Santiago, United Nations Economic Commission for Latin America and Caribbean (UNECLAC). www.cepal.org/es/publicaciones/41069-nexo-agua-la-energia-la-alimentacion-america-latina-caribe-planificacion-marco. (In Spanish.)

Emerton, L. and Bos, E. 2004. *Value: Counting Ecosystems as an Economic Part of Water Infrastructure*. Gland, Switzerland/Cambridge, UK, International Union for Conservation of Nature (IUCN). doi.org/10.13140/2.1.1470.1121.

Engels, S., Pagiola, S. and Wunder, S. 2008. Designing payments for environmental services in theory and practice: An overview of the issues. *Ecological Economics*, Vol. 65, No. 4, pp. 663–674. doi.org/10.1016/j.ecolecon.2008.03.011.

Ercin, A. E. and Hoekstra, A. Y. 2012. *Carbon and Water Footprints: Concepts, Methodologies and Policy Responses*. WWDR4, Side Publication Series No. 04. Paris, United Nations World Water Assessment Programme (WWAP), United Nations Educational, Scientific and Cultural Organization (UNESCO). www.unesco.org/new/en/natural-sciences/environment/water/wwap/publications/side-publications/carbon-and-water-footprints-concepts-methodologies-and-policy-responses/.

Escott, H., Beavis, S. and Reeves, A. 2015. Incentives and constraints to indigenous engagement in water management. *Land Use Policy*, Vol. 49, pp. 382–393. doi.org/10.1016/j.landusepol.2015.08.003.

Espey, M., Espey, J. and Shaw, W. D. 1997. Price elasticity of residential demand for water: A meta-analysis. *Water Resources Research*, Vol. 33, No. 6, pp. 1369–1374. doi.org/10.1029/97WR00571.

Esteves-Mills, J. and Cumming, O. 2016. *The Impact of WASH on Key Health & Social Outcomes*. DFID Evidence Paper. Sanitation and Hygiene Applied Research for Equity (SHARE)/United Nations Children's Fund (UNICEF). www.unicef.org/wash/files/The_Impact_of_WASH_on_Key_Social_and_Health_Outcomes_Review_of_Evidence.pdf.

European Commission. 2019a. *Fitness Check of the Water Framework Directive and the Floods Directive*. SWD (2019) 439 final, Brussels, European Union. ec.europa.eu/environment/water/fitness_check_of_the_eu_water_legislation/documents/Water%20Fitness%20Check%20-%20SWD(2019)439%20-%20web.pdf.

_____. 2019b. *EU Guidance on Integrating Ecosystems and their Services into Decision-Making*. SWD (2019) 305 final, Brussels, European Union. ec.europa.eu/environment/nature/ecosystems/pdf/SWD_2019_305_F1_STAFF_WORKING_PAPER_EN_V2_P1_1042629.PDF.

European Parliament/Council of the European Union. 2000. Directive 2000/60/EC of the European Parliament and the Council of 23 October 2000 establishing a framework for Community action in the field of water policy. *Official Journal of the European Communities*, L 327. eur-lex.europa.eu/legal-content/EN/TXT/?uri=CELEX:32000L0060.

FAO (Food and Agriculture Organization of the United Nations). 1984. *Systematic Index of International Water Resources Treaties, Declarations, Acts and Cases, by Basin*, Legislative Study No. 34. Rome, FAO. www.ircwash.org/sites/default/files/820-INT78-18710.pdf.

_____. 2004. *Economic Valuation of Water Resources in Agriculture: From the Sectoral to a Functional Perspective of Natural Resource Management*. FAO Water Report No. 27. Rome, FAO. www.fao.org/3/y5582e/y5582e00.htm.

_____. 2010a. *The Wealth of Waste: The Economics of Wastewater Use in Agriculture*. FAO Water Report No. 35. Rome, FAO. www.fao.org/3/i1629e/i1629e.pdf.

_____. 2010b. *Sustainable Diets and Biodiversity: Direction and Solution for Policy, Research and Action*. Proceedings of the International Scientific Symposium: Biodiversity and Sustainable Diets United Against Hunger, 3–5 November 2010. Rome, FAO. www.fao.org/3/a-i3004e.pdf.

____. 2011a. *The State of the World's Land and Water Resources for Food and Agriculture: Managing Systems of Risk*. London, Earthscan/Rome, FAO. www.fao.org/nr/solaw/solaw-home/en/.

____. 2011b. *Save and Grow: A Policymaker's Guide to the Sustainable Intensification of Smallholder Crop Production*. Rome, FAO. www.fao.org/3/I2215E/i2215e.pdf.

____. 2012a. *Irrigation Water Requirement and Water Withdrawal by Country*. FAO AQUASTAT Report. Rome, FAO. www.fao.org/nr/water/aquastat/water_use_agr/irrigationwateruse.pdf.

____. 2012b. *Coping with Water Scarcity: An Action Framework for Agriculture and Food Security*. FAO Water Report No. 38. Rome, FAO. www.fao.org/3/a-i3015e.pdf.

____. 2013a. *The State of Food and Agriculture 2013 – Food Systems for Better Nutrition*. Rome, FAO. www.fao.org/publications/sofa/2013/en/.

____. 2013b. *Multiple Uses of Water Services in Large Irrigation Systems. Auditing and Planning Modernization: The MASSMUS approach*. Irrigation and Drainage Paper No. 67. Rome, FAO. www.fao.org/3/i3414e/i3414e.pdf.

____. 2013c. *Climate-Smart Agriculture Sourcebook*. Rome, FAO. www.fao.org/3/i3325e/i3325e.pdf.

____. 2014a. *The State of World Fisheries and Aquaculture: Opportunities and Challenges*. Rome, FAO. www.fao.org/3/a-i3720e.pdf.

____.2014b. *Turning Family Farm Activity into Decent Work*. Information material. Rome, FAO. www.fao.org/fileadmin/user_upload/fao_ilo/pdf/FF_DRE.pdf.

____. 2014c. *The Water–Energy–Food Nexus: A New Approach in Support of Food Security and Sustainable Agriculture*. Rome, FAO. www.fao.org/3/a-bl496e.pdf.

____. 2015. *Evaporation from Artificial Lakes and Reservoirs*. FAO AQUASTAT reports. Rome, FAO. www.fao.org/documents/card/en/c/04499d76-fd6f-4360-adaf-796dfd422050/.

____. 2016. *El riego en América del Sur, Centroamérica y Caribe en cifras* [Irrigation in South America, Central America and the Caribbean in numbers]. Encuesta AQUASTAT 2015. Rome, FAO. www.fao.org/publications/card/es/c/CA3580ES. (In Spanish.)

____. 2017a. *Water for Sustainable Food and Agriculture: A Report Produced for the G20 Presidency of Germany*. Rome, FAO. www.fao.org/3/a-i7959e.pdf.

____. 2017b. *The Future of Food and Agriculture: Trends and Challenges*. Rome, FAO. www.fao.org/3/a-i6583e.pdf.

____. 2018a. *The Future of Food and Agriculture: Alternative Pathways to 2050*. Rome, FAO. www.fao.org/policy-support/tools-and-publications/resources-details/en/c/1259562/. Licence: CC BY-NC-SA 3.0 IGO.

____. 2018b. *Progress on Level of Water Stress – Global Baseline for SDG 6 Indicator 6.4.2*. Rome, FAO/UN-Water. www.unwater.org/publications/progress-on-level-of-water-stress-642/. Licence: CC BY-NC-SA 3.0 IGO.

____. 2019a. *The State of Food and Agriculture 2019. Moving Forward on Food Loss and Waste Reduction*. Rome, FAO. www.fao.org/3/ca6030en/ca6030en.pdf.

____. 2019b. *Incorporating Environmental Flows into "Water Stress" Indicator 6.4.2 – Guidelines for a Minimum Standard Method for Global Reporting*. Rome, FAO. www.fao.org/3/ca3097en/CA3097EN.pdf. Licence: CC BY-NC-SA 3.0 IGO.

____. 2019c. *Water Use in Livestock Production Systems and Supply Chains – Guidelines for Assessment (Version 1)*. Livestock Environmental Assessment and Performance (LEAP) Partnership. Rome, FAO. www.fao.org/3/ca5685en/ca5685en.pdf.

____. 2020a. *Impacts of Coronavirus on Food Security and Nutrition in Asia and the Pacific: Building more Resilient Food Systems*. Bangkok, FAO. doi.org/10.4060/ca9473en.

____. 2020b. *SMART Irrigation – SMART WASH: Solutions in Response to the Pandemic Crisis in Africa*. Land and Water Discussion Paper No. 16. Rome, FAO. www.fao.org/3/cb1306en/CB1306EN.pdf.

____. 2020c. *Setting Regional Priorities to Manage Water for Agriculture under Conditions of Water Scarcity*. FAO Regional Conference for Asia and the Pacific. Thimphu. www.fao.org/3/nb841en/nb841en.pdf.

____. 2020d. *WaPOR Database Methodology: Version 2 Release, April 2020*. Rome, FAO. doi.org/10.4060/ca9894en.

____. n.d.a. *Water and Gender*. FAO Land and Water Division. www.fao.org/land-water/water/watergovernance/water-gender/en/ (Accessed August 2020).

____. n.d.b. *Building Water Access for a COVID-19 Response: Multiple Water Use Systems, Water Stations, Air-to-Water Non Conventional Technologies*. FAO website. www.fao.org/land-water/overview/covid19/access/en/

____. n.d.c. *WaPOR: The FAO Portal to Monitor Water Productivity through Open Access of Remotely Sensed Derived Data*. wapor.apps.fao.org/home/WAPOR_2/1.

FAO/IFAD/UNICEF/WFP/WHO (Food and Agriculture Organization of the United Nations/International Fund for Agricultural Development/United Nations Children's Fund/World Food Programme/World Health Organization). 2020. *The State of Food Security and Nutrition in the World 2020: Transforming Food Systems for Affordable Healthy Diets*. Rome, FAO. doi.org/10.4060/ca9692en.

FAO/WWC (Food and Agriculture Organization of the United Nations/World Water Council). 2015. *Towards a Water and Food Secure Future: Critical Perspectives for Policy-Makers*. White Paper. Rome/Marseille, France, FAO/WWC. www.fao.org/3/a-i4560e.pdf.

Farolfi, S., Mabugu, R. E. and Ntshingila, S. N. 2007. Domestic water use and values in Swaziland: A contingent valuation analysis. *Agrekon*, Vol. 46, No. 1, pp. 157–170. doi.org/10.1080/03031853.2007.9523766.

Faurès, J. M. and Santini, G. (eds.). 2008. *Water and the Rural Poor: Interventions for Improving Livelihoods in Sub-Saharan Africa*. Rome, Food and Agriculture Organization of the United Nations. www.fao.org/3/i0132e/i0132e00.htm.

Fekete, B. M., Loose, U., Pietroniro, A. and Robarts, R. D. 2012. Rational for monitoring discharge on the ground. *Journal of Hydrometeorology*, Vol. 13, No. 6, pp. 1977–1986. doi.org/10.1175/JHM-D-11-0126.1.

Fernández-Arévalo, T., Lizarralde, I., Fdz-Polanco, F., Pérez-Elvira, S. I., Garrido, J. M., Puig, S., Poch, M., Grau and P., Ayesa, E. 2017. Quantitative assessment of energy and resource recovery in wastewater treatment plants based on plant-wide simulations. *Water Research*, Vol. 118, pp. 272–288. doi.org/10.1016/j.watres.2017.04.001.

Fischer, G. 2018. Transforming the global food system. *Nature*, Vol. 562, pp. 501–502. doi.org/10.1038/d41586-018-07094-6.

Fish, R., Church, A., Willis, C., Winter, M., Tratalos, J. A., Haines-Young, R. and Potschin, M. 2016a. Making space for cultural ecosystem services: Insights from a study of the UK nature improvement initiative. *Ecosystem Services*, Vol. 21, Part B, pp. 329–343. doi.org/10.1016/j.ecoser.2016.09.017.

Fish, R., Church, A. and Winter, M. 2016b. Conceptualising cultural ecosystem services: A novel framework for research and critical engagement. *Ecosystem Services*, Volume 21, Part B, pp. 208–217. doi.org/10.1016/j.ecoser.2016.09.002.

Foster, V., Gomez-Lobo, A. and Halpern, J. 2000. *Designing Direct Subsidies for Water and Sanitation: Panama – A Case Study*. Policy Research Working Paper No. 2344. Washington, DC, World Bank. openknowledge.worldbank.org/handle/10986/21582. License: CC BY 3.0 IGO.

Frija, A., Chebil, A. and Abdelkafi, B. 2012. Irrigation water use efficiency in collective irrigated schemes of Tunisia: Determinants and potential irrigation cost reduction. *Agricultural Economics Review*, Vol. 13, No. 1, pp. 39–48. doi.org/10.22004/ag.econ.253493.

Frijns, J., Hofman, J. and Nederlof, N. 2013. The potential of (waste)water as energy carrier. *Energy Conversion and Management*, Vol. 65, pp. 357–363. doi.org/10.1016/j.enconman.2012.08.023.

Fritz, S., See, L., Carlson, T., Haklay, M., Haklay, M., Oliver, J. L., Fraisl, D., Mondardini, R., Brocklehurst, M., Shanley, L. A., Schade, S., Wehn, U., Abrate, T., Anstee, J., Arnold, S., Billot, M., Campbell, J., Espey, J., Gold, M., Hager, G., He, S., Hepburn, L., Hsu, A., Long, D., Masó, J., McCallum, I., Muniafu, M., Moorthy, I., Obersteiner, M., Parker, A. J., Weisspflug, M. and West, S. 2019. Citizen science and the United Nations Sustainable Development Goals. *Nature Sustainability*, Vol. 2, pp. 922–930. doi.org/10.1038/s41893-019-0390-3.

GAHI (Global Atlas of Helminth Infections). n.d. *The Global Burden of Disease Study Estimates the Magnitude of Health Loss due to Diseases and Injuries*. GAHI website. London Applied & Spatial Epidemiology Research Group (LASER)/London School of Hygiene and Tropical Medicine. www.thiswormyworld.org/worms/global-burden.

Gardner, J., Doyle, M. and Patterson, L. 2017. *Estimating the Value of Public Water Data*. Working paper NI WP 17-05. Durham, NC, Duke University. nicholasinstitute.duke.edu/content/estimating-value-public-water-data.

Garrick, D. E., Hall, J., Dobson, A., Damania, R., Grafton, R., Hope, R., Hepburn, C., Bark, R., Boltz, F., De Stefano, L., O'Donnell, E., Matthews, N. and Money, A. 2017. Valuing water for sustainable development. *Science*, Vol. 358, No. 6366, pp. 1003-1005. doi.org/10.1126/science.aao4942.

Garrick, D. E., De Stefano, L., Turley, L., Jorgensen, I., Aguilar-Barajas, I., Schreiner, B., De Souza Leão, R., O'Donnell, E. and Horne, A. 2019. *Dividing the Water, Sharing the Benefits: Lessons from Rural-to-Urban Water Reallocation*. Washington, DC, World Bank. openknowledge.worldbank.org/handle/10986/32050. License: CC BY 3.0 IGO.

Garrick, D. E., Hanemann, M. and Hepburn, C. 2020a. Rethinking the economics of water: An assessment. *Oxford Review of Economic Policy*, Vol. 36, No.1, pp.1–23. doi.org/10.1093/oxrep/grz035.

Garrick, D. E., Iseman, T., Gilson, G., Brozovic, N., O'Donnell, E., Matthews, N., Miralles-Wilhelm, F., Wight, C. and Young, W. 2020b. Scalable solutions to freshwater scarcity: Advancing theories of change to incentivise sustainable water use. *Water Security*, Vol. 9, Art. 100055. doi.org/10.1016/j.wasec.2019.100055.

Gaupp, F., Hall, J. and Dadson, S. 2015. The role of storage capacity in coping with intra- and inter-annual water variability in large river basins. *Environmental Research Letters*, Vol. 10, No. 12, Art. 125001. doi.org/10.1088/1748-9326/10/12/125001.

Gaynor, N. 2014. The tyranny of participation revisited: International support to local governance in Burundi. *Community Development Journal*, Vol. 49, No. 2, pp. 295–310. doi.org/10.1093/cdj/bst031.

GCEC (Global Commission on the Economy and Climate). 2016. *The Sustainable Infrastructure Imperative: Financing for Better Growth and Development*. The 2016 New Climate Economy Report. GCEC, The New Climate Economy. newclimateeconomy.report/2016.

George, M. W., Hotchkiss, R. H. and Huffaker, R. 2017. Reservoir sustainability and sediment management. *Journal of Water Resources Planning and Management*, Vol. 143, No. 3, Art. 04016077. doi.org/10.1061/(ASCE)WR.1943-5452.0000720.

Ghani, A. N. A. 2016. Economic Assessment of Ecosystem Services –The Methodology and Findings. *Proceedings of the International Seminar on the Ecogydrology Management of Putrajaya Lake and Wetland*. Putrajaya, Malaysia, 19–20 January 2016.

GHS (Ghana Health Service). 2013. *2013 Annual report*.

Giordano, M. and Shah, T. 2014. From IWRM back to integrated water resources management. *International Journal of Water Resources Development*, Vol. 30, No. 3, pp. 364–376. doi.org/10.1080/07900627.2013.851521.

Giordano, M., Turral, H., Scheierling, S. M., Treguer, D. O. and McCornick, P. G. 2017. *Beyond 'More Crop per Drop': Evolving Thinking on Agricultural Water Productivity*. IWMI Research Report No. 169. Colombo, International Water Management Institute (IWMI)/Washington, DC, World Bank. doi.org/10.5337/2017.202.

Gilvear, D., Beevers, L., O'Keeffe, J. and Acreman, M. 2017. Environmental water regimes and natural capital – Free-flowing ecosystem services. A. C. Horne, J. A. Webb, M. J. Stewardson, B. Richter and M. Acreman (eds.), *Water for the Environment: From Policy and Science to Implementation and Management*. London, Academic Press.

Global High-Level Panel on Water and Peace. 2017. *A Matter of Survival. Report of the Global High-Level Panel on Water and Peace*. Geneva, Geneva Water Hub. www.genevawaterhub.org/resource/matter-survival.

Gonzalez Sanchez, R., Seliger, R., Fahl, F., De Felice, L., Ouarda, T. B. and Farinosi, F. 2020. Freshwater use of the energy sector in Africa. *Applied Energy*, Vol. 270, Art. 115171. doi.org/10.1016/j.apenergy.2020.115171.

Gosling, S. N. and Arnell, N. W. 2016. A global assessment of the impact of climate change on water scarcity. *Climatic Change*, Vol. 134, pp. 371–385. doi.org/10.1007/s10584-013-0853-x.

Gould, I. M. 2010. Alexander Gordon, puerperal sepsis, and modern theories of infection control – Semmelweis in perspective. *The Lancet Infectious Diseases*, Vol. 10, No, 4, pp. 275–278. doi.org/10.1016/S1473-3099(09)70304-4.

Government of New Zealand. 2019. *The Wellbeing Budget 2019*. Government of New Zealand. treasury.govt.nz/publications/wellbeing-budget/wellbeing-budget-2019.

Government of Rwanda. 2019. *Natural Capital Accounts for Water*, Version 1.0. Kigali, NISR, Ministry of Environment. doi.org/10.13140/RG.2.2.23507.32806.

Grafton, R. Q. and Wheeler, S. A. 2018. Economics of water recovery in the Murray-Darling Basin, Australia. *Annual Review of Resource Economics*, Vol. 10, No. 1, pp. 487–510. doi.org/10.1146/annurev-resource-100517-023039.

Grafton, R. Q., Williams, J., Perry, C. J., Molle, F., Ringler, C., Steduto, P., Udall, B., Wheeler, S. A., Wang, Y., Garrick, D. and Allen, R. G. 2018. The paradox of irrigation efficiency. *Science*, Vol. 361, No. 6404, pp. 748–50. doi.org/10.1126/science.aat9314.

Green, P., Vörösmarty, C., Harrison, I. and Farrell, T. 2015. Freshwater ecosystem services supporting humans: Pivoting from water crisis to water solutions. *Global Environmental Change*, Vol. 34, pp. 108–118. doi.org/10.1016/j.gloenvcha.2015.06.007.

Greve, P., Kahil, T., Mochizuki, J., Schinko, T., Satoh, Y., Burek, P., Fischer, G., Tramberend, S., Burtscher, R., Langan, S. and Wada, Y. 2018. Global assessment of water challenges under uncertainty in water scarcity projections. *Nature Sustainability*, Vol. 1, pp. 486-494. doi.org/10.1038/s41893-018-0134-9.

Grill, G., Lehner, B., Thieme, M., Geenen, B., Tickner, D., Antonelli, F., Babu, S., Borrelli, P., Cheng, L., Crochetiere, H., Ehalt Macedo, H., Filgueiras, R., Goichot, M., Higgins, J., Hogan, Z., Lip, B., McClain, M. E., Meng, J., Mulligan, M., Nilsson, C., Olden, J. D., Opperman, J. J., Petry, P., Reidy Liermann, C., Sáenz, L., Salinas-Rodríguez, S., Schelle, P., Schmitt, R. J. P., Snider, J., Tan, F., Tockner, K., Valdujo, P. H., Van Soesbergen, A. and Zarfl, C. 2019. Mapping the world's free-flowing rivers. *Nature*, Vol. 569, pp. 215–221. doi.org/10.1038/s41586-019-1111-9.

GRIPP (Groundwater Solutions Initiative for Policy and Practice). n.d. *Groundwater-Based Natural Infrastructure (GBNI)*. GRIPP website. International Water Management Institute (IWMI). gripp.iwmi.org/natural-infrastructure/. (Accessed August 2020).

Grizzetti, B., Liquete, C., Antunes, P., Carvalho, L., Geamănă, N., Giucă, R., Leone, M., McConnell, S., Predad, R., Santos, R., Turkelboom, F., Vădineanu, A. and Woods, H. 2016. Ecosystem services for water policy: Insights across Europe. *Environmental Science & Policy*, Vol. 66, pp. 179–190. doi.org/10.1016/j.envsci.2016.09.006.

Groenfeldt, D. 2019. *Water Ethics. A Values Approach to Solving the Water Crisis*. 2nd edition. London, Earthscan Routledge.

Grossman, D., Doyle, M. and Buckley, N. 2015. *Data Intelligence for 21st Century Water Management: A Report from the 2015 Aspen-Nicholas Water Forum*. Washington, DC, The Aspen Institute. www.aspeninstitute.org/publications/data-intelligence-21st-century-water-management-report-2015-aspen-nicholas-water-forum/.

Guardiola, J., García-Rubio, M. A. and Guidi-Gutiérrez, E. 2014. Water access and subjective well-being: The case of Sucre, Bolivia. *Applied Research in Quality of Life*, Vol. 9, No. 2, pp. 367–385. doi.org/10.1007/s11482-013-9218-x.

Guardiola, J., González-Gómez, F. and Lendechy Grajales, Á. 2013. The influence of water access in subjective well-being: Some evidence in Yucatan, Mexico. *Social Indicators Research*, Vol. 110, No. 1, pp. 207–218. doi.org/10.1007/s11205-011-9925-3.

Gulland, J., Hone, S. and Pohlner, H. 2020. *Position Paper on Valuing Water in Bangladesh*. Washington, DC, 2030 Water Resources Group. www.2030wrg.org/wp-content/uploads/2020/11/Position-Paper-on-Valuing-Water-in-Bangladesh.pdf.

GWOPA (Global Water Operators Partnership Alliance). 2020. *What Water and Sanitation Operators can do in the Fight against COVID-19*. GWOPA website. gwopa.org/what-water-and-sanitation-operators-can-do-in-the-fight-against-covid-19/.

GWP (Global Water Partnership). 2000. *Integrated Water Resources Management*. TAC Background paper No. 4. Stockholm, GWP. www.gwp.org/globalassets/global/toolbox/publications/background-papers/04-integrated-water-resources-management-2000-english.pdf.

_____. 2009. *A Handbook for Integrated Water Resources Management in Basins*. Stockholm, GWP/International Network of Basin Organizations (INBO). www.gwp.org/globalassets/global/toolbox/references/a-handbook-for-integrated-water-resources-management-in-basins-inbo-gwp-2009-english.pdf.

Hadj-Hammou, J., Loiselle, S., Ophof, D. and Thornhill, I. 2017. Getting the full picture: Assessing the complementarity of citizen science and agency monitoring data. *PLoS ONE*, Vol. 12, No. 12, e0188507. doi.org/10.1371/journal.pone.0188507.

Hagenvoort, J., Ortega-Reig, M., Botella, S., García, C., De Luis, A. and Palau-Salvador, G. 2019. Reusing treated waste-water from a circular economy perspective – The case of the Real Acequia de Moncada in Valencia (Spain). *Water*, Vol. 11, No. 9, No. 1830. doi.org/10.3390/w11091830.

Hagerty, N. 2019. *Liquid constrained in California: Estimating the potential gains from water markets*. MIT Working Paper.

Hanjra, M. A. and Qureshi, M. E. 2010. Global water crisis and future food security in an era of climate change. *Food Policy*, Vol. 35, No. 5, pp. 365–377. doi.org/10.1016/j.foodpol.2010.05.006.

Hansjürgens, B., Droste, N. and Tockner, K. 2016. Neglected values of major water engineering projects: Ecosystem services, social impacts, and economic valuation. R. F. Hüttl, O. Bens, C. Bismuth and S. Hoechstetter (eds.), *Society–Water–Technology: A Critical Appraisal of Major Water Engineering Projects*. Cham, Switzerland, Springer International Publishing.

Harmsworth, G., Awatere, S. and Mahuru, R. 2016. Indigenous Māori values and perspectives to inform freshwater management in Aotearoa-New Zealand. *Ecology and Society*, Vol. 21, No. 4, Art. 9. doi.org/10.5751/ES-08804-210409.

Harrington, K. 2015. *Saudi Arabia Creates New Solar-Powered Desalination Technology*. AIChEi (American Institute of Chemical Engineers), 16 October. www.aiche.org/chenected/2015/10/saudi-arabia-creates-new-solar-powered-desalination-technology.

Hasan, E., Tarhule, A., Hong, Y. Moore III, B. 2019. Assessment of physical water scarcity in Africa using GRACE and TRMM satellite data. *Remote Sensing*, Vol. 11, Art. 904. doi.org//10.3390/rs11080904.

Hayman, E. R. 2018. *Héen Aawashaayi Shaawat / Marrying the Water: The Tlingit, the Tagish, and the Making of Place*. Phd Thesis. Munich, Germany, Faculty of Geography, Ludwig-Maximilians University. doi.org/10.5282/edoc.22368.

Hein, C. (ed.). 2020. *Adaptive Strategies for Water Heritage – Past, Present and Future*. Springer International Publishing. doi.org/10.1007/978-3-030-00268-8.

Heineken. 2019a. *Heineken announces 'Every Drop' Water Ambition for 2030*. Media release. www.theheinekencompany.com/newsroom/heineken-announces-every-drop-water-ambition-for-2030/.

_____. 2019b. Every Drop Counts. Heineken website. www.theheinekencompany.com/newsroom/every-drop-counts/.

Hellegers, P. and Leflaive, X. 2015. Water allocation reform: What makes it so difficult. *Water International*, Vol. 40, No. 2, pp. 273–285. doi.org/10.1080/02508060.2015.1008266.

Hellegers, P. and Van Halsema, G. E. 2019. Weighing economic values against societal needs: Questioning the roles of valuing water in practice. *Water Policy*, Vol. 21, No. 3, pp. 514–525. doi.org/10.2166/wp.2019.048.

Helliwell, J. F., Layard, R., Sachs, J. and De Neve, J. (eds.). 2020. *World Happiness Report 2020*. New York, Sustainable Development Solutions Network. worldhappiness.report/ed/2020/.

Hellum, A., Kameri Mbote, P. and Van Koppen, B. (eds.). 2015. *Water is life: Women's human rights in national and local water governance in Southern and Eastern Africa*. Harare, Weaver Press.

Hermans, L. M., Van Halsema, G. E. and Mahoo, H. F. 2006. Building a mosaic of values to support local water resources management. *Water Policy*, Vol. 8, No. 5, pp. 415–434. doi.org/10.2166/wp.2006.051.

Hester, G., Carsell, K. and Ford, D. 2006. *Benefits of the USGS Stream Gauging Program – Users and Uses of US streamflow Data*. National Hydrologic Water Council. water.usgs.gov/osw/pubs/nhwc_report.pdf.

HLPW (High Level Panel on Water). 2017a. *Value Water*. Unpublished note.

_____. 2017b. *Bellagio Principles on Valuing Water*. Bellagio, Italy. sustainabledevelopment.un.org/content/documents/15591Bellagio_principles_on_valuing_water_final_version_in_word.pdf.

_____. 2018. *Making Every Drop Count: An Agenda for Water Action*. High Level Panel on Water Outcome Document. sustainabledevelopment.un.org/content/documents/17825HLPW_Outcome.pdf.

Hoekstra, A. Y. and Chapagain, A. K. 2007. Water footprints of nations: Water use by people as a function of their consumption pattern. *Water Resources Management*, Vol. 21, pp. 35–48. doi.org/10.1007/s11269-006-9039-x.

Hoekstra, A. Y., Chapagain, A. K., Aldaya, M. M. and Mekonnen, M. M. 2011. *The Water Footprint Assessment Manual: Setting the Global Standard*. London/Washington, DC, Earthscan.

Hoekstra, A. Y. and Mekonnen, M. M. 2012. The water footprint of humanity. *Proceedings of the National Academy of Sciences of the United States of America*, Vol. 109, No. 9, pp. 3232-3237. doi.org/10.1073/pnas.1109936109.

Hoekstra, R. 2019. *Replacing GDP by 2030 – Towards a Common Language for the Well-Being and Sustainability Community*. Cambridge, UK, Cambridge University Press. doi.org/10.1017/9781108608558.

Hoff, H. 2011. *Understanding the Nexus*. Background paper for the Bonn 2011 Conference: The Water, Energy and Food Security Nexus. Stockholm, Stockholm Environment Institute (SEI). www.sei.org/publications/understanding-the-nexus/.

House, S., Ferron, S., Sommer, M. and Cavill, S. 2014. *Violence, Gender & WASH: A Practitioner's Toolkit – Making Water, Sanitation and Hygiene Safer through Improved Programming and Services*. London, WaterAid/Sanitation and Hygiene Applied Research for Equity (SHARE).

Horne, A. C., O'Donnell, E. L., Acreman, M., McClain, M. E., Poff, N. L, Webb, J. A., Stewardson, M. J., Bond, N. R., Richter, B., Arthington, A. H., Tharme, R. E., Garrick, D. E., Daniell, K. A., Conallin, J. C., Thomas, G. A. and Hart, B. T. 2017a. Moving forward – the implementation challenge for environmental water management. A. C. Horne, J. A. Webb, M. J. Stewardson, B. Richter, and M. Acreman (eds.), *Water for the Environment: From Policy and Science to Implementation and Management*. Cambridge, Mass., Academic Press, pp. 649–673. doi.org/10.1016/B978-0-12-803907-6.00027-9.

Horne, A. C., O'Donnell, E. L. and Tharme, R. E. 2017b. Mechanisms to allocate environmental water. A. C. Horne, J. A. Webb, M. J. Stewardson, B. Richter, B. and M. Acreman (eds.), *Water for the Environment: From Policy and Science to Implementation and Management*. Cambridge, Mass., Academic Press, pp. 361–398. doi.org/10.1016/B978-0-12-803907-6.00017-6.

HRC (Human Rights Council). 2010. *Resolution adopted by the Human Rights Council. The Human Right to Safe Drinking Water and Sanitation*. Eighteenth session of Human Rights Council, A/HRC/RES/18/1.

HSAC (Hydropower Sustainability Assessment Council). 2018. *Hydropower Sustainability Assessment Protocol*. London, International Hydropower Association (IHA). www.hydrosustainability.org/assessment-protocol.

Hsiao, T. C., Steduto, P. and Fereres, E. 2007. A systematic and quantitative approach to improve water use efficiency in agriculture. *Irrigation Science*, Vol. 25, No. 3, pp. 209–231. doi.org/10.1007/s00271-007-0063-2.

Hugh, B. 2019. *By, for, and of the People: How Citizen Science Enhances Water Security*. NewSecurityBeat website. Wilson Center. www.newsecuritybeat.org/2019/12/by-for-people-citizen-science-enhances-water-security/.

Hurford, A. P., McCartney, M. P., Harou, J. J., Dalton, J., Smith, D. M. and Odada, E. 2020. Balancing services from built and natural assets via river basin trade-off analysis. *Ecosystem Services*, Vol. 45, Art. 101144. doi.org/10.1016/j.ecoser.2020.101144.

Hutton, G. 2012. *Monitoring "Affordability" of Water and Sanitation Services after 2015: Review of Global Indicator Options*. A paper submitted to the United Nations Office of the High Commission for Human Rights.

_____. 2013. Global costs and benefits of reaching universal coverage of sanitation and drinking-water supply. *Journal of Water and Health*, Vol.11, No. 1, pp. 1–12. doi.org/10.2166/wh.2012.105.

_____. 2018. Global benefits and costs of achieving universal coverage of basic water and sanitation services as part of the 2030 Agenda for Sustainable Development. B. Lomborg (ed.), *Prioritizing Development*. Cambridge, UK, Cambridge University Press, pp. 422–445. doi.org/10.1017/9781108233767.025.

Hutton, G. and Chase, C. 2017. Water supply, sanitation, and hygiene. C. N. Mock, R. Nugent, O. Kobusingye and K. R. Smith (eds.), Injury Prevention and Environmental Health Third Edition, Vol. 7, *Injury Prevention and Environmental Health*. Washington, DC, The International Bank for Reconstruction and Development/The World Bank. openknowledge.worldbank.org/handle/10986/28576. License: CC BY 3.0 IGO.

Hutton, G. and Varughese, M. 2016. *The Costs of Meeting the 2030 Sustainable Development Goal Targets on Drinking Water, Sanitation, and Hygiene Summary Report*. Washington DC, World Bank. openknowledge.worldbank.org/handle/10986/23681. License: CC BY 3.0 IGO.

IBNet Tariffs database (International Benchmarking Network for Water and Sanitation Utilities Tariffs database). 2018. *IBNET Tariffs DB*. tariffs.ib-net.org/sites.

ICOMOS (International Council of Monuments and Sites). 2015. *Cultural Heritages of Water: The Cultural Heritages of Water in the Middle East and Maghreb*. Thematic Study, first edition. Charenton-le-Pont, France, ICOMOS. www.icomos.org/images/DOCUMENTS/World_Heritage/CH%20of%20water_201507_opt.pdf.

_____. 2019. *The Future of Our Pasts: Engaging Cultural Heritage in Climate Action*. Paris, ICOMOS. www.icomos.org/en/77-articles-en-francais/59522-icomos-releases-future-of-our-pasts-report-to-increase-engagement-of-cultural-heritage-in-climate-action.

ICWE (International Conference on Water and the Environment). 1992. *The Dublin Statement and Report of the Conference*. ICWE: Development issues for the 21st century. Dublin, 26–31 January.

IDA (International Desalination Association). 2020. *Desalination and Water Reuse by the Numbers*. IDA website. idadesal.org/.

IEA (International Energy Agency). 2016. *Water Energy Nexus, Excerpt from the World Energy Outlook 2016*. Paris, Organisation for Economic Co-operation and Development (OECD)/IEA. www.iea.org/reports/water-energy-nexus.

_____. 2020. *Renewable Energy Market Update: Outlook for 2020 and 2021*. www.iea.org/reports/renewable-energy-market-update.

IFPRI (International Food Policy Research Institute). 2019. *2019 Global Food Policy Report*. Washington, DC., IFPRI. doi.org/10.2499/9780896293502.

IHA (International Hydropower Association). 2010. *Hydropower Sustainability Assessment Protocol*. London, IHA. www.hydrosustainability.org/assessment-protocol.

_____. 2020. *Hydropower Sustainability Guidelines on Good International Industry Practice*. London, IHA. www.hydropower.org/publications/hydropower-sustainability-guidelines.

Imamura, K., Takano, K. T., Mori, N., Nakashizuka, T. and Managi, S. 2016. Attitudes toward disaster-prevention risk in Japanese coastal areas: Analysis of civil preference. *Natural Hazards*, Vol. 82, pp. 209–226. doi.org/10.1007/s11069-016-2210-7.

Instituto Nacional de Estadística y Geografía. 2016. *Encuesta Nacional de Ingresos y Gastos de los Hogares* [National Survey of Household Income and Expenditure]. Mexico, Instituto Nacional de Estadística y Geografía. www.inegi.org.mx/programas/enigh/nc/2016/. (In Spanish).

International Health Conference. 1946. *Constitution of the World Health Organization*. www.who.int/governance/eb/who_constitution_en.pdf.

International Rivers. 2012. *Right Priorities for Africa's Power Sector: An Evaluation of Dams under the Programme of Infrastructure Development for Africa (PIDA)*. Pretoria, International Rivers.

IPBES (Intergovernmental Science-Policy Platform on Biodiversity and Ecosystem Services). 2019a. *Global Assessment Report on Biodiversity and Ecosystem Services of the Intergovernmental Science-Policy Platform on Biodiversity and Ecosystem Services*. E. S. Brondizio, J. Settele, S. Díaz and H. T. Ngo (eds.). Bonn, Germany, IPBES secretariat. www.ipbes.net/global-assessment.

_____. 2019b. *Summary for Policymakers of the Global Assessment Report on Biodiversity and Ecosystem Services of the Intergovernmental Science-Policy Platform on Biodiversity and Ecosystem Services*. S. Díaz, J. Settele, E. S. Brondízio, H. T. Ngo, M. Guèze, J. Agard, A. Arneth, P. Balvanera, K. A. Brauman, S. H. M. Butchart, K. M. A. Chan, L. A. Garibaldi, K. Ichii, J. Liu, S. M. Subramanian, G. F. Midgley, P. Miloslavich, Z. Molnár, D. Obura, A. Pfaff, S. Polasky, A. Purvis, J. Razzaque, B. Reyers, R. Roy Chowdhury, Y. J. Shin, I. J. Visseren-Hamakers, K. J. Willis and C. N. Zayas (eds.). Bonn, Germany, IPBES secretariat. doi.org/10.5281/zenodo.3553579.

_____. n.d. Indigenous and local knowledge in IPBES. IPBES website. ipbes.net/indigenous-local-knowledge.

IPCC (Intergovernmental Panel on Climate Change). 2018. *Global Warming of 1.5°C. An IPCC Special Report on the Impacts of Global Warming of 1.5°C above Pre-Industrial Levels and Related Global Greenhouse Gas Emission Pathways, in the Context of Strengthening the Global Response to the Threat of Climate Change, Sustainable Development, and Efforts to Eradicate Poverty*. Masson-Delmotte, V., P. Zhai, H.-O. Pörtner, D. Roberts, J. Skea, P.R. Shukla, A. Pirani, W. Moufouma-Okia, C. Péan, R. Pidcock, S. Connors, J.B.R. Matthews, Y. Chen, X. Zhou, M.I. Gomis, E. Lonnoy, T. Maycock, M. Tignor, and T. Waterfield (eds.). www.ipcc.ch/sr15/.

IWA (International Water Association). 2019. *Digital water: Industry Leaders Chart the Transformation Journey*. London, IWA. iwa-network.org/wp-content/uploads/2015/12/IWA_2019_Digital_Water_Report.pdf.

IWGIA (International Work Group for Indigenous Affairs). 2019. *The Indigenous World 2019*. Copenhagen, IWGIA. www.iwgia.org/images/documents/indigenous-world/IndigenousWorld2019_UK.pdf.

Jackson, S. 2017. How much water does a culture need? Environmental water management's cultural challenge and indigenous responses. A.C. Horne, E. L. O'Donnell, J. A. Webb, M. J. Stewardson, M. Acreman and B. Richter (eds.), *Water for the Environment: From Policy and Science to Implementation and Management*. London, Academic Press, pp. 173–188. doi.org/10.1016/B978-0-12-803907-6.00009-7.

Jackson, S. and Langton, M. 2012. Trends in the recognition of indigenous water needs in Australian water reform: The limitations of 'cultural' entitlements in achieving water equity. *Journal of Water Law*, Vol. 22, No. 2, pp. 109–123. doi.org/10.1016/j.landusepol.2020.104869.

Jägermeyr, J., Gerten, D., Heinke, J., Schaphoff, S., Kummu, M. and Lucht, W. 2015. Water savings potentials of irrigation systems: Global simulation of processes and linkages. *Hydrology and Earth System Science*, Vol. 19, pp. 3073–3091. doi.org/10.5194/hess-19-3073-2015.

Jägermeyr, J., Pastor, A., Biemans, H. and Gerten, D. 2017. Reconciling irrigated food production with environmental flows for Sustainable Development Goals implementation. *Nature Communications*, Vol. 8, Art. 15900. doi.org/10.1038/ncomms15900.

Jalava, M., Guillaume, J. H. A., Kummu, M., Porkka, M., Siebert, S. and Varis, O. 2016. Diet change and food loss reduction: What is their combined impact on global water use and scarcity? *Earth's Future*, Vol. 4, pp. 62–78. doi.org/10.1002/2015EF000327.

James, A. J., Bahadur, A. V., Verma, S., Reid, P. and Biswas, S. 2018. *Climate-Resilient Water Management: An Operational Framework from South Asia. Learning paper*. New Delhi, Action on Climate Today.

Japanese Ministry of Environment. 2010. *Conserving Water by Recharging Groundwater in Kumamoto*. www.biodic.go.jp/biodiversity/shiraberu/policy/pes/en/water/water03.html.

_____. 2015. *Groundwater Conservation and Tap Water Management: Experience of Kumamoto City, Japan*. Asia Low-Carbon Cities Platform Case Study. www.env.go.jp/earth/coop/lowcarbon-asia/english/localgov3/data/kumamoto_20150305_01.pdf.

Jax, K., Calestani, M., Chan, K. M. A., Eser, U., Keune, H., Muraca, B., O'Brien, L., Potthast, T., Voget-Kleschin, L. and Wittmer, H. 2018. Caring for nature matters: A relational approach for understanding nature's contributions to human well-being. *Current Opinion in Environmental Sustainability*, Vol. 35, pp. 1–8. doi.org/10.1016/j.cosust.2018.10.009.

Jeuland, M. 2020. The economics of dams. *Oxford Review of Economic Policy*, Vol. 36, No. 1, pp. 45–68. doi.org/10.1093/oxrep/grz028.

Jiménez, A., Molina, M. F. and Le Deunff, H. 2014. Indigenous peoples and industry water users: Mapping the conflicts worldwide. *Aquatic Procedia*, Vol. 5, pp. 69–80. doi.org/10.1016/j.aqpro.2015.10.009.

Johnston, B., Hiwasaki, L., Klaver, I., Ramos-Castillo, A. and Strang, V. (eds.). 2012. *Water, Cultural Diversity, and Global Environmental Change: Emerging Trends, Sustainable Futures?* Dordrecht, The Netherlands, Springer.

Jones, E., Qadir, M., Van Vliet, M. T. H., Smakhtin, V. and Kang, S. 2019. The state of desalination and brine production: A global outlook. *Science of The Total Environment*, Vol. 657, pp. 1343–1356. doi.org/10.1016/j.scitotenv.2018.12.076.

Justus, J., Colyvan, M., Regan, H. and Maguire, L. 2019. Buying into conservation: Intrinsic versus instrumental value. *Trends in Ecology & Evolution*, Vol. 24, No. 4, pp. 187–191. doi.org/10.1016/j.tree.2008.11.011.

K

Kablouti, G. 2015. Cost of water use: A driver of future investments into water-efficient thermal power plants? *Aquatic Procedia*, Vol. 5, pp. 31–43. doi.org/10.1016/j.aqpro.2015.10.006.

Kaliba, A. R., Norman, D. W. and Chang, Y. M. 2003. Willingness to pay to improve domestic water supply in rural areas of Central Tanzania: Implications for policy. *The International Journal of Sustainable Development & World Ecology*, Vol. 10, No. 2, pp. 119–132. doi.org/10.1080/13504500309469791.

Kendy, E., Molden, D., Steenhuis, T. S., Liu, C. and Wang, J. 2003. *Policies Drain the North China Plain: Agricultural Policy and Groundwater Depletion in Luancheng County, 1949–2000*. Research Report No. 71. Colombo, International Water management Institute (IWMI). www.iwmi.cgiar.org/Publications/IWMI_Research_Reports/PDF/pub071/Report71.pdf.

Khadem, M., Rougé, C., Harou, J. J., Hansen, K. M., Medellin-Azuara, J. and Lund, J. R. 2018. Estimating the economic value of interannual reservoir storage in water resource systems. *Water Resources Research*, Vol. 54, No. 11, pp. 8890–8908. doi.org/10.1029/2017WR022336.

Kingdom, B., Lloyd-Owen, D., Trémolet, S., Kayaga, S. and Ikeda, J. 2018. *Better Use of Capital to Deliver Sustainable Water Supply and Sanitation Services: Practical Examples and Suggested Next Steps*. Washington, DC, World Bank. openknowledge.worldbank.org/handle/10986/30870. License: CC BY 3.0 IGO.

Kingdom of Cambodia. 2015. *Cambodia Socio-Economic Survey 2015*. Phnom Penh, National Institute of Statistics/Ministry of Planning. www.nis.gov.kh/nis/CSES/Final%20Report%20CSES%202015.pdf.

Kjellén, M. 2018. Wastewater governance and the local, regional and global environments. *Water Alternatives*, Vol. 11, No. 2, pp. 219–237.

Klimes, M. and Yaari, E. A. 2019. Water security in the Middle East – Opportunities and challenges for water diplomacy. A. Jägerskog, M. Schulz and A. Swain (eds.), *Routledge Handbook on Middle East Security*. London, Routledge.

Krause, F. and Strang, V. 2016. Thinking relationships through water. *Society and Natural Resources*, Vol. 29, No. 6, pp. 633–638. doi.org/10.1080/08941920.2016.1151714.

Kumamoto City. 2020a. *A World-Class Pure Groundwater City Kumamoto, Japan*. Kumamoto City website. www.city.kumamoto.jp/kankyo/hpkiji/pub/Detail.aspx?c_id=5&id=20548.

_____. 2020b. 第３次熊本市地下水保全プラン [R2(2020)年度～R6(2024)年度] [The 3rd Kumamoto City Groundwater Conservation Plan 2020-2024]. www.city.kumamoto.jp/common/UploadFileDsp.aspx?c_id=5&id=27658&sub_id=1&flid=201535. (In Japanese.)

_____. 2020c. *A World Class Pure Groundwater City Kumamoto, Japan*. www.city.kumamoto.jp/kankyo/common/UploadFileDsp.aspx?c_id=5&id=20442&set_doc=1&set_file_field=1. (In Japanese.)

_____. 2020d. 白川中流域水田を活用した地下水かん養事業 [Groundwater Recharge in Kumamoto City]. www.city.kumamoto.jp/common/UploadFileDsp.aspx?c_id=5&id=20453&sub_id=3&flid=218653. (In Japanese.)

Kummu, M., De Moel, H., Porkka, M., Siebert, S., Varis, O. and Ward, P. J. 2012. Lost food, wasted resources: Global food supply chain losses and their impacts on freshwater, cropland, and fertiliser use. *Science of The Total Environment*, Vol. 438, pp. 477–489. doi.org/10.1016/j.scitotenv.2012.08.092.

Kummu, M., Ward, P. J., De Moel, H. and Varis, O. 2010. Is physical water scarcity a new phenomenon? Global assessment of water shortage over the last two millennia. *Environmental Research Letters*, Vol. 5, No. 3, Art. 034006. doi.org/10.1088/1748-9326/5/3/034006.

Lackey, K. and Fillmore, L. 2017. *Energy Management for Water Utilities in Latin America and the Caribbean: Exploring Energy Efficiency and Energy Recovery Potential in Wastewater Treatment Plants*. Washington, DC/Alexandria, Va., The World Bank Group/Water Environment Research Foundation. pubdocs.worldbank.org/en/392871496427784755/Task-B-WERF1T14-web.pdf.

Laituri, M. and Sternlieb, F. 2014. Water data systems: Science, practice, and policy. *Journal of Contemporary Water Research & Education*, Vol. 153, No. 1, pp. 1–3. doi.org/10.1111/j.1936-704X.2014.03174.x.

Lamers, J. P. A. and Khamzina, A. 2008. Fuelwood production in the degraded agricultural areas of the Aral Sea Basin, Uzbekistan. *Bois et Forêts des Tropiques*, Vol. 297, No. 3, pp. 47–57.

Lange, G. M. 2006. Water valuation case studies in Namibia. G. M. Lange and R. M. Hassan, *The Economics of Water Management in Southern Africa: An Environmental Accounting Approach*. Cheltenham, United Kingdom, Edward Elgar Publishing, pp. 44–113.

Lary, D. 2001. Drowned earth: The strategic breaching of the Yellow River Dyke, 1938. *War in History*, Vol. 8, No. 2, pp. 191–207.

Laurent, F., Leturcq, G., Mello, I., Corbonnois, J. and Verdum, R. 2011. La diffusion du semis direct au Brésil, diversité des pratiques et logiques territoriales: L'exemple de la région d'Itaipu au Paraná [The spread of direct seeding in Brazil, diversity of practices and territorial approaches: The example of the Itaipu region in Paraná]. *Confins*, Vol. 12. doi.org/10.4000/confins.7143. (In French.)

LeRoy Poff, N., Brown, C. M., Grantham, T. E., Matthews, J. H., Palmer, M. A., Spence, C. M., Wilby, R., Haasnoot, M., Mendoza, G. F., Dominique, K. C. and Baeza, A. 2015. Sustainable water management under future uncertainty with eco-engineering decision scaling. *Nature Climate Change*, Vol. 6, pp. 25–34. doi.org/10.1038/nclimate2765.

Levidow, L., Zaccaria, D., Maia, R., Vivas, E., Todorovic, M. and Scardigno, A. 2014. Improving water-efficient irrigation: Prospects and difficulties of innovative practices. *Agricultural Water Management*, Vol. 146, pp. 84–94. doi.org/10.1016/j.agwat.2014.07.012.

Lewis, T. 2020. Eight persistent myths about the COVID-19 pandemic and why people believe them. *Scientific American*, 12 October 2020. www.scientificamerican.com/article/eight-persistent-covid-19-myths-and-why-people-believe-them/.

Liebenberg, L., Steventon, J., Brahman, N., Benadie, K., Minye, J., Langwane, H. and Xhukwe, Q. 2017. Smartphone Icon User Interface design for non-literate trackers and its implications for an inclusive citizen science. *Biological Conservation*, Vol. 208, pp. 155–162. doi.org/10.1016/j.biocon.2016.04.033.

Lipper, L., Thornton, P., Campbell, B. M., Baedeker, T., Braimoh, A., Bwalya, M., Caron, P., Cattaneo, A., Garrity, D., Henry, K., Hottle, R., Jackson, L., Jarvis, A., Kossam, F., Mann, W., McCharty, N., Meyback, A., Neufeldt, H., Remington, T., Sen, P. T., Sessa, R., Shula, R., Tibu, A. and Torquebiau, E. F. 2014. Climate-smart agriculture for food security. *Nature Climate Change*, Vol. 4, pp. 1068–1072. doi.org/10.1038/nclimate2437.

Liu, X., Feng, X., Ciais, P. and Fu, B. 2019. Widespread decline in terrestrial water storage and its link to teleconnections across Asia and Eastern Europe. *Hydrology and Earth System Sciences*, Vol. 24, pp. 3663–3676. doi.org/10.5194/hess-2019-281.

López, S. T., De los Angeles Barrionuevo, M. and Rodríguez-Labajos, B. 2019. Water accounts in decision-making processes of urban water management: Benefits, limitations and implications in a real implementation. *Sustainable Cities and Society*, Vol. 50, Art. 101676. doi.org/10.1016/j.scs.2019.101676.

Lopez-Gunn, E., Zorrilla, P., Prieto, F. and Llamas, M. R. 2012. Lost in translation? Water efficiency in Spanish agriculture. *Agricultural Water Management*, Vol. 108, pp. 83–95. doi.org/10.1016/j.agwat.2012.01.005.

Lu, C. and Tian, H. 2017. Global nitrogen and phosphorus fertilizer use for agriculture production in the past half century: Shifted hot spots and nutrient imbalance. *Earth System Science Data*, Vol. 9, pp. 181–192. doi.org/10.5194/essd-9-181-2017.

Lubell, M. and Edelenbos, J. 2013. Integrated Water Resources Management. *International Journal of Water Governance*, Vol. 1, No. 3–4, pp. 177–196. doi.org/10.7564/13-IJWG14.

Luo, T., Krishnan, D. and Sen, S. 2018. *Parched Power: Water Demands, Risks, and Opportunities for India's Power Sector*. Working Paper. Washington, DC, World Resources Institute (WRI). www.wri.org/publication/parched-power.

Mach, K. J., Kraan, C. M., Adger, W. N., Buhaug, H., Burke, M., Fearon, J. D., Field, C. B., Hendrix, C. S., Maystadt, J., O'Loughlin, J., Roessler, P., Scheffran, J., Schultz, K. A. and Von Uexkull, N. 2019. Climate as a risk factor for armed conflict. *Nature*, Vol. 571, pp. 193–197. doi.org/10.1038/s41586-019-1300-6.

Maclean, K., Robinson, C. J. and Natcher, D. 2014. Consensus building or constructive conflict? Aboriginal discursive strategies to enhance participation in natural resource management in Australia and Canada. *Society & Natural Resources*, Vol. 28, No. 2, pp. 1–15. doi.org/10.1080/08941920.2014.928396.

Maclean, K. and The Bana Yarralji Bubu Inc. 2015. Crossing cultural boundaries: Integrating Indigenous water knowledge into water governance through co-research in the Queensland Wet Tropics, Australia. *Geoforum*, Vol. 59, pp. 142–152. doi.org/10.1016/j.geoforum.2014.12.008.

Maes, J., Teller, A., Erhard, M., Grizzetti, B., Barredo, J. I., Paracchini, M. L., Condé, S., Somma, F., Orgiazzi, A., Jones, A., Zulian, A., Vallecilo, S., Petersen, J. E., Marquardt, D., Kovacevic, V., Abdul Malak, D., Marin, A. I., Czúcz, B., Mauri, A., Loffler, P., Bastrup-Birk, A., Biala, K., Christiansen, T. and Werner, B. 2018. *Mapping and Assessment of Ecosystems and their Services: An Analytical Framework for Ecosystem Condition*. Luxembourg, Publications office of the European Union. ec.europa.eu/environment/nature/knowledge/ecosystem_assessment/pdf/5th%20MAES%20report.pdf.

Mahasuweerachai, P. and Pangjai, S. 2018. Does piped water improve happiness? A case from Asian rural communities. *Journal of Happiness Studies*, Vol. 19, No. 5, pp. 1329–1346. doi.org/10.1007/s10902-017-9875-9.

Mahdavi, T., Bagheri, A. and Hosseini, S. A. 2019. Applying the System of Environmental and Economic Accounts for Water (SEEA-Water) for integrated assessment of water security in an aquifer scale – Case study: Azarshahr aquifer, Iran. *Groundwater for Sustainable Development*, Vol. 9, Art. 100261. doi.org/10.1016/j.gsd.2019.100261.

Makey, L. and Awatere, S. 2018. *He mahere pāhekoheko mō Kaipara Moana* – Integrated ecosystem-based management for Kaipara Harbour, Aotearoa New Zealand. *Society & Natural Resources*, Vol. 31, No. 12, pp. 1400–1418. doi.org/10.1080/08941920.2018.1484972.

Makondo, C. C. and Thomas, D. S. G. 2018. Climate change adaptation: Linking indigenous knowledge with western science for effective adaptation. *Environmental Science & Policy*, Vol. 88, pp. 83–91. doi.org/10.1016/j.envsci.2018.06.014.

Makropoulos, C., Nikolopoulos, D., Palmen, L., Kools, S., Segrave, A., Vries, D., Koop, S., Van Alphen, H. J., Vonk, E., Van Thienen, P. and Rozos, E. 2018. A resilience assessment method for urban water systems. *Urban Water Journal*, Vol. 15, No. 4, pp. 316–328. doi.org/10.1080/1573062X.2018.1457166.

Maktabifard, M., Zaborowska, E. and Makinia, J. 2018. Achieving energy neutrality in wastewater treatment plants through energy savings and enhancing renewable energy production. *Reviews in Environmental Science and Biotechnology*, Vol. 17, pp. 655–689. doi.org/10.1007/s11157-018-9478-x.

Mandela, D. 2020. Construction of Agadir desalination project in Morocco on track. *Construction Review Online*, 3 March 2020. constructionreviewonline.com/2020/03/construction-of-agadir-desalination-project-in-morocco-on-track/.

Manson, R., Barrantes, G. and Bauche Petersen, P. 2013. Lecciones de Costa Rica y México para el desarrollo y fortalecimiento de programas de pago por servicios ambientales hidrológicos en América Latina [Lessons from Costa Rica and Mexico for the development and strengthening of payment for hydrological environmental services programmes in Latin America]. A. Lara, P. Laterra, R. Manson and G. Barrantes (eds.), *Servicios ecosistémicos hídricos: estudios de caso en América Latina y el Caribe* [Water ecosystem services: Case studies from Latin America and the Caribbean]. Valdivia, Chile, Red ProAgua CYTED Imprenta América. (In Spanish.)

Markantonis, V., Dondeynaz, C., Latinopoulos, D., Bithas, K., Trichakis, I., M'Po, Y. N. T. and Carmona Moreno, C. 2018. Values and preferences for domestic water use: A study from the transboundary river basin of Mékrou (West Africa). *Water*, Vol. 10, No. 9, p. 1232. doi.org/10.3390/w10091232.

Mayer, B. K., Baker, L. A., Boyer, T. H., Drechsel, P., Gifford, M., Hanjra, M. A., Parameswaran, P., Stoltzfus, J., Westerhoff, P. and Rittmann, B. E. 2016. Total value of phosphorus recovery. *Environmental Science & Technology*, Vol. 50, pp. 6606–6620. doi.org/10.1021/acs.est.6b01239.

Mayor, B. 2020. Unraveling the historical economies of scale and learning effects for desalination technologies. *Water Resources Research*, Vol. 56, e2019WR025841. doi.org/10.1029/2019WR025841.

McCabe, M. F., Rodell, M., Alsdorf, D. E., Miralles, D. G., Uijlenhoet, R., Wagner, W., Lucieer, A., Houborg, R., Verhoest, N. E. C., Franz, T. E., Shi, J., Gao, H. and Wood, E. F. 2017. The future of earth observation in hydrology. *Hydrology and Earth System Sciences*, Vol. 21, pp. 3879–3914. doi.org/10.5194/hess-21-3879-2017.

McCartney, M., Foudi, S., Muthuwatta, L., Sood, A., Simons, G., Hunink, J., Vercruysse, K., Omuombo, C. 2019. *Quantifying the Services of Natural and Built Infrastructure in the Context of Climate Change: The Case of the Tana River Basin, Kenya*. IWMI Research Report No. 174. Colombo, International Water Management Institute (IWMI). doi.org/10.5337/2019.200.

McDonald, R. I. and Shemie, D. 2014. *Urban Water Blueprint: Mapping Conservation Solutions to the Global Water Challenge*. Washington, DC, The Nature Conservancy. water.nature.org/waterblueprint/#/intro=true.

McKinley, D. C., Miller-Rushing, A. J., Ballard, H. L., Bonney, R., Brown, H., Cook-Patton, S. C., Evans, D. M., French, R. A., Parrish, J. K., Phillips, T. B., Ryan, S. F., Shanley, L. A., Shirk, J. L., Stepenuck, K. F., Weltzin, J. F., Wiggins, A., Boyle, O. D., Briggs, R. D., Chapin III, S. F., Hewitt, D. A., Preuss, P. W. and Soukup, M. A. 2017. Citizen science can improve conservation science, natural resource management, and environmental protection. *Biological Conservation*, Vol. 208, pp. 15–28. doi.org/10.1016/j.biocon.2016.05.015.

McKinsey & Company. 2011. *Resource Revolution: Meeting the World's Energy, Materials, Food, and Water Needs*. McKinsey & Company. www.mckinsey.com/business-functions/sustainability/our-insights/resource-revolution.

Mekonnen, M. and Hoekstra A. 2011a. The green, blue and grey water footprint of crops and derived crop products. *Hydrology and Earth System Sciences*, Vol. 15, pp. 1577–1600. doi.org/10.5194/hess-15-1577-2011.

_____. 2011b. *Average Water Footprint of Industrial Products per Unit of Industrial Value Added (1996-2005)*. Dataset. 4TU.ResearchData. Delft, The Netherlands, Delft University of Technology. doi.org/10.4121/uuid:44c6e294-3a56-4bb4-b288-9588ca01d0c5.

_____. 2016. Four billion people facing severe water scarcity. *Science Advances*, Vol. 2, No. 2, e1500323. doi.org/10.1126/sciadv.1500323.

Mekonnen, M. M., Pahlow, M., Aldaya, M. M., Zarate, E. and Hoekstra, A. Y. 2015. Sustainability, efficiency and equitability of water consumption and pollution in Latin America and the Caribbean. *Sustainability*, Vol. 2, No. 7, pp. 2086–2112. doi.org/10.3390/su7022086.

Meldrum, J., Nettles-Anderson, S., Heath, G. and Macknick, J. 2013. Life cycle water use for electricity generation: A review and harmonization of literature estimates. *Environmental Research Letters*, Vol. 8, No. 1, Art. 015031. doi.org/10.1088/1748-9326/8/1/015031.

Mello, I. and Van Raij, B. 2006. No-till for sustainable agriculture in Brazil. *Proceedings of the World Association for Soil and Water Conservation*, P1, pp. 49–57.

Molden, D., Oweis, T., Steduto, P., Bindraban, P. S., Hanjra, M. A. and Kijne, J. 2010. Improving agricultural water productivity: Between optimism and caution. *Agricultural Water Management*, Vol. 97, No. 4, pp. 528–535. doi.org/10.1016/j.agwat.2009.03.023.

Molle, F. and Tanouti, O. 2017. Squaring the circle: Agricultural intensification vs. water conservation in Morocco. *Agricultural Water Management*, Vol. 192, pp. 170–179. doi.org/10.1016/j.agwat.2017.07.009.

Mommen, B., Humphries-Waaand, K. and Gwavuya, S. 2017. Does women's participation in water committees affect management and water system performance in rural Vanuatu? *Waterlines*, Vol. 36, No. 3, pp. 216–232. doi.org/10.3362/1756-3488.16-00026.

Morgan, A., Laporte-Bisquit, M., Williams, T. and Maggo, D. 2020. *Right Tool for the Job: Tools and Approaches for Companies and Investors to Assess Water Risks and Shared Water Challenges*. Gland/Geneva, Switzerland, WWF International/World Business Council for Sustainable Development (WBCSD). www.wbcsd.org/Programs/Food-and-Nature/Water/Resources/Right-tool-for-the-job.

Morimoto, R. and Hope, C. 2004. Applying a cost-benefit analysis model to the Three Gorges project in China. *Impact Assessment and Project Appraisal*, Vol. 22, No. 3, pp. 205–220. doi.org/10.3152/147154604781765888.

Mukherjee, P. 2020. *India's Vulnerable and Voiceless Groups speak out at Rishikesh*. Water Supply and Sanitation Collaborative Council (WSSCC) website. www.wsscc.org/2020/01/14/indias-vulnerable-and-voiceless-groups-speak-out-at-rishikesh/.

Muller, M., Biswas, A., Martin-Hurtado, R. and Tortajada, C. 2015. Built infrastructure is essential. *Science*, Vol. 349, No. 6248, pp. 585–586. doi.org/10.1126/science.aac7606.

MunichRe. 2020. *Tropical Cyclones cause Highest Losses: Natural Disasters of 2019 in Figures*. MunichRe website. www.munichre.com/topics-online/en/climate-change-and-natural-disasters/natural-disasters/natural-disasters-of-2019-in-figures-tropical-cyclones-cause-highest-losses.html.

N

Nadeem, A. M., Cheo, R. and Shaoan, H. 2018. Multidimensional analysis of water poverty and subjective well-being: A case study on local household variation in Faisalabad, Pakistan. *Social Indicators Research*, Vol. 138, pp. 207–224. doi.org/10.1007/s11205-017-1652-y.

NASAC (Network of African Science Academies). 2014. *The Grand Challenge of Water Security in Africa: Recommendations to Policymakers*. NASAC. nasaconline.org/wp-content/uploads/2016/05/The-Grand-Challenge-of-Water-Security-in-Africa-Recommendations-to-Policymakers.pdf.

National Action Plan on Business and Human Rights. n.d. *Small & Medium-Sized Enterprises*. National Action Plan on Business and Human Right website. globalnaps.org/issue/small-medium-enterprises-smes/.

National Water Commission. 2004. *Intergovernmental Agreement on a National Water Initiative between the Commonwealth of Australia and the Governments of New South Wales, Victoria, Queensland, South Australia, the Australian Capital Territory and the Northern Territory*. www.pc.gov.au/inquiries/completed/water-reform/national-water-initiative-agreement-2004.pdf.

Natural Capital Coalition. 2016. *Natural Capital Protocol*. www.naturalcapitalcoalition.org/protocol.

Nauges, C. and Whittington, D. 2010. Estimation of water demand in developing countries: An overview. *The World Bank Research Observer*, Vol. 25, No. 2, pp. 263–94. doi.org/10.1093/wbro/lkp016.

_____. 2017. Evaluating the performance of alternative municipal water tariff designs: Quantifying the tradeoffs between equity, economic efficiency, and cost recovery. *World Development*, Vol. 91, pp. 125–143. doi.org/10.1016/j.worlddev.2016.10.014.

Newborne, P. and Dalton, J. 2016. *Water Management and Stewardship: Taking Stock of Corporate Water Behaviour*. Gland, Switzerland/London, International Union for Conservation of Nature/Overseas Development Institute (IUCN/ODI). doi.org/10.2305/IUCN.CH.2016.16.en.

_____. 2019. *Corporate Water Management and Stewardship – Signs of Evolution towards Sustainability*. ODI briefing note. London, Overseas Development Institute (ODI). www.odi.org/sites/odi.org.uk/files/resource-documents/12994.pdf.

Novo, C. 2019. Africa's largest desalination plant to be built in Morocco. *Smart Water Magazine*, 8 July 2019. smartwatermagazine.com/news/smart-water-magazine/africas-largest-desalination-plant-be-built-morocco.

O

O'Brien, G. C., Dickens, C., Hines, E., Wepener, V., Stassen, R., Quayle, L., Fouchy, K., MacKenzie, J., Graham, P. M. and Landis, W. G. 2018. A regional-scale ecological risk framework for environmental flow evaluations. *Hydrology and Earth System Sciences*, Vol. 22, No. 2, pp. 957–975. doi.org/10.5194/hess-22-957-2018.

O'Brien, G. C., Dickens, C., Stassen, R., Van Weert, F. 2020. Sustainable floodplains: Linking e-flows to floodplain management, ecosystems and livelihoods. *Sustainability*, Vol. 12, Art. 10578. doi.org/10.3390/su122410578.

O'Donnell, M. 2011. *NAILSMA – TRaCK Project 6.2: Indigenous Rights in Water in Northern Australia*. Darwin, Australia, Charles Darwin University/Tropical Rivers and Coastal Knowledge/The North Australian Indigenous Land and Sea Management Alliance Ltd (TraCK/NAILSMA). www.nespnorthern.edu.au/wp-content/uploads/2016/02/TRaCKPub6.2Final_Mar11-Michael-ODonnel.web_.pdf.

OECD (Organisation for Economic Co-operation and Development). 2012. *OECD Environmental Outlook to 2050: The Consequences of Inaction. Key Facts and Figures*. Paris, OECD Publishing. www.oecd.org/env/indicators-modelling-outlooks/49910023.pdf.

_____. 2014. *Greening Household Behaviour: Overview from the 2011 Survey – Revised edition, OECD Studies on Environmental Policy and Household Behaviour*. Paris, OECD Publishing. doi.org/10.1787/9789264214651-en.

_____. 2015a. *The Potential Benefits of Trans-Boundary Cooperation in Georgia and Azerbaijan-Kura River Basin*. Final Report. www.oecd.org/env/outreach/EAP(2015)%2011%20%20THE%20POTENTIAL%20BENEFITS%20OF%20TRANS.pdf.

_____. 2015b. *Stakeholder Engagement for Inclusive Water Governance*. OECD Studies on Water. Paris, OECD Publishing. doi.org/10.1787/9789264231122-en.

_____. 2016. *Better Policies for Sustainable Development 2016: A New Framework for Policy Coherence*. Paris, OECD Publishing. doi.org/10.1787/9789264256996-en.

_____. 2017a. *Diffuse Pollution, Degraded Waters: Emerging Policy Solutions*. Paris, OECD Publishing. doi.org/10.1787/9789264269064-en.

_____. 2017b. *Technical Note on Estimates of Infrastructure Investment Needs. Background note to the report Investing in Climate, Investing in Growth*. OECD. www.oecd.org/env/cc/g20-climate/Technical-note-estimates-of-infrastructure-investment-needs.pdf.

_____. 2017c. *Getting Governments Organised to Deliver on the Sustainable Development Goals*. Summary Report and Next Steps. New York, OECD. www.oecd.org/gov/SDGs-Summary-Report-WEB.pdf.

_____. 2018. *Financing Water: Investing in Sustainable Growth*. Policy Perspectives. OECD Environment Policy Paper No.11. OECD. www.oecd.org/water/Policy-Paper-Financing-Water-Investing-in-Sustainable-Growth.pdf.

_____. 2019. *Biodiversity: Finance and the Economic and Business Case for Action*. Report prepared for the G7 Environment Ministers' Meeting, 5–6 May 2019. www.oecd.org/env/resources/biodiversity/biodiversity-finance-and-the-economic-and-business-case-for-action.htm.

_____. 2020. *Financing Water Supply, Sanitation and Flood Protection: Challenges in EU Member States and Policy Options*. OECD Studies on Water. Paris, OECD Publishing. doi.org/10.1787/6893cdac-en.

Oestigaard, T. 2005. *Water and World Religions: An Introduction*. Bergen, Norway, SFU & SMR.

Onder, H. and Yilmaz, M. 2005. Underground dams: A tool of sustainable development and management of groundwater resources. *European Water*, Vol. 11, No. 12, pp. 35–45.

Onuma, A. and Tsuge, T. 2018. Comparing green infrastructure as ecosystem-based disaster risk reduction with gray infrastructure in terms of costs and benefits under uncertainty: A theoretical approach. *International Journal of Disaster Risk Reduction*, Vol. 32, pp. 22–28. doi.org/10.1016/j.ijdrr.2018.01.025.

Opperman, J., Grill, G., and Hartmann, J. 2015. *The Power of Rivers: Finding Balance between Energy and Conservation in Hydropower Development*. Washington, DC, The Nature Conservancy. www.nature.org/media/freshwater/power-of-rivers-report.pdf.

Oweis, T. 2014. The need for a paradigm change: Agriculture in the water-scarce MENA region. G. Holst-Warhaft, T. Steenhuis and F. de Châtel (eds.), *Water Scarcity, Security and Democracy: A Mediterranean Mosaic*. Global Water Partnership (GWP) Mediterranean/Cornell University/The Atkinson Center for a Sustainable Future. www.gwp.org/globalassets/global/gwp-med-files/news-and-activities/various/gwp-med-final-publication-online_with-cover.pdf.

P

Pahl-Wostl, C. 2020. Adaptive and sustainable water management: From improved conceptual foundations to transformative change. *International Journal of Water Resources Development*, Vol. 36, No. 2–3, pp. 397–415. doi.org/10.1080/07900627.2020.1721268.

Pahl-Wostl, C., Knieper, C., Lukat, E., Meergans, F., Schoderer, M., Schütze, N., Schweigatz, D., Dombrowsky, I., Lenschow, A., Steine, U., Thield, A., Tröltzsche, J. and Thiel, A. 2020. Enhancing the capacity of water governance to deal with complex management challenges: A framework of analysis. *Environmental Science & Policy*, Vol. 107, pp. 23–35. doi.org/10.1016/j.envsci.2020.02.011.

Pakistan Bureau of Statistics, n.d. *Household Integrated Economic Survey/Household Integrated Income and Consumption Survey 2015-16*. Government of Pakistan. www.pbs.gov.pk/content/hies-hiics-2015-16-microdata.

Palatnik, R. R. 2019. The economic value of seawater desalination – The case of Israel. G. Wittwer (ed.), *Economy-Wide Modeling of Water at Regional and Global Scales*. Singapore, Springer. pp. 193–208.

Parliament of New Zealand. 2017. *Te Awa Tupua (Whanganui River Claims Settlement) Act 2017*. www.legislation.govt.nz/act/public/2017/0007/latest/whole.html.

Parsons, M. and Fisher, K. 2019. Indigenous peoples and transformations in freshwater governance and management. *Current Opinion in Environmental Sustainability*, Vol. 20, pp. 1–16. doi.org/10.1016/j.cosust.2020.03.006.

Parsons, M., Nalau, J., Fisher, K. and Brown, C. 2019. Disrupting path dependency: Making room for indigenous knowledge in river management. *Global Environmental Change*, Vol. 56, pp. 95–113. doi.org/10.1016/j.gloenvcha.2019.03.008.

PBL Netherlands Environmental Assessment Agency. 2018. *The Geography of Future Water Challenges*. The Hague, PBL Netherlands Environmental Assessment Agency. www.pbl.nl/en/publications/the-geography-of-future-water-challenges.

Pedrero, F., Aziz, F. and Hussein, H. 2018. Mediterranean Youth for Water Network (MedYWat): Connecting the youth from the MED. *Journal on Food, Agriculture and Society*, Vol. 6, No. 2, pp. 70–71. www.thefutureoffoodjournal.com/index.php/FOFJ/article/view/43/36.

Perez-Pineda, F. and Quintanilla-Armijo, C. 2013. Estimating willingness-to-pay and financial feasibility in small water projects in El Salvador. *Journal of Business Research*, Vol. 66, No. 10, pp. 1750–1758. doi.org/10.1016/j.jbusres.2013.01.014.

Pistocchi, A., Bleninger, T., Breyer, C., Caldera, U., Dorati, C., Ganora, D., Millan, M. M., Paton, C., Poullis, D., Herrero, F. S. and Sapiano, M. 2020. Can seawater desalination be a win-win fix to our water cycle? *Water Research*, Vol. 182, Art. 115906. doi.org/10.1016/j.watres.2020.115906.

PMNCH (The Partnership for Maternal, Newborn and Child Health). 2014. *PMNCH Knowledge Summary #30: Water, Sanitation and Hygiene – The Impact on RMNCH*. www.who.int/pmnch/knowledge/publications/summaries/ks30/en/.

Poff, N. L., Tharme, R. E. and Arthington, A. H. 2017. Evolution of environmental flows assessment science, principles, and methodologies. A.C. Horne, E. L. O'Donnell, J. A. Webb, M. J. Stewardson, M. Acreman and B. Richter (eds.), *Water for the Environment: From Policy and Science to Implementation and Management*. London, Academic Press, pp. 203–236. doi.org/10.1016/B978-0-12-803907-6.00011-5.

Priscoli, J. D. 2012. Reflections on the nexus of politics, ethics, religion and contemporary water resources decisions. *Water Policy*, Vol. 14, No. S1, pp. 21–40. doi.org/10.2166/wp.2012.002.

Priscoli, J. D. and Wolf, A. T. 2009. *Managing and Transforming Water Conflicts*. Cambridge, UK, Cambridge University Press. doi.org/10.1017/CBO9780511551536.

Prosser, I. (ed.). 2010. *Water: Science and Solutions for Australia*. Collingwood, Australia, CSIRO Publishing. www.publish.csiro.au/book/6557.

Prüss-Üstün, A., Bos, R., Gore, F. and Bartram, J. 2008. *Safer Water, Better Health: Costs, Benefits and Sustainability of Interventions to Protect and Promote Health*. Geneva, World Health Organization (WHO). apps.who.int/iris/handle/10665/43840.

Prüss-Üstün, A., Wolf, J., Bartram, J., Clasen, T., Cumming, O., Freeman, M., Gordon, B., Hunter, P. R., Medlicott, K. and Johnston, R. 2019. Burden of disease from inadequate water, sanitation and hygiene for selected adverse health outcomes: An updated analysis with a focus on low- and middle-income countries. *International Journal of Hygiene and Environmental Health*, Vol. 222, No. 5, pp. 765–777. doi.org/10.1016/j.ijheh.2019.05.004.

Qadir, M., Drechsel, P., Cisneros, B. J., Kim, Y., Pramanik, A., Mehta, P. and Olaniyan, O. 2020. Global and regional potential of wastewater as a water, nutrient, and energy source. *Natural Resources Forum*, Vol. 44, No. 1, pp. 40–51. doi.org/10.1111/1477-8947.12187.

Qadir, M., Martius, C., Khamzina, A. and Lamers, J. P. A. 2010. Harnessing renewable energy from abandoned salt-affected lands and saline drainage networks in the dry areas. A. El-Beltagy and M. C. Saxena (eds.), *Proceedings of the Ninth International Conference on Development of Drylands: Sustainable Development in Drylands – Meeting the Challenge of Global Climate Change, 7–10 November 2008, Alexandria, Egypt*. International Dryland Development Commission (IDDC), pp. 836-845.

Ramazotti, M. 1996. *Readings in African Customary Water Law*. FAO Legislative Study No. 58. Rome, Food and Agriculture Organization of the United Nations (FAO). www.fao.org/publications/card/fr/c/W0046B/.

Reig, P., Larson, W., Vionnet S. and Bayart, J. B. 2019. *Volumetric Water Benefit Accounting (VBWA): A Method for Implementing and Valuing Water Stewardship Activities*. WRI Working Paper. Washington, DC, World Resources Institute (WRI). www.wri.org/publication/volumetric-water-benefit-accounting.

Renzetti, S. and Dupont, D. 2003. *The Value of Water in Manufacturing*, CSERGE Working Paper ECM 03-03. Norwich, UK, University of East Anglia's Centre for Social and Economic Research on the Global Environment.

Republic of Zambia Central Statistical Office. 2016. *2015 Living Conditions Monitoring Survey Report*. Lusaka. www.zamstats.gov.zm/phocadownload/Living_Conditions/2015%20Living%20Conditions%20Monitoring%20Survey%20Report.pdf.

République française. 2015. *Code de l'action sociale et des familles* [Legal framework on social action and families]. www.legifrance.gouv.fr/codes/texte_lc/LEGITEXT000006074069/. (In French.)

____. 2019. *Loi n° 2019-1461 du 27 décembre 2019 relative à l'engagement dans la vie locale et à la proximité de l'action publique* [Law nr. 2019-1416 of 27 December 2019 regarding involvement in local life and the proximity of public action]. www.legifrance.gouv.fr/jorf/id/JORFTEXT000039681877/#JORFARTI000039681967. (In French.)

Richey, A. S., Thomas, B. F., Lo, M., Reager, J. T., Famiglietti, J. S., Voss, K., Swenson, S. and Rodell, M. 2015. Quantifying renewable groundwater stress with GRACE. *Water Resources Research*, Vol. 51, No. 7, pp. 5217–5238. doi.org/10.1002/2015WR017349.

Ringler, C. and Zhu, T. 2015. Water resources and food security. *Agronomy Journal*, Vol. 107, No. 4, pp. 1533–1538. doi.org/10.2134/agronj14.0256.

Ritchie, H. and Roser, M. 2018. Water use and stress. *OurWorldInData.org*. ourworldindata.org/water-use-stress.

Rockström, J., Hatibu, N., Oweis, T. Y., Wani, S. P., Barron, J., Bruggeman, A., Farahani, J., Karlsberg, L. and Qiang, Z. 2007. Managing water in rainfed agriculture. Comprehensive Assessment of Water Management in Agriculture, *Water for Food, Water for Life: A Comprehensive Assessment of Water Management in Agriculture*. Colombo, International Water Management Institute (IWMI), pp. 315–352.

Rockström, J., Karlberg, L., Wani, S. P., Barron, J., Hatibu, N., Oweis, T., Bruggeman, A., Farahani, J. and Qiang, Z. 2010. Managing water in rainfed agriculture – The need for a paradigm shift. *Agricultural Water Management*, Vol. 97, No. 4, pp. 543–550. doi.org/10.1016/j.agwat.2009.09.009.

Q

R

Rodriguez, D. J., Serrano, H. A., Delgado, A., Nolasco, D. and Saltiel, G. 2020. *From Waste to Resource: Shifting Paradigms for Smarter Wastewater Interventions in Latin America and the Caribbean*. Washington, DC, World Bank. openknowledge.worldbank.org/handle/10986/33436. License: CC BY 3.0 IGO.

Rogers, P., Bhatia, R. and Huber, A. 1998. *Water as a Social and Economic Good: How to put the Principle into Practice*. Paper prepared for the meeting of the Technical Advisory Committee of the Global Water Partnership in Namibia. Washington, DC, World Bank.

Roidt, M. and Avellán, T. 2019. Learning from integrated management approaches to implement the Nexus. *Journal of Environmental Management*, Vol. 237, No. 5, pp. 609–616. doi.org/10.1016/j.jenvman.2019.02.106.

Rosegrant, M. W., Ringler, C., Msangi, S., Sulser, T. B., Zhu, T. and Cline, S. A. 2008. *International Model for Policy Analysis of Agricultural Commodities and Trade (IMPACT): Model Description*. Washington, DC, International Food Policy Research Institute (IFPRI).

Russi, D., Ten Brink, P., Farmer, A., Badura, T., Coates, D., Förster, J., Kumar, R. and Davidson, N. 2013. *The Economics of Ecosystems and Biodiversity for Water and Wetlands*. London/Brussels/Gland, Institute for European Environmental Policy (IEEP)/Ramsar Secretariat. teebweb.org/publications/water-wetlands/.

Rüßmann, M., Lorenz, M., Gerbert, P., Waldner, M., Justus, J., Engel, P. and Harnisch, M. 2015. *Industry 4.0: The Future of Productivity and Growth in Manufacturing Industries*. The Boston Consulting Group. image-src.bcg.com/Images/Industry_40_Future_of_Productivity_April_2015_tcm74-61694.pdf.

S

Sadoff, C. W. and Grey, D. 2003. Beyond the river: The benefits of cooperation on international rivers. *Water Policy*, Vol. 4, No. 6, pp. 389–403. doi.org/10.2166/wst.2003.0365.

_____. 2005. Cooperation on international rivers: A continuum for securing and sharing benefits. *Water International*, Vol. 30, No. 4, pp. 420–427. doi.org/10.1080/02508060508691886.

Sadoff, C. W., Hall, J., Grey, D., Aerts, J., Ait-Kadi, M., Brown, C., Cox, A., Dadson, S., Garrick, D. and Kelman, J. 2015. *Securing Water, Sustaining Growth*. Report of the GWP/OECD Task Force on Water Security and Sustainable Growth. Oxford, UK, University of Oxford. gwp.org/globalassets/global/about-gwp/publications/the-global-dialogue/securing-water-sustaining-growth.pdf.

Salminen, J. M., Veiste, P. J., Koskiaho, J. T. and Tikkanen, S. 2018. Improving data quality, applicability and transparency of national water accounts – A case study for Finland. *Water Resources and Economics*, Vol. 24, pp. 25–39. doi.org/10.1016/j.wre.2018.05.001.

Sánchez, A. M. R. 2015. Los pagos por servicios ambientales hidrológicos. Examen de las experiencias de Costa Rica, México, Ecuador y Colombia [Payment for hydrological environmental services: Analysis of the experiences of Costa Rica, Mexico, Ecuador and Colombia]. *Ambiente y Desarrollo* [Environment and Development], Vol. 19, No. 36, pp. 110–115.

Saravia-Matus, S. L., Aguirre Hörmann, P. and Berdegué, J. A. 2019. Environmental efficiency in the agricultural sector of Latin America and the Caribbean 1990–2015: Are greenhouse gas emissions reducing while agricultural production is increasing? *Ecological Indicators*, Vol. 102, pp. 338–348. doi.org/10.1016/j.ecolind.2019.02.050.

Sato, T., Qadir, M., Yamamoto, S., Endo, T. and Zahoor, A. 2013. Global, regional, and country level need for data on wastewater generation, treatment, and use. *Agricultural Water Management*, Vol. 130, pp. 1–13. doi.org/10.1016/j.agwat.2013.08.007.

Scanlon, B. R., Zhang, Z., Save, H., Sun, A. Y., Schmied, H. M., Van Beek, L. P., Wiese, D. N., Wada, Y., Long, D., Reedy, R. C. and Longuevergne, L. 2018. Global models underestimate large decadal declining and rising water storage trends relative to GRACE satellite data. *Proceedings of the National Academy of Sciences of the United States of America*, Vol. 115, No. 6, pp. E1080–E1089. doi.org/10.1073/pnas.1704665115.

Schaar, J. 2019. *A Confluence of Crises: On Water, Climate and Security in the Middle East and North Africa*. Stockholm International Peace Research Institute (SIPRI) Insights on Peace and Security No. 2019/4. Solna, Sweden, SIPRI. www.sipri.org/publications/2019/sipri-insights-peace-and-security/confluence-crises-water-climate-and-security-middle-east-and-north-africa.

Scheierling, S. M. and Tréguer, D. O. 2018. *Beyond Crop per Drop: Assessing Agricultural Water Productivity and Efficiency in a Maturing Water Economy*. International Development in Focus. Washington, DC, World Bank. openknowledge.worldbank.org/handle/10986/29922. License: CC BY 3.0 IGO.

Schenk, C., Roquier, B., Soutter, M. and Mermoud, A. 2009. A system model for water management. *Environmental Management*, Vol. 43, No. 3, pp. 458–469. doi.org/10.1007/s00267-008-9254-8.

Schiffler, M. 2014. *The Economics of Groundwater Management in Arid Countries: Theory, International Experience and a Case Study of Jordan* (No. 11). London, Routledge.

Schreiner, B. and Van Koppen, B. 2018. *Establishing Hybrid Water Use Right Systems in Sub-Saharan Africa: A Practical Guide for Managers*. Pretoria, Pegasys Institute/International Water Management Institute (IWMI).

Schulz, C., Martin-Ortega, J. and Glenk, K. 2018. Value landscapes and their impact on public water policy preferences. *Global Environmental Change-Human and Policy Dimensions*, Vol. 53, pp. 209–224. doi.org/10.1016/j.gloenvcha.2018.09.015.

Scott, C. A., Vicuña, S., Blanco-Gutiérrez, I., Meza, F. and Varela-Ortega, C. 2014. Irrigation efficiency and water-policy implications for river basin resilience. *Hydrology and Earth System Sciences*, Vol. 18, No. 4, pp. 1339–1348. doi.org/10.5194/hess-18-1339-2014.

Scottish Government. n.d. *Non-Market Values*. Scottish Forestry website. forestry.gov.scot/sustainable-forestry/economic-research/non-market-values.

Seidl, C., Wheeler, S. A. and Zuo, A. 2020a. Treating water markets like stock markets: Key water market reform lessons in the Murray-Darling Basin. *Journal of Hydrology*, Vol. 581, Art. 124399. doi.org/10.1016/j.jhydrol.2019.124399.

_____. 2020b. High turbidity: Water valuation and accounting in the Murray-Darling Basin. *Agricultural Water Management*, Vol. 230, Art. 105929. doi.org/10.1016/j.agwat.2019.105929.

Shah, T. 2005. Groundwater and human development: Challenges and opportunities in livelihoods and environment. *Water, Science & Technology*, Vol. 51, No. 8, pp. 27–37. doi.org/10.2166/wst.2005.0217.

Shokhrukh-Mirzo, J., Varis, O. and Keskinen, M. 2015. Sharing benefits in transboundary rivers: An experimental case study of Central Asian water-energy-agriculture nexus. *Water*, Vol. 7, pp. 4778–4805. doi.org/10.3390/w7094778.

Siebert, S., Burke, J., Faures, J. M., Frenken, K., Hoogeveen, J., Döll, P. and Portmann, F. T. 2010. Groundwater use for irrigation – a global inventory. *Hydrology and Earth System Science*, Vol. 14, pp. 1863–1880. doi.org/10.5194/hess-14-1863-2010.

SIWI (Stockholm International Water Institute). 2018. *Building a Resilient Future through Water.* Policy Brief. www.siwi.org/wp-content/uploads/2018/06/building-a-resilient-future_20180704_WEB.pdf.

Skinner, J. and Haas, L. J. 2014. *Watered Down? A Review of Social and Environmental Safeguards for Large Dam Projects*. Natural Resource Issues No. 28. London, International Institute for Environment and Development (IIED). pubs.iied.org/17517IIED/.

Sommer, M., Chandraratna, S., Cavill, S., Mahon, T. and Phillips-Howard, P. 2016. Managing menstruation in the workplace: An overlooked issue in low- and middle-income countries. International Journal for Equity in Health, Vol. 15, No. 86. doi.org/10.1186/s12939-016-0379-8.

Son, H. N., Chi, D. T. L. and Kingsbury, A. 2019. Indigenous knowledge and climate change adaptation of ethnic minorities in the mountainous regions of Vietnam: A case study of the Yao people in Bac Kan Province. *Agricultural Systems*, Vol. 176, Art. 102683. doi.org/10.1016/j.agsy.2019.102683.

Springmann, M., Clark, M., Mason-D'Croz, D., Wiebe, K., Bodirsky, B. L., Lassaletta, L., De Vries, W., Vermeulen, S. J., Herrero, M., Carlson, K. M., Jonell, M., Troell, M., DeClerck, F., Gordon, L. J., Zurayk, R., Scarborough, P., Rayner, M., Loken, B., Fanzo, J., Godfray, H. G. J., Tilman, D., Rockström, J. and Willett, W. 2018. Options for keeping the food system within environmental limits. *Nature*, Vol. 562, pp. 519–525. doi.org/10.1038/s41586-018-0594-0.

Stacklin, C. 2012. *The Value of Wastewater: An Econometric Evaluation of Recoverable Resources in Wastewater for Reuse.* WEF Proceedings, New Orleans, La., New Orleans Morial Convention Center.

Statistics Canada. 2016. *Human Activity and the Environment: Freshwater in Canada*. Ottawa, Minister of Industry. www150.statcan.gc.ca/n1/en/pub/16-201-x/16-201-x2017000-eng.pdf?st=z39q7UEE.

_____. 2018. *Physical Flow Accounts: Water Use, 2015*. www150.statcan.gc.ca/n1/daily-quotidien/180711/dq180711c-eng.htm.

_____. 2020a. *Total Water Costs in Manufacturing Industries, by Water Cost Component and Industry (x 1,000)*. Table 38-10-0064-01 (formerly CANSIM 153-0076). doi.org/10.25318/3810006401-eng.

_____. 2020b. *Total Water Costs in Mineral Extraction and Thermal-Electric Power Generation Industries, by Water Cost Component, by Industry (x 1,000)*. Table 38-10-0085-01 (formerly CANSIM 153-0097). doi.org/10.25318/3810008501-eng.

Stats NZ. 2017. *Asset Value of Water and Other Renewables for Electricity Generation: 2007–15*. Wellington, Stats NZ Tatauranga Aotearoa. www.stats.govt.nz/reports/asset-value-of-water-and-other-renewables-for-electricity-generation-200715.

Stevenson, E. G. J., Greene, L. E., Maes, K. C., Ambelu, A., Alemu, Y., Rheingans, T. R. and Hadley, C. 2012. Water insecurity in 3 dimensions: An anthropological perspective on water and women's psychosocial distress in Ethiopia. *Social Science & Medicine*, Vol. 75, No. 2, pp. 392–400. doi.org/10.1016/j.socscimed.2012.03.022.

Stewart, B. 2015. Measuring what we manage – the importance of hydrological data to water resources management. *Proceedings of the International Association of the Hydrological Sciences*, Vol. 366, pp. 80–85. doi.org/10.5194/piahs-366-80-2015.

Stillwell, A. S. 2019. *Is Water Price an Effective Means to Reduce Cooling Water Consumption at Thermal Power Plants?* Global Water Forum website. globalwaterforum.org/2019/07/15/is-water-price-an-effective-means-to-reduce-cooling-water-consumption-at-thermal-power-plants/.

Stokstad, E. 1999. Scarcity of rain, stream gages threatens forecasts. *Science*, Vol. 285, No. 5431, pp. 1199–1200. doi.org/10.1126/science.285.5431.1199.

Sun, Q., Miao, C., Duan, Q., Ashouri, H., Sorooshian, S. and Hsu, K. L. 2018. A review of global precipitation data sets: Data sources, estimation, and intercomparisons. *Reviews of Geophysics*, Vol. 56, No. 1, pp. 79-107. doi.org/10.1002/2017RG000574.

Søreide, T. 2016. *Corruption and Criminal Justice: Bridging Economic and Legal Perspectives*. Cheltenham, UK/Northampton, Mass., Edward Elgar. doi.org/10.4337/9781784715984.

T

Tarallo, S., Shaw, A., Kohl, P. and Eschborn, R. 2015. *A Guide to Net-Zero Energy Solutions for Water Resource Recovery Facilities* (ENER1C12). Alexandria, Va./London, Water Environment Research Foundation (WERF)/International Wate Association (IWA) Publishing.

Teague, J., Johnston, E. A. and Graham, J. P. 2014. Water, sanitation, hygiene, and nutrition: Successes, challenges, and implications for integration. *International Journal of Public Health*, Vol. 59, No. 6, pp. 913–921. doi.org/10.1007/s00038-014-0580-8.

Te Aho, L. 2018. Te Mana o te Wai: An indigenous perspective on rivers and river management. *River Research and Application,* Vol. 35, No. 10, pp. 1–7. doi.org/10.1002/rra.3365.

TEEB (The Economics of Ecosystems and Biodiversity). 2010. *The Economics of Ecosystems and Biodiversity in Local and Regional Policy and Management*. London and Washington, DC, Earthscan. www.teebweb.org/publication/teeb-for-local-and-regional-policy-makers-2/.

Teichmann, M. and Berghöfer, A. 2010. TEEBcase River Elbe flood regulation options with ecological benefits, Germany. Largely based on: Grossmann, M., Hartje, V. and Meyerhoff, J. 2010. *Ökonomische Bewertung naturverträglicher Hochwasservorsorge an der Elbe: Naturschutz und biologische Vielfalt* [Economic assessment of nature-compatible flood prevention on the Elbe. Nature conservation and biological diversity] 89. Bonn, Germany, Federal Agency for Nature Conservation. www.teebweb.org/wp-content/uploads/2013/01/River-Elbe-flood-regulation-options-with-ecological-benefits-Germany.pdf. (In German.)

Tetzlaff, D., Carey, S. K., McNamara, J. P., Laudon, H. and Soulsby, C. 2017. The essential value of long-term experimental data for hydrology and water management. *Water Resources Research*, Vol. 53, No. 4, pp. 2598–2604. doi.org/10.1002/2017WR020838.

Thakar, K. 2019. Women are visibly missing from the water dialogue. *Smart Water Magazine,* 12 November 2019. smartwatermagazine.com/news/siwi/kanika-thakar-siwi-women-are-visibly-missing-water-dialogue.

Tharakan, J. 2015. Indigenous knowledge systems – A rich appropriate technology resource. *African Journal of Science, Technology, Innovation and Development*, Vol. 7, No. 1, pp. 52–57. doi.org/10.1080/20421338.2014.987987.

The Rockefeller Foundation/Arup. 2014. *City Resilience Framework: City Resilience Index*. The Rockefeller Foundation/Arup. www.rockefellerfoundation.org/wp-content/uploads/City-Resilience-Framework-2015.pdf.

The Value of Water Campaign. 2017. *The Economic Benefits of Investing in Water Infrastructure*. http://thevalueofwater.org/sites/default/files/Economic%20Impact%20of%20Investing%20in%20Water%20Infrastructure_VOW_FINAL_pages.pdf.

Thünen Institute. n.d. *Data Base Forest Service*. Institute of International Forestry and Forest Economics. Thünen Institute website. www.thuenen.de/en/wf/figures-facts/environmental-valuation/data-base-for%adest-services/. (Accessed October 2020).

Tilman, D. and Clark, M. 2014. Global diets link environmental sustainability and human health. *Nature,* Vol. 515, pp. 518–522. doi.org/10.1038/nature13959.

Timboe, I., Pharr, K. and Matthews, J. H. 2019. *Watering the NDCs: National Climate Planning for 2020 and Beyond. How Water-Aware Climate Policies can Strengthen Climate Change Mitigation & Adaptation Goals*. Corvallis, Oreg., Alliance for Global Water Adaptation (AGWA). www.wateringthendcs.org.

Tipa, G. and Nelson, K. 2012. Environmental flow assessments: A participatory process enabling Mauri cultural values to inform flow regime setting. B. Johnston, L. Hiwasaki, I. Klaver, A. Ramos Castillo and V. Strang (eds.), *Water, Cultural Diversity, and Global Environmental Change*. Dordrecht, The Netherlands, Springer, pp. 467–491. doi.org/10.1007/978-94-007-1774-9_32.

TNC (The Nature Conservancy). 2018. *Water Funds*. Field Guide. Washington, DC. TNC. s3.amazonaws.com/tnc-craft/library/2018-WF-Field-Guide_online-final.pdf?mtime=20190314215347.

Trivedi, A. 2018. *Women Are the Secret Weapon for Better Water Management*. Water Resources Institute website. www.wri.org/blog/2018/10/women-are-secret-weapon-better-water-management.

U

Uganda Bureau of Statistics. 2020. *Uganda National Panel Survey 2015-2016*. Kampala.

UNDESA (United Nations Department for Economic and Social Affairs). 2012. *SEEA-Water. System of Environment-Economic Accounting for Water.* New York, United Nations. unstats.un.org/unsd/publication/seriesf/Seriesf_100e.pdf.

____. n.d.a. *Transboundary Waters*. International Decade for Action 'Water for Life' 2005–2015. www.un.org/waterforlifedecade/transboundary_waters.shtml.

____. n.d.b. *United Nations Global SDG Database*. unstats.un.org/sdgs/indicators/database/ (Accessed November 2020.)

UNDP (United Nations Development Programme). 2005. *Central Asia Human Development Report. Bringing Down Barriers: Regional Cooperation for Human Development and Human Security*. Bratislava, UNDP. hdr.undp.org/sites/default/files/central_asia_2005_en.pdf.

____. 2006. *Human Development Report 2006 – Beyond Scarcity: Power, Poverty and the Global Water Crisis*. New York, UNDP. www.undp.org/content/undp/en/home/librarypage/hdr/human-development-report-2006.html.

____. 2020. *Human Development Report 2020. The Next Frontier: Human Development and the Anthropocene*. New York, UNDP. hdr.undp.org/sites/default/files/hdr2020.pdf.

UNDP (United Nations Development Programme)/Huairou Commission. 2012. *Seeing Beyond the State: Grassroots Women's Perspectives on Corruption and Anti-Corruption.* New York, UNDP/Huairou Commission. www.undp.org/content/dam/undp/library/Democratic%20Governance/Anti-corruption/Grassroots%20women%20and%20anti-corruption.pdf.

UNECA/AU/AfDB (United Nations Economic Commission for Africa/African Union/African Development Bank). 2003. *Africa Water Vision for 2025: Equitable and Sustainable Use of Water for Socioeconomic Development.* Addis Ababa, UNECA. www.afdb.org/fileadmin/uploads/afdb/Documents/Generic-Documents/african%20water%20vision%202025%20to%20be%20sent%20to%20wwf5.pdf.

UNECE (United Nations Economic Commission for Europe). 1992. *Convention on the Protection and Use of Transboundary Watercourses and International Lakes.* Helsinki, 17 March 1992, UNECE. unece.org/environment-policy/water/about-the-convention/introduction.

_____. 2015. *Policy Guidance Note on the Benefits of Transboundary Water Cooperation: Identification, Assessment and Communication.* New York/Geneva, United Nations. unece.org/fileadmin/DAM/env/water/publications/WAT_Benefits_of_Transboundary_Cooperation/ECE_MP.WAT_47_PolicyGuidanceNote_BenefitsCooperation_1522750_E_pdf_web.pdf.

_____. 2017. *Assessment of the Water-Food-Energy-Ecosystem Nexus and Benefits of Transboundary Cooperation in the Drina River Basin.* New York/Geneva, United Nations.

_____. 2019. *Scoping the Benefits of Transboundary Water Cooperation in the NWSAS Basin.* Policy Brief – Draft annotated outline. Geneva, UNECE. www.unece.org/fileadmin/DAM/env/water/meetings/2019/18-19_June_Tunis/ENG-18062019-NWSAS_benefits_policy_brief_twopager_final.pdf.

UNECLAC (United Nations Commission for Latin America and the Caribbean). Forthcoming. *Flagship of Natural Resources and Development.*

UN Environment (United Nations Environment Programme). 2019. *Global Environment Outlook – GEO-6: Healthy Planet, Healthy People.* Cambridge, UK, Cambridge University Press. doi.org/10.1017/9781108627146.

UNEP (United Nations Environment Programme). 2002. *Vital Water Graphics: An Overview of the State of the World's Fresh and Marine Waters.* Nairobi, UNEP. digitallibrary.un.org/record/491441.

_____. 2016. *A Snapshot of the World's Water Quality: Towards a Global Assessment.* Nairobi, UNEP. uneplive.unep.org/media/docs/assessments/unep_wwqa_report_web.pdf.

UNEP/UNEP-DHI/IUCN/TNC (United Nations Environment Programme/UNEP-DHI Partnership – Centre on Water and Environment/International Union for Conservation of Nature/The Nature Conservancy). 2014. *Green Infrastructure Guide for Water Management.* Ecosystem-based management approaches for water-related infrastructure projects. UNEP. wedocs.unep.org/bitstream/handle/20.500.11822/9291/-Green%20infrastructure%3a%20guide%20for%20water%20management%20%20-2014unep-dhigroup-green-infrastructure-guide-en.pdf?sequence=3&isAllowed=y.

UNEP-WCMC (United Nations Environment Programme – World Conservation Monitoring Centre). 2016. *The State of Biodiversity in Latin America and the Caribbean: A Mid-Term Review of Progress towards the Aichi Biodiversity Targets.* Paris, UNEP. www.cbd.int/gbo/gbo4/outlook-grulac-en.pdf.

UNESCAP (United Nations Economic and Social Commission for Asia and the Pacific). 2019. *Tackling Water Pollution and Promoting Efficient Water Use in Industries.* Regional perspectives – Environment and Development Policy Brief 2019/3. UNESCAP. www.unescap.org/sites/default/files/Policy%20Brief%202_12June.pdf.

UNESCAP/UNESCO/ILO/UN Environment (United Nations Economic and Social Commission for Asia and the Pacific/United Nations Educational, Scientific and Cultural Organization/International Labour Organization/United Nations Environmental Programme). 2018. *SDG6 Goal Profile. Clean Water and Sanitation – Ensure Availability and Sustainable Management of Water and Sanitation for all.* UN-Water. www.unescap.org/sites/default/files/SDG%206%20Goal%20Profile_0.pdf.

UNESCO (United Nations Educational, Scientific and Cultural Organization). 2002. *Records of the General Conference, 31st session, Paris, 15 October to 3 November 2001, Vol. 1: Resolutions.* Paris, UNESCO. unesdoc.unesco.org/ark:/48223/pf0000124687.page=67.

_____. 2011. Water. Its role in human evolution. *World Heritage*, No. 59. Paris, UNESCO.

_____. 2017. *Global Education Monitoring Report Summary 2017/18: Accountability in Education: Meeting Our Commitments.* Paris, UNESCO. unesdoc.unesco.org/ark:/48223/pf0000259338.

_____. n.d. *Local and Indigenous Knowledge Systems (LINKS).* Paris, UNESCO. en.unesco.org/links.

UNESCO Bangkok Office. 2017. *Cultural Mapping.* UNESCO Bangkok Office website. bangkok.unesco.org/content/cultural-mapping.

UNESCO Regional Office for Eastern Africa. 2020. *Biennial Programme Synthesis Report: Implementation Period 2018–2019.* Nairobi, UNESCO Regional Office for Eastern Africa. en.unesco.org/sites/default/files/natural_science_nairobi_office_biennial_report_2018-19.pdf.

UNESCO/UNECE/UN-Water. 2018. *Progress on Transboundary Water Cooperation – Global Baseline for SDG Indicator 6.5.2.* Paris, UNESCO. www.unwater.org/publications/progress-on-transboundary-water-cooperation-652/.

UNESCO/UN-Water. 2020. *The United Nations World Water Development Report 2020: Water and Climate Change.* Paris, UNESCO. en.unesco.org/themes/water-security/wwap/wwdr/2020.

UNESCWA (United Nations Economic and Social Commission for Western Asia). 2017. *Wastewater: An Arab Perspective*. Beirut, UNESCWA. www.unescwa.org/sites/www.unescwa.org/files/page_attachments/l1700174_web_-_waste_water_-_march_2017_0.pdf.

____. 2019a. *Moving towards Water Security in the Arab Region*. Beirut, UNESCWA. www.unescwa.org/publications/moving-towards-achieving-water-security-arab-region.

____. 2019b. *Status Report on the Implementation of Integrated Water Resources Management in the Arab Region: Progress on SDG indicator 6.5.1*. Beirut, UNESCWA. www.unescwa.org/sites/www.unescwa.org/files/publications/files/implementation-integrated-water-resources-management-arab-countries-english.pdf.

____. 2020a. *Arab Sustainable Development Report 2020*. Beirut, UNESCWA. asdr.unescwa.org/.

____. 2020b. *Regional Emergency Response to Mitigate the Impact of COVID-19*. Policy Brief. UNESCWA. www.unescwa.org/sites/www.unescwa.org/files/publications/files/20-00116_rer_mitigatingimpact_covid-19_eng_april8.pdf#overlay-context=publications/socioeconomic-impact-covid-19-policy-briefs.

UNESCWA et al. 2017. *Arab Climate Change Assessment Report: Main Report*. Beirut, UNESCWA. www.riccar.org/sites/default/files/riccar/RICCAR%20Publications/Pdfs/Main%20Report/Arab%20Climate%20Change%20Assessment%20Report-%20Main%20Report_2017.pdf.

UNFPA (United Nations Population Fund). n.d. *The Human Rights-Based Approach*. UNFPA website. www.unfpa.org/human-rights-based-approach.

UNGA (United Nations General Assembly). 2007. *United Nations Declaration on the Rights of Indigenous Peoples*. Resolution adopted by the General Assembly on 13 September 2007. Sixty-first session. A/RES/61/295. http://undocs.org/en/A/RES/61/295.

____. 2010. *The Human Right to Water and Sanitation*. Resolution adopted by the General Assembly on 28 July 2010. Sixty-fourth Session. A/RES/64/292. undocs.org/A/RES/64/292.

____. 2015. *Transforming Our World: The 2030 Agenda for Sustainable Development*. Resolution adopted by the General Assembly on 25 September 2015. Seventieth session, A/RES/70/1. undocs.org/A/RES/70/1.

____. 2016. *The Human Rights to Safe Drinking Water and Sanitation*. Resolution adopted by the General Assembly on 17 December 2015. Seventieth Session. A/RES/70/169. undocs.org/A/RES/70/169.

____. 2019. *Report of the Special Rapporteur on the Human Rights to Safe Drinking Water and Sanitation*. Sixty-fourth session. A/74/197. undocs.org/A/74/197.

UN-Habitat (United Nations Human Settlements Programme). 2020. *Cities and COVID-19*. unhabitat.org/sites/default/files/2020/05/13_may_2020_-_key_messages_un-habitat_and_covid-19.pdf.

UN-Habitat/UNICEF (United Nations Human Settlement Programme/United Nations Children's Fund). 2020. *Interim Technical Note on Water, Sanitation and Hygiene for COVID-19 Response in Slums and Informal Urban Settlements*. UN-Habitat/UNICEF. unhabitat.org/sites/default/files/2020/05/un-habitat-unicef_wash_technical_note-_urban_wash_for_covid_in_informal_settlements.pdf.

UNICEF (United Nations Children's Fund). 2012. *Water, Sanitation and Hygiene (WASH) in Schools*. New York, United Nations Children's Fund. www.unicef.org/publications/files/CFS_WASH_E_web.pdf.

____. 2016. *Collecting Water is often a Colossal Waste of Time for Women and Girls*. Press release, 29 August. UNICEF website. www.unicef.org/press-releases/unicef-collecting-water-often-colossal-waste-time-women-and-girls.

____. 2019a. *Water under Fire: For every Child, Water and Sanitation in Complex Emergencies*. New York, UNICEF. www.unicef.org/media/51286/file.

____. 2019b. *Guide to Menstrual Hygiene Materials*. New York, UNICEF. www.unicef.org/wash/files/UNICEF-Guide-menstrual-hygiene-materials-2019.pdf.

UNICEF/WHO (United Nations Children's Fund/World Health Organization). 2021. *The Measurement and Monitoring of Water Supply, Sanitation and Hygiene (WASH) Affordability: A Missing Element of Monitoring of Sustainable Development Goal (SDG) Targets 6.1 and 6.2*. New York/Geneva, UNICEF/WHO.

UNICEF/WHO/The World Bank Group (United Nations Children's Fund/World Health Organization). 2020. *Levels and Trends in Child Malnutrition: Key Findings of the 2020 Edition of the Joint Child Malnutrition Estimates*. Geneva, WHO. www.who.int/publications/i/item/jme-2020-edition.

UNIDO (United Nations Industrial Development Organization). 2017. *Accelerating Clean Energy through Industry 4.0: Manufacturing the Next Revolution*. T. Nagasawa, C. Pillay, G. Beier, K. Fritzsche, F. Pougel, T. K. Takama and I. Bobashev. Vienna, UNIDO. www.unido.org/sites/default/files/2017-08/REPORT_Accelerating_clean_energy_through_Industry_4.0.Final_0.pdf.

____. n.d. *Fostering Eco-Industrial Parks in Viet Nam*. UNIDO website. www.unido.org/stories/fostering-eco-industrial-parks-viet-nam.

UNISDR (The United Nations Office for Disaster Risk Reduction). 2015. *Sendai Framework for Disaster Risk Reduction 2015–2030*. Geneva, UNISDR. www.undrr.org/publication/sendai-framework-disaster-risk-reduction-2015-2030.

United Nations. 2013. *Basin Wide Groundwater Management using the System of Nature: Kumamoto City, Japan.* 'Water for Life' UN-Water Best Practices Award, 2013 edition: Winners. www.un.org/waterforlifedecade/winners2013.shtml.

_____. 2014. *System of Environmental- Economic Accounting 2012— Central Framework.* United Nations, New York. unstats.un.org/unsd/envaccounting/seearev/seea_cf_final_en.pdf.

_____. 2018. *Sustainable Development Goal 6: Synthesis Report 2018 on Water and Sanitation.* New York, United Nations. www.unwater.org/publication_categories/sdg-6-synthesis-report-2018-on-water-and-sanitation/.

United Nations/UNESCO (United Nations Educational, Scientific and Cultural Organization). 2018. *Progress on Transboundary Water Cooperation 2018 Global Baseline for SDG Indicator 6.5.2.* Paris/New York, United Nations/UNESCO.

University of Cambridge. n.d. *What is a Value Chain? Definitions and Characteristics.* Cambridge Institute for Sustainability Leadership. University of Cambridge website. www.cisl.cam.ac.uk/education/graduate-study/pgcerts/value-chain-defs.

UNPFA (United Nations Population Fund). 2014. *The Power of 1.8 Billion – Adolescents, Youth and the Transformation of the Future.* UNPFA State of World Population 2014. New York, UNFPA www.unfpa.org/sites/default/files/pub-pdf/EN-SWOP14-Report_FINAL-web.pdf.

UNSDG (United Nations Sustainable Development Group). 2020. *Policy Brief: COVID-19 in an Urban World.* unsdg.un.org/resources/policy-brief-covid-19-urban-world.

UN-Water. 2020. *UN-Water launch Analytical Brief on Unconventional Water Resources.* Geneva, Switzerland, UN-Water. www.unwater.org/un-water-launch-analytical-brief-on-unconventional-water-resources/.

Uphoff, N. and Dazzo, F. B. 2016. Making rice production more environmentally-friendly. *Environments*, Vol. 3, No. 2, Art. 12. doi.org/10.3390/environments3020012.

V

Van der Ploeg, S. and De Groot, R. S. 2010. *The TEEB Valuation Database: A Searchable Database of 1310 Estimates of Monetary Values of Ecosystems Services.* Wageningen, The Netherlands, Foundation for Sustainable Development.

Van Vliet, M. T. H., Flörke, M. and Wada, Y. 2017. Quality matters for water scarcity. *Nature Geoscience*, Vol. 10, pp. 800–802. doi.org/10.1038/ngeo3047.

Van Wesenbeeck, B. K., Lange, G. M., Jongman, B., Bosche, L. V., Nieboer, H., Meliane, I., Holm-Nielsen, N. B., IJff, S., Balog, S. A. B., Kurukulasuriya, P. H., Kaupa, S. M. and Taishi, Y. 2017. *Implementing Nature-Based Flood Protection: Principles and Implementation Guidance.* Washington, DC, World Bank. documents1.worldbank.org/curated/en/739421509427698706/pdf/Implementing-nature-based-flood-protection-principles-and-implementation-guidance.pdf.

Vásquez, W. F. and Espaillat, R. 2016. Willingness to pay for reliable supplies of safe drinking water in Guatemala: A referendum contingent valuation study. *Urban Water Journal*, Vol. 13, No. 3, pp. 284–292. doi.org/10.1080/1573062X.2014.991741.

Villarroel Walker, R., Beck, M. B. and Hall, J. W. 2012. Water – and nutrient and energy – systems in urbanizing watersheds. *Frontiers of Environmental Science & Engineering*, Vol. 6, No. 5, pp. 596–611. doi.org/10.1007/s11783-012-0445-4.

Vilmin, L., Mogollón, J. M., Beusen, A. H. W. and Bouwman, A. F. 2018. Forms and subannual variability of nitrogen and phosphorus loading to global river networks over the 20th century. *Global Planetary Change*, Vol. 163, pp. 67–85. doi.org/10.1016/j.gloplacha.2018.02.007.

Völker, S. and Kistemann, T. 2011. The impact of blue space on human health and well-being – Salutogenetic health effects of inland surface waters: A review. *International Journal of Hygiene and Environmental Health*, Vol. 214, No. 6, pp. 449–460. doi.org/10.1016/j.ijheh.2011.05.001.

Von Lossow, T. 2016. The Rebirth of Water as a Weapon: IS in Syria and Iraq. *The International Spectator*, Vol. 51, No. 3, pp. 82–99. doi.org/10.1080/03932729.2016.1213063.

Vörösmarty, C. J., McIntyre, P. B., Gessner, M. O., Dudgeon, D., Prusevich, A., Green, P., Glidden, S., Bunn, S. E., Sullivan, C. A., Liermann, C. R. and Davies, P. M. 2010. Global threats to human water security and river biodiversity. *Nature*, Vol. 467, pp. 555–561. doi.org/10.1038/nature09440.

Vörösmarty, C. J., Rodríguez Osuna, V., Cak, A. D., Bhaduri, A., Bunn, S. E., Corsi, F., Gastelumendi, J., Green, P. A., Harrison, I., Lawford, R., Marcotullio, P. J., McClain, M., McDonald, R., McIntyre, P., Palmer, M., Robarts, R. D., Szöllösi-Nagy, A., Tessler, Z. and Uhlenbrook, S. 2018. Ecosystem-based water security and the Sustainable Development Goals (SDGs). *Ecohydrology & Hydrobiology*, Vol. 18, No. 4, pp. 317–333. doi.org/10.1016/j.ecohyd.2018.07.004.

Voulvoulis, N. 2018. Water reuse from a circular economy perspective and potential risks from an unregulated approach. *Current Opinion in Environmental Science & Health*, Vol. 2, pp. 32–45. doi.org/10.1016/j.coesh.2018.01.005.

VWI (Valuing Water Initiative). 2020. *Valuing Water: A Conceptual Framework for making Better Decisions Impacting Water.* Valuing Water Initiative.

W

Wada, Y. 2016. Modeling groundwater depletion at regional and global scales: Present state and future prospects. *Surveys in Geophysics*, Vol. 37, pp. 419–451. doi.org/10.1007/s10712-015-9347-x.

Wada, Y., Van Beek, L. P. H., Wanders, N. and Bierkens, M. F. P. 2013. Human water consumption intensifies hydrological drought worldwide. *Environmental Research Letters*, Vol. 8, No. 3, Art. 034036. doi.org/10.1088/1748-9326/8/3/034036.

Waitangi Tribunal. 1999. *The Waitangi River Report*. Wellington, GP Publications.

Walker, I., Ordonez, F., Serrano, P. and Halpern, J. 2000. *Pricing, Subsidies and the Poor: Demand for Improved Water Services in Central America*. World Bank Policy Research Working Paper, No. 2468. Washington, DC, World Bank. openknowledge.worldbank.org/handle/10986/19770. License: CC BY 3.0 IGO.

Wang, C. 2018. Scientific culture and the construction of a world leader in science and technology. *Cultures of Science*, Vol. 1, No. 1, pp. 1–13. doi.org/10.1177/209660831800100102.

Ward, A. J., Arola, K., Brewster, E. T., Mehta, C. M. and Batstone, D. J. 2018. Nutrient recovery from wastewater through pilot scale electrodialysis. *Water Research*, Vol. 135, pp. 57–65. doi.org/10.1016/j.watres.2018.02.021.

Ward, F. A. and Pulido-Velazquez, M. 2008. Water conservation in irrigation can increase water use. *Proceedings of the National Academy of Sciences of the United States of America*, Vol. 105, No. 47, pp. 18215–18220. doi.org/10.1073/pnas.0805554105.

_____. 2009. Incentive pricing and cost recovery at the basin scale. *Journal of Environmental Management*, Vol 90, pp. 293–313. doi.org/10.1016/j.jenvman.2007.09.009.

Water Footprint Network. n.d. *What is a Water Footprint?* Water Footprint Network website. waterfootprint.org/en/water-footprint/what-is-water-footprint/.

Water Integrity Network. 2016. *The Water Integrity Global Outlook 2016*. Berlin, Water Integrity Network. www.waterintegritynetwork.net/wigo/.

Waterlution. 2020. *Impact & Learnings of the Great Canoe Journey*. Oakville, Ont., Waterlution. waterlution.org/wp-content/uploads/2020/05/GCJ-Impact-and-Learning-Report-1.pdf.

WBCSD (World Business Council for Sustainable Development). 2012. *Water Valuation: Building the Business Case*. Geneva/Washington, DC, WBCSD. www.wbcsd.org/Programs/Food-and-Nature/Water/Resources/Water-valuation-Building-the-business-case.

_____. 2013. *Business Guide to Water Valuation: An Introduction to Concepts and Techniques*. Geneva/Washington, DC, WBCSD. www.wbcsd.org/Programs/Food-and-Nature/Water/Resources/Business-Guide-to-Water-Valuation-an-introduction-to-concepts-and-techniques.

_____. 2018. *WASH Pledge Impact Report: Maximizing the Business Contribution towards Water, Sanitation and Hygiene*. Geneva, WBCSD. www.wbcsd.org/Programs/Food-and-Nature/Water/Water-stewardship/WASH-access-to-water-sanitation-and-hygiene/Resources/WASH-Pledge-impact-report-Maximizing-the-business-contribution-towards-water-sanitation-and-hygiene.

Wehn de Montalvo, U. and Alaerts, G. 2013. Leadership in knowledge and capacity development in the water sector: A status review. *Water Policy*, Vol. 15, No. S2, pp. 1–14. doi.org/10.2166/wp.2013.109.

Wheeler, S. A., Carmody, E., Grafton, R. Q., Kingsford, R. T. and Zuo, A. 2020. The rebound effect on water extraction from subsidising irrigation infrastructure in Australia. *Resources, Conservation and Recycling*, Vol. 159, Art. 104755. doi.org/10.1016/j.resconrec.2020.104755.

Whitelaw, E. and MacMullan, E. 2002. A Framework for Estimating the Costs and Benefits of Dam Removal: Sound cost–benefit analyses of removing dams account for subsidies and externalities, for both the short and long run, and place the estimated costs and benefits in the appropriate economic context. *BioScience*, Vol. 52, No. 8, pp. 724–730. doi.org/10.1641/0006-3568(2002)052[0724:AFFETC]2.0.CO;2.

Whittington, D., Nauges, C., Fuente, D. and Wu, X. 2015. A diagnostic tool for estimating the incidence of subsidies delivered by water utilities in low- and medium-income countries, with illustrative simulations. *Utilities Policy*, Vol. 34, pp. 70–81. doi.org/10.1016/j.jup.2014.12.007.

WHO (World Health Organization). 2012. *Global Costs and Benefits of Drinking-Water Supply and Sanitation Interventions to Reach the MDG Target and Universal Coverage*. Geneva, World Health Organisation. www.who.int/water_sanitation_health/publications/global_costs/en/.

_____. 2015. *Investing to Overcome the Global Impact of Neglected Tropical Diseases*. Third WHO report on neglected tropical diseases. Geneva, WHO. www.who.int/neglected_diseases/9789241564861/en/.

_____. 2017. *UN-Water Global Analysis and Assessment of Sanitation and Drinking-Water (GLAAS) 2017 Report: Financing Universal Water, Sanitation and Hygiene under the Sustainable Development Goals*. Geneva, WHO. www.unwater.org/publications/un-water-glaas-2017-financing-universal-water-sanitation-hygiene-sustainable-development-goals/.

_____. 2020a. *Recommendations to Member States to Improve Hand Hygiene Practices to Help Prevent the Transmission of the COVID-19 Virus*. Interim guidance 1 April 2020. WHO. www.who.int/publications/i/item/recommendations-to-member-states-to-improve-hand-hygiene-practices-to-help-prevent-the-transmission-of-the-covid-19-virus.

_____. 2020b. *Schistosomiasis. Key Facts*. WHO website. www.who.int/news-room/fact-sheets/detail/schistosomiasis.

_____. 2020c. *Trachoma. Key Facts*. WHO website. www.who.int/news-room/fact-sheets/detail/trachoma.

_____. 2020d. *Soil-Transmitted Helminth Infections. Key Facts*. WHO website. www.who.int/news-room/fact-sheets/detail/soil-transmitted-helminth-infections.

_____. 2020e. *Hygiene: UN-Water GLAAS Findings on National Policies, Plans, Targets and Finance*. Geneva, WHO. www.unwater.org/publications/hygiene-un-water-glaas-findings-on-national-policies-plans-targets-and-finance/. Licence: CC BY-NC-SA 3.0 IGO.

_____. n.d. *Burden of Disease SDG 3.9.2 – Mortality Rate attributed to Unsafe Water, Unsafe Sanitation and Lack of Hygiene (Exposure to Unsafe Water, Sanitation and Hygiene for All (WASH))*. Global Health Observatory data repository, WHO. apps.who.int/gho/data/node.main.INADEQUATEWSH?lang=en.

WHO/UNICEF (World Health Organization/United Nations Children's Fund). 2016. *Inequalities in Sanitation and Drinking Water in Latin America and the Caribbean*. washdata.org/report/lac-snapshot-wash-2016-en.

_____. 2017a. *Progress on Drinking Water, Sanitation and Hygiene: 2017 Update and SDG Baselines*. Geneva/New York, WHO/UNICEF. www.unicef.org/publications/index_96611.html.

_____. 2017b. *WASH in the 2030 Agenda: New Global Indicators for Drinking Water, Sanitation and Hygiene*. Geneva/New York, WHO/UNICEF. www.who.int/water_sanitation_health/monitoring/coverage/wash-post-2015-brochure/en/.

_____. 2018. *Drinking Water, Sanitation and Hygiene in Schools: Global Baseline Report 2018*. New York/Geneva, UNICEF/WHO. www.unicef.org/media/47671/file/JMP-WASH-in-Schools-ENG.pdf.

_____. 2019a. *Progress on Household Drinking Water, Sanitation and Hygiene 2000–2017. Special Focus on Inequalities*. New York, UNICEF/WHO. data.unicef.org/resources/progress-drinking-water-sanitation-hygiene-2019/.

_____. 2019b. *Water, Sanitation and Hygiene in Health Care Facilities: Practical Steps to Achieve Universal Access*. Geneva, World Health Organization. apps.who.int/iris/handle/10665/311618.

WHO/UNICEF/UNFPA/World Bank/UN Population Division (World Health Organization/United Nations Children's Fund/United Nations Population Fund). 2019. *Trends in Maternal Mortality: 2000 to 2017*. Geneva, WHO. https://apps.who.int/iris/handle/10665/327596.

Willems, W. and Van Schaik, H. (eds.). 2015. *Water and Heritage: Material, Conceptual and Spiritual Connections*. Leiden, The Netherlands, Sidestone Press. www.sidestone.com/books/water-heritage.

Willett, W., Rockström, J., Loken, B., Springmann, M., Lang, T., Vermeulen, S., Garnett, T., Tilman, D., DeClerck, F., Wood, A., Jonell, M., Clarck, M., Gornon, L. J., Fanzo, J., Hawkes, C., Zurayk, R., Rivera, J. A., De Vries, J., Sibanda, L. M., Afshim, A., Chaudhary, A., Herrero, M., Agustina, R., Branca, F., Lartey, A., Fan, S., Crona, B., Fox, E., Bignet, V., Troell, M., Lindahl, T., Singh, S., Cornell, S. E., Reddy, K. S., Narain, S., Nishtar, S. and Murray, C. J. L. 2019. Food in the Anthropocene: The EAT–Lancet Commission on healthy diets from sustainable food systems. *Lancet*, Vol. 393, No. 10170, pp. 447–492. doi.org/10.1016/S0140-6736(18)31788-4.

Wisser, D., Frolking, S., Hagen, S. and Bierkens, M. F. 2013. Beyond peak reservoir storage? A global estimate of declining water storage capacity in large reservoirs. *Water Resources Research*, Vol. 49, No. 9, pp. 5732–5739. doi.org/10.1002/wrcr.20452.

WMO (World Meteorological Organization), 2009. *Guide to Hydrological Practices Volume II: Management of Water Resources and Application of Hydrological Practices*. WMO-No. 168, Sixth edition. Geneva, WMO. library.wmo.int/index.php?lvl=notice_display&id=543.

_____. 2019. *Guidance on Environmental Flows: Integrating E-flow Science with Fluvial Geomorphology to Maintain Ecosystem Services*. Geneva, WMO. library.wmo.int/doc_num.php?explnum_id=9808.

Wolf, A. 2017. *The Spirit of Dialogue: Lessons from Faith Traditions in Transforming Conflict*. Washington, DC, Island Press.

Wolf, J., Hunter P. R., Freeman, M. C., Cumming, O., Clasen, T., Bartram, J., Higgins, J. P. T., Johnston, R., Medlicott, K., Boisson, S. and Prüss-Ustün, A. 2018. Impact of drinking water, sanitation and handwashing with soap on childhood diarrhoeal disease: Updated meta-analysis and meta-regression. *Tropical Medicine and International Health*. Vol. 23, No. 5, pp. 508–525. doi.org/10.1111/tmi.13051.

World Bank. 2003. *Capacity Enhancement Indicators: Review of the Literature*. WBI Evaluation Studies No. EG03-72. Washington, DC, World Bank. documents.worldbank.org/en/publication/documents-reports/documentdetail/651641468762909851/capacity-enhancement-indicators-review-of-the-literature.

_____. 2007. *World Development Report 2008: Agriculture for Development*. Washington, DC, World Bank. openknowledge.worldbank.org/handle/10986/5990. License: CC BY 3.0 IGO.

_____. 2015. *Economic Assessment of Sanitation Interventions in Southeast Asia: A Six-Country Study conducted in Cambodia, Indonesia, Lao PDR, the Philippines, Vietnam and Yunnan Province (China) under the Economics of Sanitation Initiative*. Washington, DC, World Bank. www.wsp.org/sites/wsp/files/publications/WSP-ESI-EAP-Synthesis-Report.pdf.

_____. 2016a. *High and Dry: Climate Change, Water, and the Economy*. Washington, DC, World Bank. openknowledge.worldbank.org/handle/10986/23665. License: CC BY 3.0 IGO.

_____. 2016b. *Poverty and Shared Prosperity 2016: Taking on Inequality*. Washington, DC, World Bank. openknowledge.worldbank.org/handle/10986/25078. License: CC BY 3.0 IGO.

_____. 2016c. *Regional Power Trade. Unrealized Benefits for Central Asia for 2010–2014*. Washington, DC, World Bank. www.carecprogram.org/uploads/Regional-Power-Trade-Unrealized-Benefits-for-Central-Asia-for-2010-2014.pdf.

_____. 2017. *Implementing Nature-Based Flood Protection: Principles and Implementation Guidance*. Washington, DC, World Bank. documents1.worldbank.org/curated/en/739421509427698706/pdf/Implementing-nature-based-flood-protection-principles-and-implementation-guidance.pdf.

_____. 2018. *Menstrual Hygiene Management Enables Women and Girls to Reach Their Full Potential*. World Bank website. www.worldbank.org/en/news/feature/2018/05/25/menstrual-hygiene-management.

_____. 2019. *Women in Water Utilities: Breaking Barriers*. Washington, DC, World Bank. openknowledge.worldbank.org/handle/10986/32319. License: CC BY 3.0 IGO.

_____. 2020. *World Bank Open Data*. data.worldbank.org/ (Accessed September 2020)

World Commission on Dams. 2000. *Dams and Development: A New Framework for Decision-Making: The Report of the World Commission on Dams*. London, Earthscan.

World Economic Forum. 2018. *Harnessing the Fourth Industrial Revolution for Water*. Geneva, World Economic Forum. www3.weforum.org/docs/WEF_WR129_Harnessing_4IR_Water_Online.pdf.

_____. 2019. *The Global Risks Report 2019*. World Economic Forum. www.weforum.org/reports/the-global-risks-report-2019.

Worthington, A. C. and Hoffman, M. 2008. An empirical survey of residential water demand modelling. *Journal of Economic Surveys*, Vol. 22, No. 5, pp. 842–871. doi.org/10.1111/j.1467-6419.2008.00551.x.

WRI (World Resources Institute). 2019. WRI Aqueduct website. www.wri.org/aqueduct.

WWAP (UNESCO World Water Assessment Programme). 2012. *The United Nations World Water Development Report 4: Managing Water under Uncertainty and Risk*. Paris, UNESCO. www.unesco.org/new/en/natural-sciences/environment/water/wwap/wwdr/wwdr4-2012/.

_____. 2015. *The United Nations World Water Development Report 2015: Water for a Sustainable World*. Paris, UNESCO. www.unesco.org/new/en/natural-sciences/environment/water/wwap/wwdr/2015-water-for-a-sustainable-world/.

_____. 2016. *The United Nations World Water Development Report 2016: Water and Jobs*. Paris, UNESCO. unesdoc.unesco.org/ark:/48223/pf0000243938.

_____. 2017. *The United Nations World Water Development Report 2017. Wastewater: The Untapped Resource*. Paris, UNESCO. www.unesco.org/new/en/natural-sciences/environment/water/wwap/wwdr/2017-wastewater-the-untapped-resource/.

WWAP (World Water Assessment Programme)/UN-Water. 2018. *The United Nations World Water Development Report 2018: Nature-Based Solutions for Water*. Paris, UNESCO. www.unesco.org/new/en/natural-sciences/environment/water/wwap/wwdr/2018-nature-based-solutions/.

_____. 2019. *The United Nations World Water Development Report 2019: Leaving No One Behind*. Paris, UNESCO. en.unesco.org/themes/water-security/wwap/wwdr/2019.

WWC/OECD (World Water Council/Organisation for Economic Co-operation and Development). 2015. *Water: Fit to Finance? Catalyzing National Growth through Investment in Water Security*. Report of the High Level Panel of Financing Infrastructure for a Water-Secure World. World Water Council/Organisation for Economic Co-operation and Development (WWC/OECD). www.worldwatercouncil.org/sites/default/files/Thematics/WWC_OECD_Water_fit_to_finance_Report.pdf.

WWF (World Wide Fund for Nature). 2003. *An Investor's Guide to Dams*. DamRight! WWF's Dams Initiative. London, WWF. wwfint.awsassets.panda.org/downloads/investorsguidedams.pdf.

_____. 2019a. *Linking Water Risk and Financial Value – Part II: Review of Water Risk Valuation Tools*. WWF Germany. wwfint.awsassets.panda.org/downloads/wwf_waterrisk_financialvalue_part2_web.pdf.

_____. 2019b. *Valuing Water Database*. waterriskfilter.panda.org/en/Value/ValuationApproachFinder. (Accessed November 2020)

WWF/IFC (World Wildlife Fund/International Finance Corporation). 2015. *The Value of Water: A Framework for Understanding Water Valuation, Risk and Stewardship*. Discussion draft, August 2015. WWF/IFC. wwfint.awsassets.panda.org/downloads/the_value_of_water_discussion_draft_final_august_2015.pdf.

X

Xie, J. 2009. *Addressing China's Water Scarcity: Recommendations for Selected Water Resource Management Issues*. Washington DC, World Bank. openknowledge.worldbank.org/handle/10986/2585. License: CC BY 3.0 IGO.

Y

Yao, H., You, Z. and Liu, B. 2016. Economic estimation of the losses caused by surface water pollution accidents in China from the perspective of water bodies' functions. *International Journal of Environmental Research and Public Health*, Vol. 13, No. 2, Art. 154. doi.org/10.3390/ijerph13020154.

Yokwe, S. 2009. Water productivity in smallholder irrigation schemes in South Africa. *Agricultural Water Management*, Vol. 96, No. 8, pp. 1223–1228. doi.org/10.1016/j.agwat.2009.03.012.

Young, R. 1996. *Measuring Economic Benefits for Water Investments and Policies*. World Bank Technical Paper No. 338. Washington, DC, World Bank. elibrary.worldbank.org/doi/abs/10.1596/0-8213-3745-9.

Young, R. and Loomis, J. 2014. *Determining the Economic Value of Water: Concepts and Methods*. Second edition. Abingdon, UK, RFF Press and Routledge.

Yu, W. H. 2008. *Benefit Sharing in International Rivers: Findings from the Senegal River Basin, the Columbia River Basin, and the Lesotho Highlands Water Project*. Report no. 46456, Africa Region Water Resources Unit Working Paper 1. The World Bank. documents1.worldbank.org/curated/en/159191468193140438/pdf/464560NWP0P1121g0AFTWR0YU301PUBLIC1.pdf.

Zhu, T., Ringler, C. and Rosegrant, M. W. 2019. Viewing agricultural water management through a systems analysis lens. *Water Resources Research*, Vol. 55, No. 3, pp. 1778–1791. doi.org/10.1029/2017WR021007.

Zheng, Y., Ross, A., Villholth, K. G. and Dillon, P. (eds.). Forthcoming. *Managing Aquifer Recharge: A Showcase for Resilience and Sustainability*. UNESCO/IAH-GRIPP.

Zhulidov, A. V., Khlobystov, V. V., Robarts, R. D. and Pavlov, D. F. 2000. Critical analysis of water quality monitoring in the Russian Federation and former Soviet Union. *Canadian Journal of Fisheries and Aquatic Sciences*, Vol. 57, No. 9, pp. 1932–1939. doi.org/10.1139/cjfas-57-9-1932.

Abbreviations and acronyms

AWS	Alliance for Water Stewardship
BAFWAC	Business Alliance for Water and Climate
BCE	Before the Common Era
BCR	Benefit–Cost Ratio
BOD	Biological Oxygen Demand
CAPEX	Capital Expenditures
CAREC	Central Asia Regional Environmental Centre
CBA	Cost–Benefit Analysis, or Cost-Based Approach (in Section 8.1)
CDP	formerly the Carbon Disclosure Project
CE	Common Era
COSVF	Carryover Storage Value Functions
COVID-19	Coronavirus Disease 2019
CSP	Concentrated Solar Power
CSR	Corporate Social Responsibility
CV	Contingent Valuation
DALYs	Disability-Adjusted Life Years
DRR	Disaster Risk Reduction
EBA	Ecosystem-Based Approach
EBITDA	Earnings before Interest, Taxes, Depreciations and Amortization
ECSA	European Citizen Science Association
EDD	Environmental Enteric Dysfunction
EDF	Électricité de France – France Electricity
EIB	Energy, Industry and Business
ESD	Education for Sustainable Development
ESG	Environmental, Social and Governance
EU	European Union
EWS	Early Warning System
FAO	Food and Agriculture Organization of the United Nations
FLW	Food Loss and Waste
FONAFIFO	Fondo Nacional de Financiamiento Forestal – National Fund for Forestry Financing (Costa Rica)
FP2E	Fédération Professionnelle des Entreprises de l'Eau – Federation of Private Water Operators (France)
FSL	Fonds de Solidarité pour le Logement – Housing Solidarity Fund (France)
GCC	Gulf Cooperation Council
GDP	Gross Domestic Product
GEMS	Global Environmental Monitoring System
GHG	Greenhouse Gas
GLAAS	Global Analysis and Assessment of Sanitation and Drinking-Water
GRDC	Global Runoff Data Center
GWI	Global Water Intelligence
GWOPA	Global Water Operators Partnership Alliance
HLPW	High Level Panel on Water
HRBA	Human Rights-Based Approach
HSAC	Hydropower Sustainability Assessment Protocol
HSE	Health, Safety and Environment
ICT	Information and Communication Technology
IBT	Increasing Block Tariff
IEA	International Energy Agency
IFC	International Finance Corporation
IPBES	Intergovernmental Science-Policy Platform on Biodiversity and Ecosystem Services
IW:LEARN	International Waters Learning Exchange and Resource Network
IWRM	Integrated Water Resources Management
LAC	Latin America and the Caribbean

LIK	Local and Indigenous Knowledge
MAR	Managed Aquifer Recharge
MDGs	Millennium Development Goals
MHM	Menstrual Hygiene Management
NGO	Non-Governmental Organization
NOAA	National Oceanic and Atmospheric Administration
NTD	Neglected Tropical Disease
OECD	Organisation for Economic Co-operation and Development
O&M	Operation & Maintenance
OMVS	Organisation pour la mise en valeur du fleuve Sénégal – Senegal River Basin Development Authority
OPEC	Organization of Petroleum-Exporting Countries
OPEX	Operational Expenditures
PCCP	From Potential Conflict to Cooperation Potential
PES	Payment for Ecosystem Services
PIDA	Programme for Infrastructure Development in Africa
PIMMS	Point d'information médiation multi-services – Multi-Services Points of Information (France)
POP	Persistent Organic Pollutant
RBO	River Basin Organization
RECP	Resource Efficient and Cleaner Production
RVM	Residual Valuation Method
SDGs	Sustainable Development Goals
SEEA	System of Environmental Economic Accounting
SIWI	Stockholm International Water Institute
SMEs	Small and Medium-sized Enterprises
SRI	System of Rice Intensification
STH	Soil-Transmitted Helminthiases
SWPA	Surface Water Pollution Accident
TBNA	Transboundary Basin Nexus Assessment
TEEB	The Economics of Ecosystems and Biodiversity
TEV	Total Economic Value
UK	United Kingdom
UN	United Nations
UNDP	United Nations Development Programme
UNECE	United Nations Economic Commission for Europe
UNESCO	United Nations Educational, Scientific and Cultural Organization
UNGA	United Nations General Assembly
UNIDO	United Nations Industrial Development Organization
URV	Unit Reference Value
USA	United States of America
VWBA	Volumetric Water Benefit Accounting
VWI	Valuing Water Initiative
WaPOR	Water Productivity Open Access Portal
WARMA	Water Resources Management Authority (Zambia)
WASH	Water, Sanitation and Hygiene
WAVES	Wealth Accounting and the Valuation of Ecosystem Services
WBCSD	World Business Council for Sustainable Development
WFD	Water Framework Directive
WHO	World Health Organization
WMO	World Meteorological Organization
WSP	Water Service Provider
WPS	Water, Peace and Security
WTA	Willing to Accept
WTP	Willingness to Pay
WWAP	World Water Assessment Programme
WWF	World Wide Fund for Nature

THE UNITED NATIONS WORLD WATER DEVELOPMENT REPORT

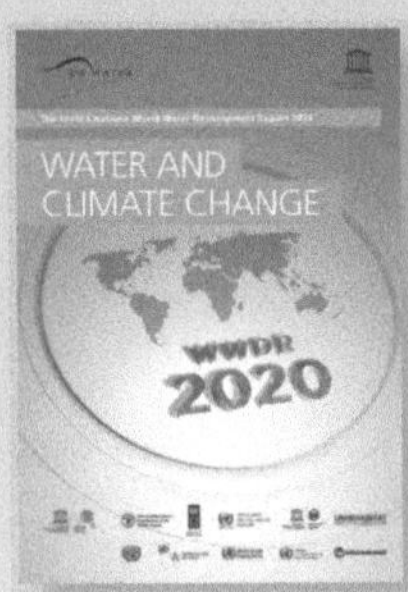

ISBN 978-92-3-100371-4

236 pages
Price: EUR 45.00

WWDR 2020 Full colour, with boxes, figures, maps, tables, notes, photographs, references, and list of abbreviations and acronyms, as well as Forewords by UNESCO Director-General Audrey Azoulay and UN-Water Chair and IFAD President Gilbert F. Houngbo

ISBN 978-92-3-100434-6

208 pages
Price: EUR 45.00

WWDR 2021 Full colour, with boxes, figures, maps, tables, notes, photographs, references, and list of abbreviations and acronyms, as well as Forewords by UNESCO Director-General Audrey Azoulay and UN-Water Chair and IFAD President Gilbert F. Houngbo

To download the PDF format of the report and associated publications, WWDR previous editions and media material, please visit: www.unesco.org/water/wwap

USB key content: WWDR 2021, Executive Summary in 11 languages, Facts and Figures in five languages and WWDR previous editions

ASSOCIATED PUBLICATIONS

Executive Summary of the WWDR 2020
12 pages
Available in Arabic, Chinese, English, French, German, Hindi, Italian, Korean, Portuguese, Russian and Spanish

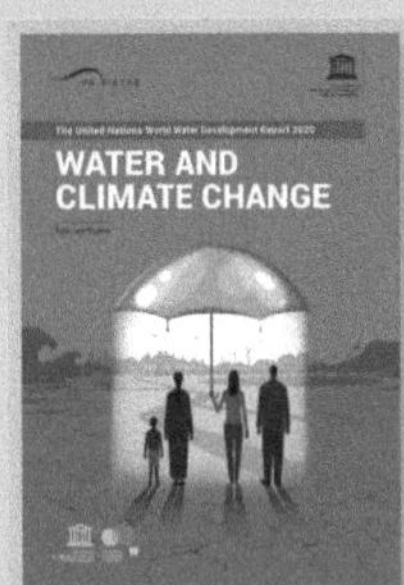

Facts and Figures from the WWDR 2020
16 pages
Available in English, French, Italian, Portuguese and Spanish

Executive Summary of the WWDR 2021
12 pages
Available in Arabic, Chinese, English, French, German, Hindi, Italian, Korean, Portuguese, Russian and Spanish

Facts and Figures from the WWDR 2021
12 pages
Available in English, French, Italian, Portuguese and Spanish

To download these documents, please visit: www.unesco.org/water/wwap

United Nations Educational, Scientific and Cultural Organization
World Water Assessment Programme

UN-Water coordinates the efforts of United Nations entities and international organizations working on water and sanitation issues. By doing so, UN-Water seeks to increase the effectiveness of the support provided to Member States in their efforts towards achieving international agreements on water and sanitation. UN-Water publications draw on the experience and expertise of UN-Water's Members and Partners.

SDG 6 Progress Update 2021 – brief
This brief will which will provide an executive update on progress towards all of the SDG 6 (based on new data on the SDG 6 global indicators) and identify priority areas for acceleration.

SDG 6 Progress Update 2021 – 8 reports, by SDG 6 global indicator
This series of reports will provide an in-depth update and analysis of progress towards the different SDG 6 targets (based on new data on the SDG 6 global indicators) and identify priority areas for acceleration: Progress on Drinking Water, Sanitation and Hygiene; Progress on Wastewater Treatment; Progress on Ambient Water Quality; Progress on Water-use Efficiency; Progress on Level of Water Stress; Progress on Integrated Water Resources Management; Progress on Transboundary Water Cooperation; Progress on Water-related Ecosystems.

United Nations World Water Development Report
The United Nations World Water Development Report (WWDR) is UN-Water's flagship report on water and sanitation issues, focusing on a different theme each year. The report is published by UNESCO, on behalf of UN-Water and its production is coordinated by the UNESCO World Water Assessment Programme. The report gives insight on main trends concerning the state, use and management of freshwater and sanitation, based on work done by the Members and Partners of UN-Water. Launched in conjunction with World Water Day, the report provides decision-makers with knowledge and tools to formulate and implement sustainable water policies. It also offers best practices and in-depth analyses to stimulate ideas and actions for better stewardship in the water sector and beyond.

UN-Water Global Analysis and Assessment of Sanitation and Drinking-Water (GLAAS)
GLAAS is produced by the World Health Organization (WHO) on behalf of UN-Water. It provides a global update on the policy frameworks, institutional arrangements, human resource base, and international and national finance streams in support of sanitation and drinking water. It is a substantive input into the activities of Sanitation and Water for All (SWA).

The progress report of the WHO/UNICEF Joint Monitoring Programme for Water Supply, Sanitation and Hygiene (JMP)
This report is affiliated with UN-Water and presents the results of the global monitoring of progress towards access to safe and affordable drinking water, and adequate and equitable sanitation and hygiene. Monitoring draws on the findings of household surveys and censuses usually supported by national statistics bureaus in accordance with international criteria and increasingly draws on national administrative and regulatory datasets.

Policy and Analytical Briefs
UN-Water's Policy Briefs provide short and informative policy guidance on the most pressing freshwater-related issues that draw upon the combined expertise of the United Nations system. Analytical Briefs provide an analysis of emerging issues and may serve as basis for further research, discussion and future policy guidance.

UN-WATER PLANNED PUBLICATIONS 2021

- UN-Water Policy Brief on Gender and Water
- Update of UN-Water Policy Brief on Transboundary Waters Cooperation
- UN-Water Analytical Brief on Water Efficiency

More information on UN-Water Reports at: www.unwater.org/unwater-publications

WORLD WATER DAY AND THE UNITED NATIONS WORLD WATER DEVELOPMENT REPORT

The United Nations designates specific days, weeks, years and decades as occasions to mark particular events or topics in order to promote, through awareness and action, the objectives of the Organization.

International observances are occasions to educate the general public on issues of concern, to mobilize political will and resources to address global problems, and to celebrate and reinforce achievements of humanity.

The majority of observances have been established by resolutions of the United Nations General Assembly. World Water Day (22 March) dates back to the 1992 United Nations Conference on Environment and Development where an international observance for water was recommended. The United Nations General Assembly responded by designating 22 March 1993 as the first World Water Day. It has been held annually since then and is one of the most popular international days together with International Women's Day (8 March), the International Day of Peace (21 September) and Human Rights Day (10 December).

Every year, UN-Water — the UN's coordination mechanism on water and sanitation — sets a theme for World Water Day corresponding to a current or future water-related challenge. This theme also defines the theme of the United Nations World Water Development Report that is presented on World Water Day. The publication is UN-Water's flagship report and provides decision-makers with tools to formulate and implement sustainable water policies. The report also gives insight on main trends including the state, use and management of freshwater and sanitation, based on work by the Members and Partners in UN-Water.

The report is published by UNESCO, on behalf of UN-Water, and its production is coordinated by the UNESCO World Water Assessment Programme.